Dwayne Wright

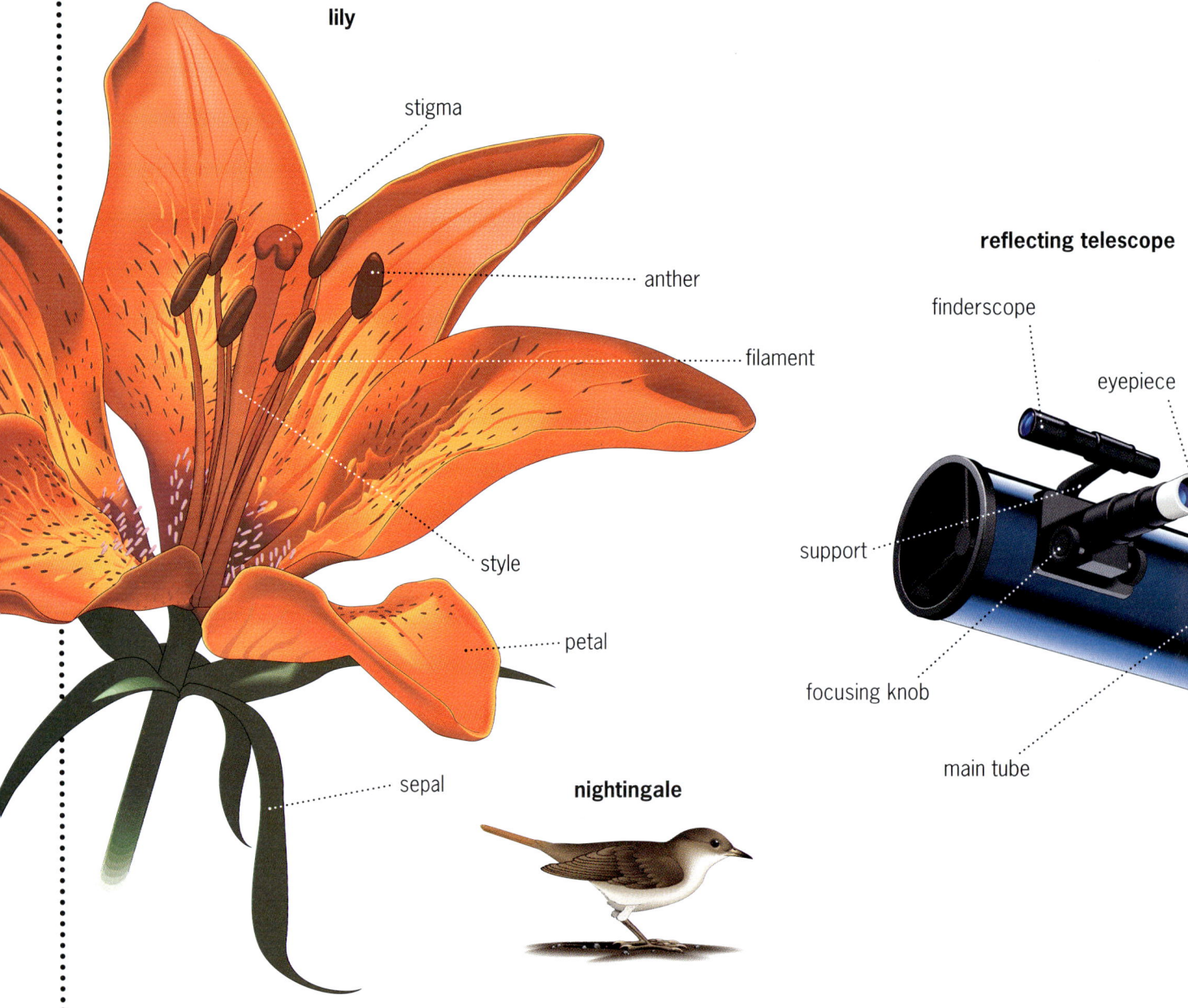

lily
- stigma
- anther
- filament
- style
- petal
- sepal

nightingale

reflecting telescope
- finderscope
- eyepiece
- support
- focusing knob
- main tube
- counterweight

Canadian Cataloguing in Publication Data

Corbeil, Jean-Claude, 1932-

The junior visual dictionary

Includes index.

ISBN 0-590-12477-3

1. Picture dictionaries, English - Juvenile literature.
2. English language - Dictionaries, Juvenile.
I. Archambault, Ariane, 1936-   . II. Title.

PE1629.C67   1998   j423'.1   C98-930277-6

Created and produced by QA International

Published by Scholastic Canada Ltd.,
175 Hillmount Road,
Markham, Ontario L6C 1Z7

Copyright © 1994 Les Éditions Québec Amérique Inc.

All rights reserved. No part of this publication may be reproduced or transmitted in any form or by any means, electronic or mechanical, including photocopying, recording or by any information storage and retrieval system, without permission in writing from the Publisher.

Printed and bound in Canada.

10 9 8 7 6 5 4 3 2   02 01 00 99

JEAN-CLAUDE CORBEIL • ARIANE ARCHAMBAULT

THE JUNIOR VISUAL DICTIONARY

Authors
Jean-Claude Corbeil
Ariane Archambault

Director of Computer Graphics
François Fortin

Art Directors
Jean-Louis Martin
François Fortin

Graphic Designer
Anne Tremblay

Computer Graphics Designers
Marc Lalumière
Jean-Yves Ahern
Rielle Lévesque
Anne Tremblay

*Jacques Perrault
Jocelyn Gardner
Christiane Beauregard
Michel Blais
Stéphane Roy
Alice Comtois
Benoît Bourdeau*

Computer Programming
Yves Ferland

Data Capture
Serge D'Amico

Page Make-up
Lucie Mc Brearty
Pascal Goyette

Technical Support
Gilles Archambault

Production
Tony O'Riley

Scholastic Canada Ltd.

THEMES AND SUBJECTS

SKY
solar system 6
Sun 8
Moon 9
comet 10
solar eclipse 10
lunar eclipse 10
reflecting telescope 11
refracting telescope 11

EARTH
Earth coordinate system 12
structure of the Earth 12
earthquake 13
cave 13
coastal features 14
volcano 15
glacier 16
mountain 17
the continents 18
seasons of the year 20
structure of the biosphere 20
elevation zones and vegetation 20
climates of the world 21
weather 22
meteorological measuring instruments 23
cartography 24
compass card 27
ecology 28

VEGETABLE KINGDOM
plant and soil 34
soil profile 34
germination 34
mushroom 35
structure of a plant 36
flowers 38
tree 40
conifer 43

FRUITS AND VEGETABLES
fleshy fruits: berry fruits 44
fleshy stone fruits 45
fleshy pome fruits 46
fleshy fruits: citrus fruits 47
tropical fruits 48
vegetables 49

GARDENING
gardening 54

ANIMAL KINGDOM
insects and spider 56
butterfly 57
honeybee 58
amphibians 60
crustaceans 61
fishes 62
reptiles 64
cat 66
dog 66
horse 67
farm animals 68
types of jaws 70
major types of horns 71
major types of tusks 71
types of hoofs 71
wild animals 72
bird 74
examples of birds 76

HUMAN BODY
human body, anterior view 78
human body, posterior view 79
skeleton 80
human anatomy 81
eye: the organ of sight 82
hand: the organ of touch 82
ear: the organ of hearing 83
nose: the organ of smell 84
mouth: the organ of taste 84
human denture 85

ARCHITECTURE
traditional houses 86
mosque 87
castle 88
gothic cathedral 89
downtown 90

HOUSE
house 92
window 94
bed 95
seats 96
table and chairs 97
lights 98
lighting 99
glassware 100
dinnerware 100
silverware 101
kitchen utensils 102
cooking utensils 104
kitchen appliances 105
refrigerator 106
cooking appliances 107

DO-IT-YOURSELF
carpentry tools 108
electric tools 110
painting upkeep 111

CLOTHING
men's clothing 112
women's clothing 114
sweaters 117
gloves and stockings 118
shoes 119
sportswear 120

PERSONAL ARTICLES
hairdressing 122
dental care 122
glasses 123
leather goods 123
umbrella 123

COMMUNICATIONS
communication by telephone 124
photography 125
television 126

THEMES AND SUBJECTS

video............................127
stereo system 128
portable sound systems 129

ROAD TRANSPORT
car............................130
trucking......................134
motorcycle.................135
bicycle.......................136

RAIL TRANSPORT
diesel-electric locomotive 138
types of freight cars..............138
highway crossing 140
high-speed train 140

MARITIME TRANSPORT
four-masted bark 141
hovercraft 141
cruise liner 142
harbor......................................142

AIR TRANSPORT
plane 144
helicopter.................145
airport......................146

SPACE TRANSPORT
space shuttle..............148
spacesuit 149

SCHOOL
school supplies........................150

school equipment......................152
geometry..................................156
drawing....................................157

MUSIC
traditional musical instruments 158
keyboard instruments 159
musical notation..............................160
stringed instruments 162
wind instruments.............................164
percussion instruments 166
symphony orchestra........................167

TEAM GAMES
baseball 168
football....................170
soccer......................172
cricket......................174
field hockey..............175
ice hockey................176
basketball................178
volleyball.................179
tennis......................180

WATER SPORTS
swimming...............182
sailboard.................184

WINTER SPORTS
skating....................185
skiing......................186

ATHLETICS
gymnastics..............188

CAMPING
tents 190
sleeping equipment 191
camping equipment..................192

INDOOR GAMES
card games..............194
dominoes.................194
dice..........................194
chess........................195
backgammon............196
checkers..................196
video entertainment system 197
game of darts..........197

MEASURING DEVICES
measure of time 198
measure of temperature...............199
measure of weight 200

ENERGY
oil 202
hydroelectric energy 204
nuclear energy........................206
solar energy 208
wind energy............................209

HEAVY MACHINERY
fire prevention 210
heavy vehicles........................212
heavy machinery....................214

SYMBOLS
common symbols 216
safety symbols 216
protection 216

5

SKY

SOLAR SYSTEM

planets and moons

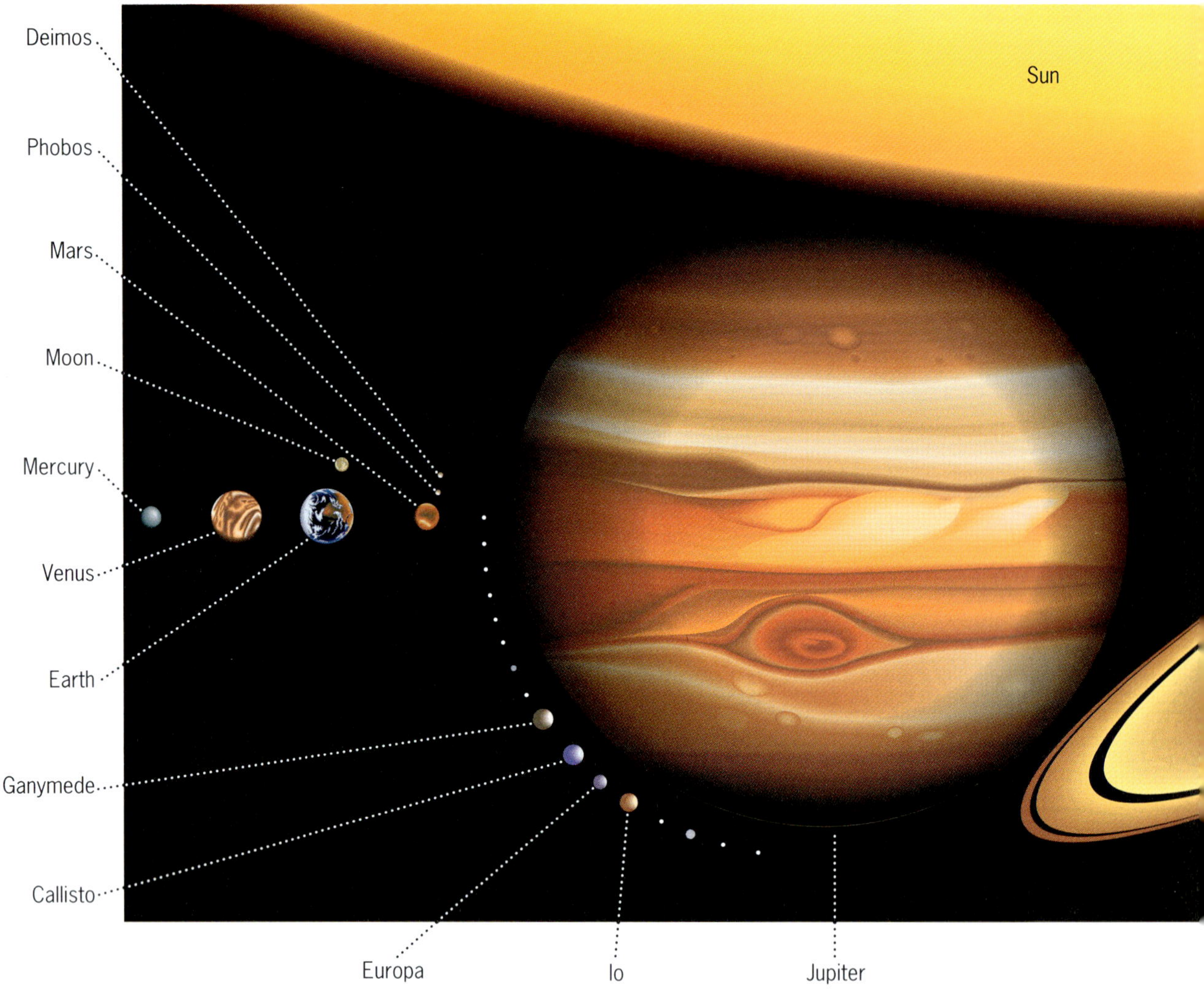

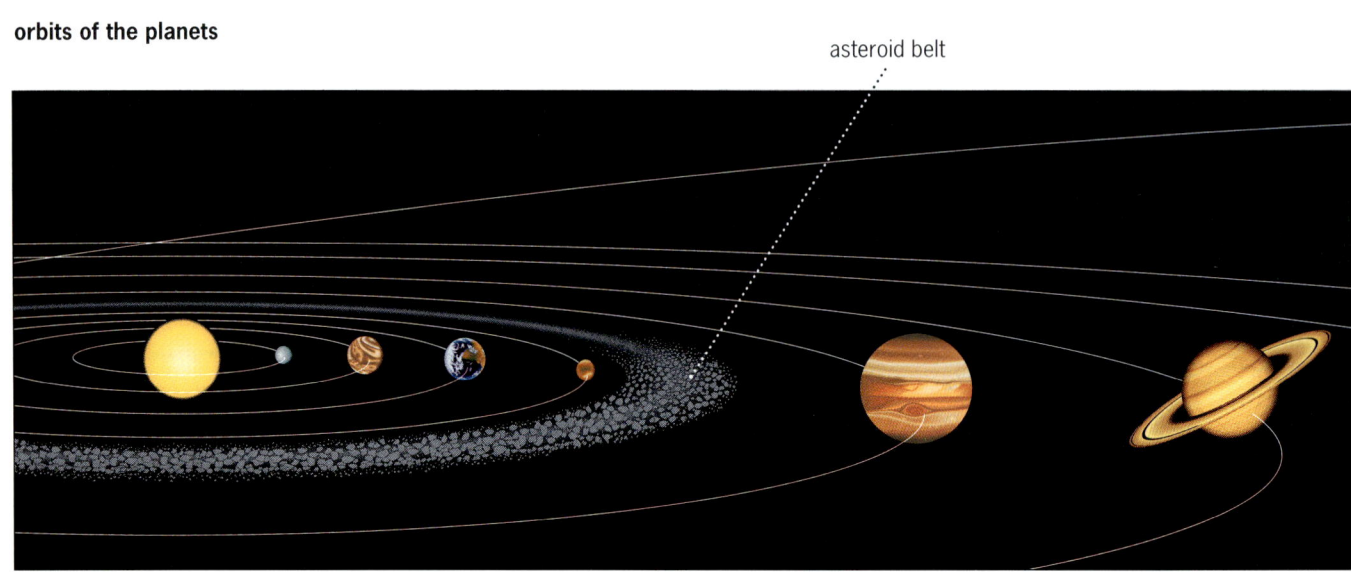

orbits of the planets

SOLAR SYSTEM

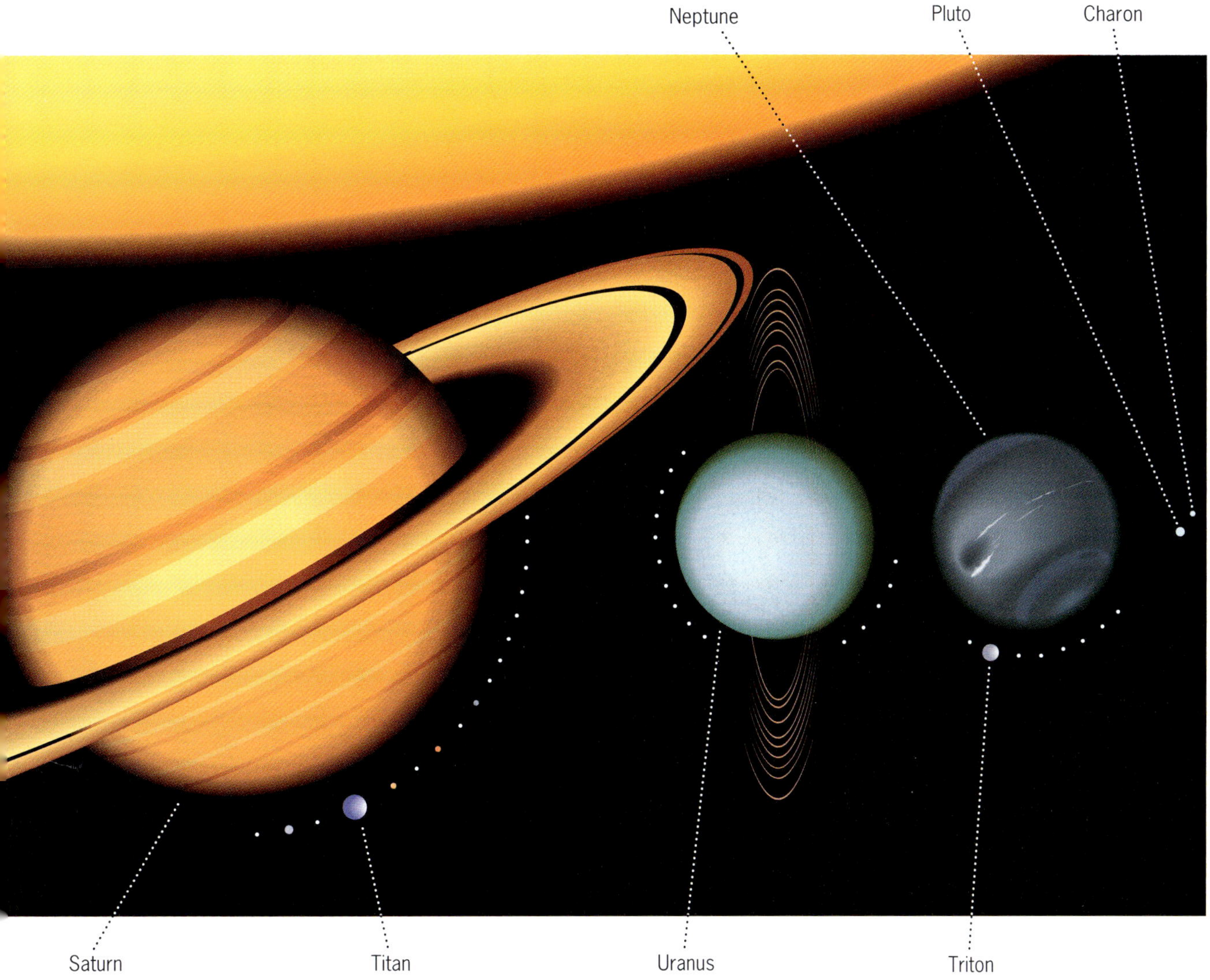

SKY

Neptune · · · · · · · · · · Pluto · · · · · · · · · · Charon

Saturn · · · · · · · · · · Titan · · · · · · · · · · Uranus · · · · · · · · · · Triton

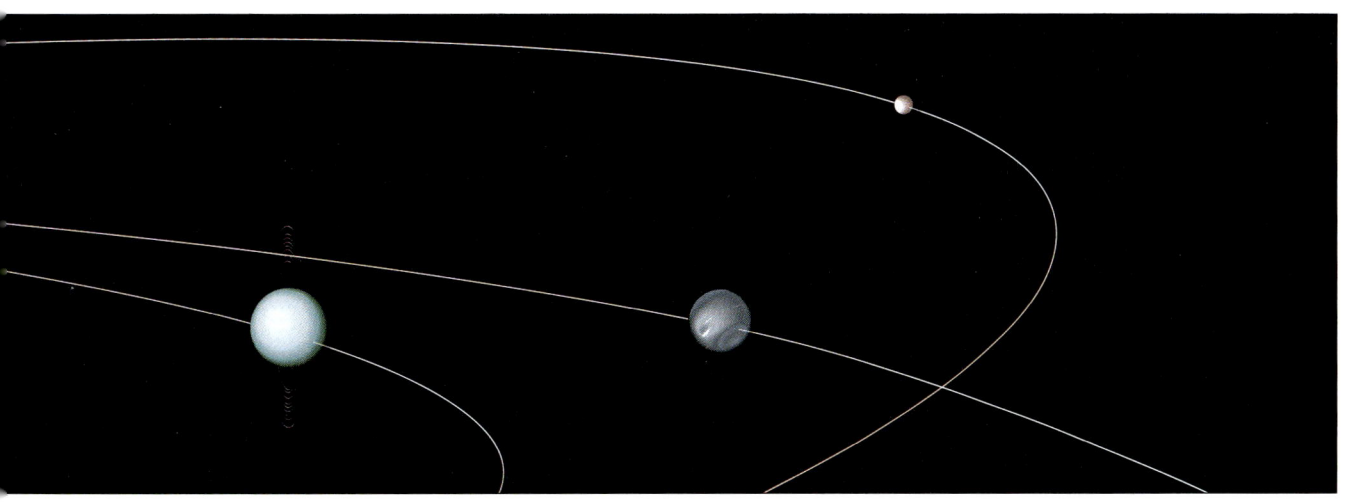

SKY

SUN

structure of the Sun

radiation zone convection zone Sun's surface corona

prominence sunspot core flare

MOON

SKY

lunar features

- bay
- cliff
- ocean
- lake
- sea
- mountain range
- crater
- wall
- cirque

PHASES OF THE MOON

new Moon — new crescent — first quarter — waxing gibbous Moon — full Moon — waning gibbous Moon — last quarter — old crescent

SKY

COMET

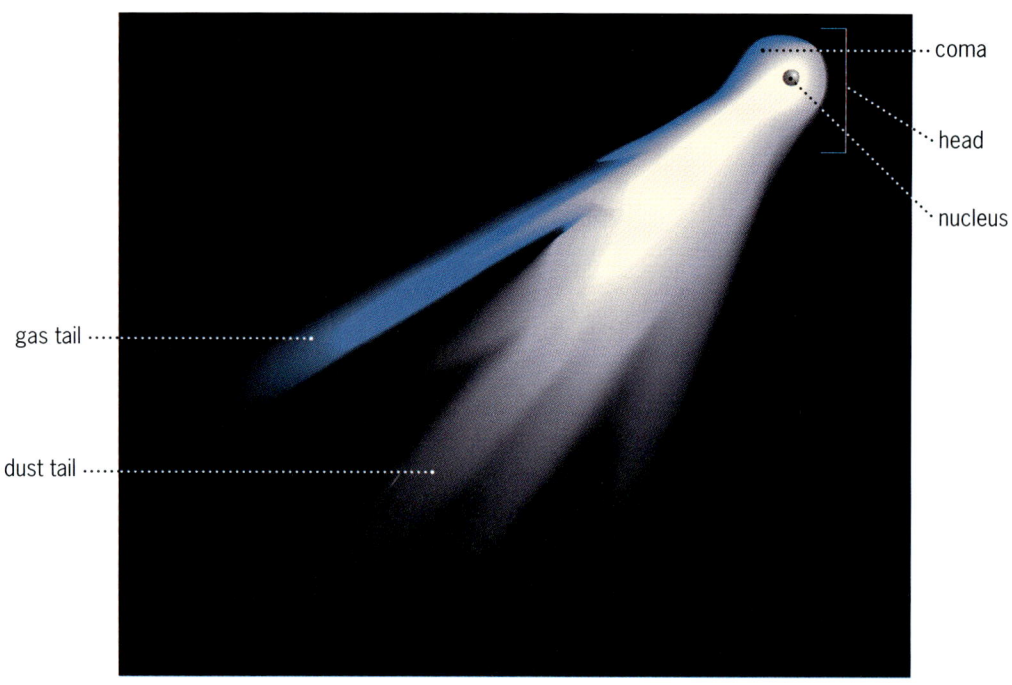

SOLAR ECLIPSE

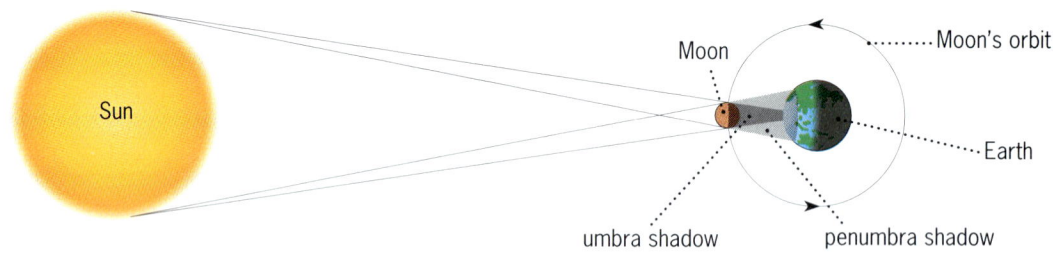

TYPES OF SOLAR ECLIPSES

 **total eclipse**  **annular eclipse**  **partial eclipse**

LUNAR ECLIPSE

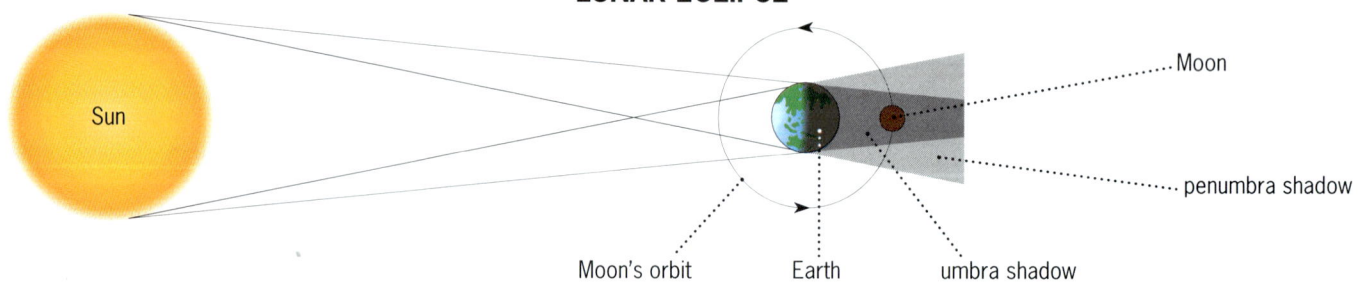

TYPES OF LUNAR ECLIPSES

partial eclipse  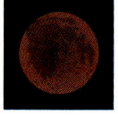 **total eclipse**

REFLECTING TELESCOPE

cross section of a reflecting telescope

REFRACTING TELESCOPE

cross section of a refracting telescope

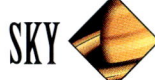

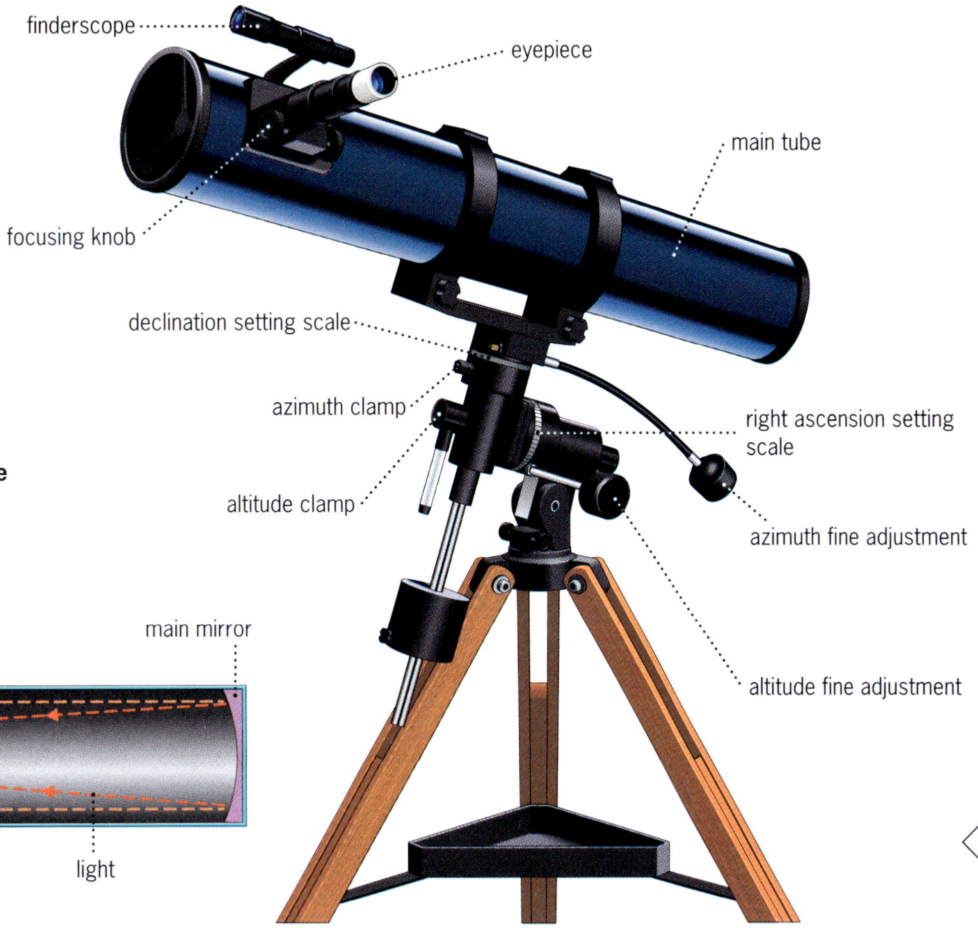

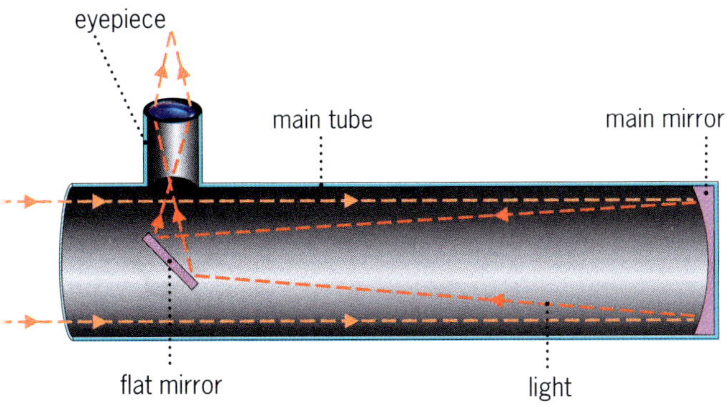

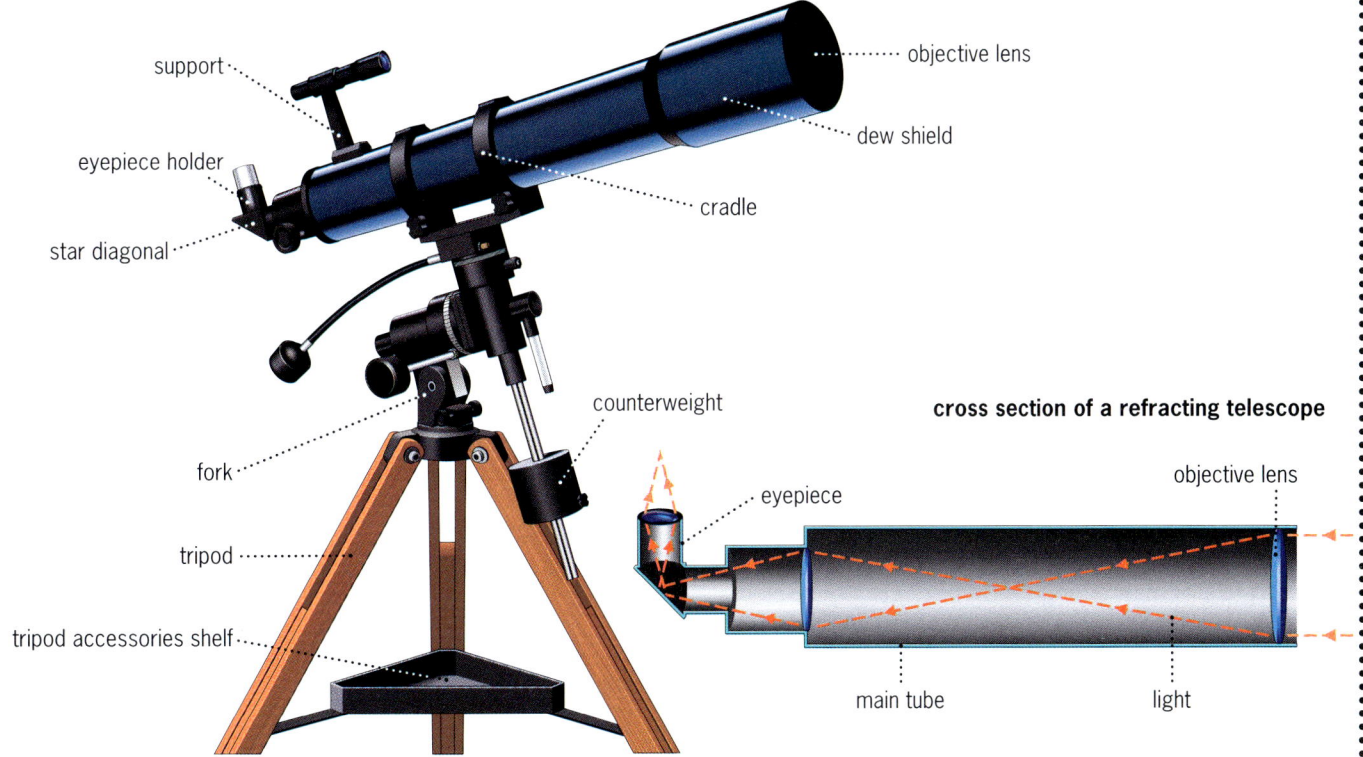

EARTH

EARTH COORDINATE SYSTEM

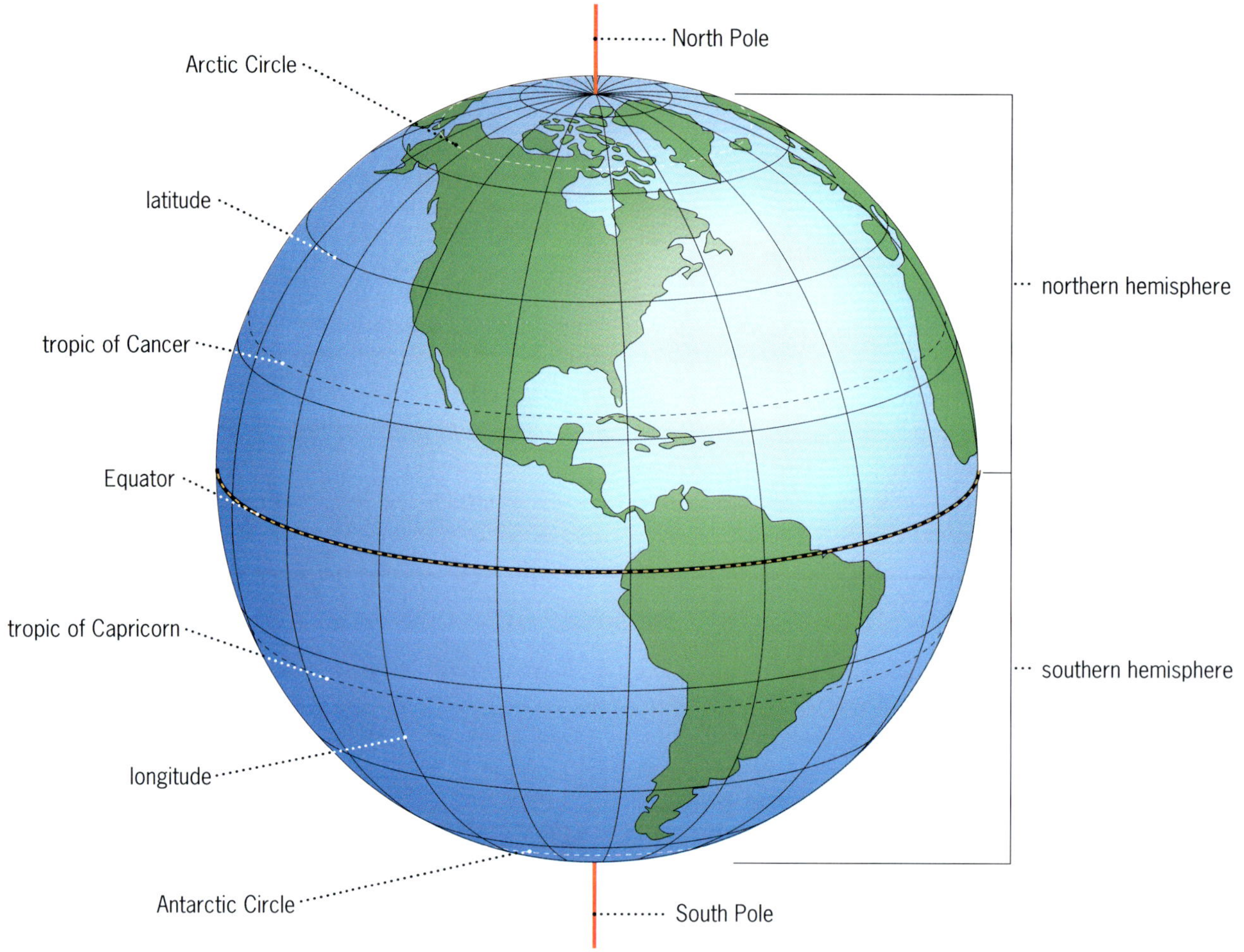

- North Pole
- Arctic Circle
- latitude
- tropic of Cancer
- Equator
- tropic of Capricorn
- longitude
- Antarctic Circle
- South Pole
- northern hemisphere
- southern hemisphere

STRUCTURE OF THE EARTH

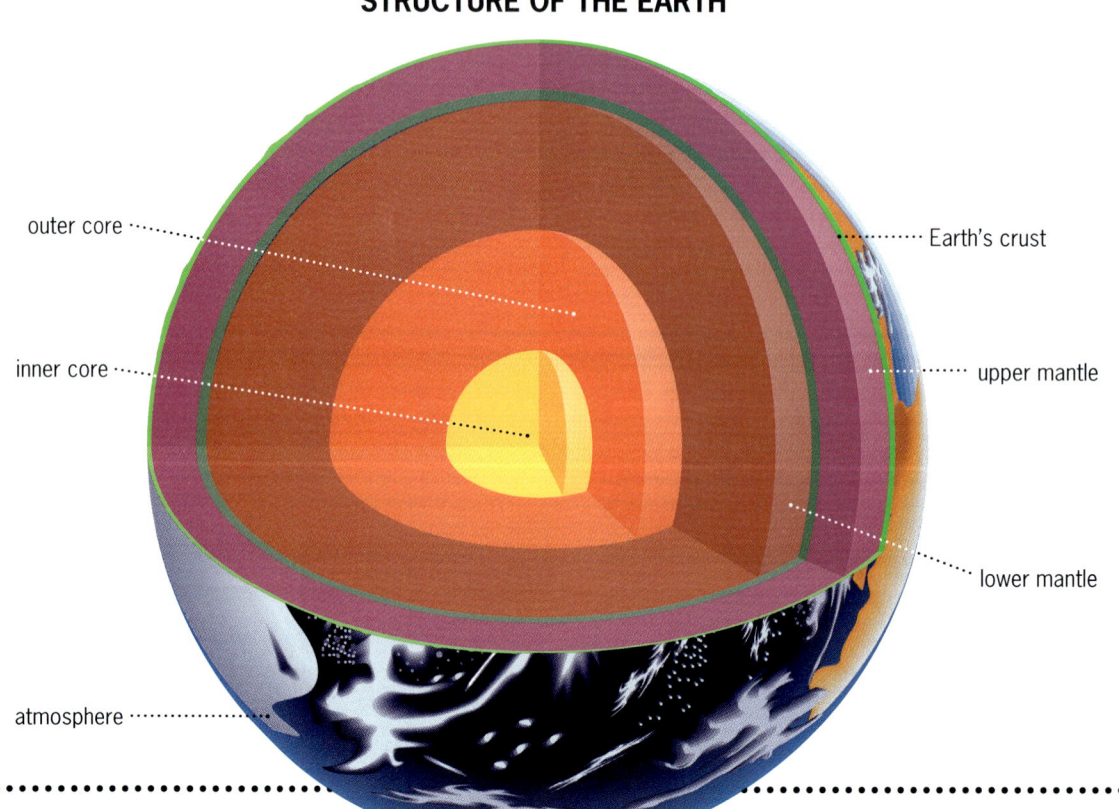

- outer core
- inner core
- atmosphere
- Earth's crust
- upper mantle
- lower mantle

 EARTH

EARTHQUAKE

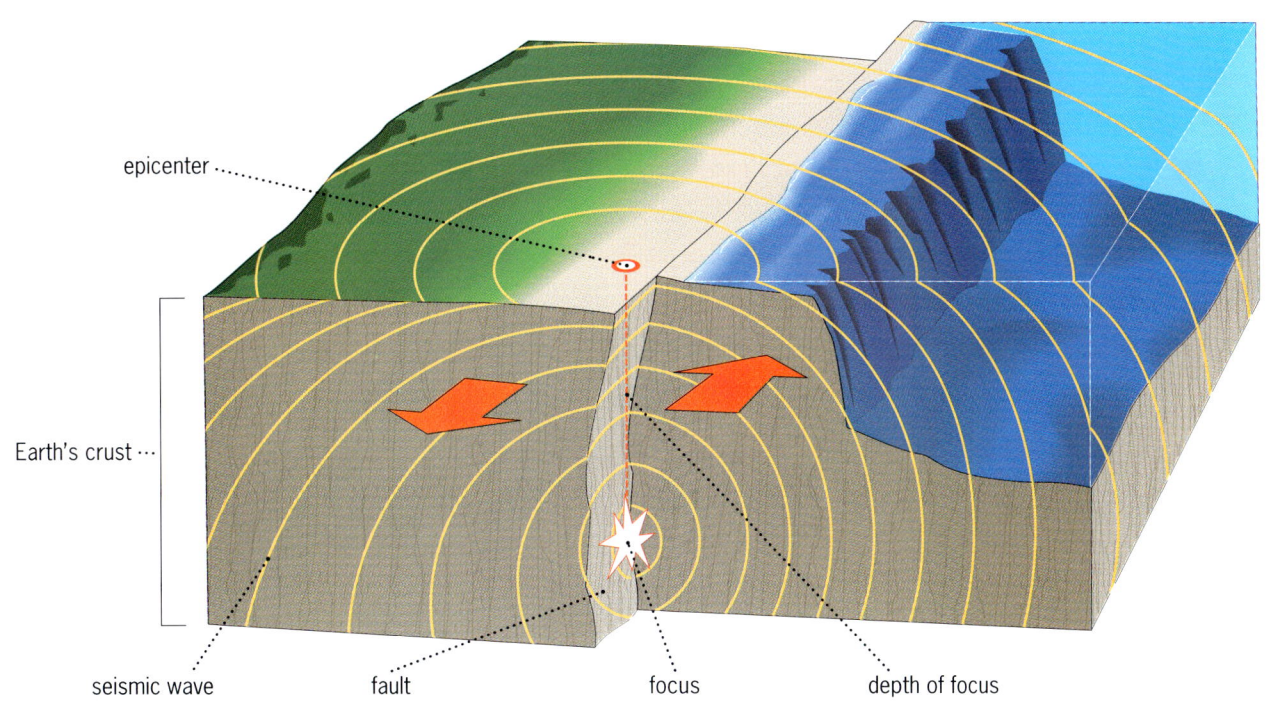

epicenter
Earth's crust
seismic wave
fault
focus
depth of focus

CAVE

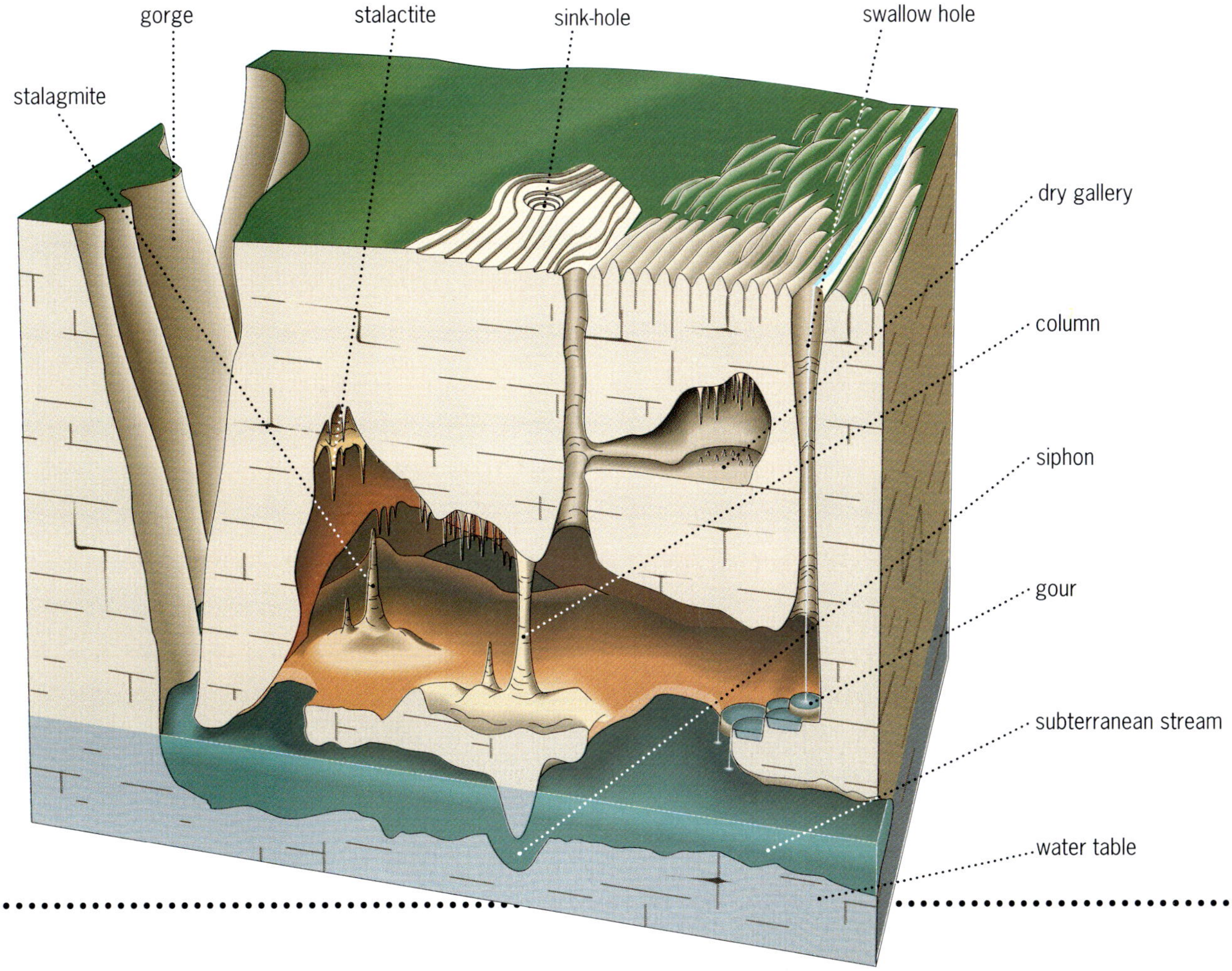

gorge
stalactite
sink-hole
swallow hole
stalagmite
dry gallery
column
siphon
gour
subterranean stream
water table

13

EARTH

COASTAL FEATURES

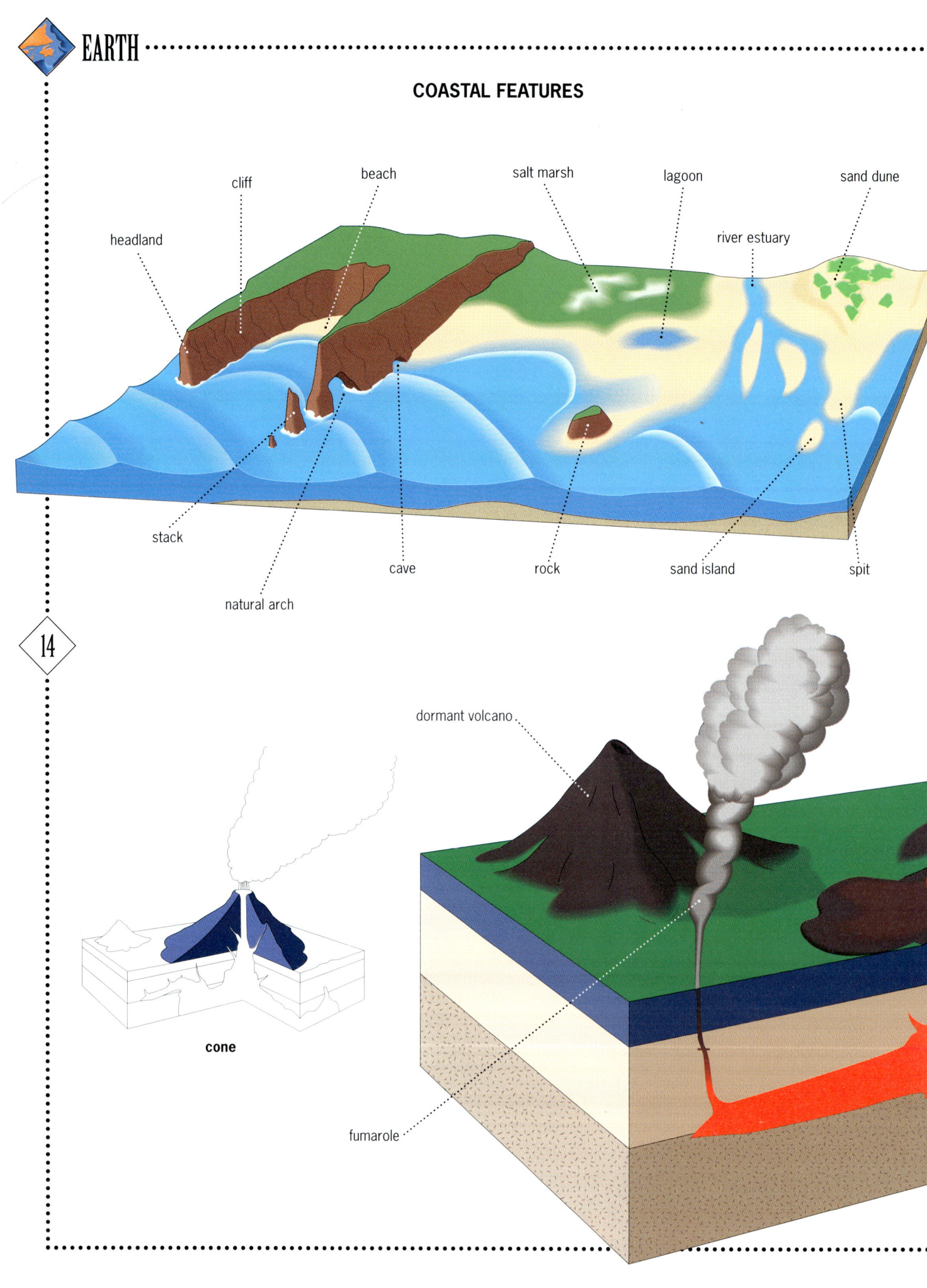

cone

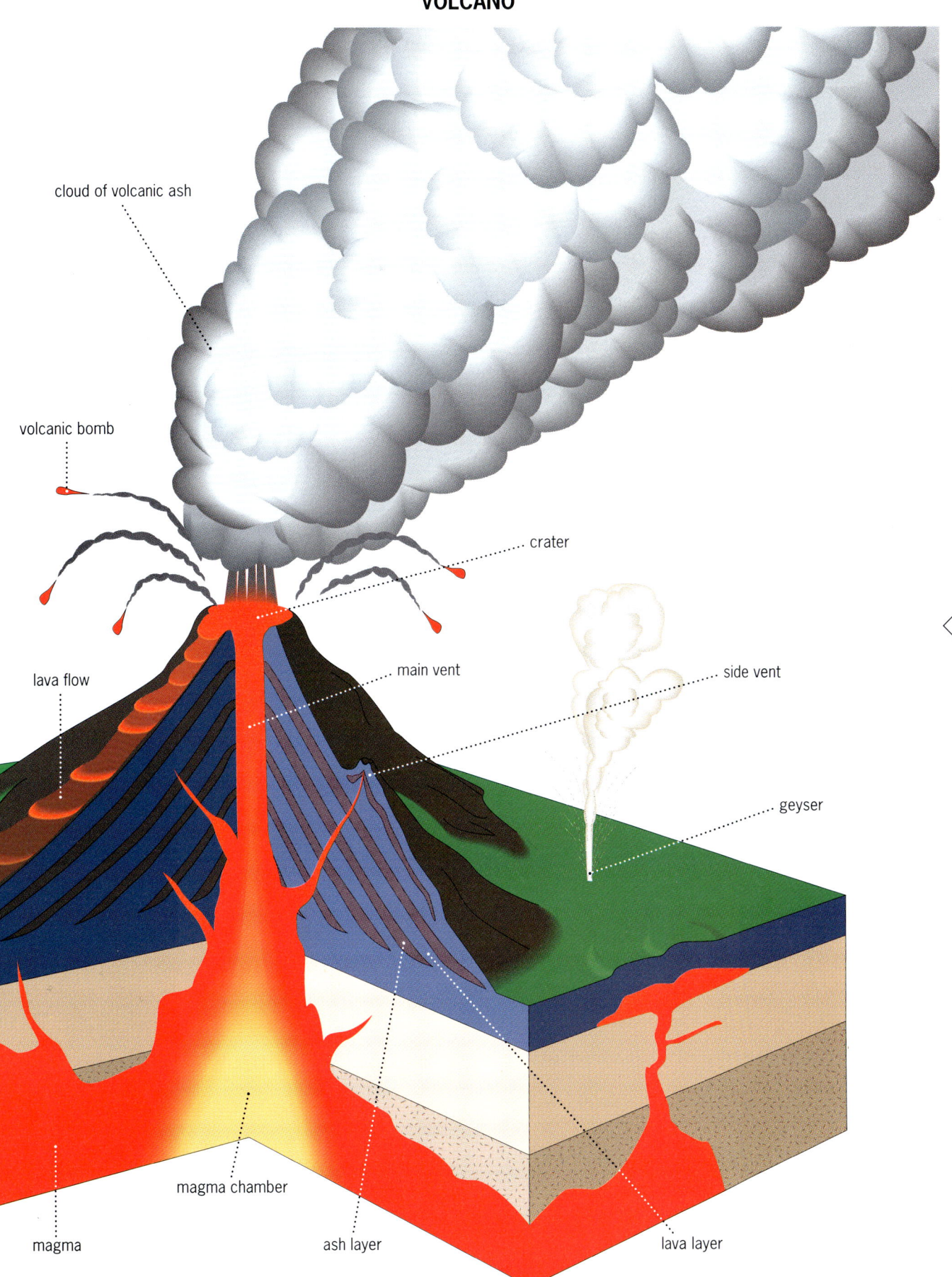

GLACIER

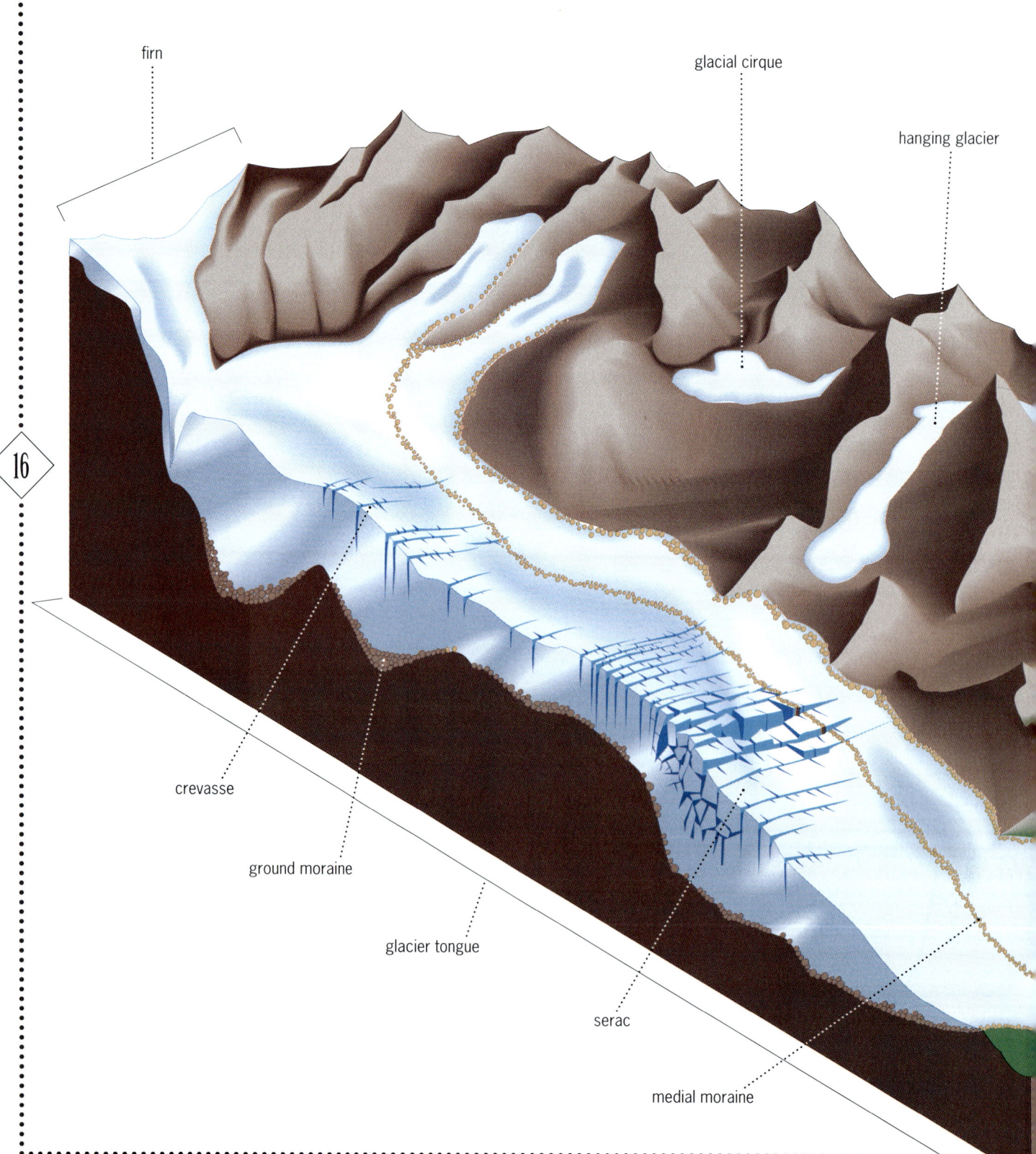

EARTH

MOUNTAIN

- summit
- perpetual snows
- pass
- spur
- mountain torrent
- waterfall
- hill
- ridge
- crest
- peak
- mountain slope
- cliff
- plateau
- forest
- valley
- lake
- lateral moraine
- terminal moraine
- meltwater
- outwash plain

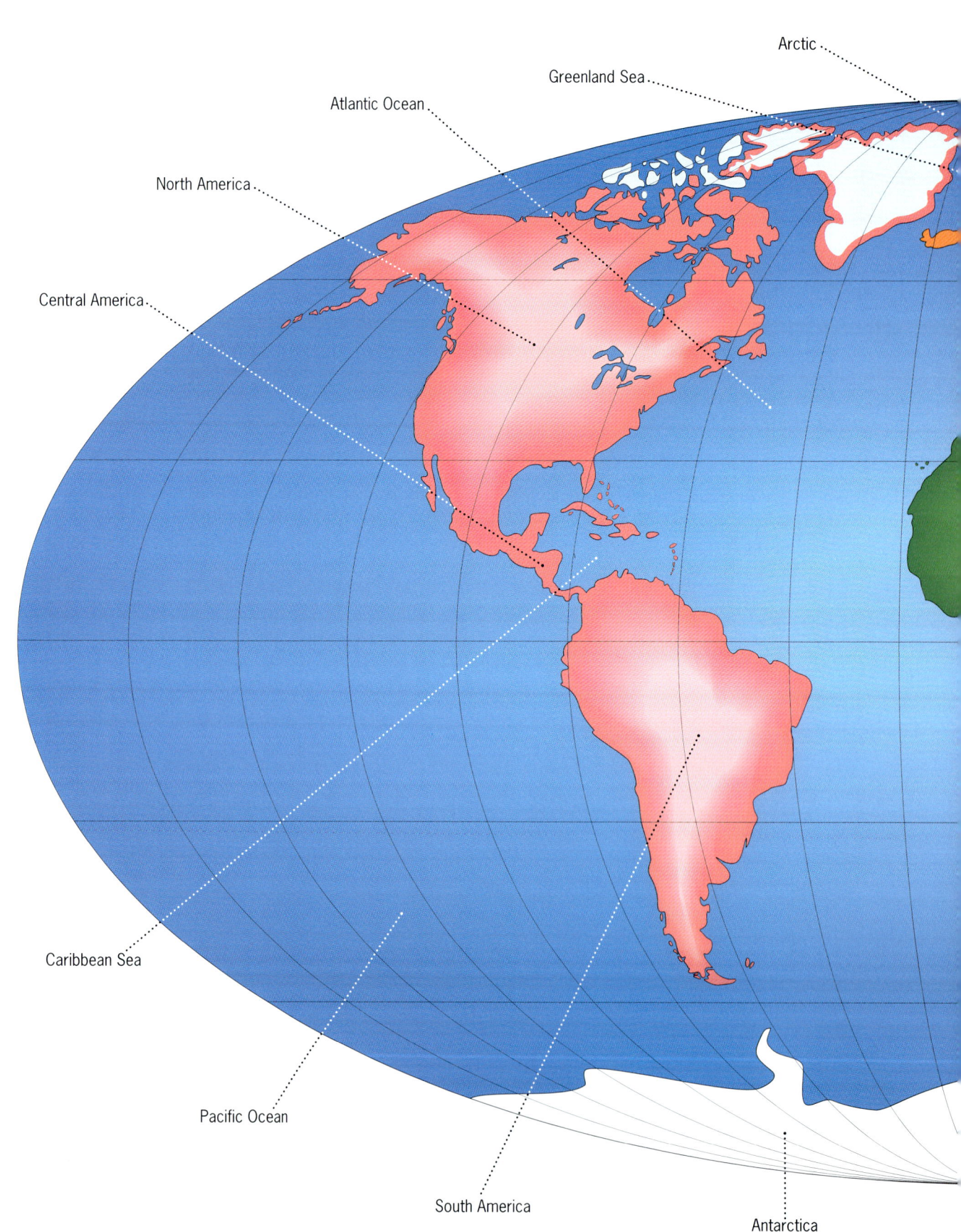

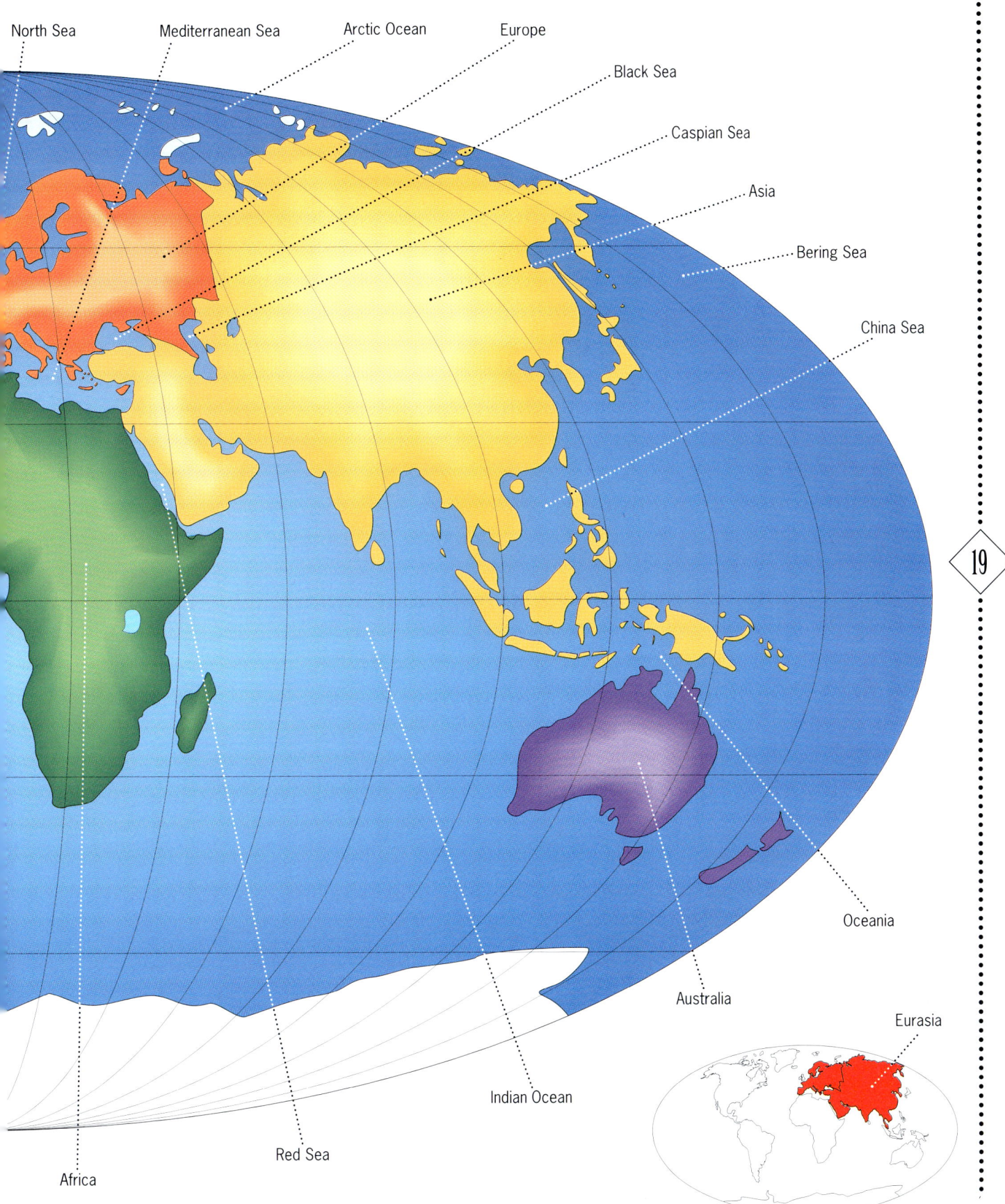

EARTH

SEASONS OF THE YEAR

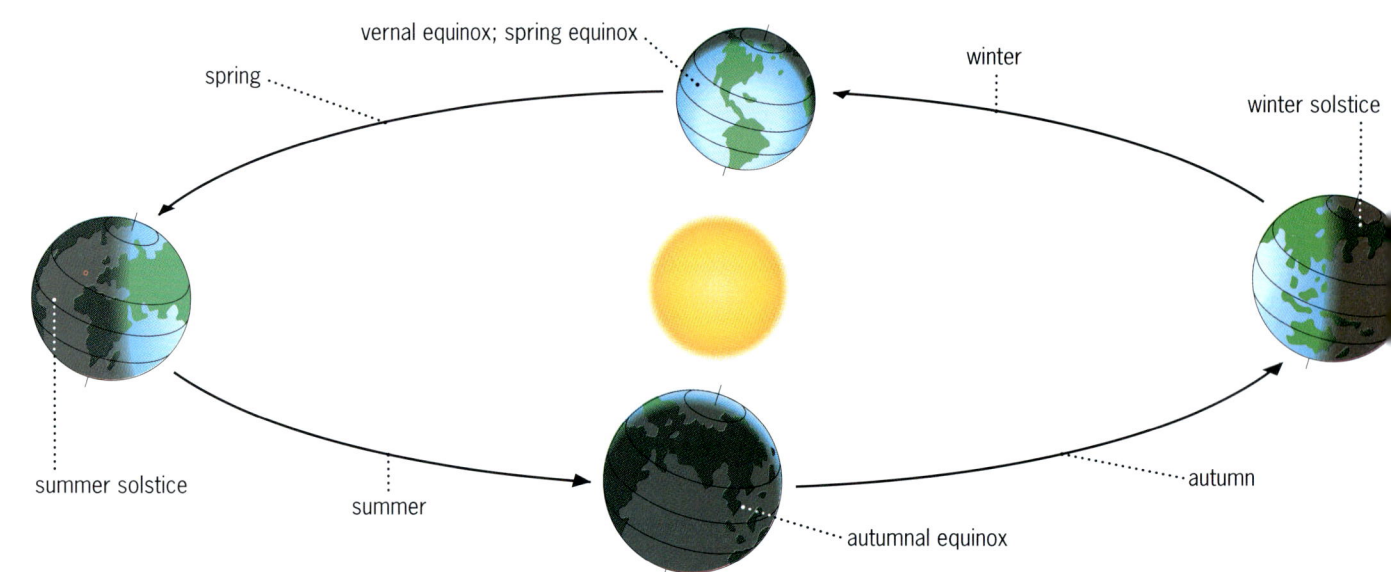

STRUCTURE OF THE BIOSPHERE

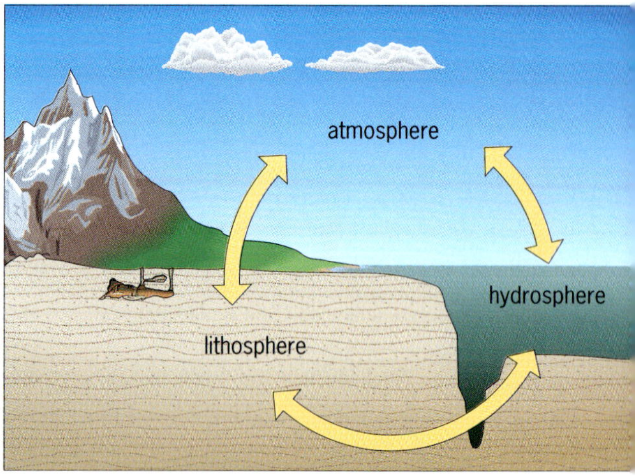

ELEVATION ZONES AND VEGETATION

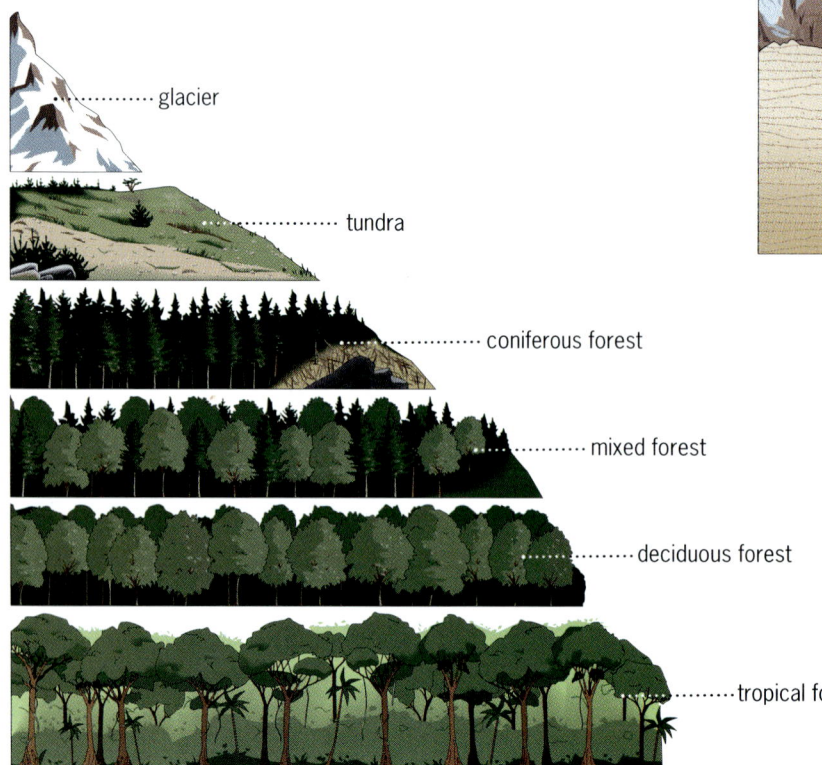

CLIMATES OF THE WORLD

tropical climates
- tropical rain forest
- tropical savanna
- steppe
- desert

temperate climates
- humid - long summer
- humid - short summer
- marine

polar climates
- polar tundra
- polar ice cap

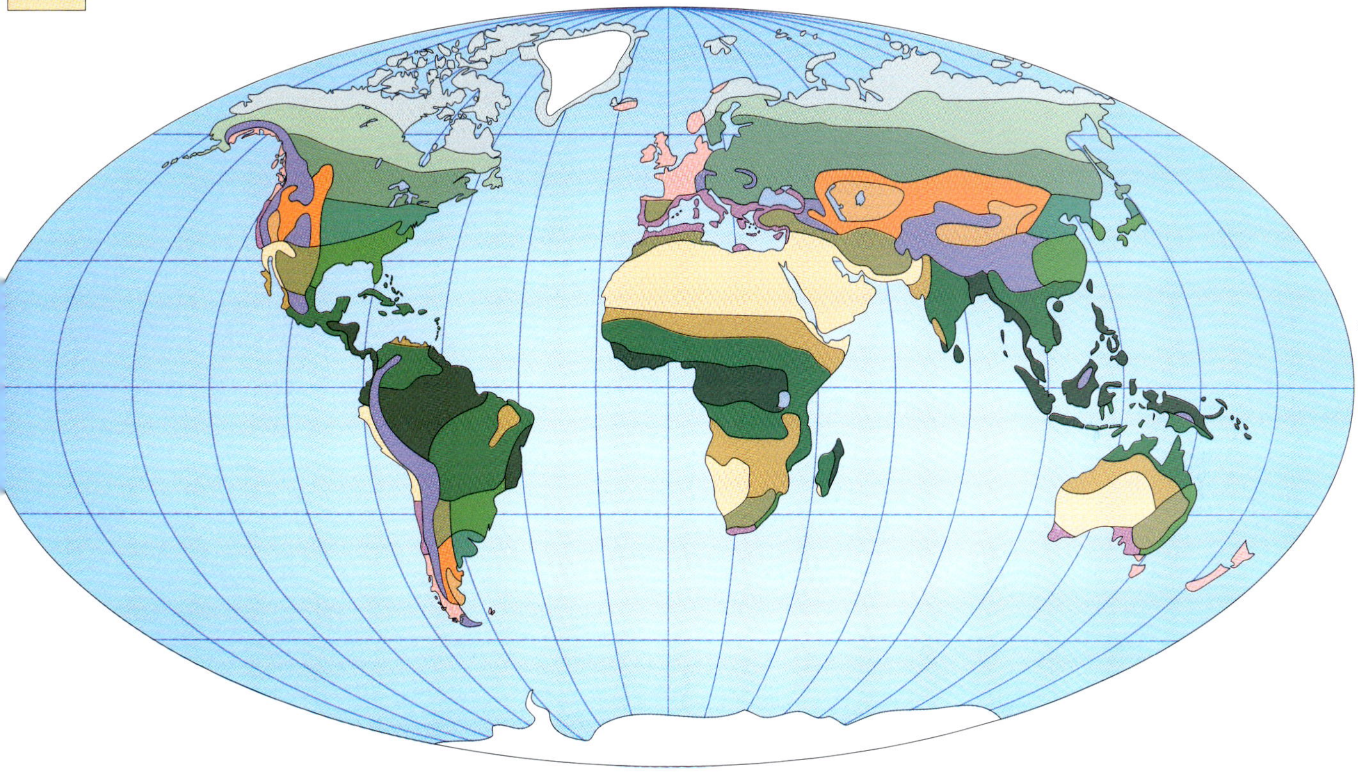

subtropical climates
- Mediterranean subtropical
- humid subtropical
- dry subtropical

continental climates
- dry continental - arid
- dry continental - semiarid

highland climates
- highland climates

subarctic climates
- subarctic climates

EARTH

WEATHER

mist

fog

dew

glazed frost

stormy sky

| rainbow | cloud | rain | raindrop | lightning |

METEOROLOGICAL MEASURING INSTRUMENTS

MEASURE OF WIND DIRECTION
wind vane

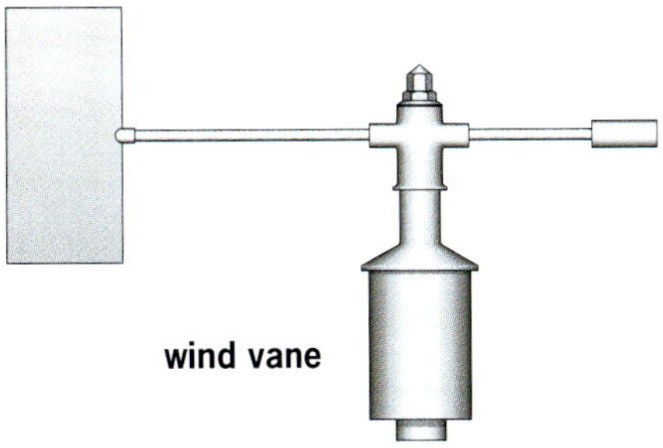

MEASURE OF WIND STRENGTH
anemometer

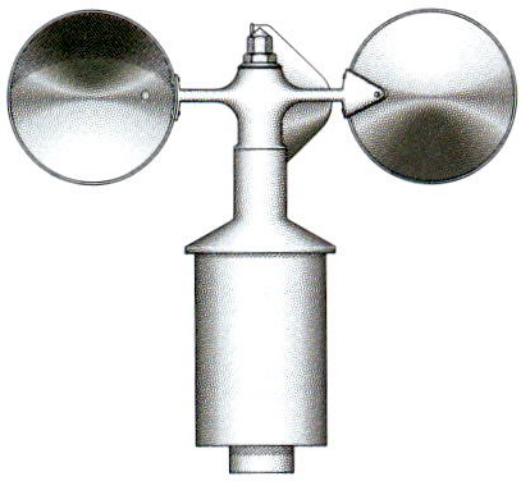

MEASURE OF HUMIDITY
hygrograph

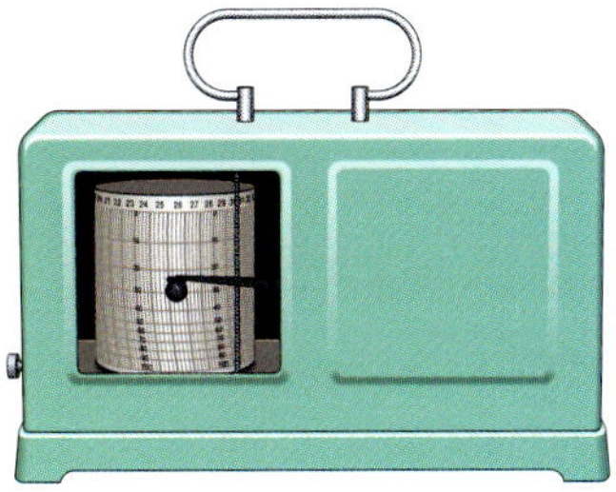

MEASURE OF RAINFALL

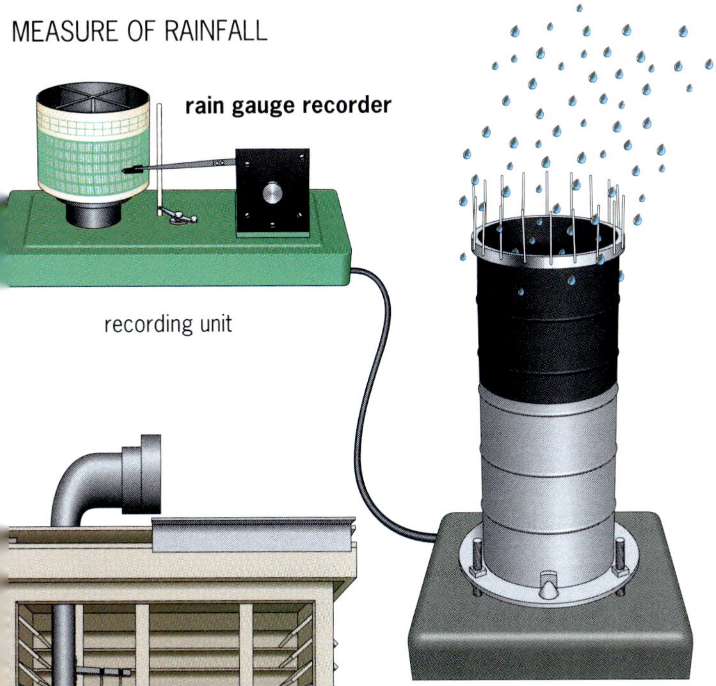

rain gauge recorder
recording unit

direct-reading rain gauge
- collecting funnel
- measuring tube
- support
- tightening band
- container

collecting vessel

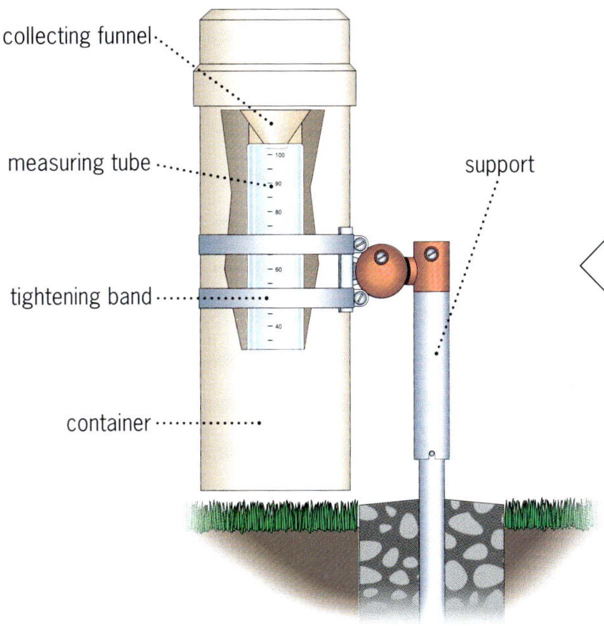

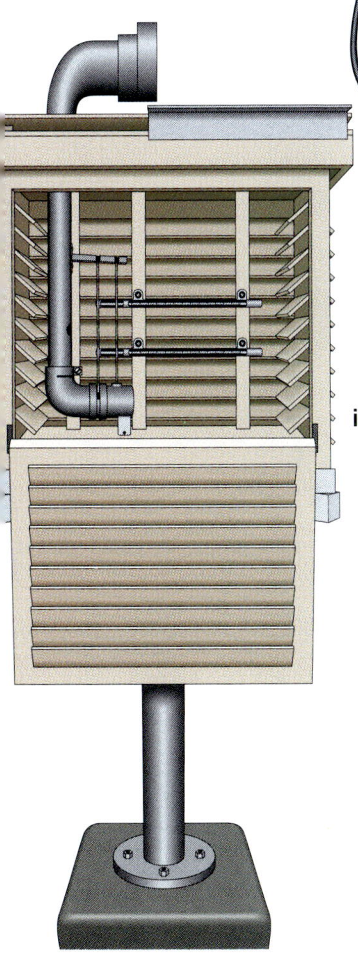

instrument shelter

MEASURE OF TEMPERATURE
minimum thermometer

maximum thermometer

mercury barometer

MEASURE OF AIR PRESSURE
barograph

EARTH

CARTOGRAPHY

hemispheres

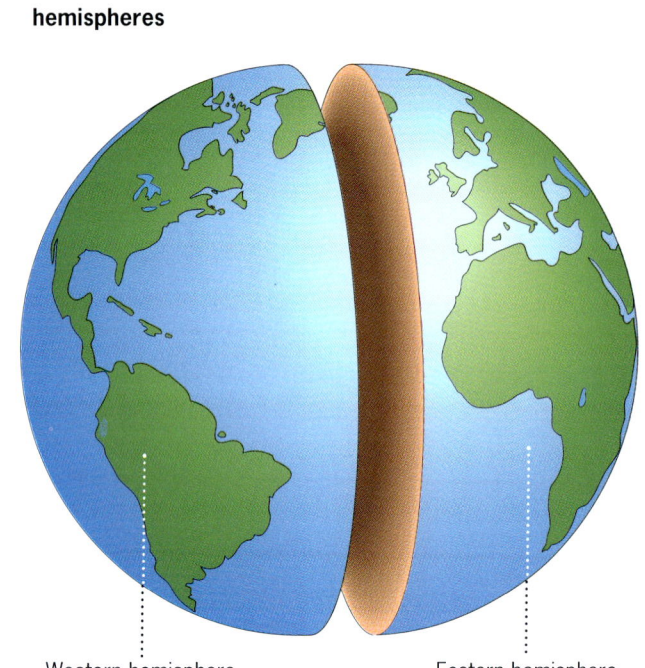

Western hemisphere · Eastern hemisphere

Northern hemisphere

Southern hemisphere

GRID SYSTEM

lines of latitude

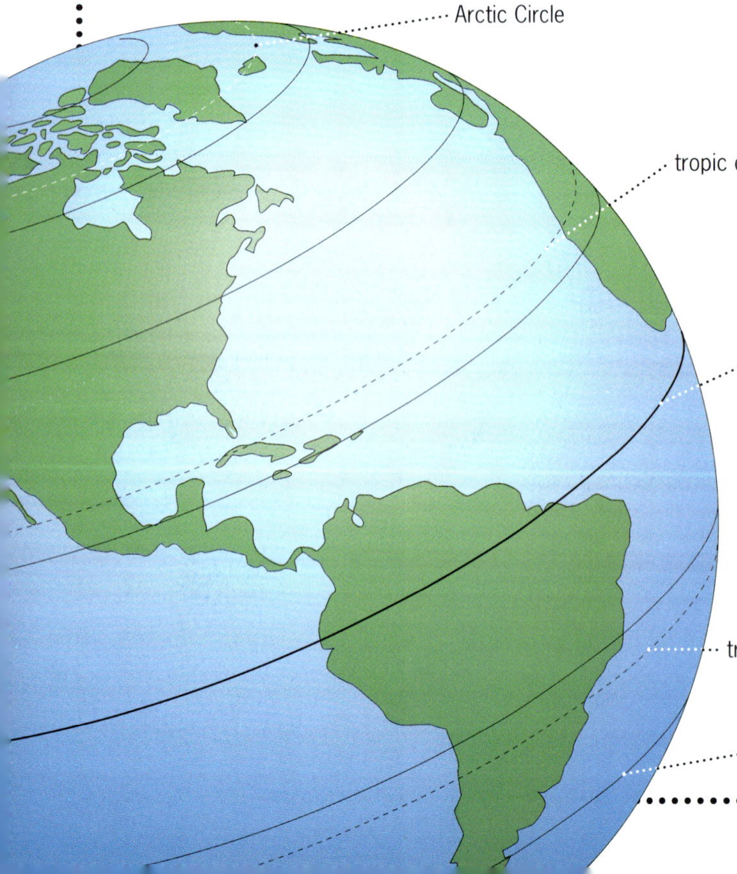

- Arctic Circle
- tropic of Cancer
- Equator
- tropic of Capricorn
- parallel

lines of longitude

- Western meridian
- Eastern meridian
- prime meridian

MAP PROJECTIONS

interrupted projection

plane projection

cylindrical projection

conical projection

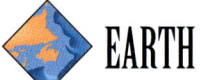

CARTOGRAPHY

political map

internal boundary
province
international boundary
country
city
capital
state
ALASKA
CANADA
UNITED STATES
MEXICO
Edmonton
Calgary
Vancouver
Winnipeg
Seattle
Montréal
Ottawa
Toronto
Detroit
New York
Chicago
Washington
San Francisco
Denver
Los Angeles
San Diego
Atlanta
Dallas
Houston
Miami
Monterrey
Guadalajara
Mexico

physical map

mountain range
bay
prairie
mountain range
ocean
river
river
gulf
cape
sea
strait
river estuary
island
lake
plain
peninsula
archipelago
plateau
isthmus

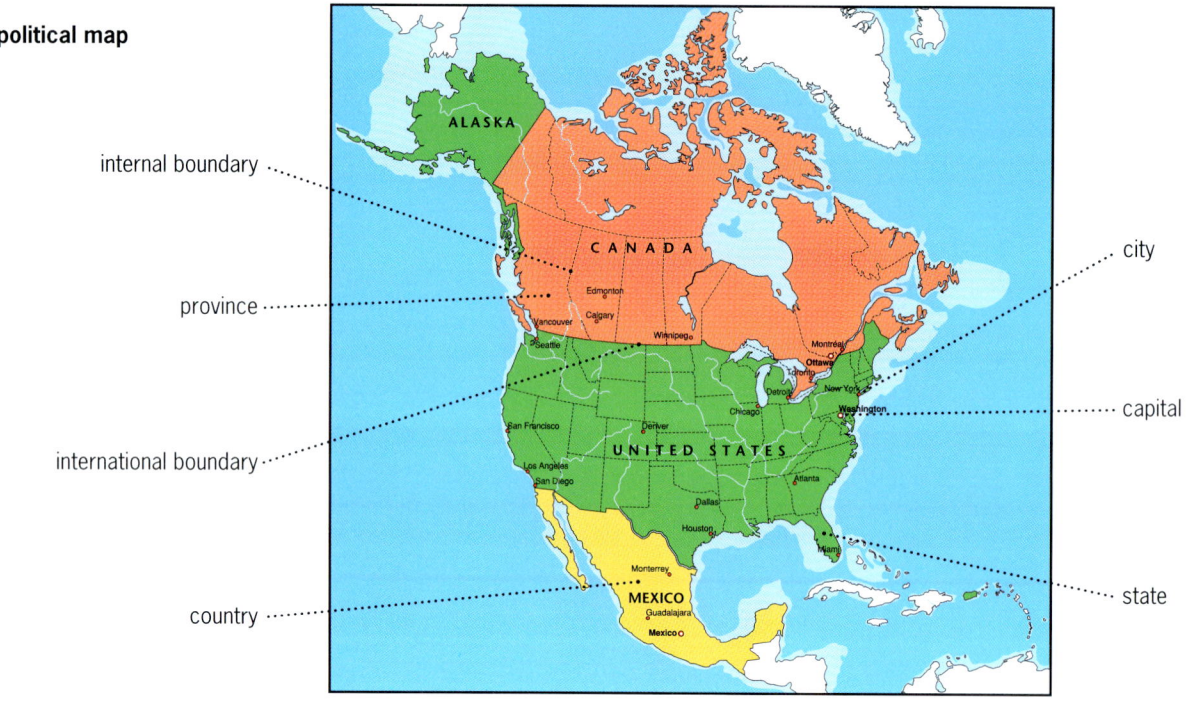

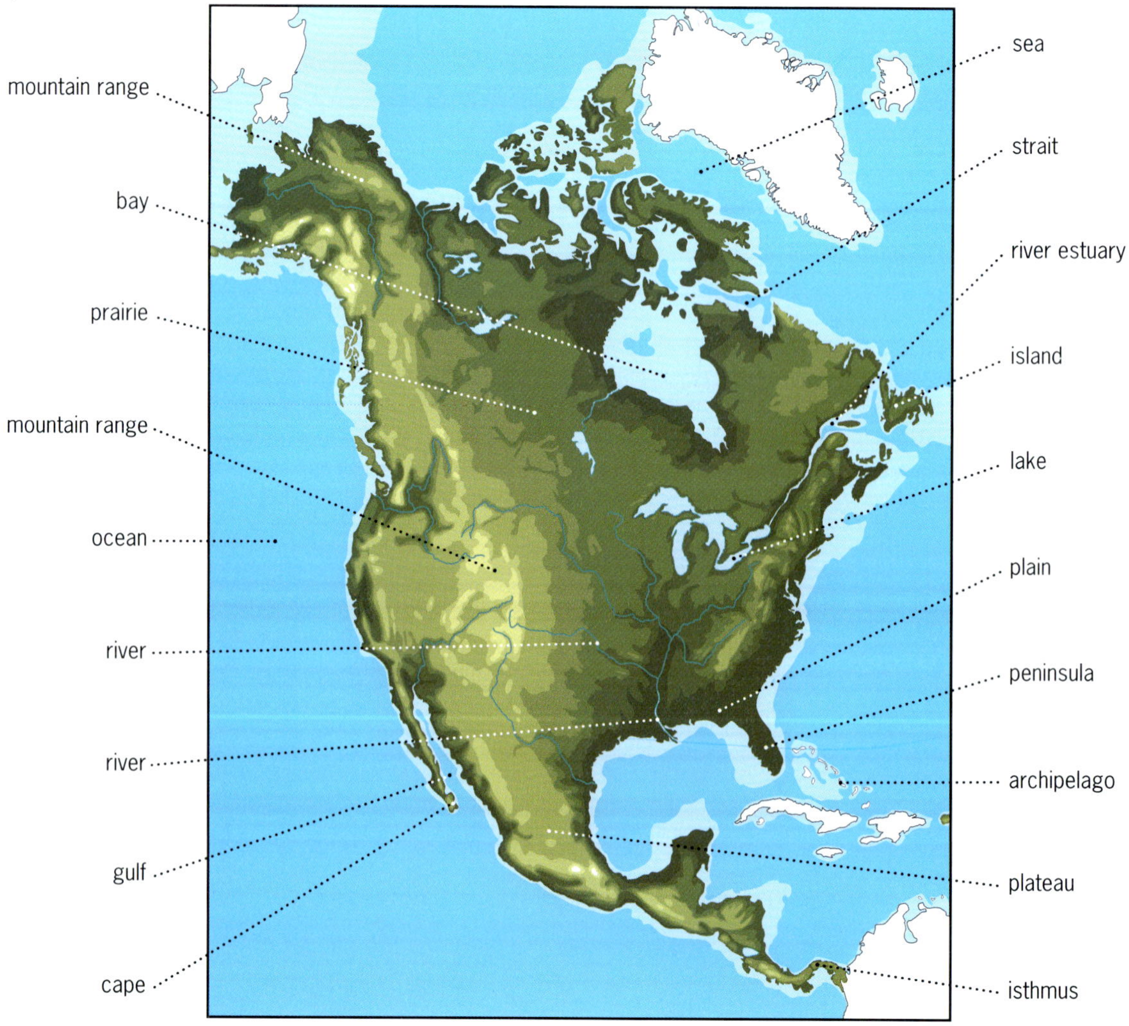

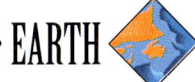

road map

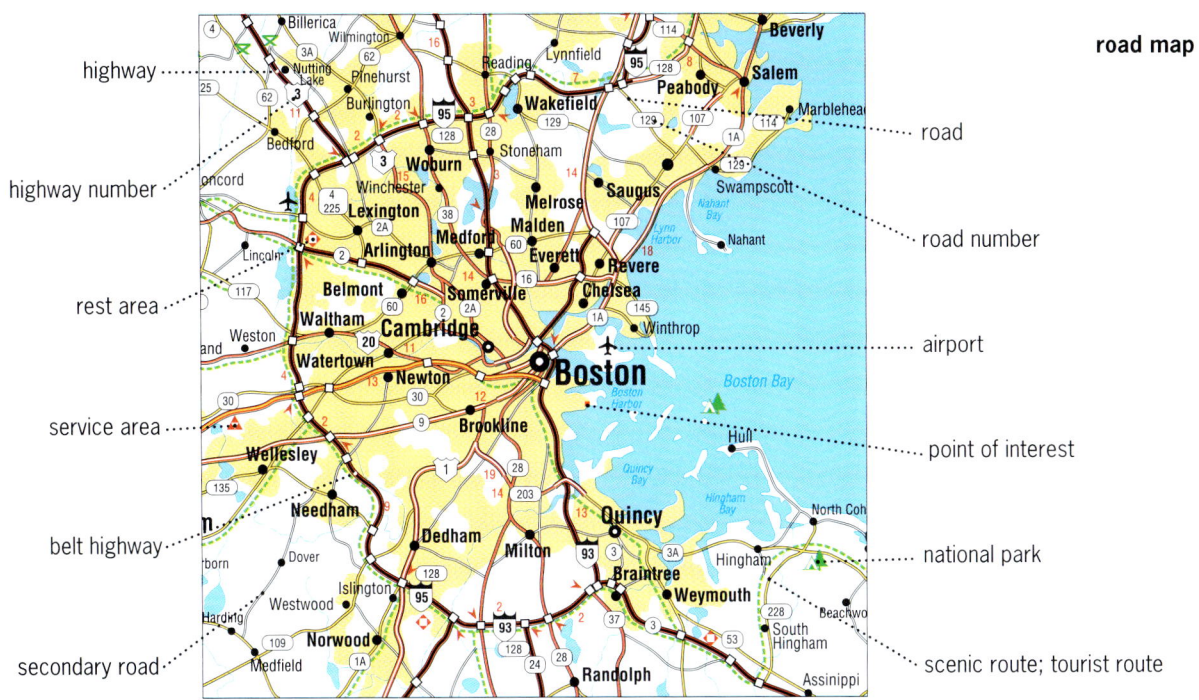

highway
highway number
rest area
service area
belt highway
secondary road
road
road number
airport
point of interest
national park
scenic route; tourist route
Billerica
Wilmington
Reading
Lynnfield
Beverly
Salem
Peabody
Marblehead
Nutting Lake
Pinehurst
Burlington
Wakefield
Bedford
Woburn
Stoneham
Winchester
Lexington
Melrose
Saugus
Swampscott
Malden
Medford
Arlington
Everett
Revere
Nahant
Lincoln
Belmont
Somerville
Chelsea
Waltham
Cambridge
Winthrop
Weston
Watertown
Boston
Boston Bay
Newton
Brookline
Hull
Wellesley
Needham
Quincy
Dedham
Milton
Dover
Hingham
Braintree
Weymouth
Islington
Westwood
Norwood
South Hingham
Medfield
Randolph
Assinippi

COMPASS CARD

North
North-northwest
North-northeast
Northwest
Northeast
West-northwest
East-northeast
West
East
West-southwest
East-southeast
Southwest
Southeast
South-southwest
South-southeast
South

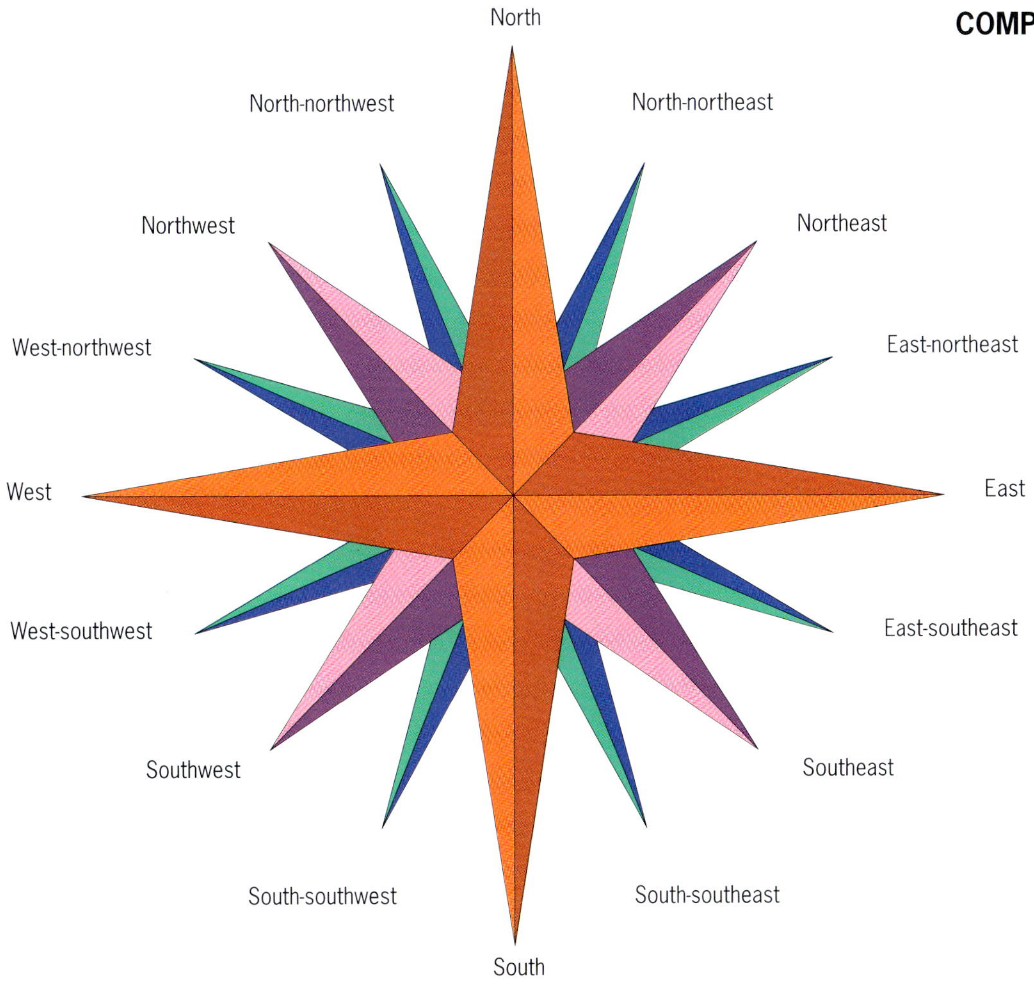

EARTH

ECOLOGY

greenhouse effect

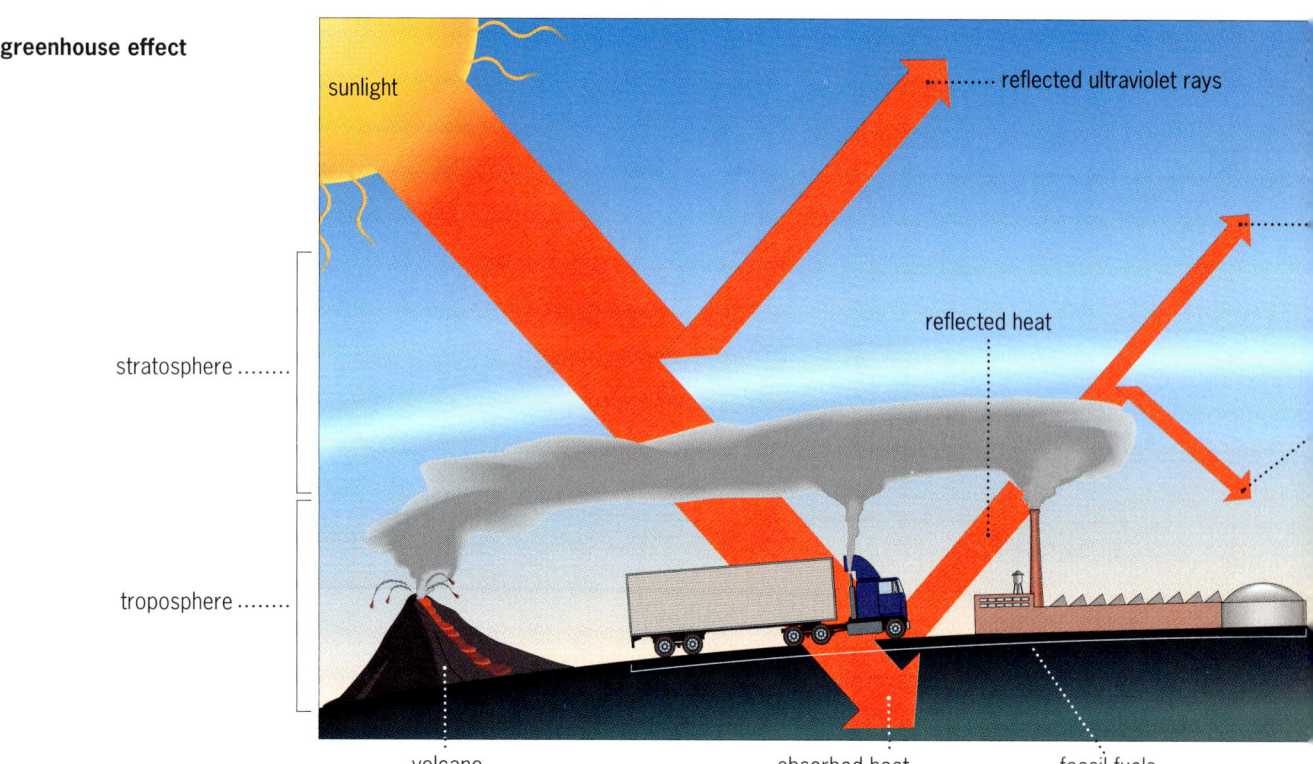

food chain

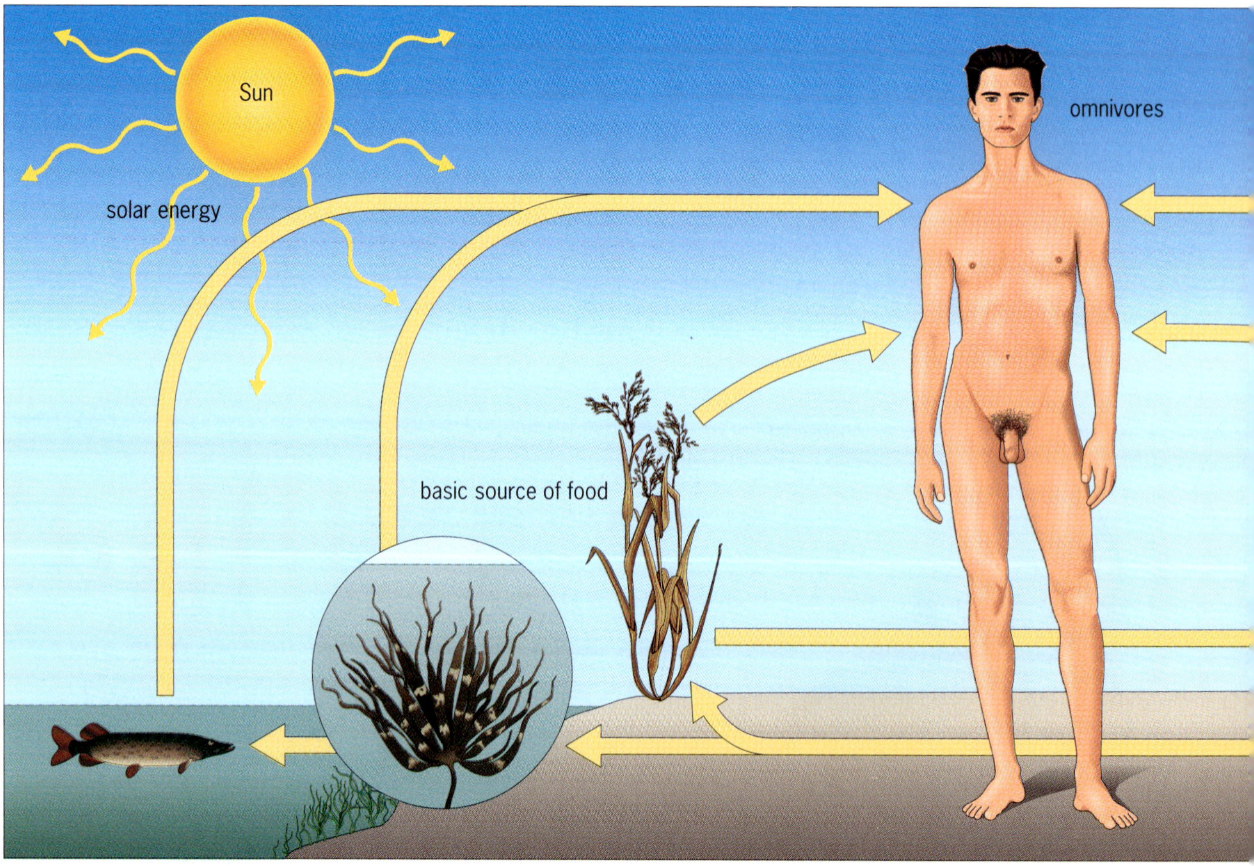

EARTH

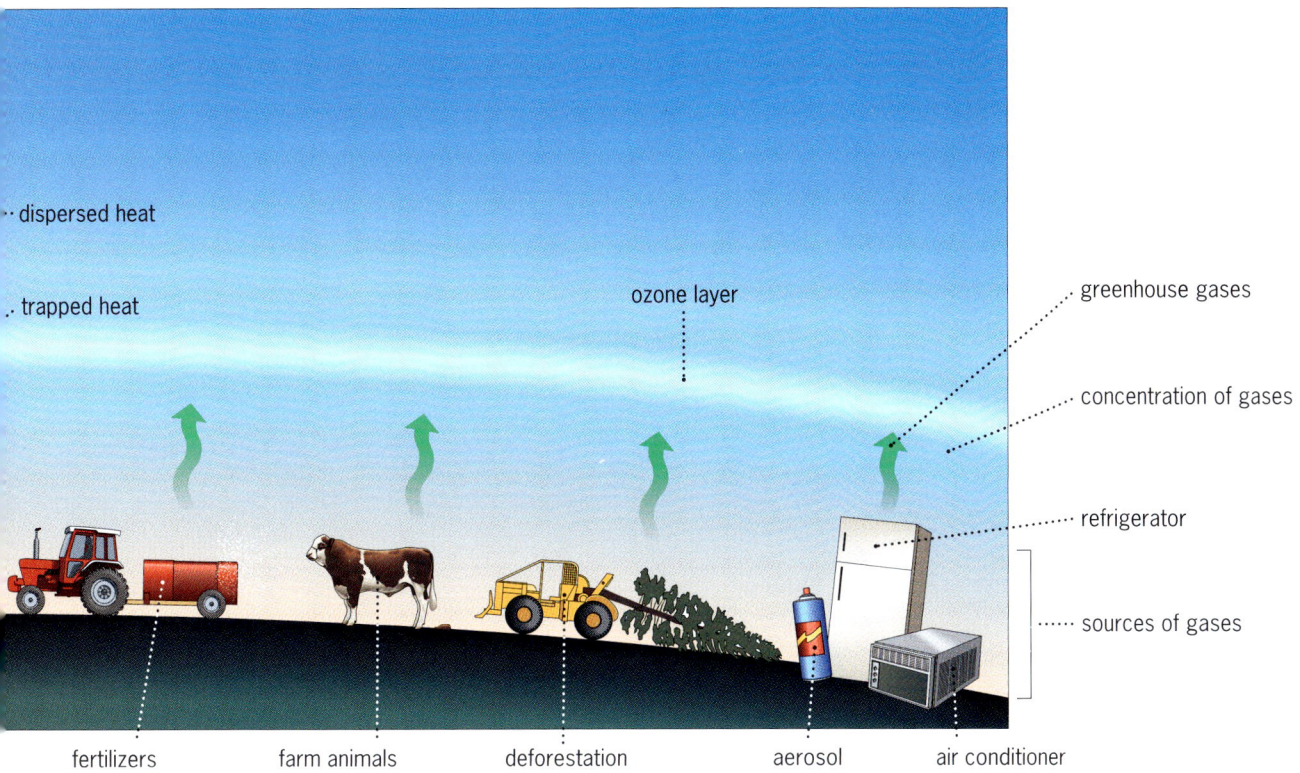

dispersed heat
trapped heat
ozone layer
greenhouse gases
concentration of gases
refrigerator
sources of gases

fertilizers | farm animals | deforestation | aerosol | air conditioner

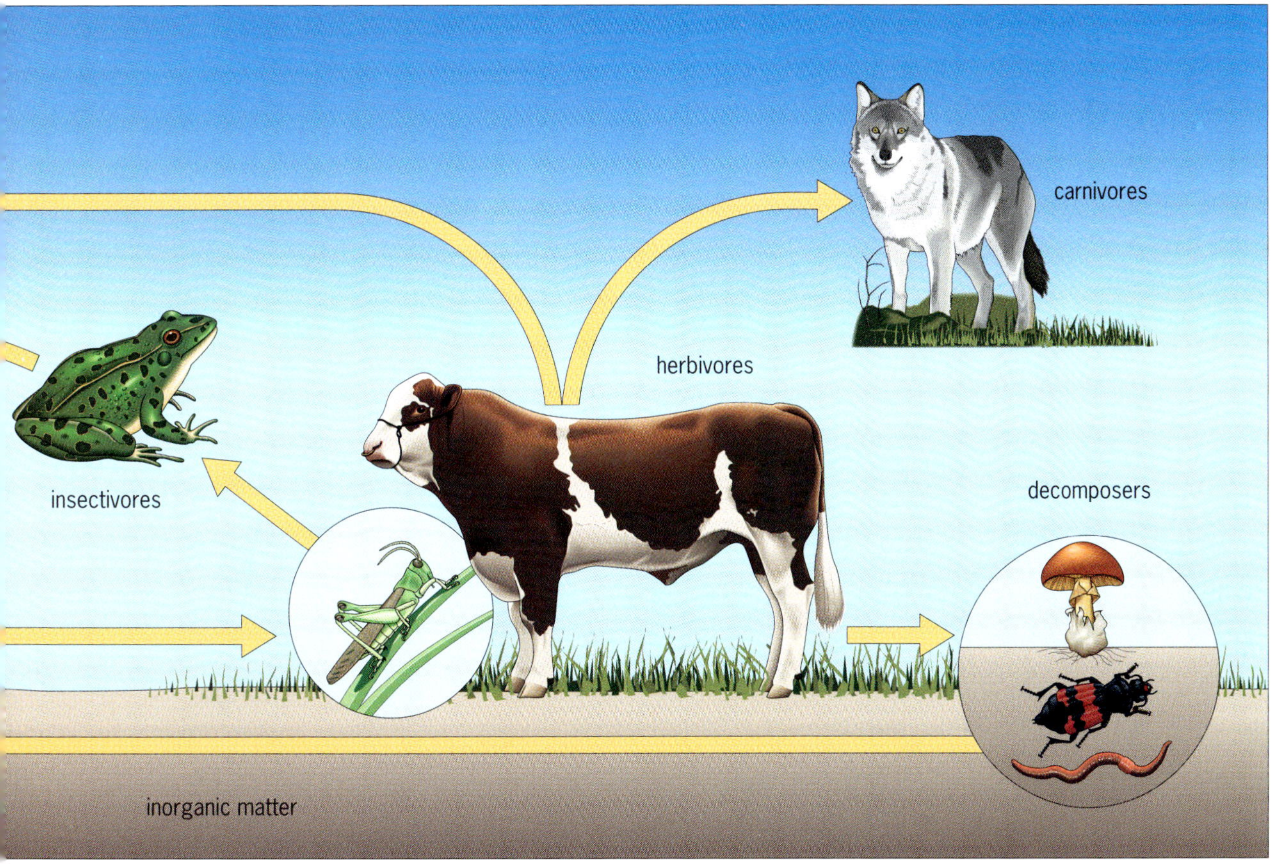

carnivores
herbivores
insectivores
decomposers
inorganic matter

ECOLOGY

atmospheric pollution

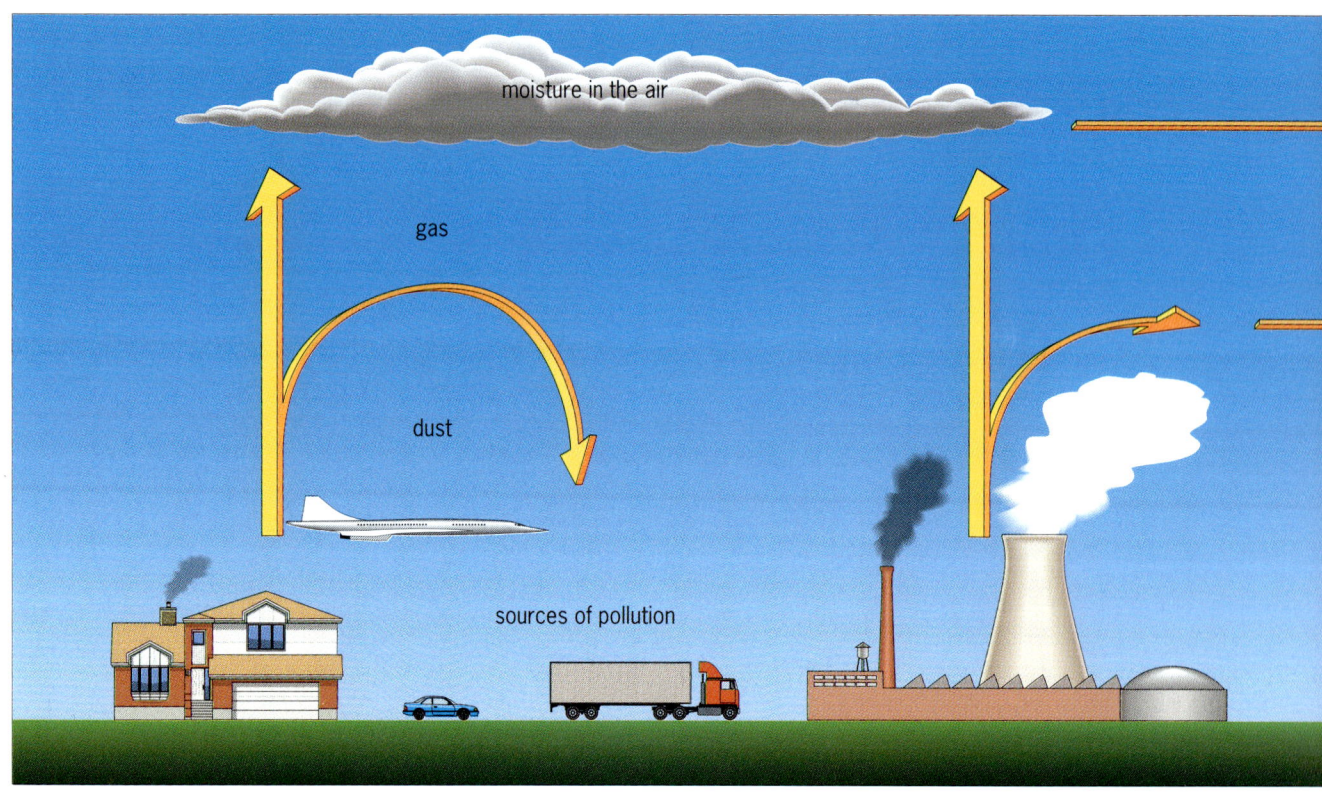

water cycle

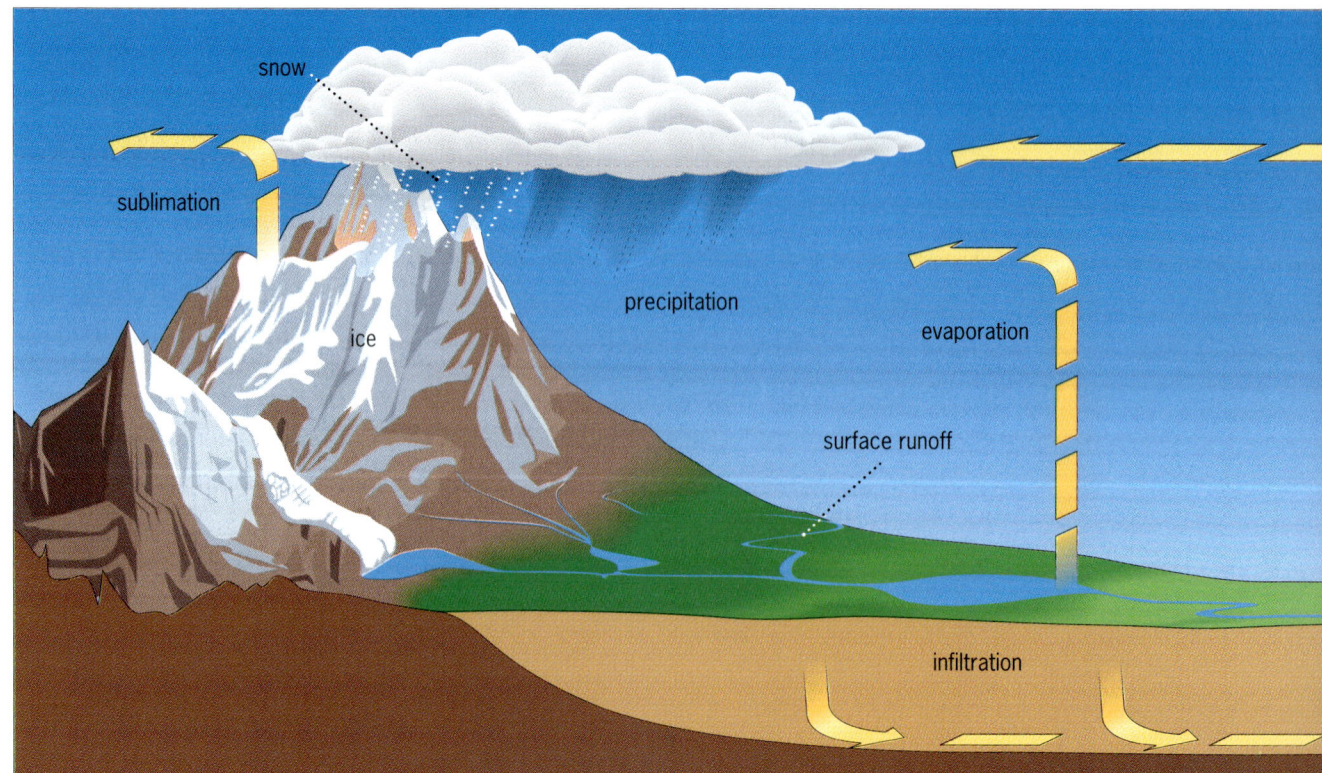

EARTH

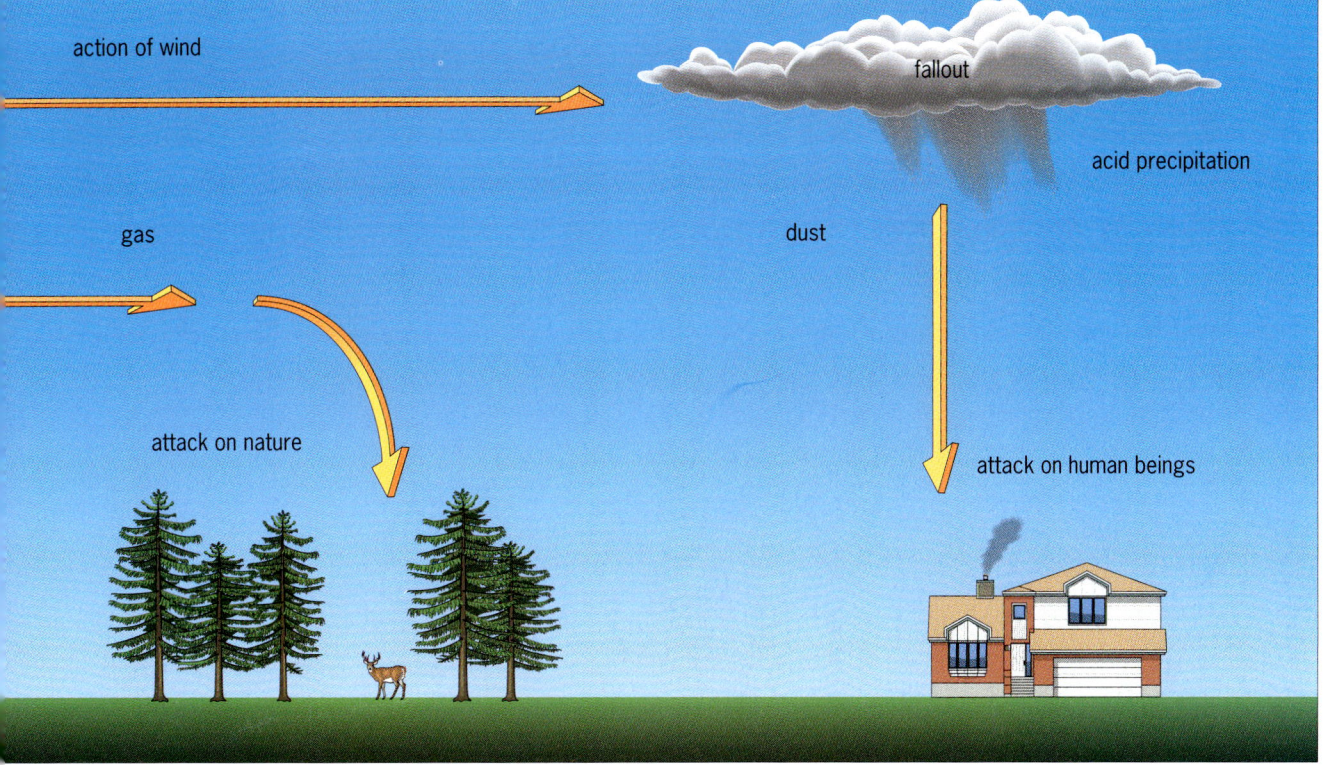

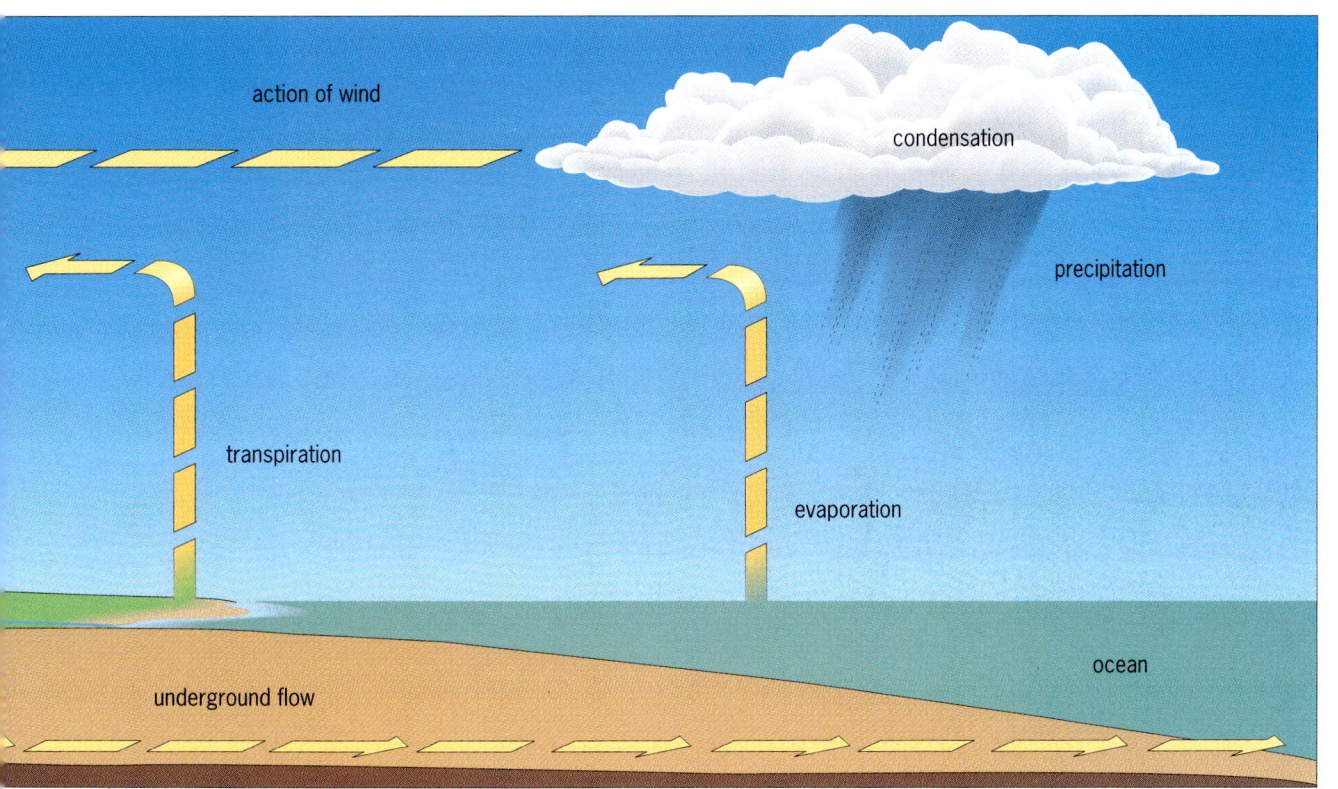

EARTH

ECOLOGY

food pollution on ground

food pollution in water

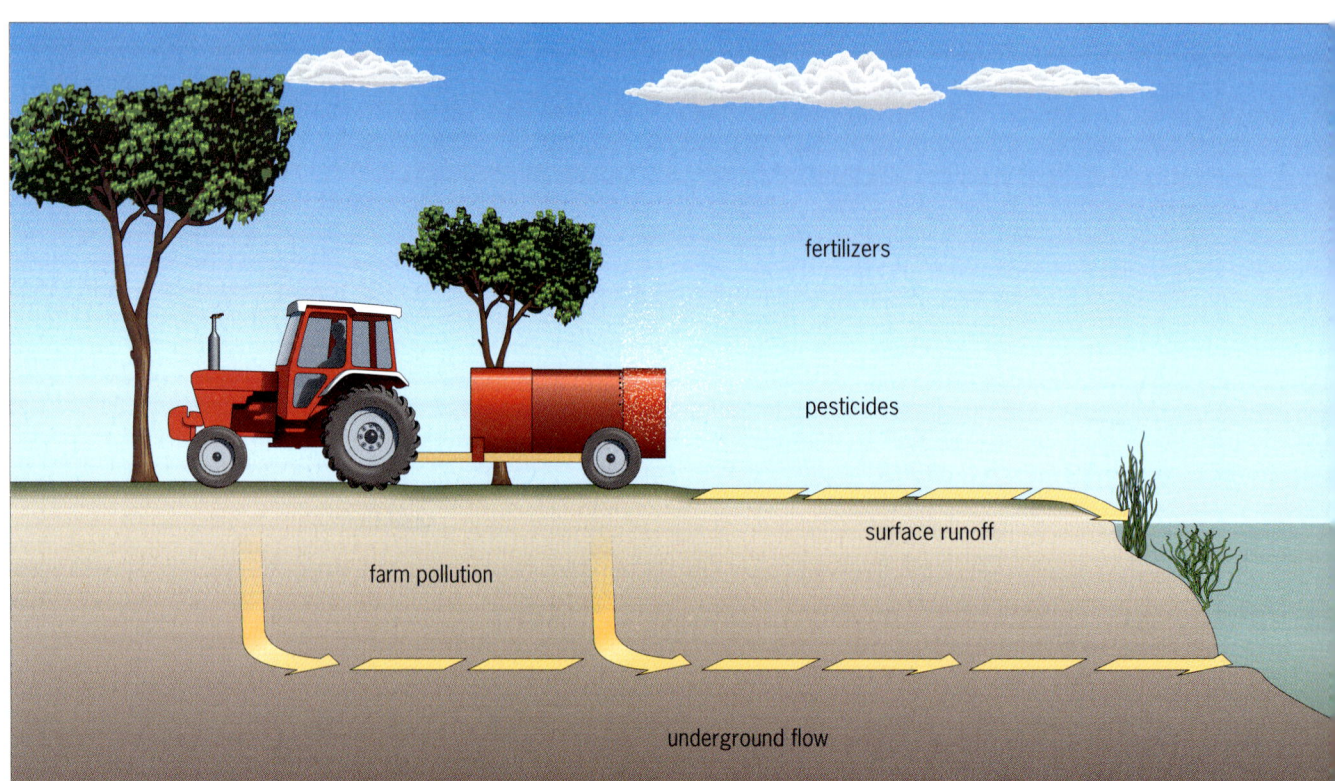

ECOLOGY

vegetables
meat
dairy products

acid rain
industrial pollution
carbon dioxide
metals
carnivores
herbivores

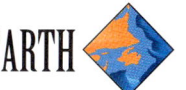

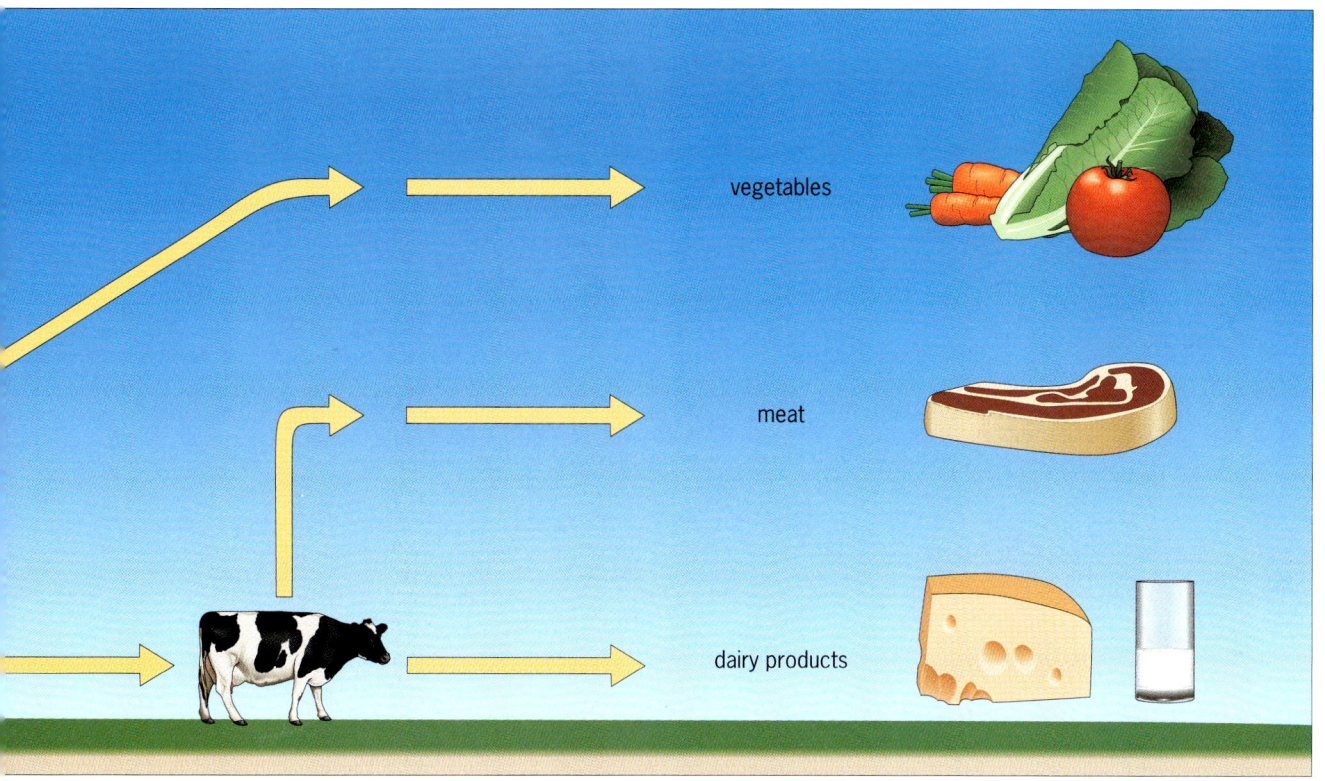

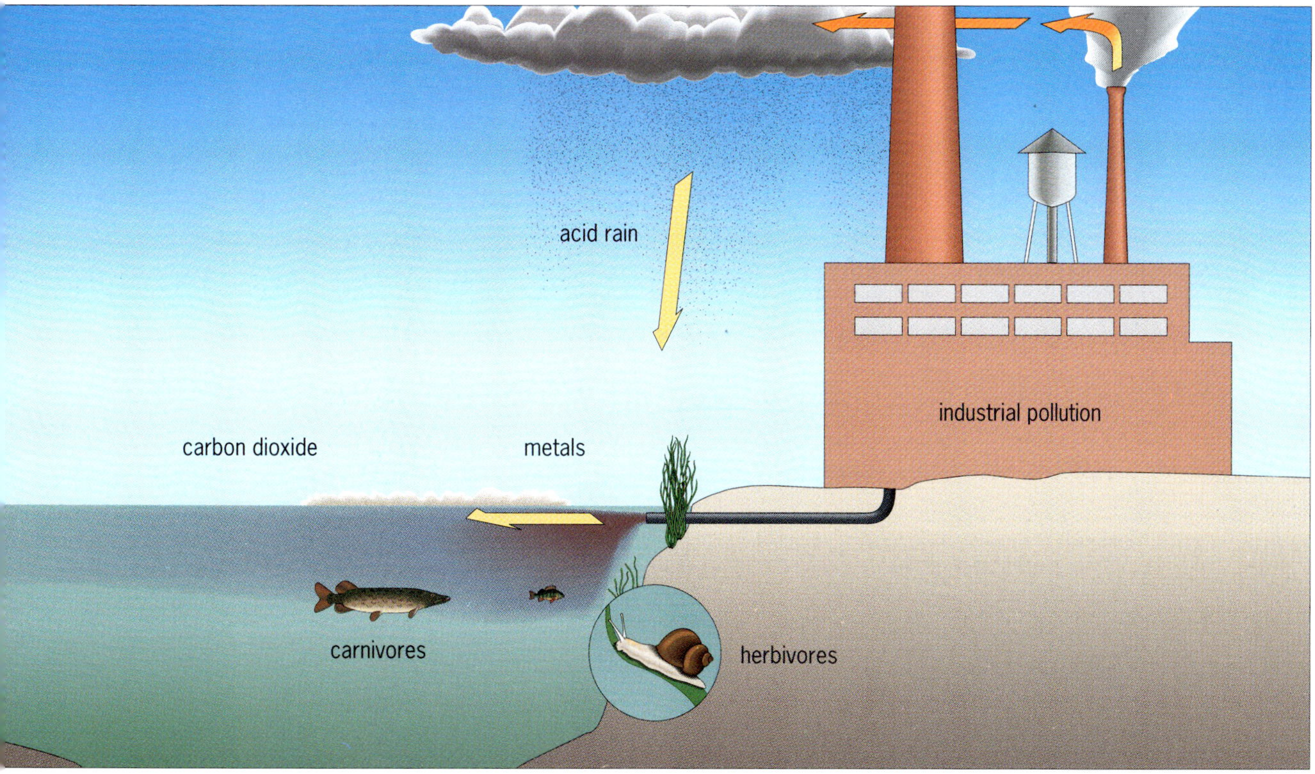

VEGETABLE KINGDOM

PLANT AND SOIL

SOIL PROFILE

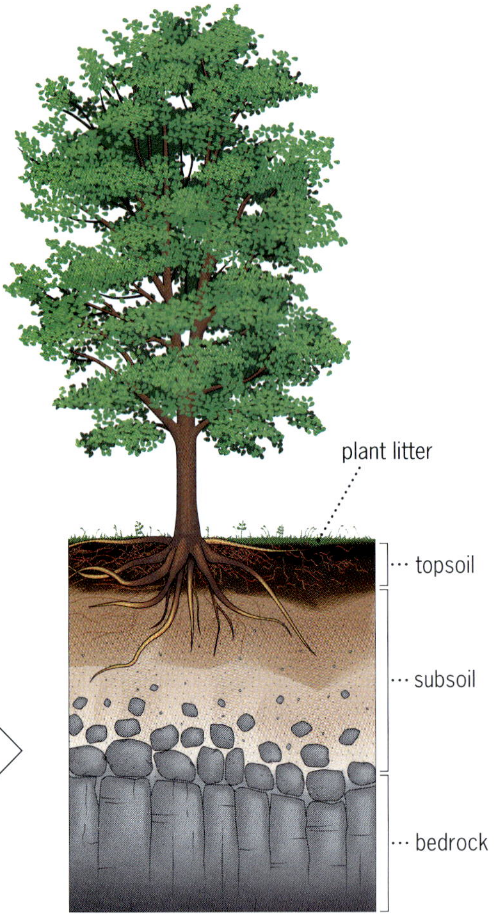

- plant litter
- topsoil
- subsoil
- bedrock

GERMINATION

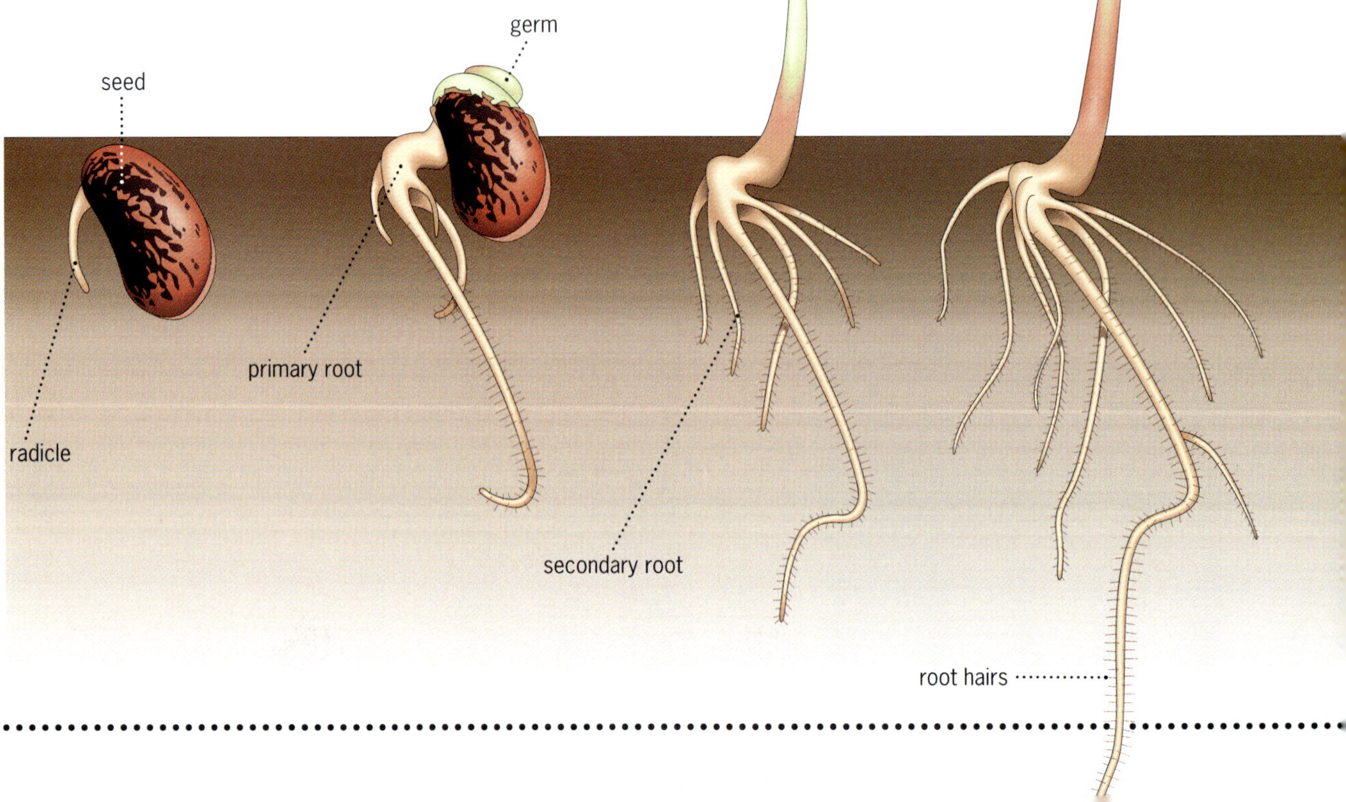

- leaf
- terminal bud
- first leaves
- cotyledons
- seed
- germ
- radicle
- primary root
- secondary root
- root hairs

VEGETABLE KINGDOM

MUSHROOM

structure of a mushroom

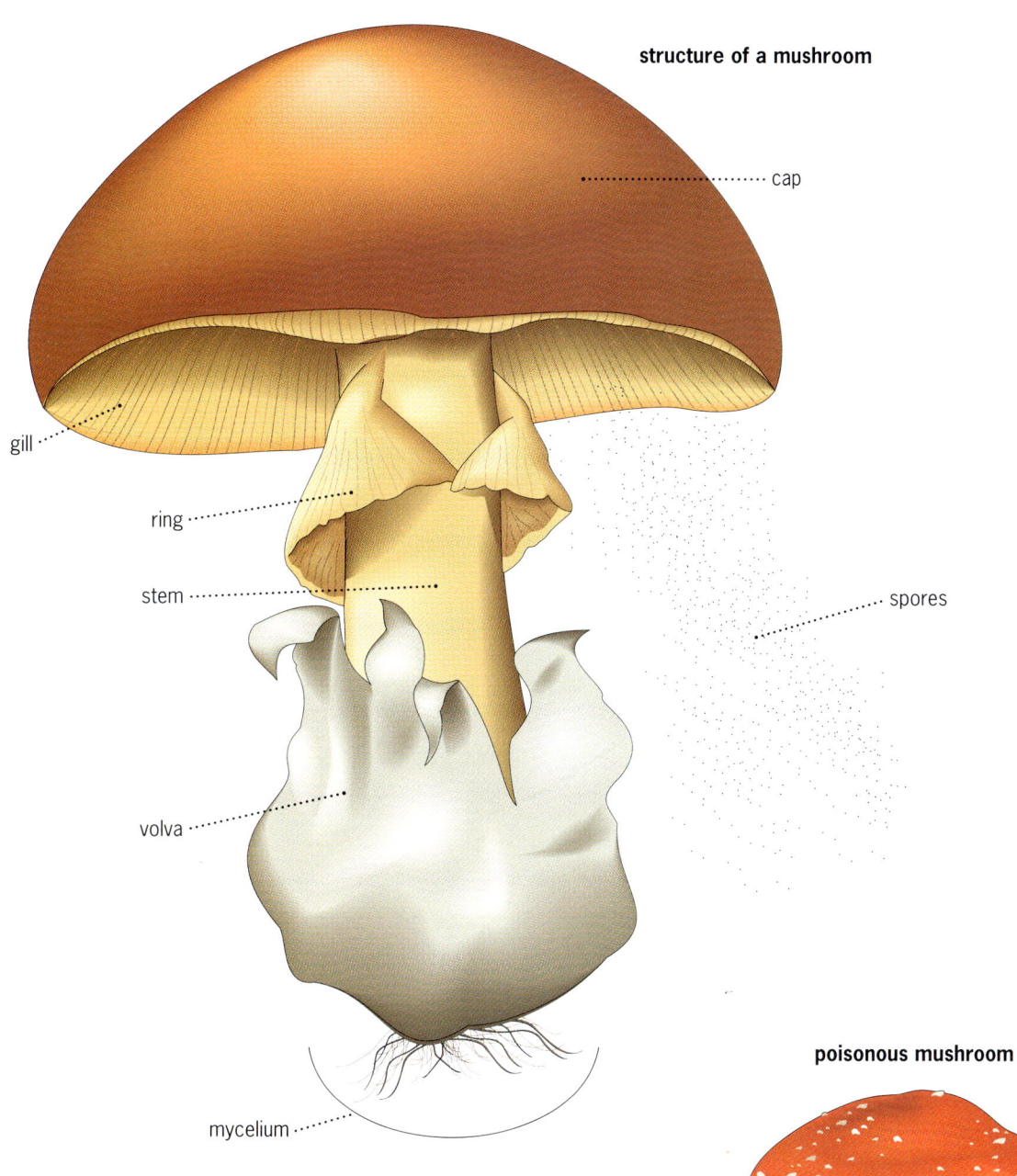

cap

gill

ring

stem

spores

volva

mycelium

edible mushroom

cultivated mushroom

deadly mushroom

destroying angel

poisonous mushroom

fly agaric

35

VEGETABLE KINGDOM

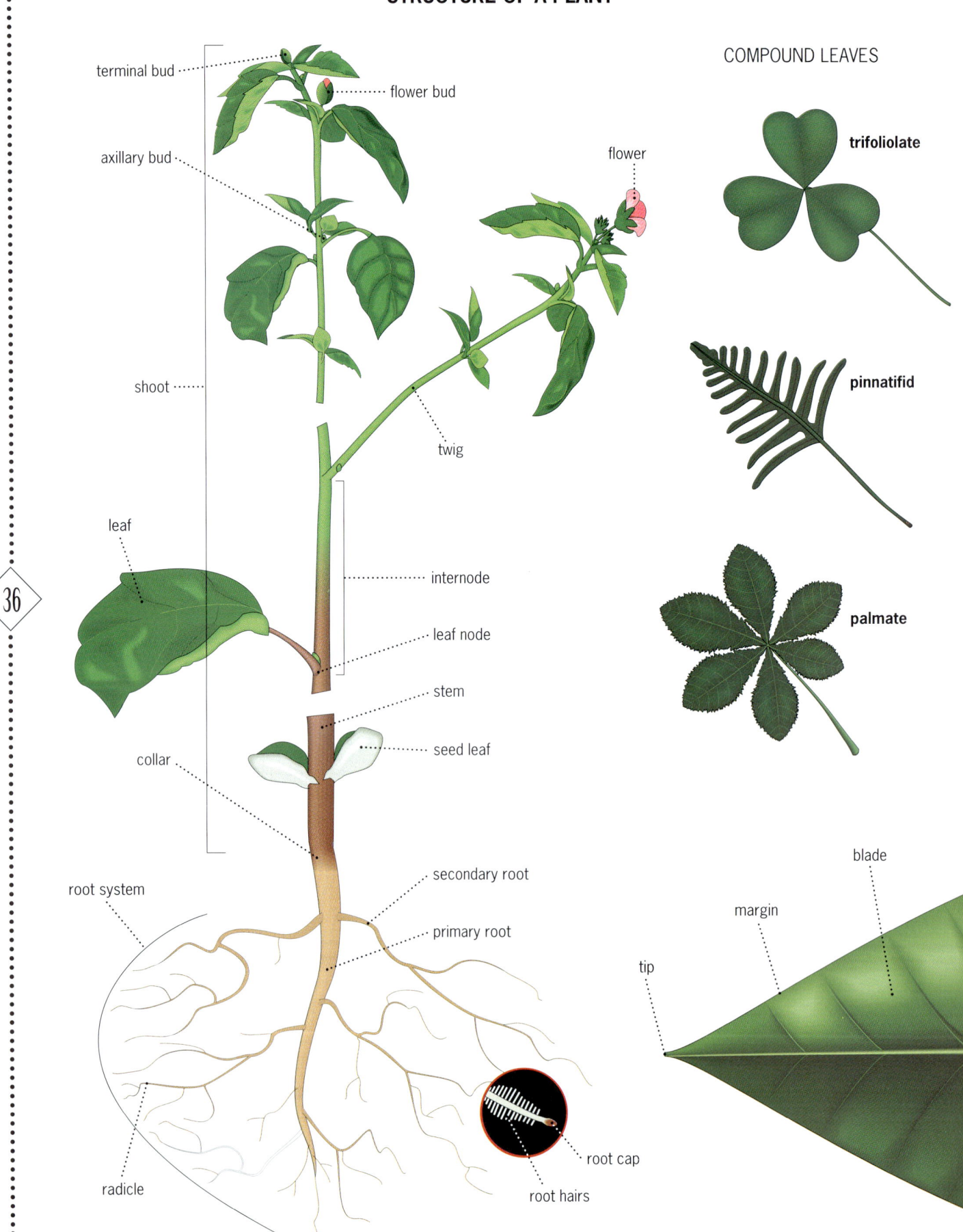

STRUCTURE OF A PLANT

- terminal bud
- flower bud
- axillary bud
- flower
- shoot
- twig
- leaf
- internode
- leaf node
- stem
- seed leaf
- collar
- secondary root
- primary root
- root system
- root cap
- root hairs
- radicle

COMPOUND LEAVES

- **trifoliolate**
- **pinnatifid**
- **palmate**

- tip
- margin
- blade

STRUCTURE OF A PLANT

VEGETABLE KINGDOM

SIMPLE LEAVES

linear

lanceolate

orbiculate

LEAF MARGINS

entire

ciliate

lobate

crenate

dentate

vein

midrib

petiole

leaf

sheath

stipule

leaf axil

37

VEGETABLE KINGDOM

FLOWERS

structure of a flower

- stigma
- filament
- petal
- sepal
- receptacle
- anther
- ovary
- style
- ovule
- pedicel

corolla

stamen

pistil

calyx

EXAMPLES OF FLOWERS

orchid

tulip

violet

begonia

poppy

rose

38

VEGETABLE KINGDOM

lily

sunflower

lily of the valley

39

crocus

carnation

daffodil

VEGETABLE KINGDOM

TREE

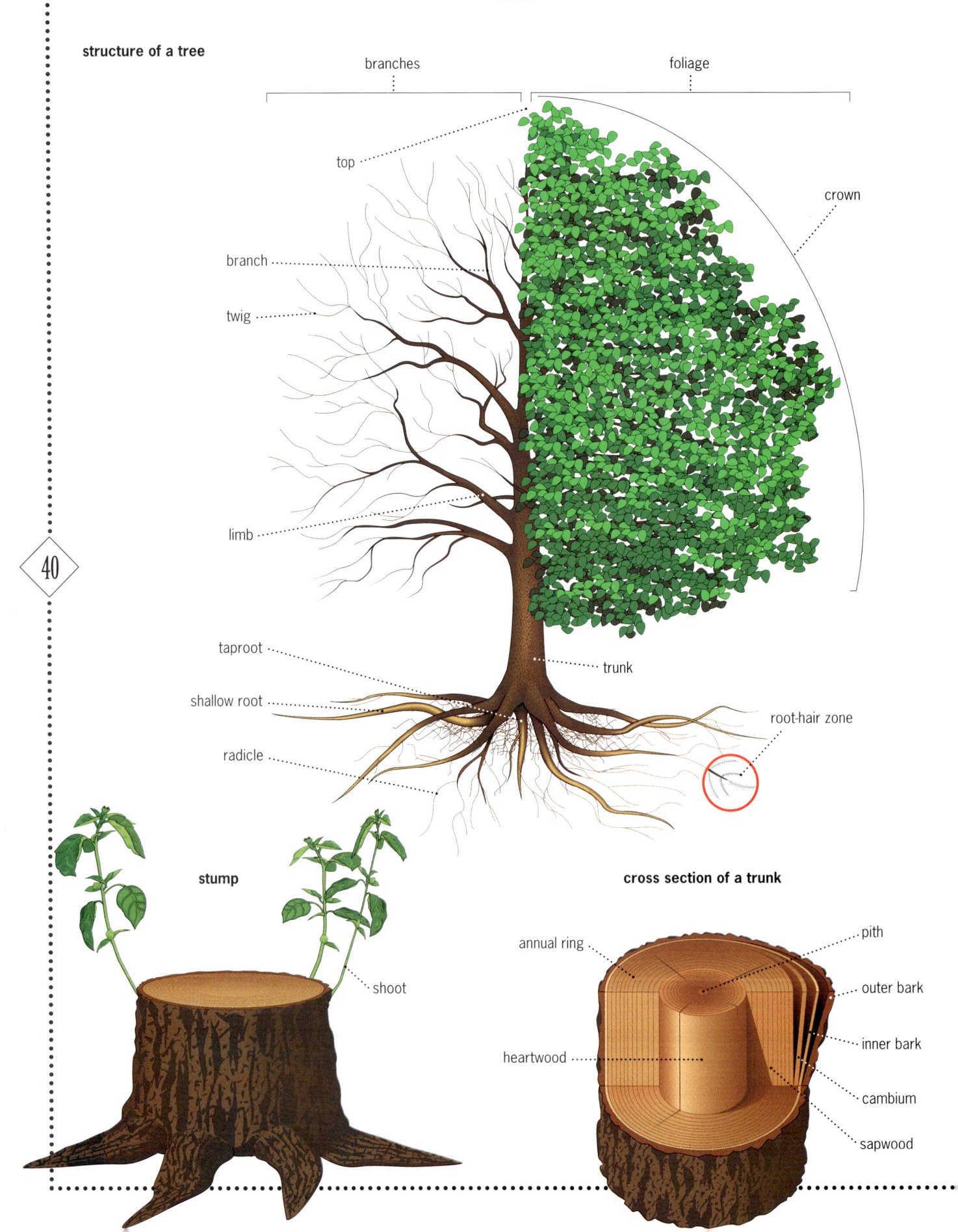

structure of a tree

- branches
  - top
  - branch
  - twig
  - limb
- foliage
  - crown
- taproot
- shallow root
- radicle
- trunk
- root-hair zone

stump
- shoot

cross section of a trunk
- annual ring
- pith
- outer bark
- inner bark
- cambium
- sapwood
- heartwood

40

VEGETABLE KINGDOM

EXAMPLES OF TREES

poplar

oak

maple

41

VEGETABLE KINGDOM

palm tree

weeping willow

birch

VEGETABLE KINGDOM

CONIFER

larch

umbrella pine

cone

pine seeds

TYPES OF LEAVES

fir needles

cypress scalelike leaves

pine needles

branch

female cone

male cone

43

FRUITS AND VEGETABLES

FLESHY FRUITS: BERRY FRUITS

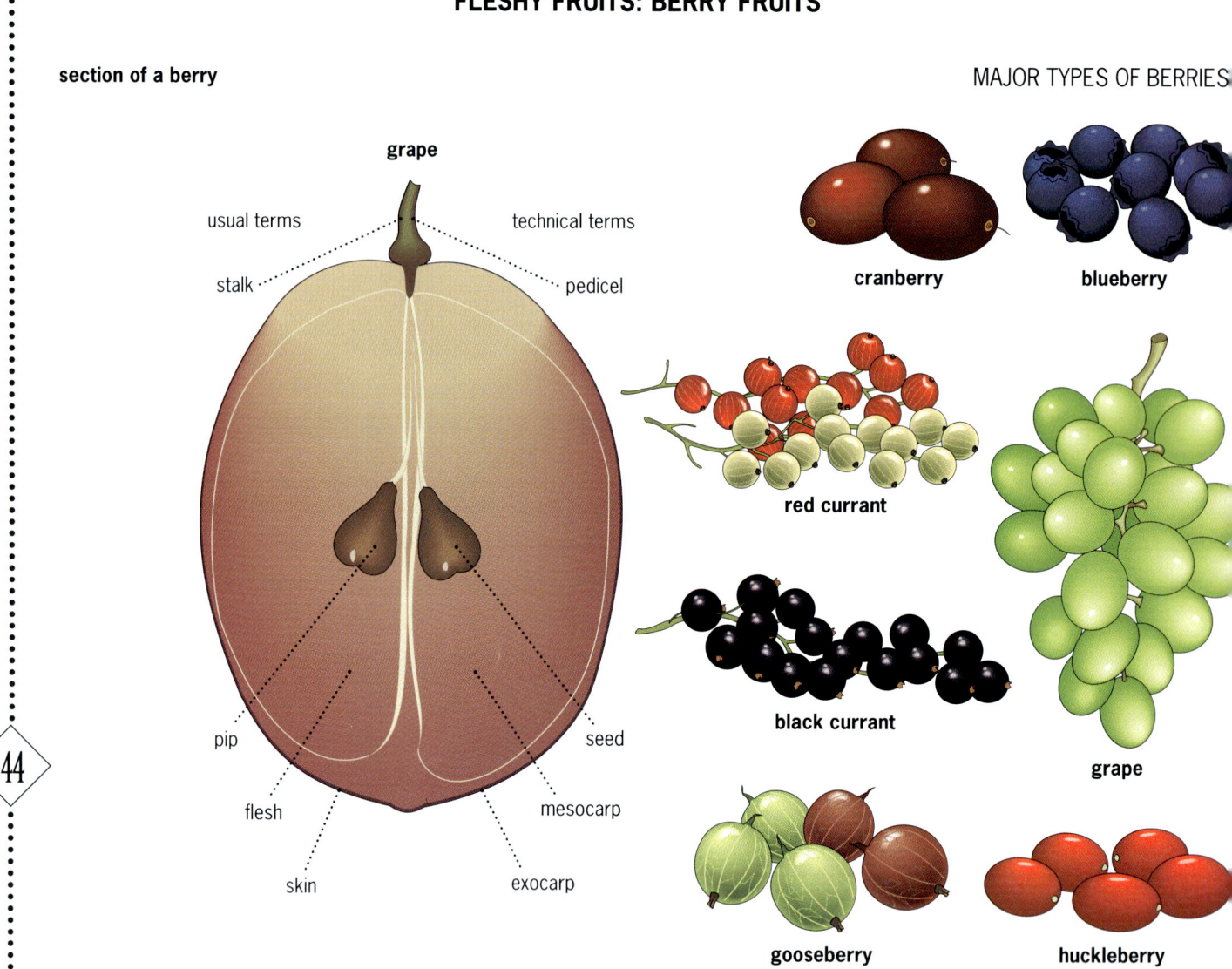

section of a berry

MAJOR TYPES OF BERRIES

grape

usual terms — technical terms
stalk — pedicel
pip — seed
flesh — mesocarp
skin — exocarp

cranberry

blueberry

red currant

black currant

grape

gooseberry

huckleberry

section of a strawberry

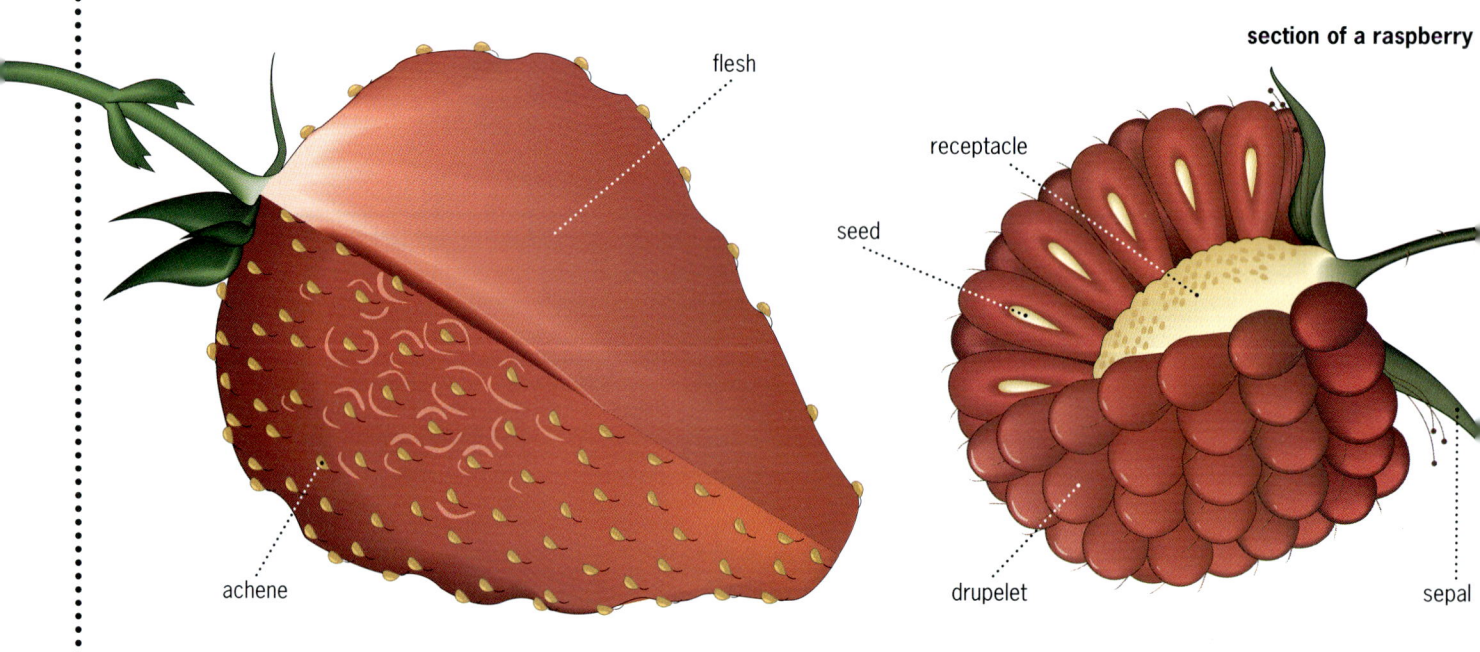

flesh

achene

section of a raspberry

receptacle

seed

drupelet

sepal

FRUITS AND VEGETABLES

FLESHY STONE FRUITS

section of a stone fruit

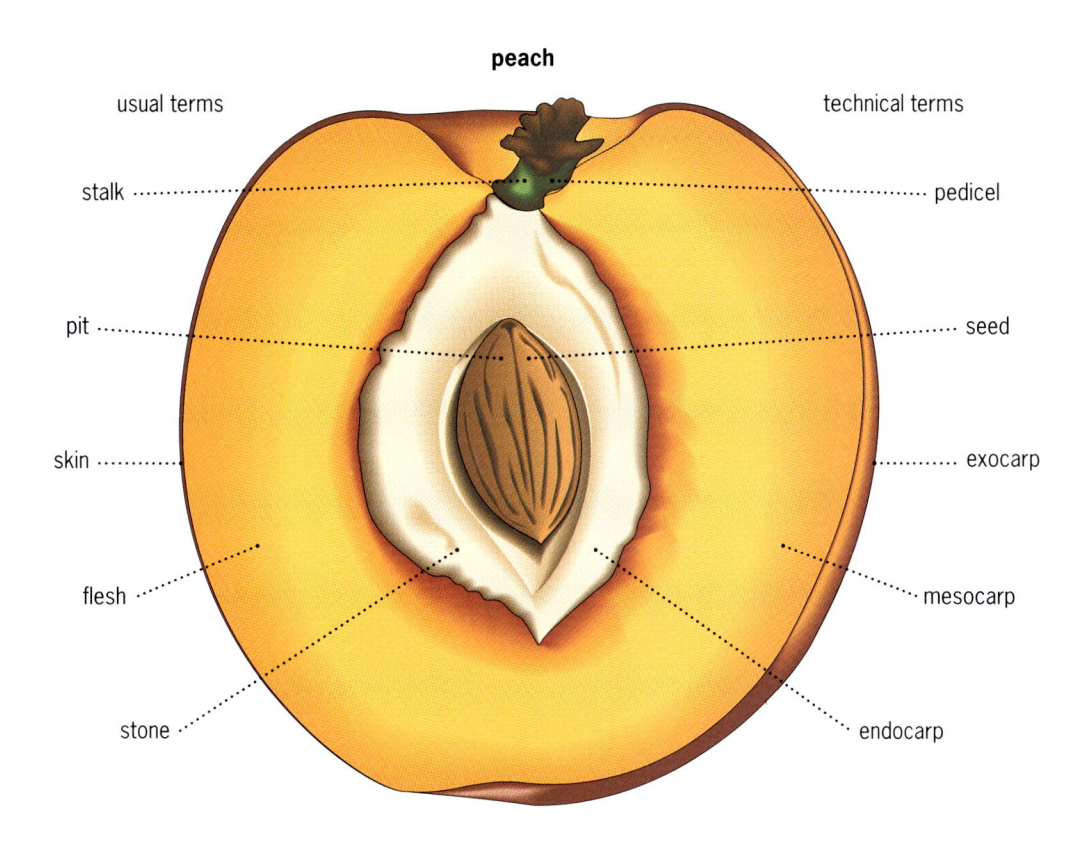

peach

usual terms | technical terms

- stalk — pedicel
- pit — seed
- skin — exocarp
- flesh — mesocarp
- stone — endocarp

MAJOR TYPES OF STONE FRUITS

- apricot
- nectarine
- peach
- mango
- olive
- plum
- cherry
- date

45

FRUITS AND VEGETABLES

FLESHY POME FRUITS

section of a pome fruit

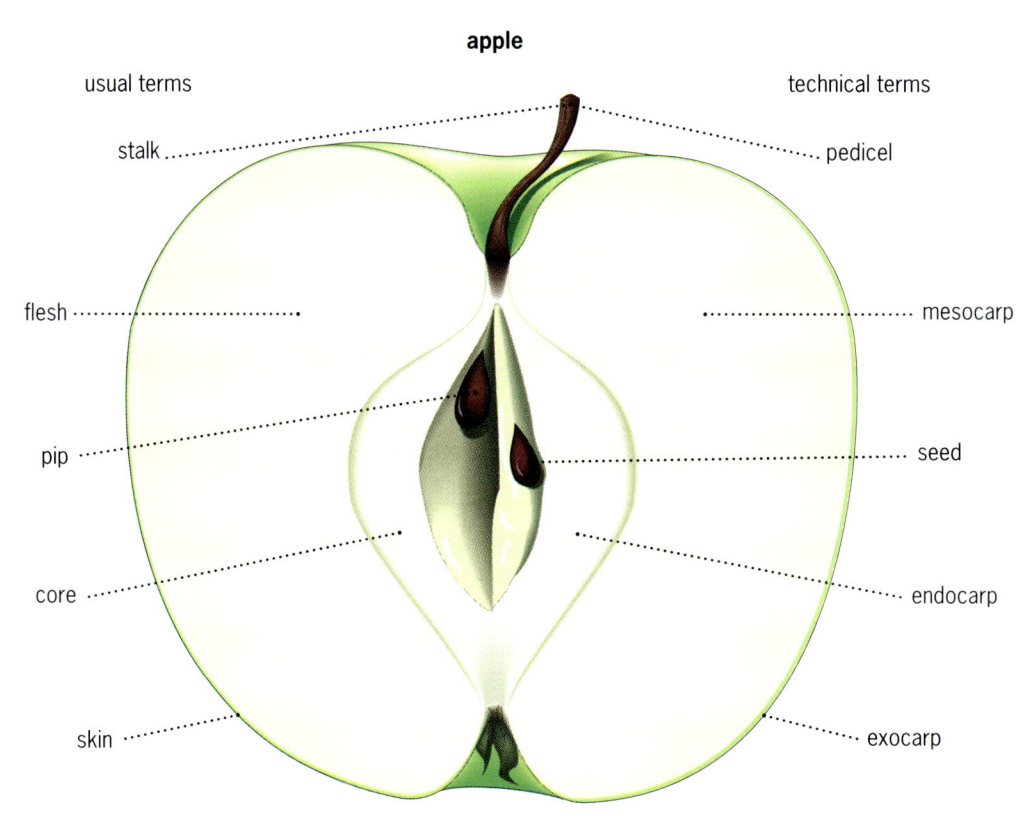

apple

usual terms — technical terms

- stalk — pedicel
- flesh — mesocarp
- pip — seed
- core — endocarp
- skin — exocarp

MAJOR TYPES OF POME FRUITS

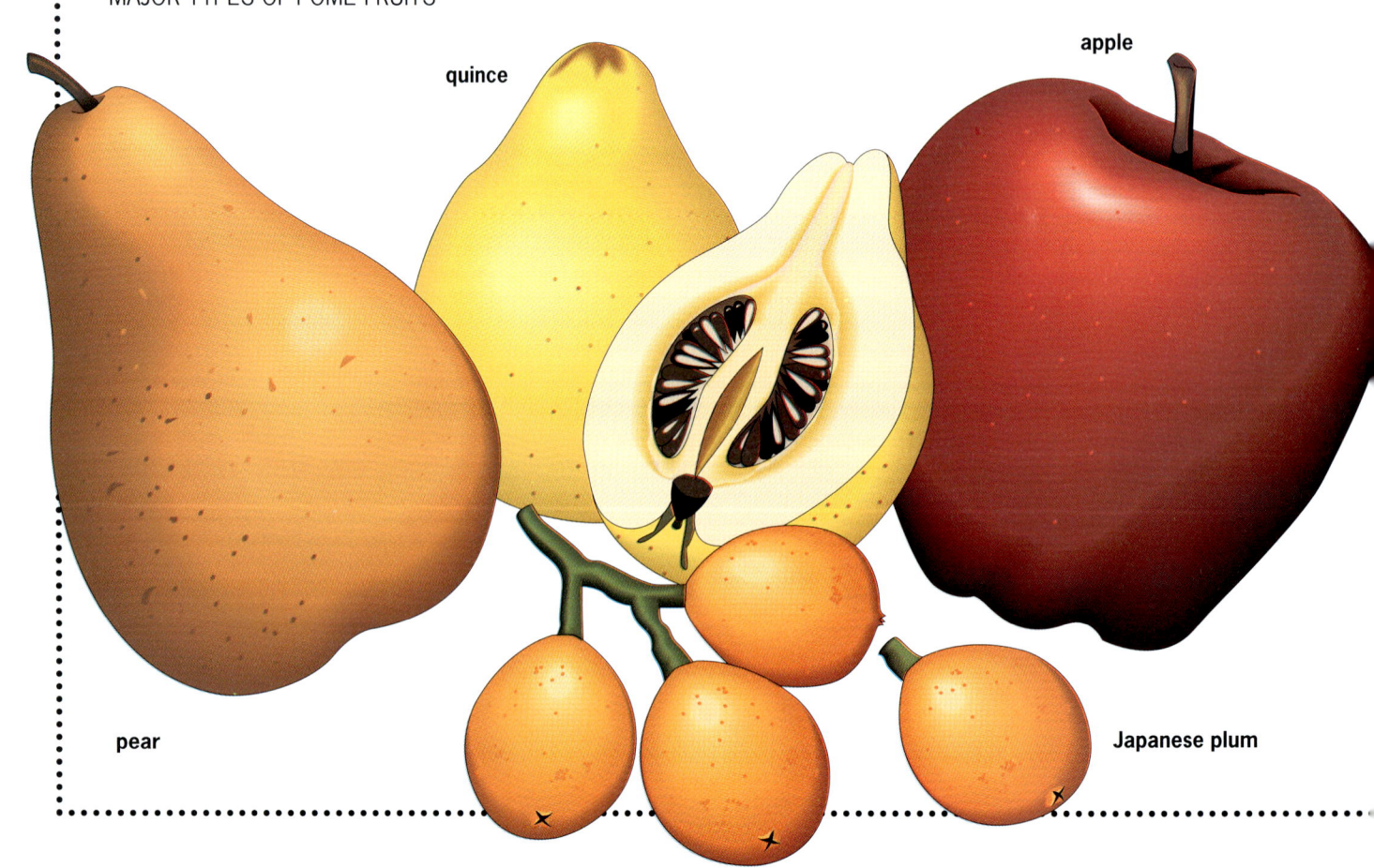

quince

apple

pear

Japanese plum

FRUITS AND VEGETABLES

FLESHY FRUITS: CITRUS FRUITS

section of a citrus fruit

orange

usual terms | technical terms

- zest
- segment
- pip
- pulp
- rind

- wall
- seed
- mesocarp
- pericarp

47

MAJOR TYPES OF CITRUS FRUITS

lemon

lime

orange

grapefruit

mandarin

… FRUITS AND VEGETABLES

TROPICAL FRUITS

MAJOR TYPES OF TROPICAL FRUITS

litchi

kiwi

guava

Japanese persimmon

Indian fig

cherimoya

fig

papaya

pomegranate

banana

avocado

pineapple

FRUITS AND VEGETABLES

VEGETABLES

INFLORESCENT VEGETABLES

cauliflower

broccoli

artichoke

FRUIT VEGETABLES

watermelon

autumn squash

pumpkin

cantaloupe

muskmelon

eggplant

summer squash

cucumber

zucchini

okra

green bean

sweet pepper; green pepper

tomato

hot pepper; chilli

49

FRUITS AND VEGETABLES

VEGETABLES

section of a bulb

- bud
- bulbil
- scale leaf
- fleshy leaves
- underground stem
- root

BULB VEGETABLES

- **garlic**
- **leek**
- **shallot**
- **yellow onion**
- **pickling onion**
- **chives**
- **scallion**

FRUITS AND VEGETABLES

TUBER VEGETABLES

- potato
- sweet potato
- Jerusalem artichoke

ROOT VEGETABLES

- beet
- celeriac
- kohlrabi
- swede
- turnip
- horseradish
- parsnip
- carrot
- radish
- salsify

FRUITS AND VEGETABLES

VEGETABLES

STALK VEGETABLES

- rhubarb
- cardoon
- Swiss chard
- fennel
- celery
- asparagus

SEED VEGETABLES

- sweet corn
  - silk
  - cob
  - husk
  - kernel
- broad beans
- sweet peas
- green peas
- lentils
- chick peas
- soy beans
- bean sprouts

52

FRUITS AND VEGETABLES

LEAF VEGETABLES

- green cabbage
- curly endive
- white cabbage
- romaine lettuce
- broad-leaved endive
- cabbage lettuce
- spinach
- chicory
- Chinese cabbage
- curly kale
- garden sorrel
- watercress
- Brussels sprouts
- dandelion
- corn salad
- vine leaf

53

GARDENING

GARDENING

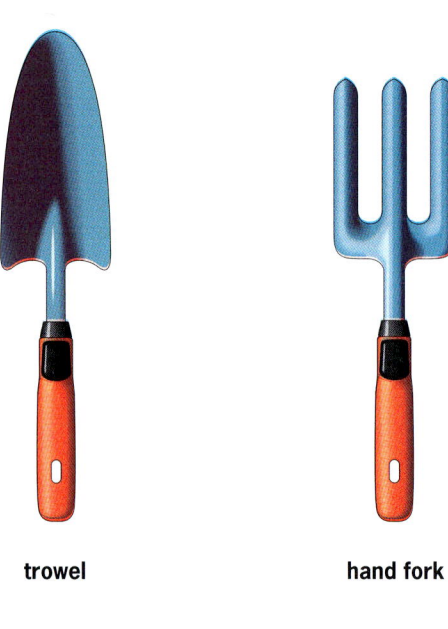

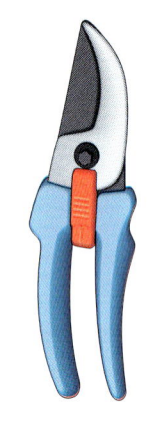

trowel

hand fork

hand cultivator

pruning shears

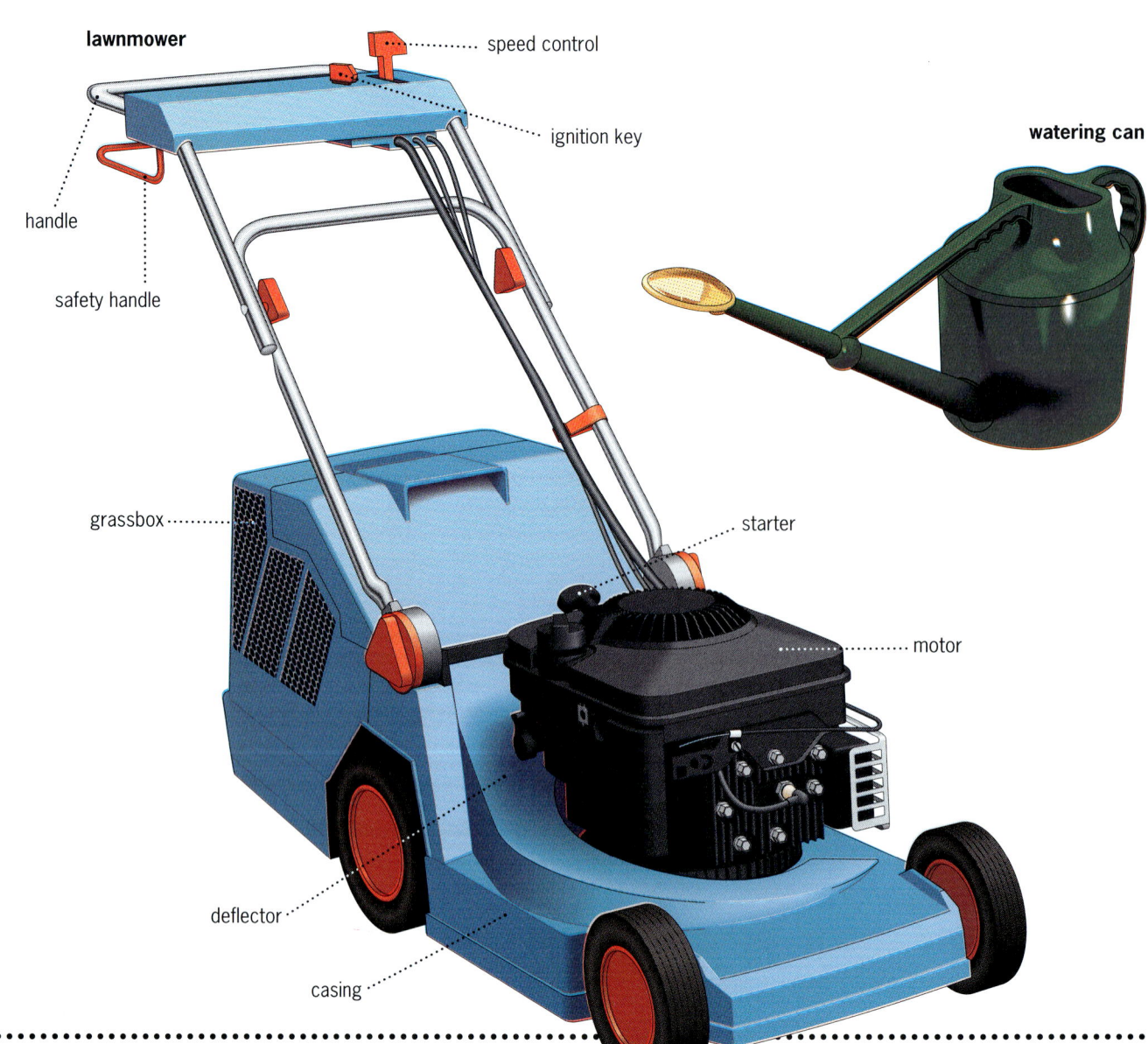

lawnmower

speed control

ignition key

handle

safety handle

watering can

grassbox

starter

motor

deflector

casing

GARDENING

rake

garden fork

spade

shovel

lawn rake

wheelbarrow

compost bin

55

ANIMAL KINGDOM

INSECTS AND SPIDER

ant

ladybug

fly

spider

grasshopper

dragonfly

56

ANIMAL KINGDOM

BUTTERFLY

caterpillar

- head
- simple eye
- mandible
- walking leg
- proleg

chrysalis

- forewing
- wing vein
- cell
- thorax
- head
- antenna
- labial palp
- compound eye
- proboscis
- foreleg
- middle leg
- claw
- hind wing
- abdomen
- hind leg

BUTTERFLY

57

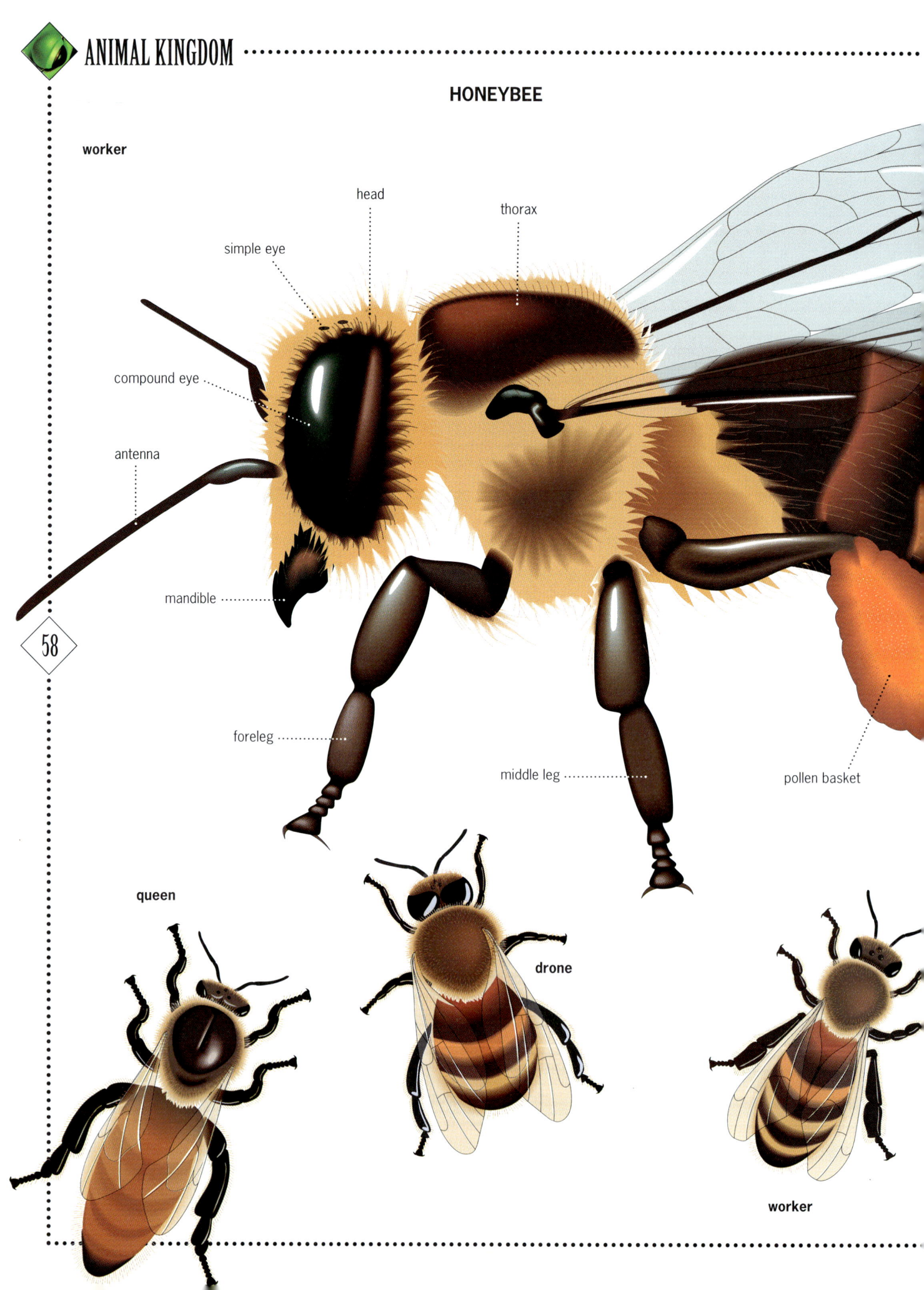

ANIMAL KINGDOM

HONEYBEE

worker

- head
- simple eye
- thorax
- compound eye
- antenna
- mandible
- foreleg
- middle leg
- pollen basket

queen

drone

worker

ANIMAL KINGDOM

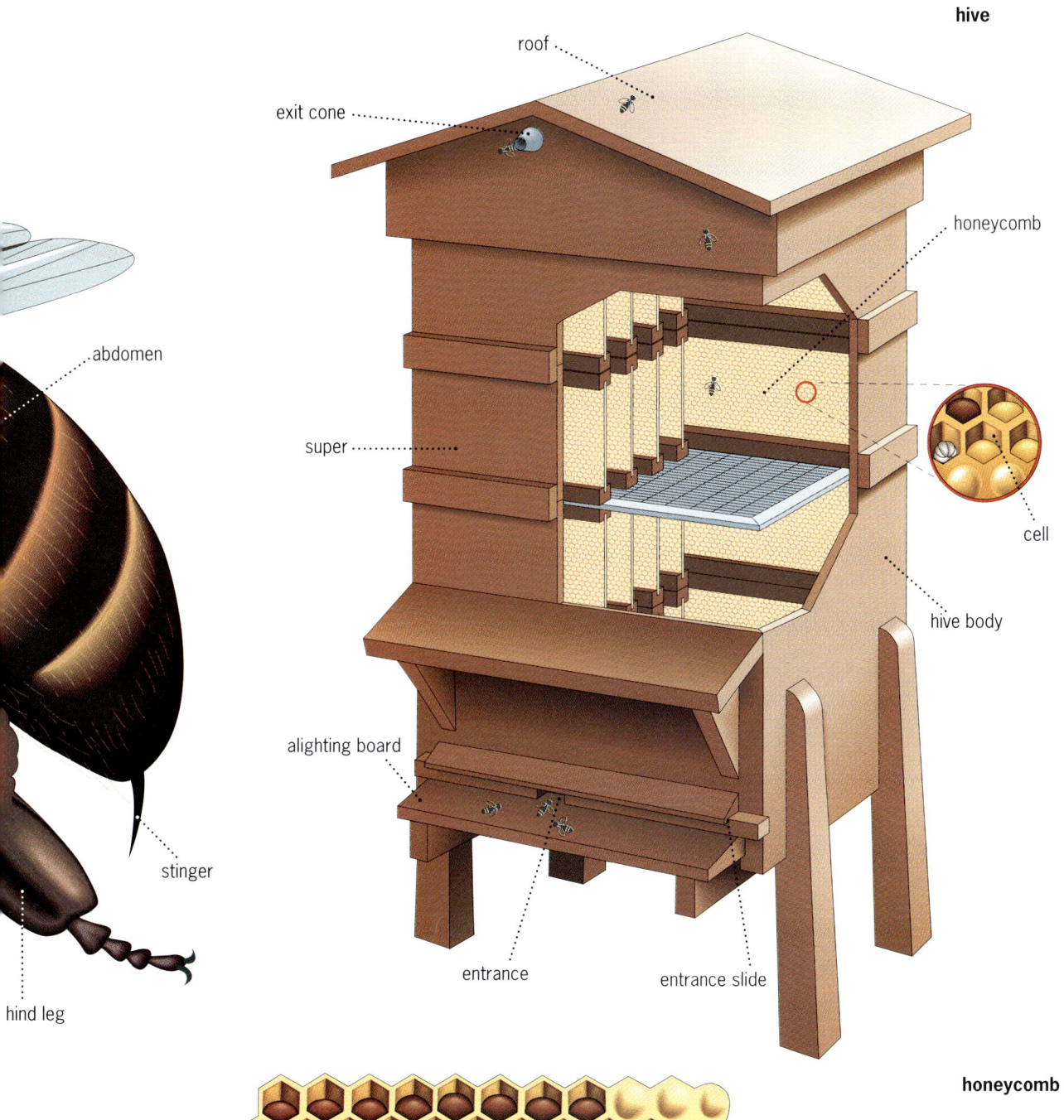

hive

- roof
- exit cone
- honeycomb
- super
- cell
- hive body
- alighting board
- abdomen
- stinger
- hind leg
- entrance
- entrance slide

honeycomb section

- honey cell
- pollen cell
- sealed cell
- chrysalis
- egg
- queen cell

ANIMAL KINGDOM

AMPHIBIANS

frog

- upper eyelid
- snout
- nostril
- eyeball
- mouth
- lower eyelid
- skin
- eardrum
- forelimb
- digit
- webbed foot
- web
- hind limb

60

LIFE CYCLE OF THE FROG

eggs

tadpole
- external gills

- operculum
- hind limb

- forelimb

MAJOR AMPHIBIANS

tree frog

toad

salamander

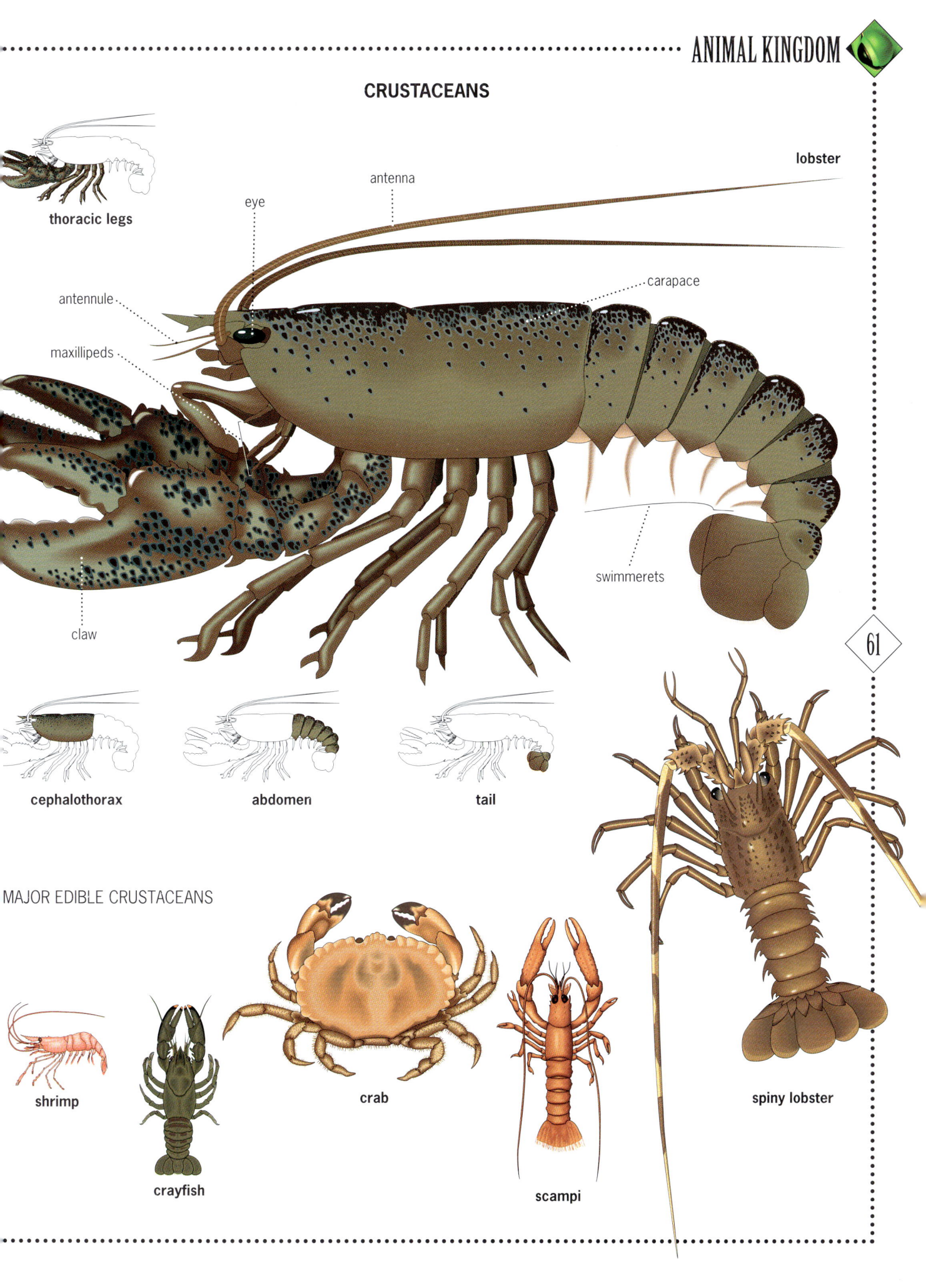

ANIMAL KINGDOM

CRUSTACEANS

thoracic legs

lobster

antenna

eye

antennule

carapace

maxillipeds

swimmerets

claw

cephalothorax **abdomen** **tail**

61

MAJOR EDIBLE CRUSTACEANS

shrimp **crayfish** **crab** **scampi** **spiny lobster**

ANIMAL KINGDOM

FISHES

MORPHOLOGY

gills

sea horse

first dorsal fin

nostril

mandible

maxilla

pectoral fin

pelvic fin

trout

swordfish

tuna

ANIMAL KINGDOM

eel

second dorsal fin

black bass

caudal fin

anal fin

flounder

scale

63

shark

cod

pike

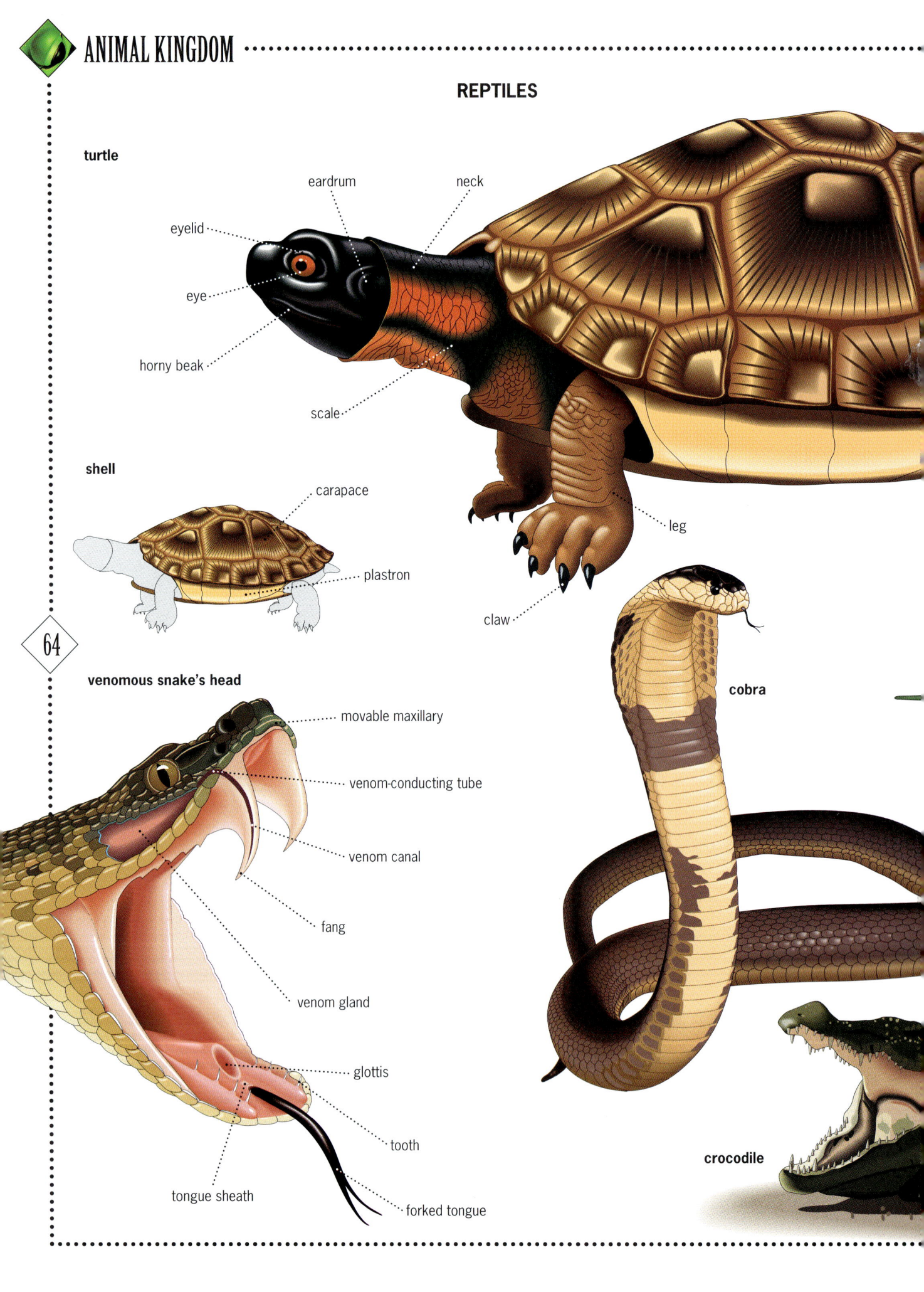

ANIMAL KINGDOM

REPTILES

turtle

- eyelid
- eardrum
- neck
- eye
- horny beak
- scale
- leg
- claw

shell

- carapace
- plastron

venomous snake's head

- movable maxillary
- venom-conducting tube
- venom canal
- fang
- venom gland
- glottis
- tooth
- tongue sheath
- forked tongue

cobra

crocodile

64

ANIMAL KINGDOM

shield

tail

chameleon

lizard

rattlesnake

65

ANIMAL KINGDOM

CAT

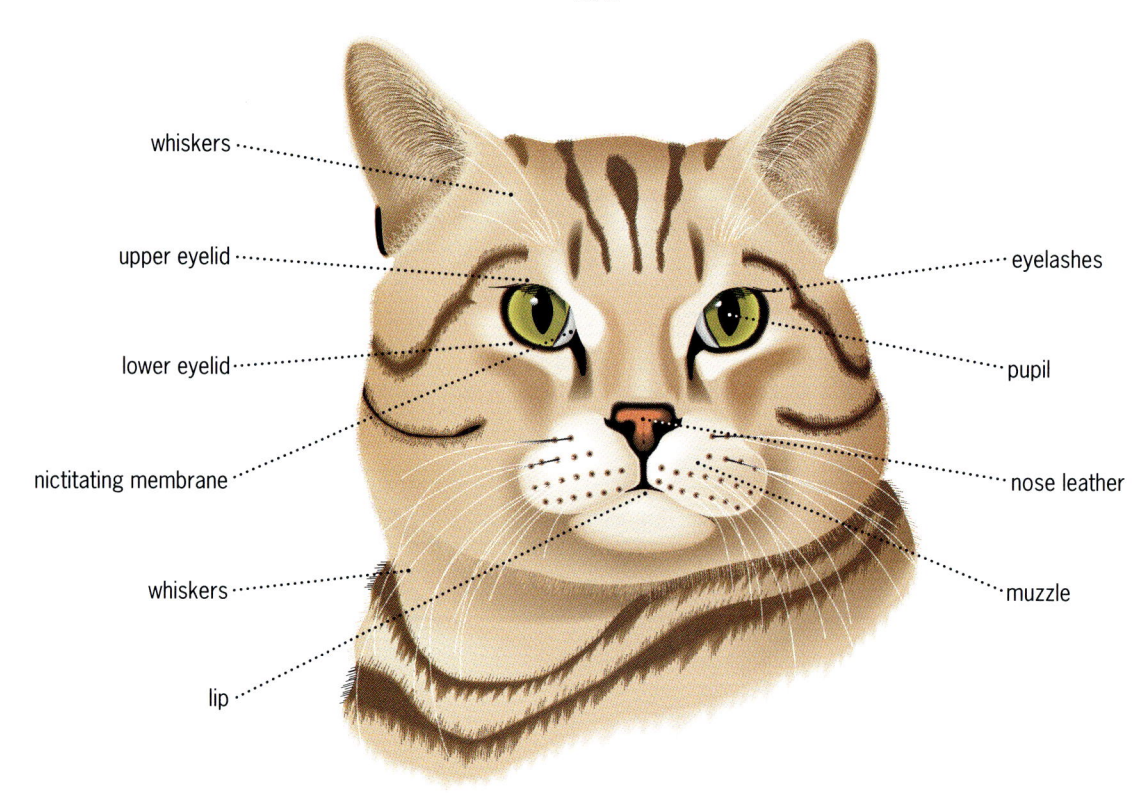

- whiskers
- upper eyelid
- lower eyelid
- nictitating membrane
- whiskers
- lip
- eyelashes
- pupil
- nose leather
- muzzle

DOG

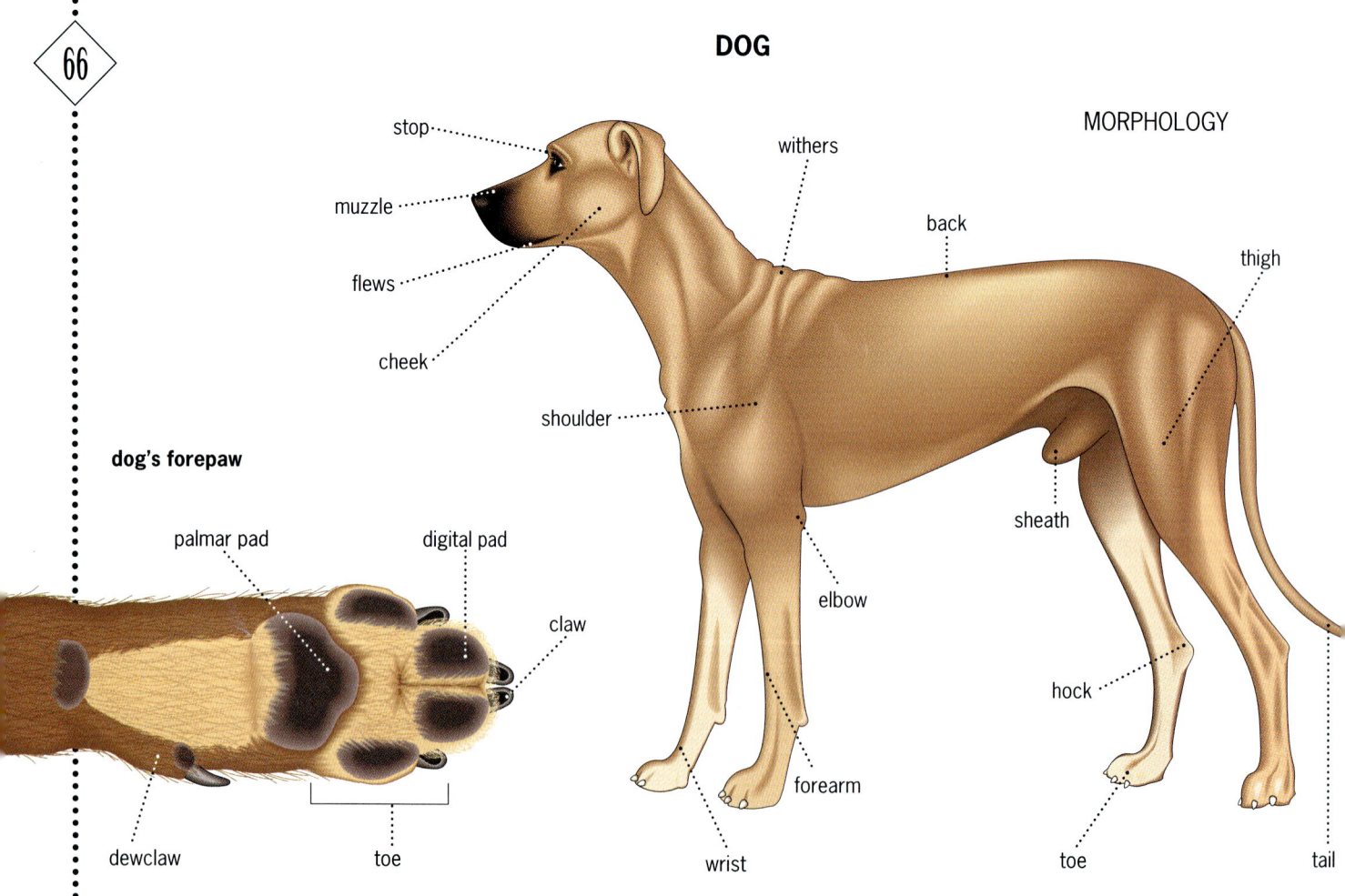

MORPHOLOGY

- stop
- muzzle
- flews
- cheek
- withers
- back
- thigh
- shoulder
- sheath
- elbow
- hock
- forearm
- wrist
- toe
- tail

dog's forepaw

- palmar pad
- digital pad
- claw
- dewclaw
- toe

66

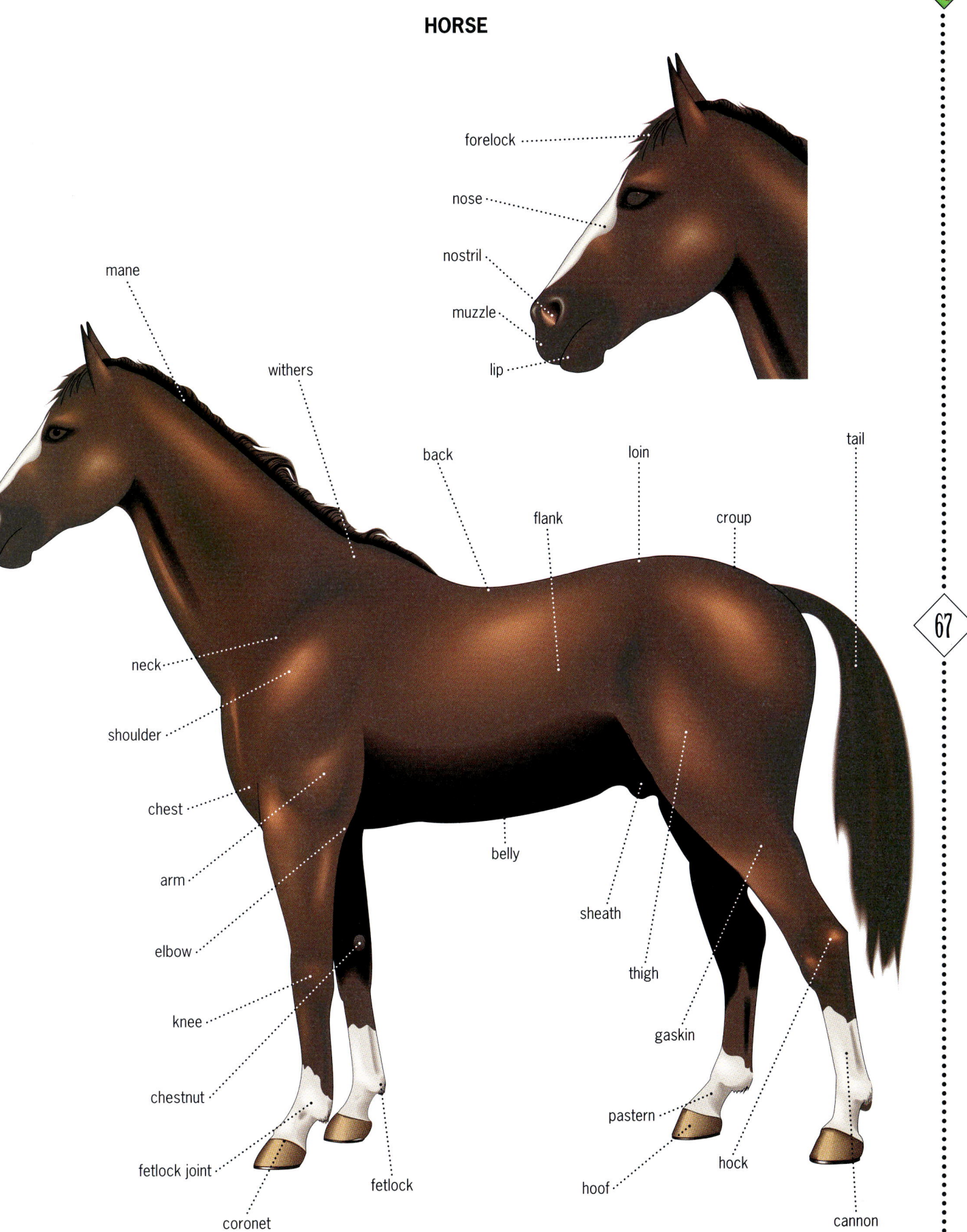

ANIMAL KINGDOM

HORSE

- forelock
- nose
- nostril
- muzzle
- lip
- mane
- withers
- back
- loin
- tail
- flank
- croup
- neck
- shoulder
- chest
- arm
- belly
- elbow
- sheath
- thigh
- knee
- gaskin
- chestnut
- pastern
- fetlock joint
- hock
- fetlock
- hoof
- coronet
- cannon

ANIMAL KINGDOM

FARM ANIMALS

hen

chick

rooster; cock

duck

goose

turkey

cow

calf

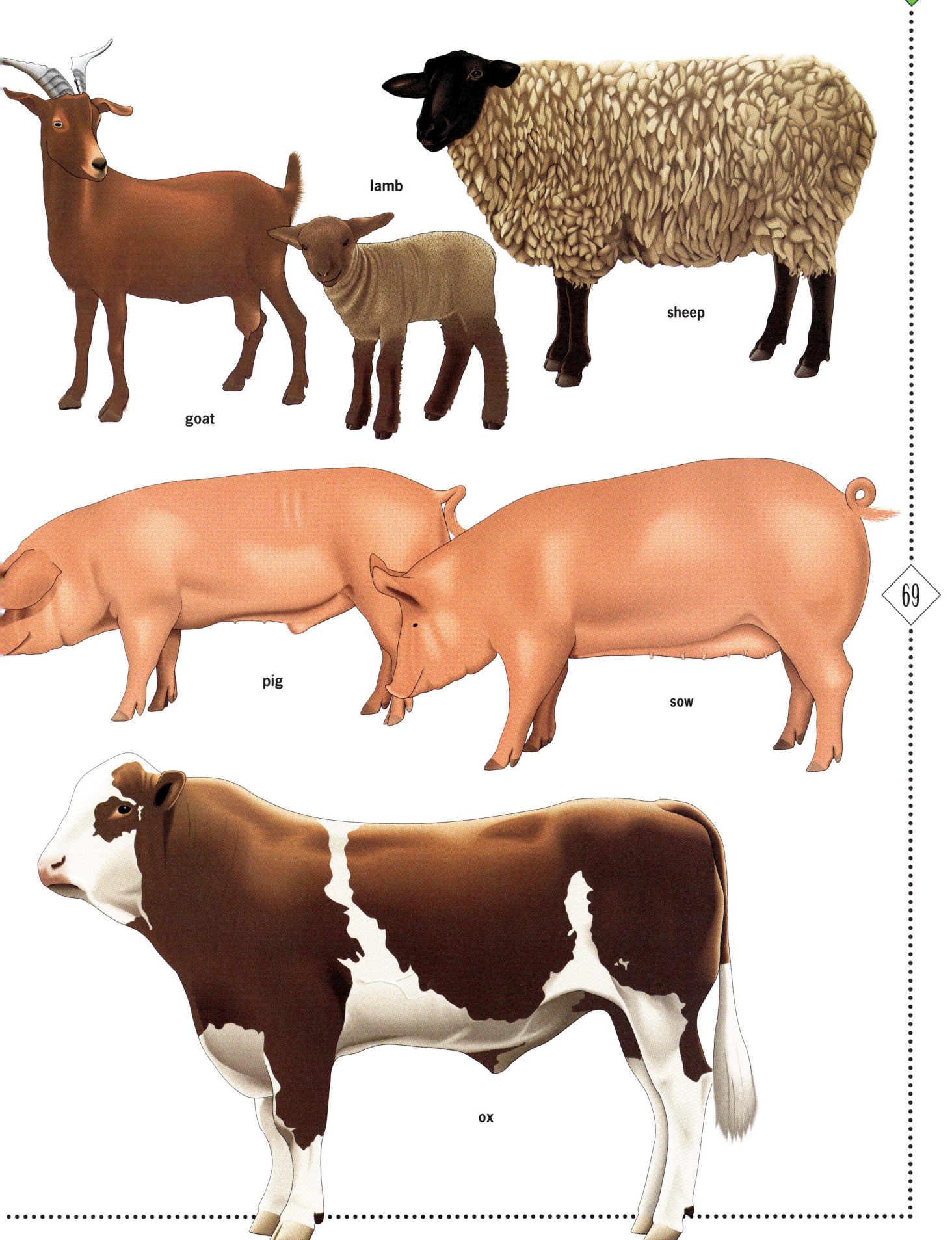

ANIMAL KINGDOM

goat

lamb

sheep

pig

sow

ox

69

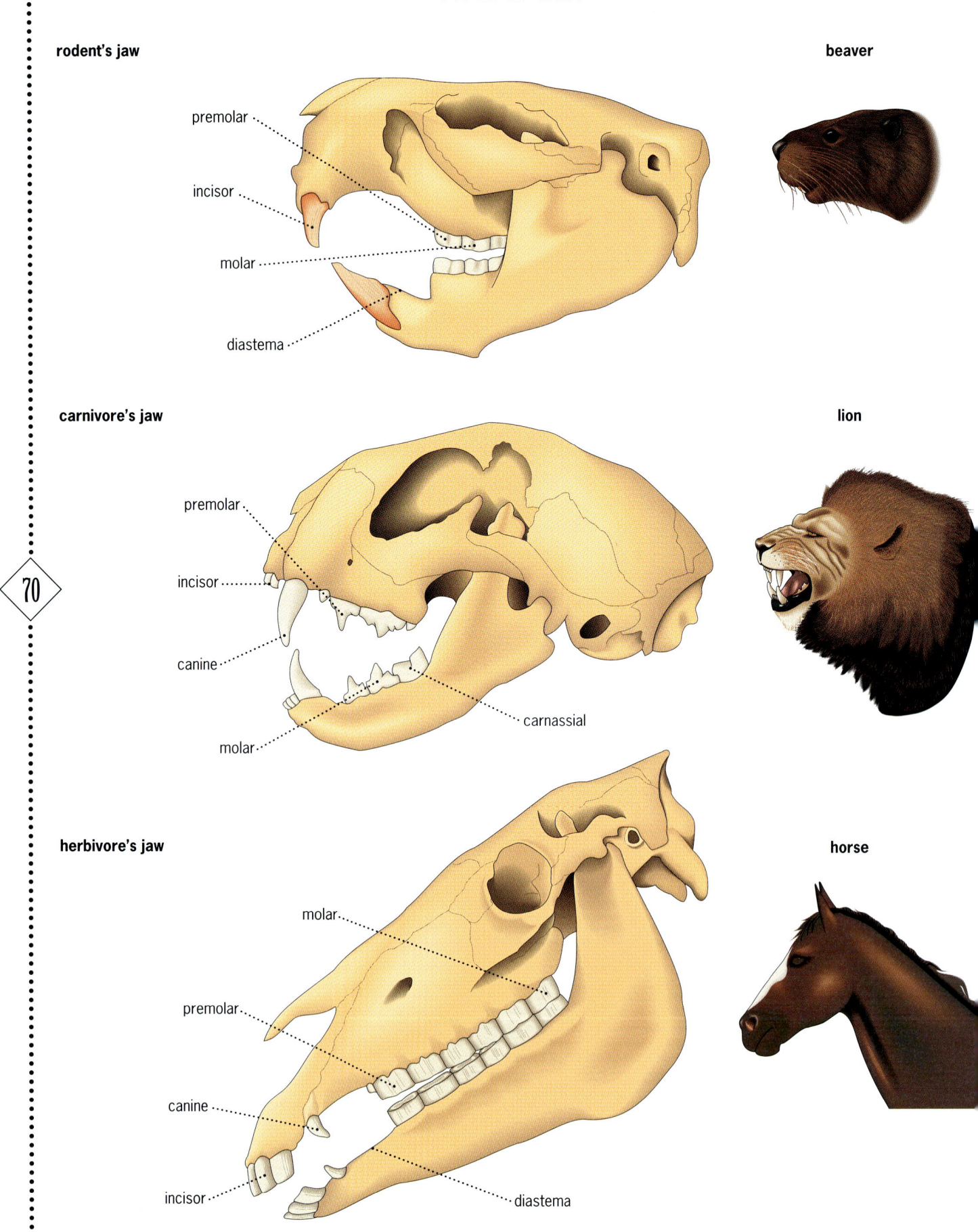

ANIMAL KINGDOM

TYPES OF JAWS

rodent's jaw

- premolar
- incisor
- molar
- diastema

beaver

carnivore's jaw

- premolar
- incisor
- canine
- carnassial
- molar

lion

herbivore's jaw

- molar
- premolar
- canine
- incisor
- diastema

horse

TYPES OF JAWS

ANIMAL KINGDOM

MAJOR TYPES OF HORNS

horns of mouflon

horns of giraffe

horns of rhinoceros

MAJOR TYPES OF TUSKS

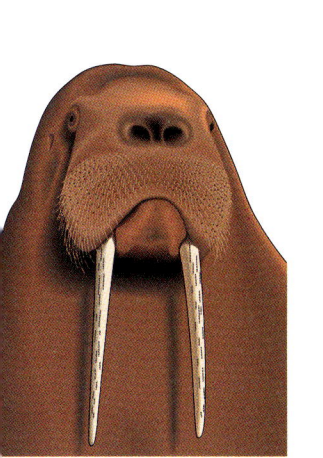

tusks of walrus

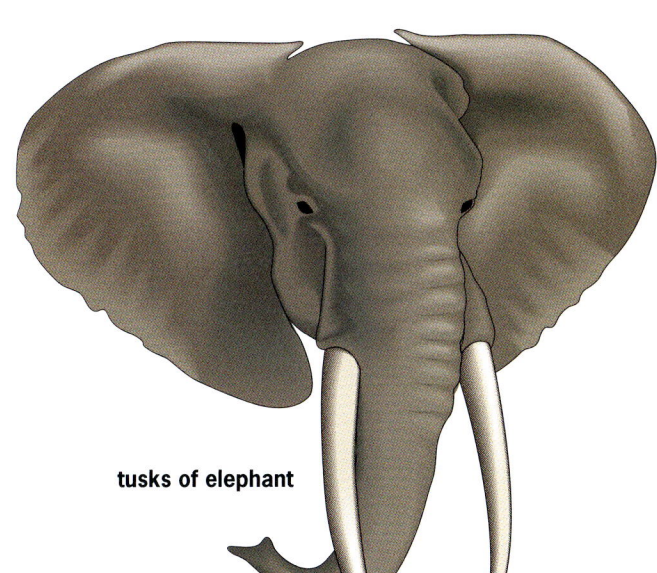

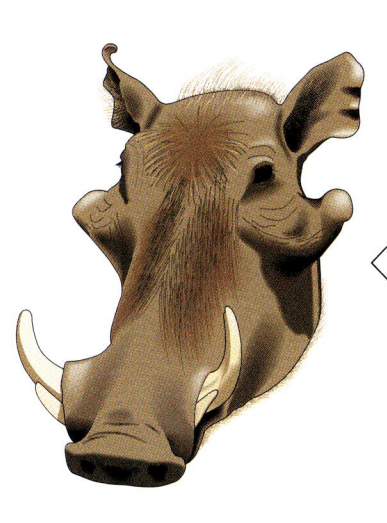

tusks of elephant

tusks of wart hog

TYPES OF HOOFS

one-toe hoof

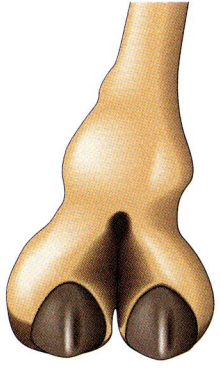

two-toed hoof

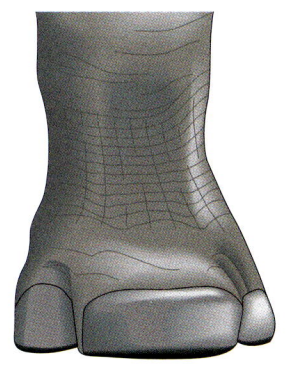

three-toed hoof

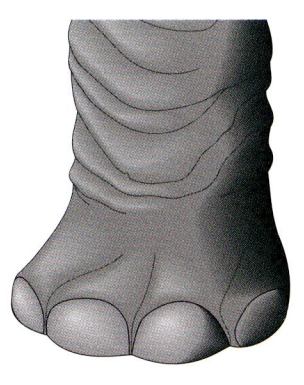

four-toed hoof

71

ANIMAL KINGDOM

WILD ANIMALS

giraffe

polar bear

monkey

lion

dolphin

whale

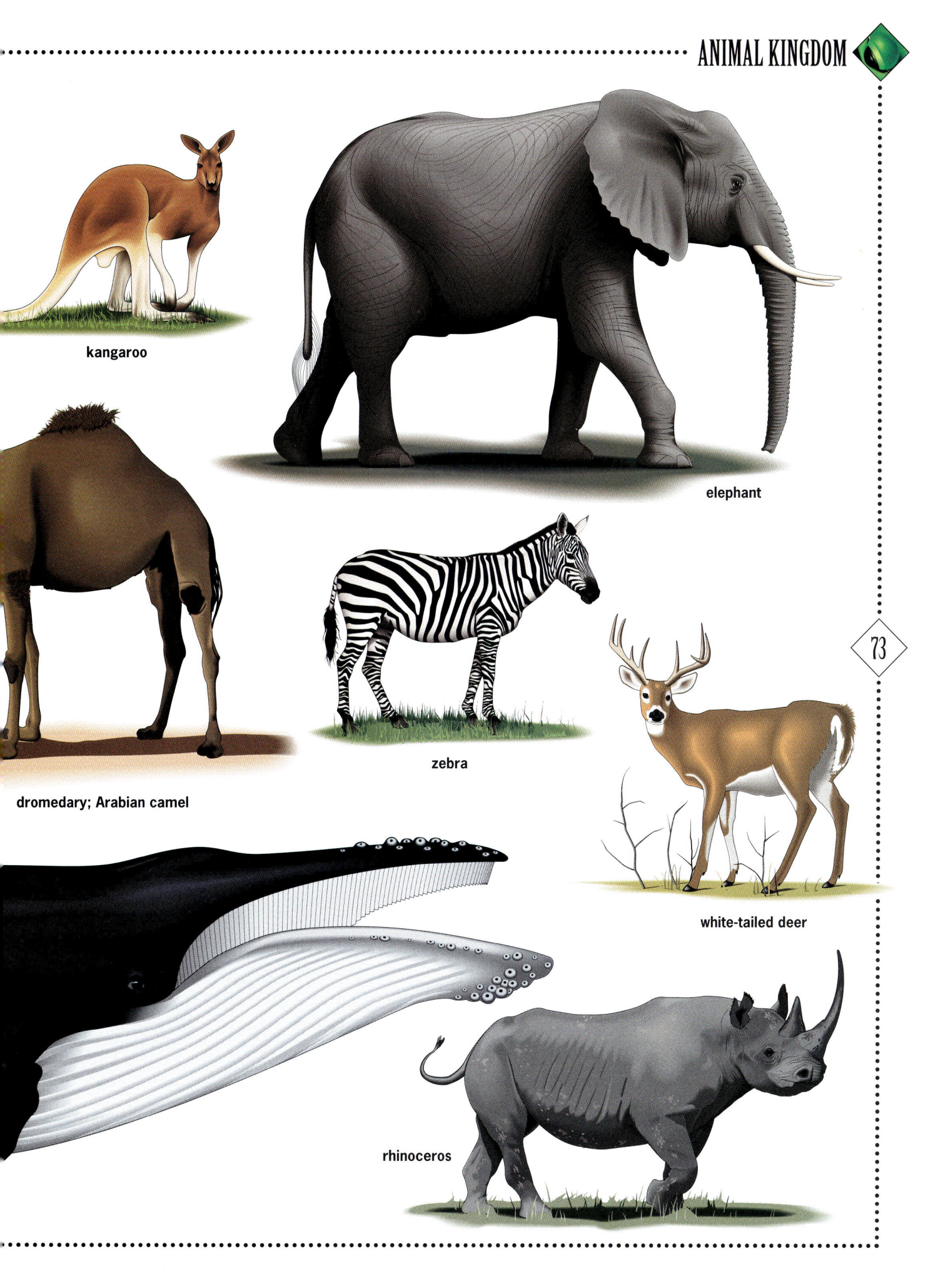

ANIMAL KINGDOM

kangaroo

elephant

dromedary; Arabian camel

zebra

white-tailed deer

rhinoceros

73

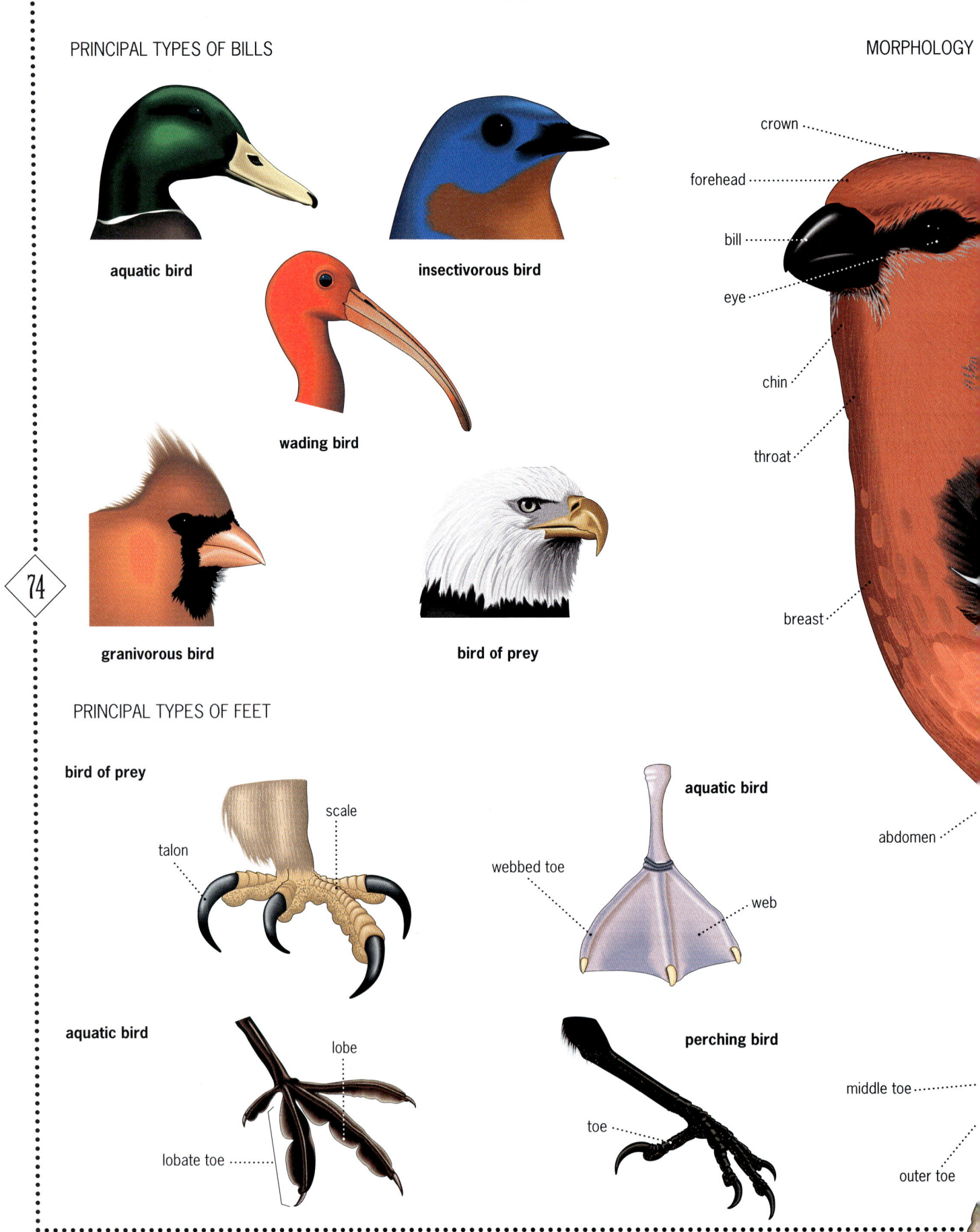

ANIMAL KINGDOM

BIRD

PRINCIPAL TYPES OF BILLS

aquatic bird

insectivorous bird

wading bird

granivorous bird

bird of prey

MORPHOLOGY

crown

forehead

bill

eye

chin

throat

breast

abdomen

middle toe

outer toe

PRINCIPAL TYPES OF FEET

bird of prey

talon

scale

aquatic bird

webbed toe

web

aquatic bird

lobe

lobate toe

perching bird

toe

BIRD

ANIMAL KINGDOM

bird's nest

birdhouse

bird feeder

nape

back

wing

cylinder

seeds

perch

75

rump

tail

flank

under tail covert

upper tail covert

foot

egg

hind toe

blastodisc

shell

air space

claw

yolk

albumen

ANIMAL KINGDOM

EXAMPLES OF BIRDS

crow

parrot

stork

swallow

ostrich

flamingo

ANIMAL KINGDOM

European robin

blue jay

nightingale

hummingbird

owl

peacock

HUMAN BODY

HUMAN BODY, ANTERIOR VIEW

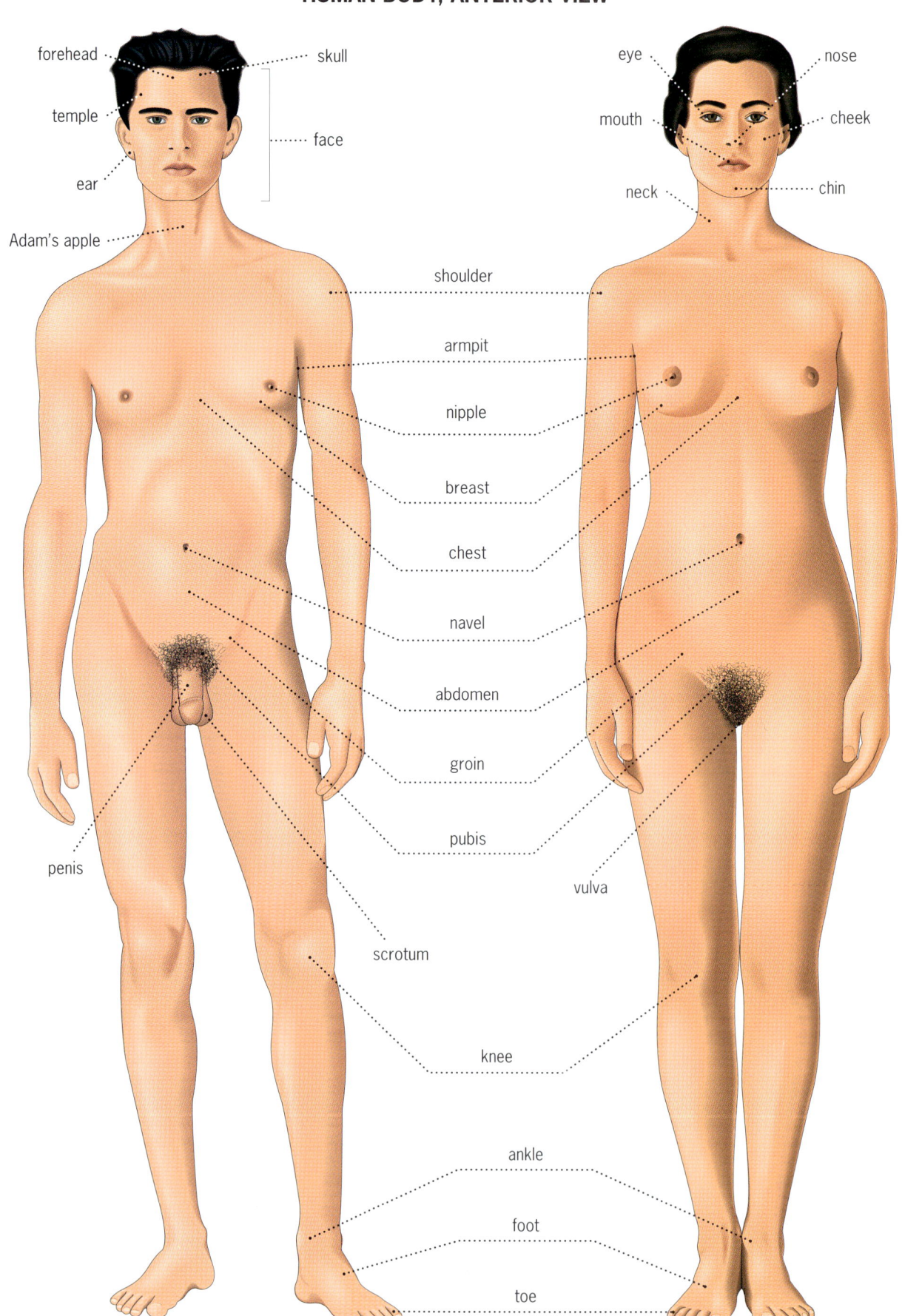

- forehead
- skull
- temple
- face
- ear
- Adam's apple
- eye
- nose
- mouth
- cheek
- neck
- chin
- shoulder
- armpit
- nipple
- breast
- chest
- navel
- abdomen
- groin
- pubis
- penis
- vulva
- scrotum
- knee
- ankle
- foot
- toe

78

HUMAN BODY

HUMAN BODY, POSTERIOR VIEW

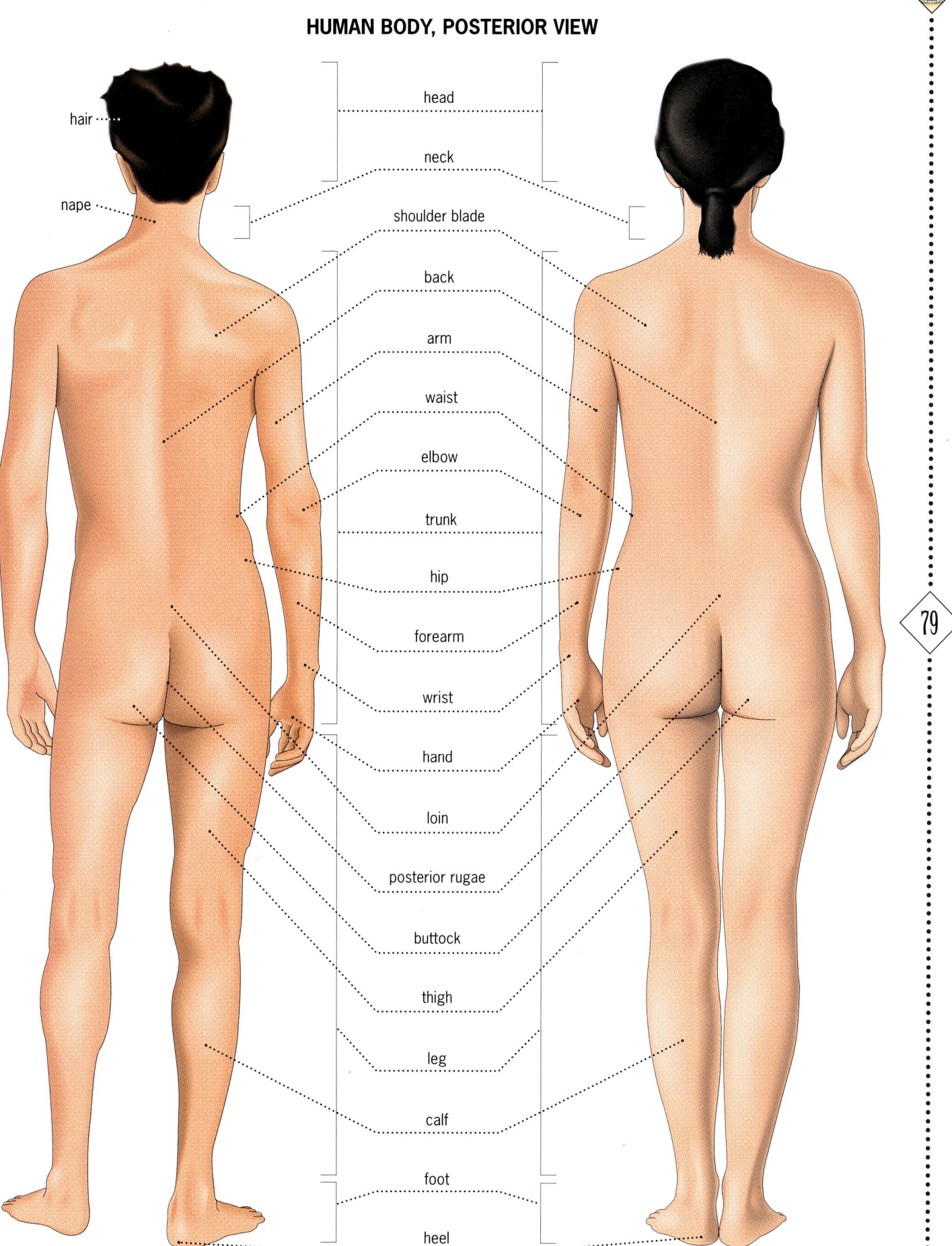

- hair
- nape
- head
- neck
- shoulder blade
- back
- arm
- waist
- elbow
- trunk
- hip
- forearm
- wrist
- hand
- loin
- posterior rugae
- buttock
- thigh
- leg
- calf
- foot
- heel

79

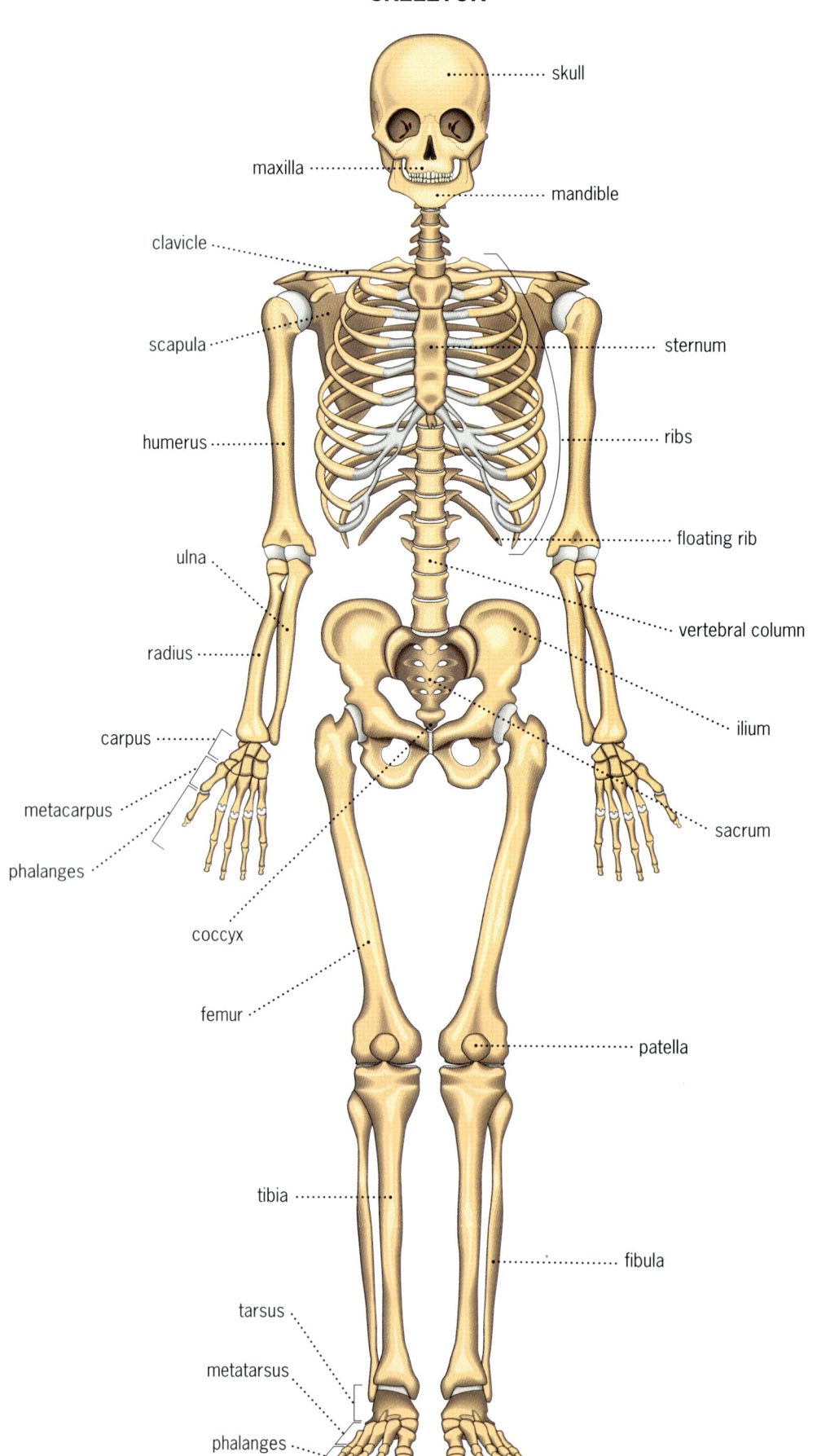

HUMAN BODY

SKELETON

- skull
- maxilla
- mandible
- clavicle
- scapula
- sternum
- humerus
- ribs
- floating rib
- ulna
- vertebral column
- radius
- ilium
- carpus
- metacarpus
- sacrum
- phalanges
- coccyx
- femur
- patella
- tibia
- fibula
- tarsus
- metatarsus
- phalanges

SKELETON

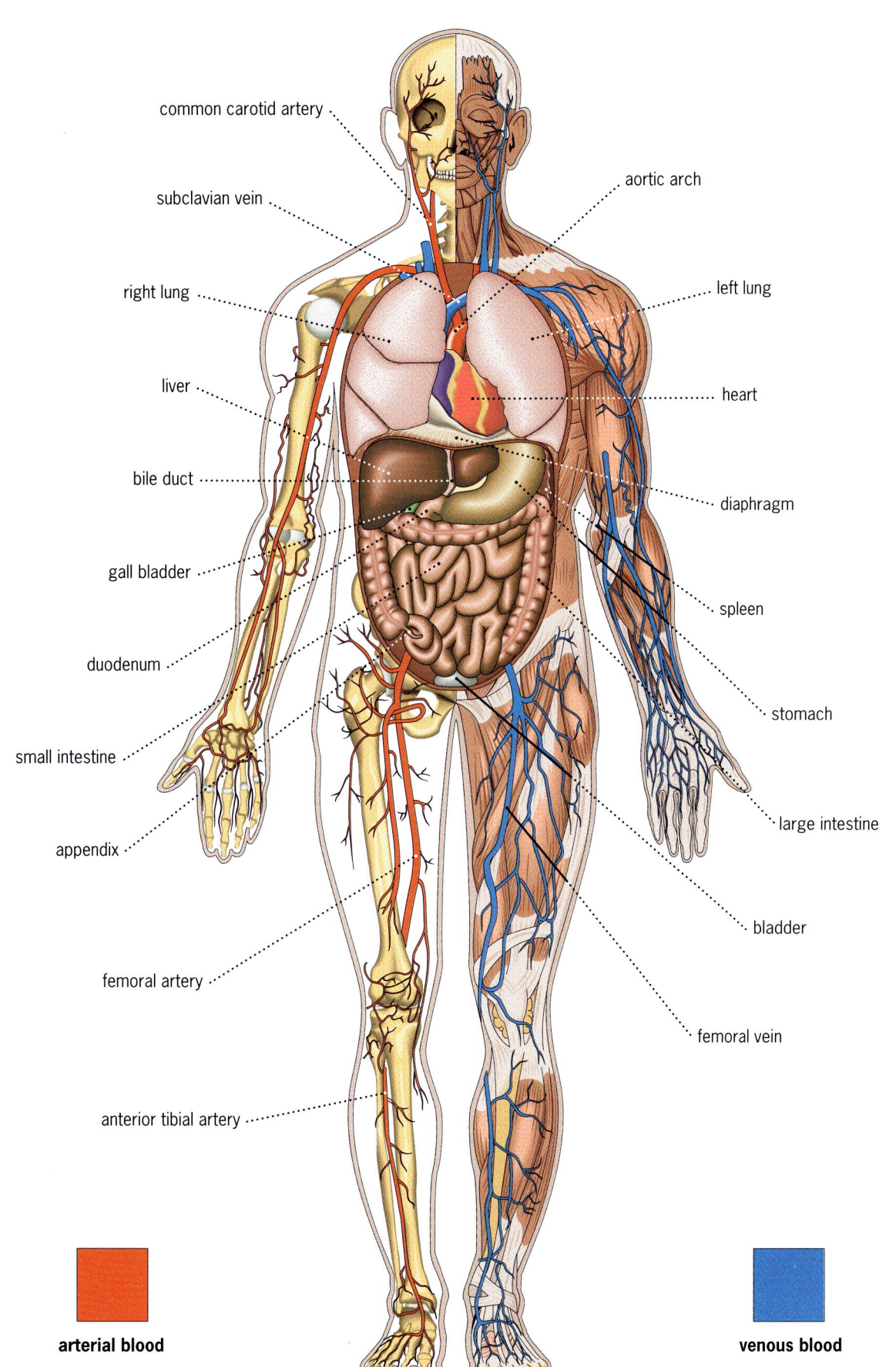

HUMAN BODY

HUMAN ANATOMY

- common carotid artery
- subclavian vein
- right lung
- liver
- bile duct
- gall bladder
- duodenum
- small intestine
- appendix
- femoral artery
- anterior tibial artery

- aortic arch
- left lung
- heart
- diaphragm
- spleen
- stomach
- large intestine
- bladder
- femoral vein

arterial blood

venous blood

HUMAN ANATOMY

81

HUMAN BODY

EYE: THE ORGAN OF SIGHT

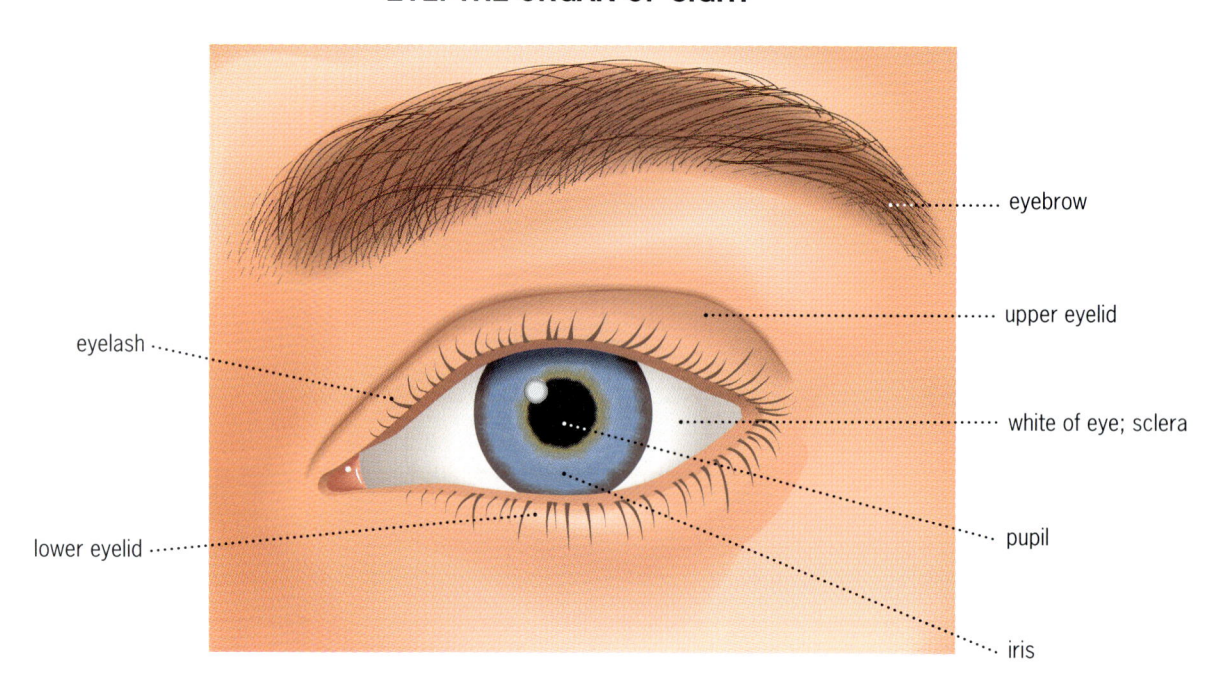

- eyebrow
- upper eyelid
- eyelash
- white of eye; sclera
- lower eyelid
- pupil
- iris

HAND: THE ORGAN OF TOUCH

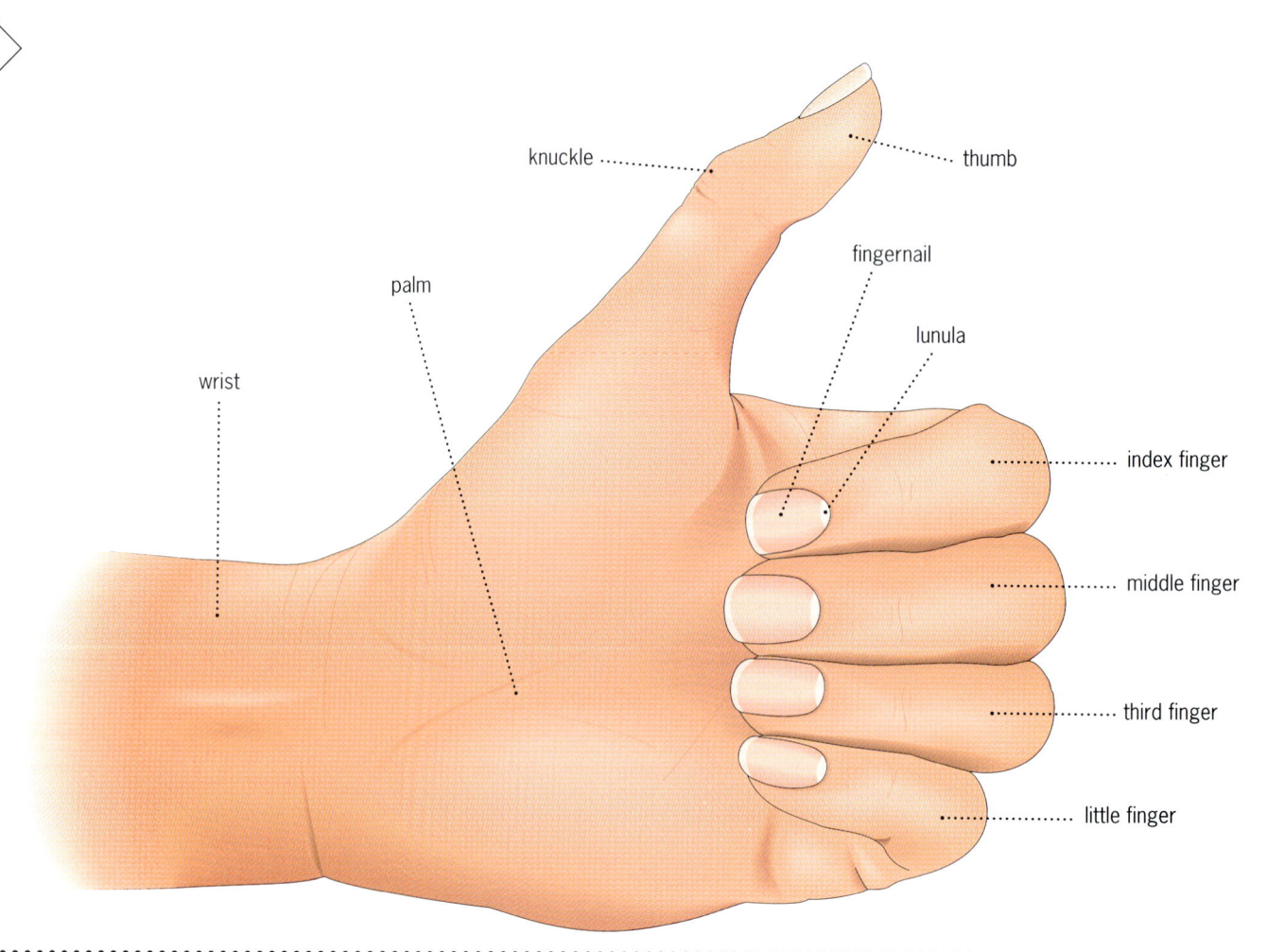

- knuckle
- thumb
- palm
- fingernail
- lunula
- wrist
- index finger
- middle finger
- third finger
- little finger

82

HUMAN BODY

EAR: THE ORGAN OF HEARING

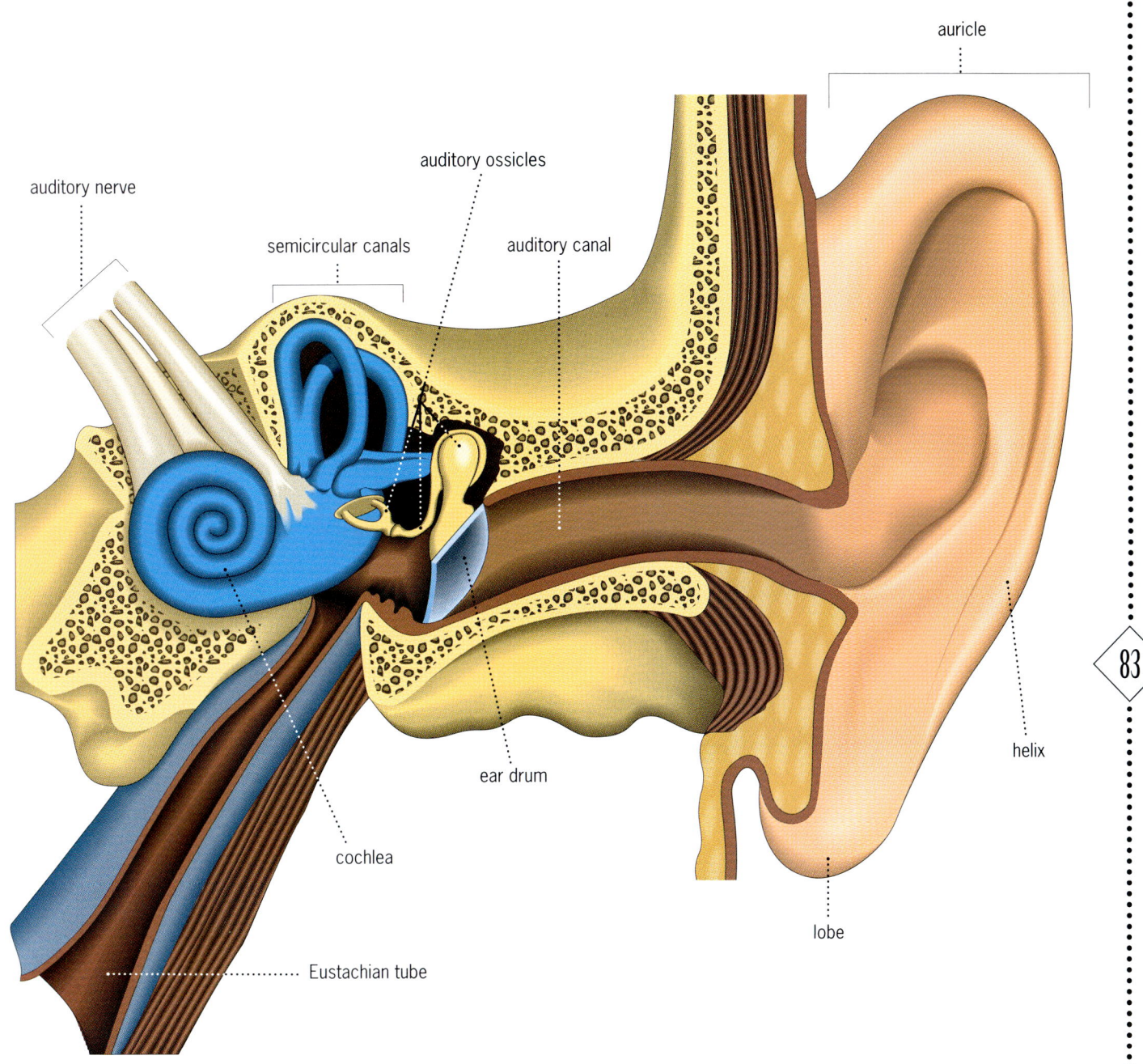

- auricle
- auditory nerve
- auditory ossicles
- semicircular canals
- auditory canal
- ear drum
- cochlea
- Eustachian tube
- helix
- lobe

PARTS OF THE EAR

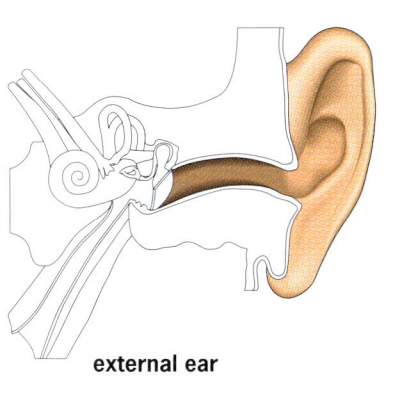

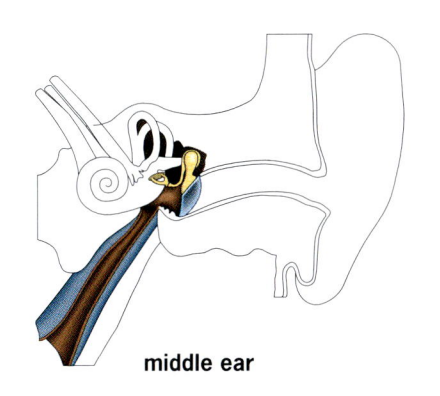

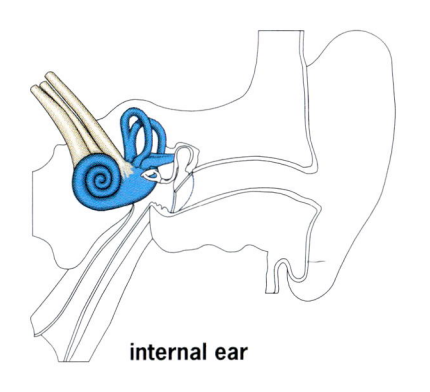

external ear   **middle ear**   **internal ear**

83

HUMAN BODY

NOSE: THE ORGAN OF SMELL

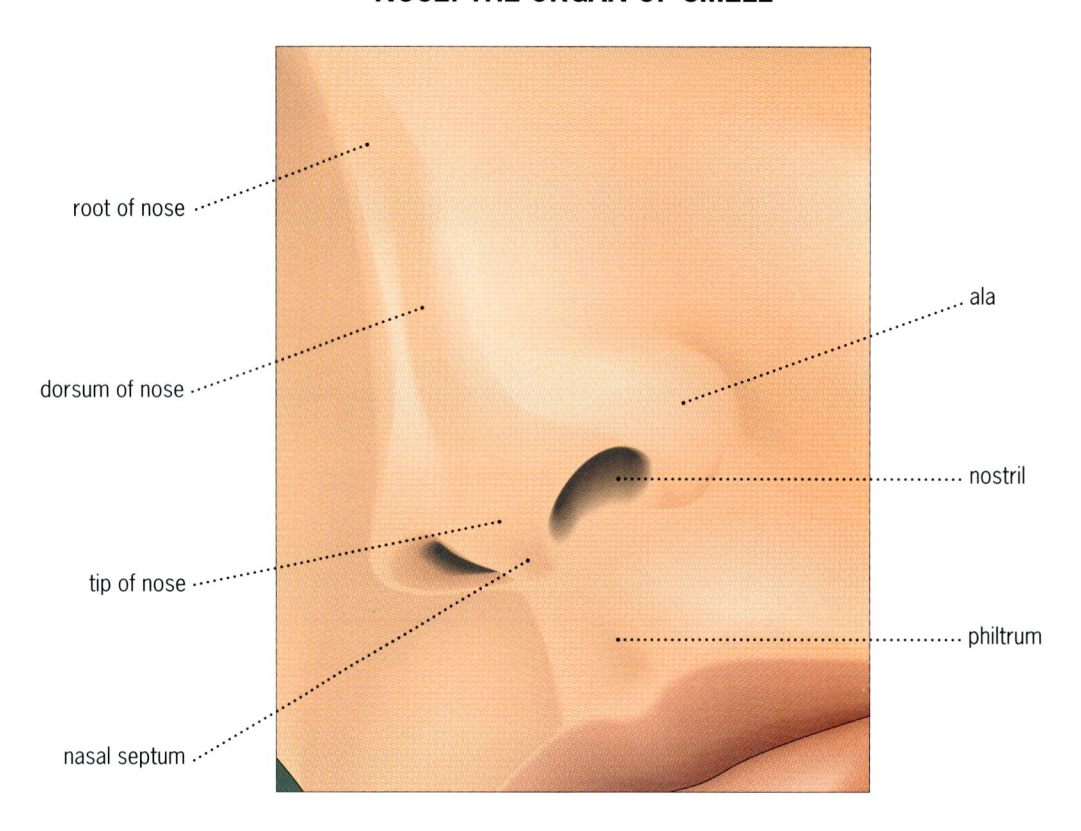

- root of nose
- dorsum of nose
- tip of nose
- nasal septum
- ala
- nostril
- philtrum

MOUTH: THE ORGAN OF TASTE

- upper lip
- gum
- hard palate
- commissure of lips
- tonsil
- tongue
- lower lip
- tooth
- soft palate
- fauces
- uvula

taste sensations

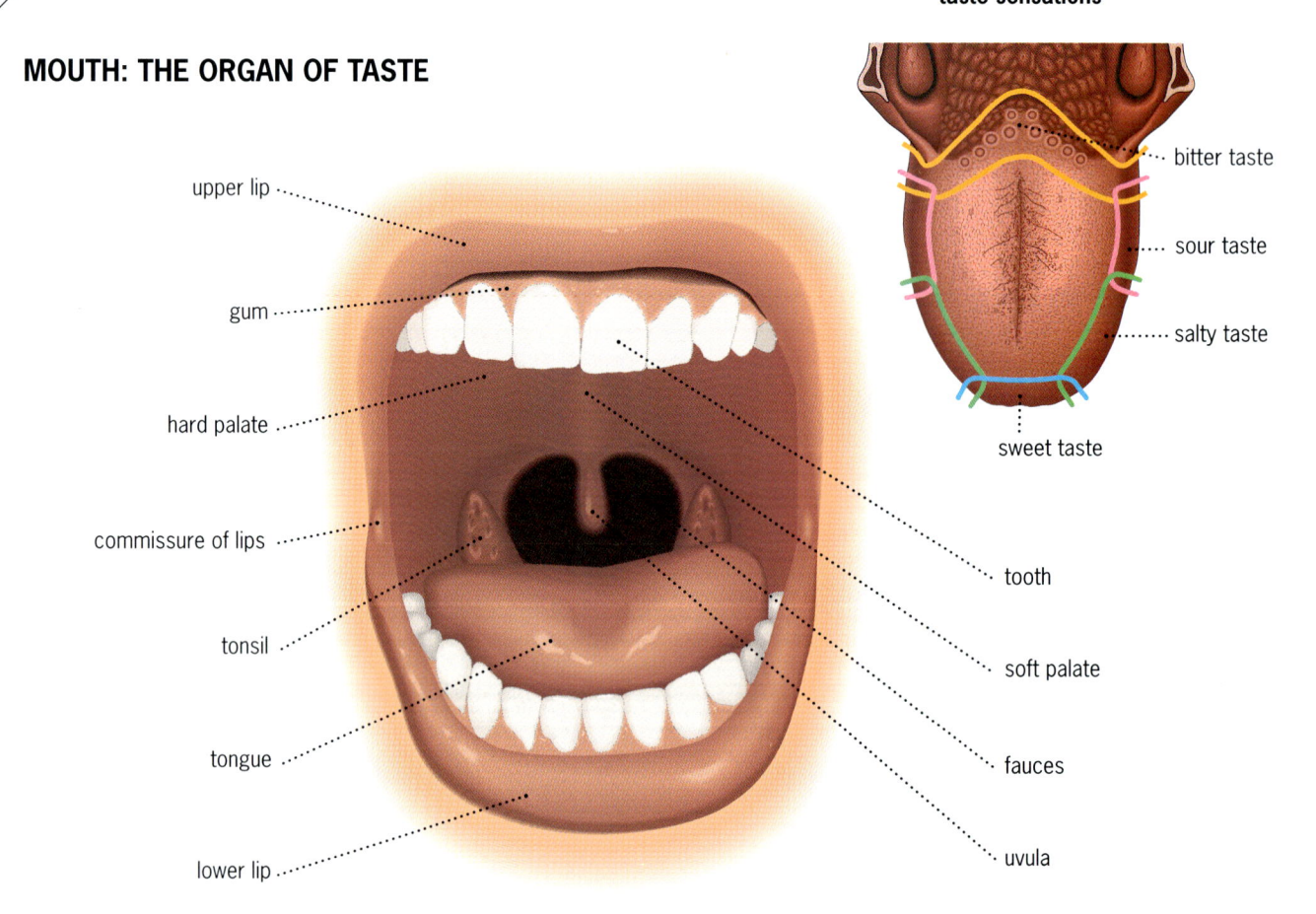

- bitter taste
- sour taste
- salty taste
- sweet taste

HUMAN BODY

HUMAN DENTURE

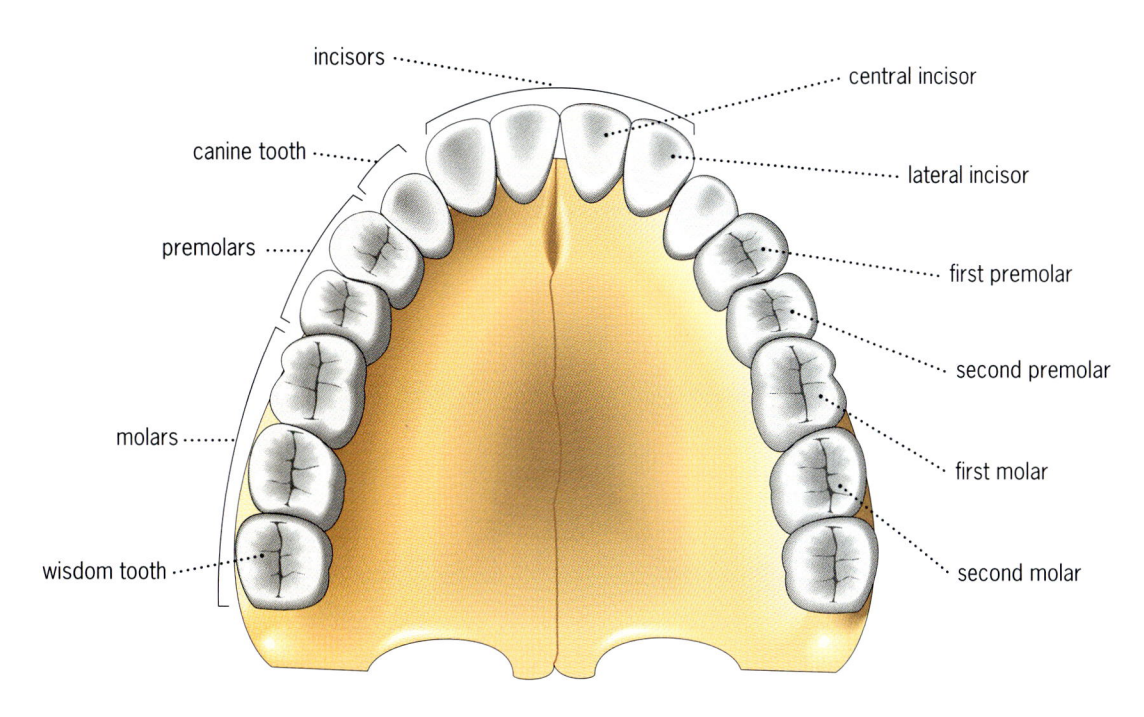

- incisors
- canine tooth
- premolars
- molars
- wisdom tooth
- central incisor
- lateral incisor
- first premolar
- second premolar
- first molar
- second molar

cross section of a molar

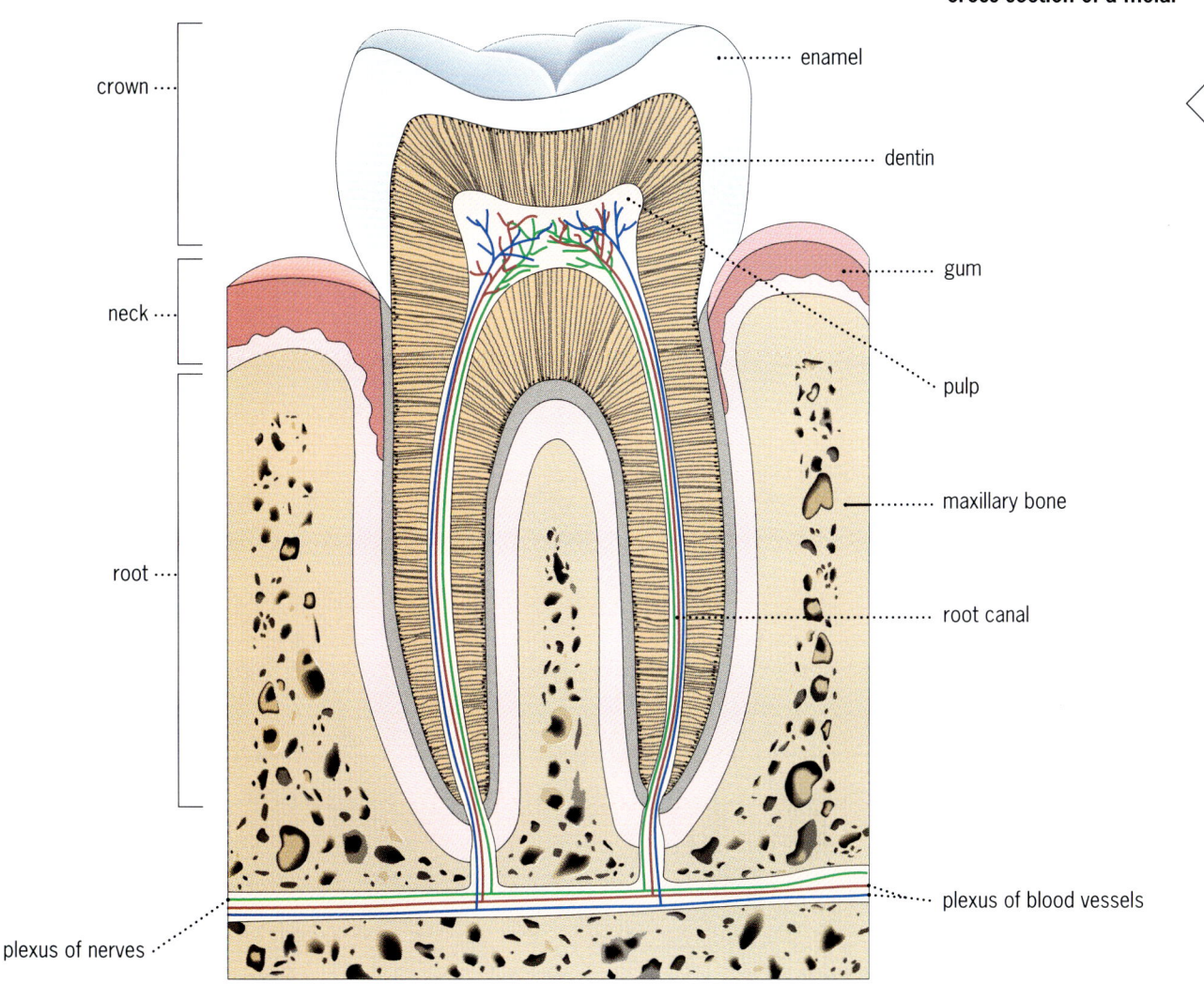

- crown
- neck
- root
- enamel
- dentin
- gum
- pulp
- maxillary bone
- root canal
- plexus of blood vessels
- plexus of nerves

85

ARCHITECTURE

TRADITIONAL HOUSES

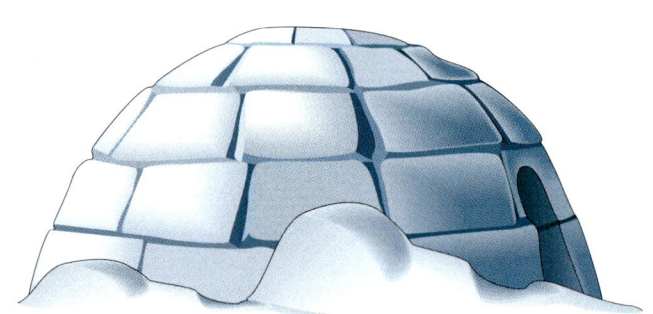

igloo

wigwam

log cabin

mud hut

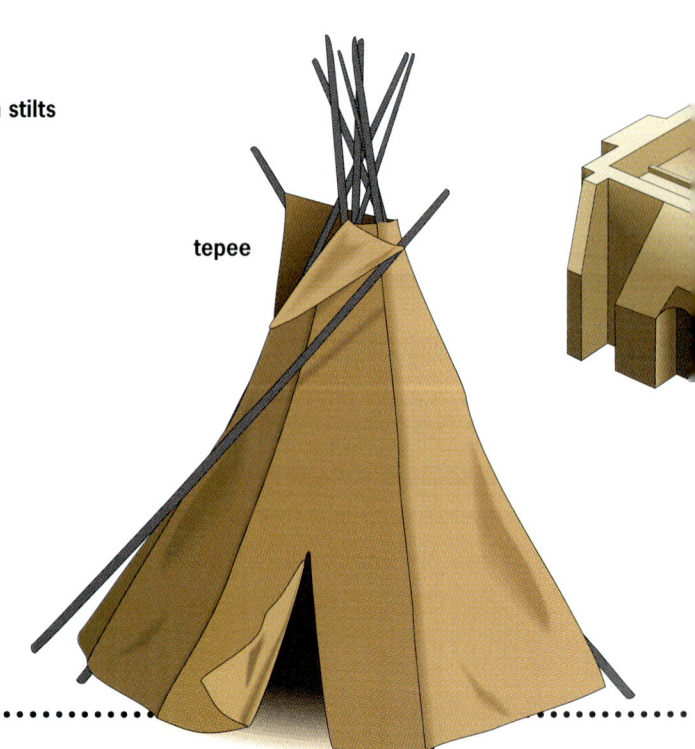

house on stilts

tepee

ARCHITECTURE

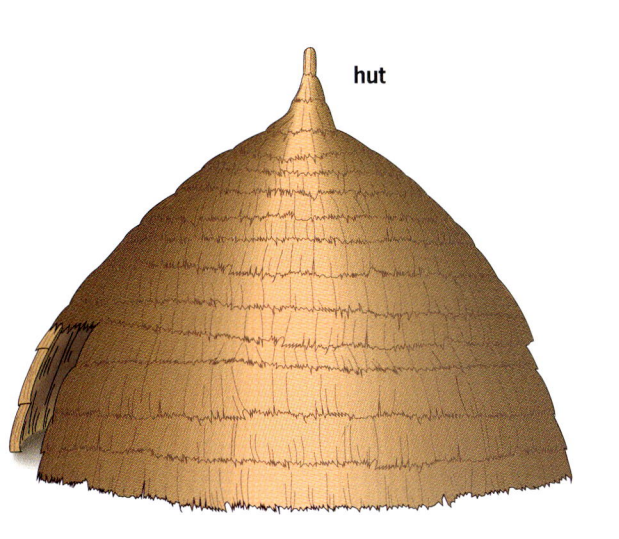

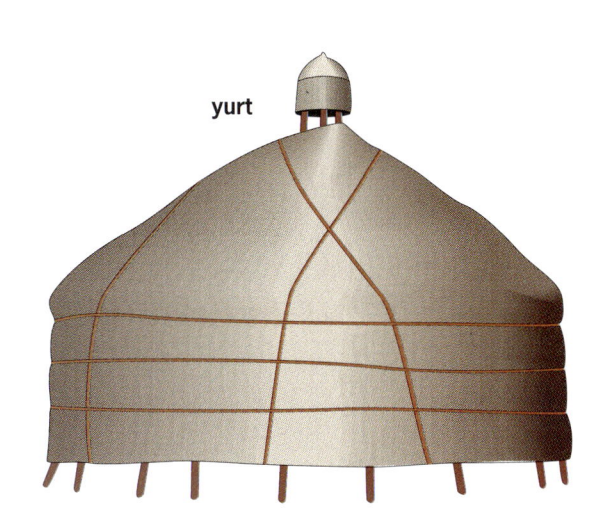

hut

yurt

MOSQUE

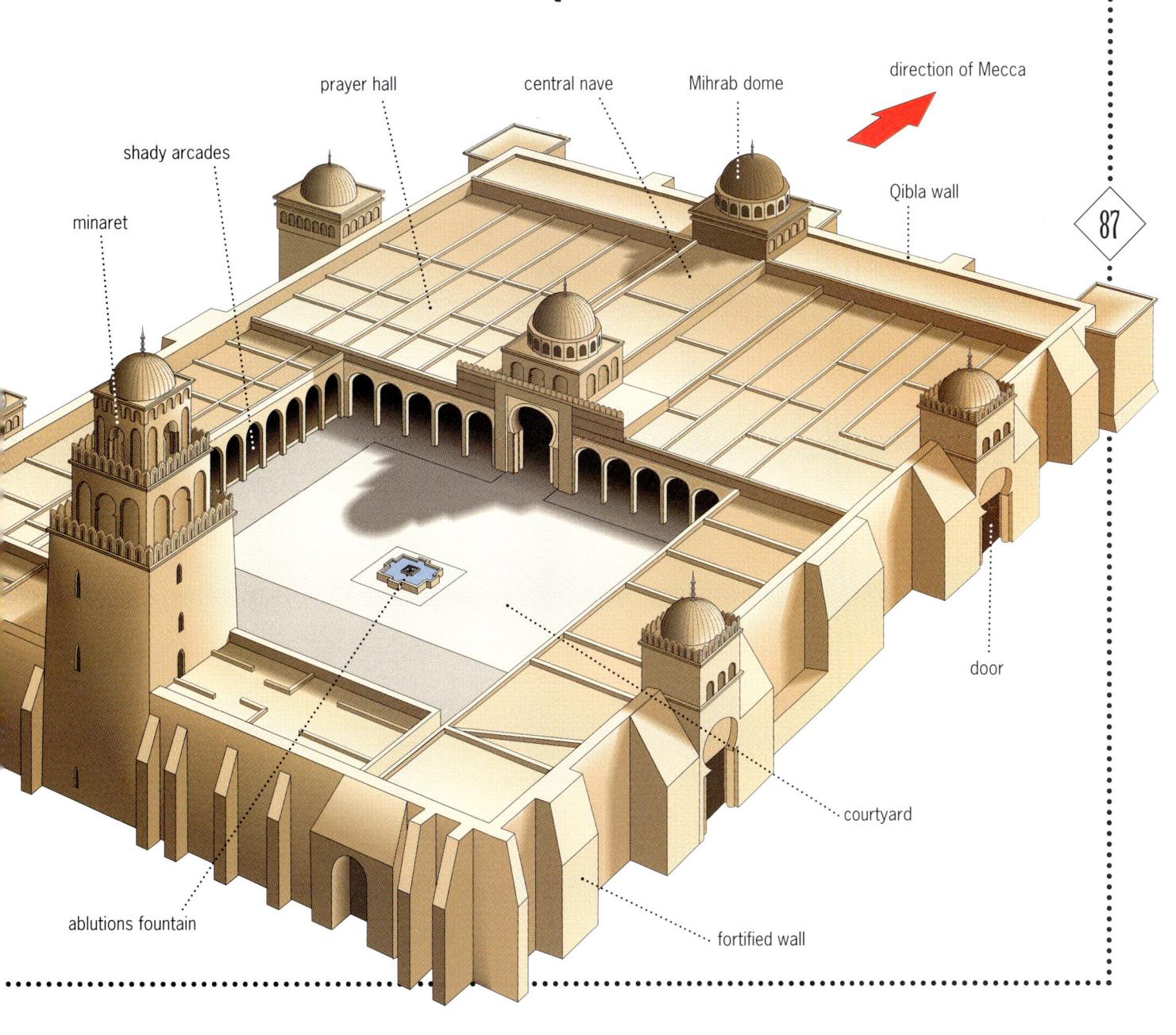

- minaret
- shady arcades
- prayer hall
- central nave
- Mihrab dome
- direction of Mecca
- Qibla wall
- door
- courtyard
- fortified wall
- ablutions fountain

87

ARCHITECTURE

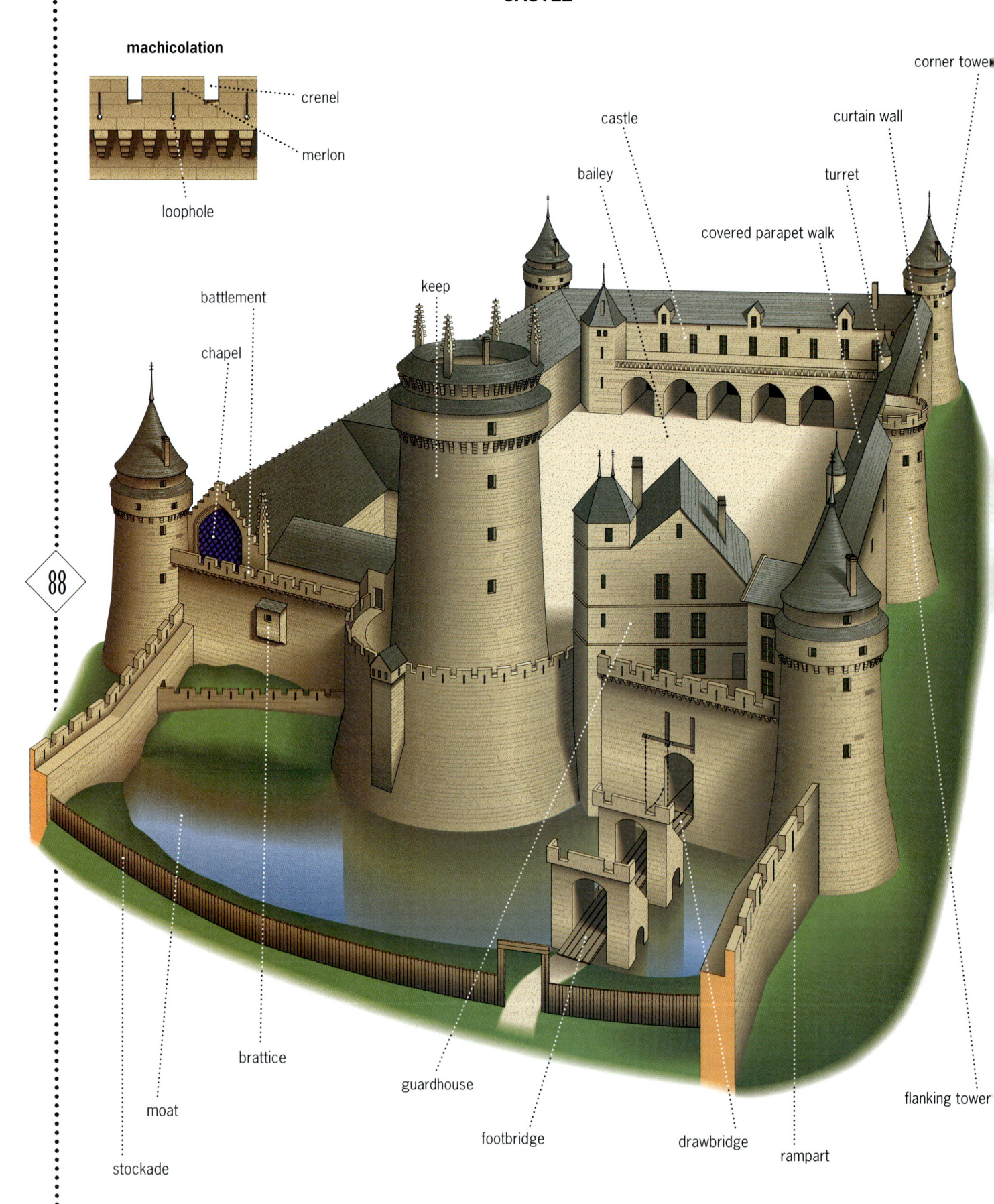

CASTLE

machicolation

- crenel
- merlon
- loophole

- corner tower
- curtain wall
- turret
- castle
- bailey
- covered parapet walk
- keep
- battlement
- chapel
- brattice
- moat
- stockade
- guardhouse
- footbridge
- drawbridge
- rampart
- flanking tower

CASTLE

ARCHITECTURE

GOTHIC CATHEDRAL

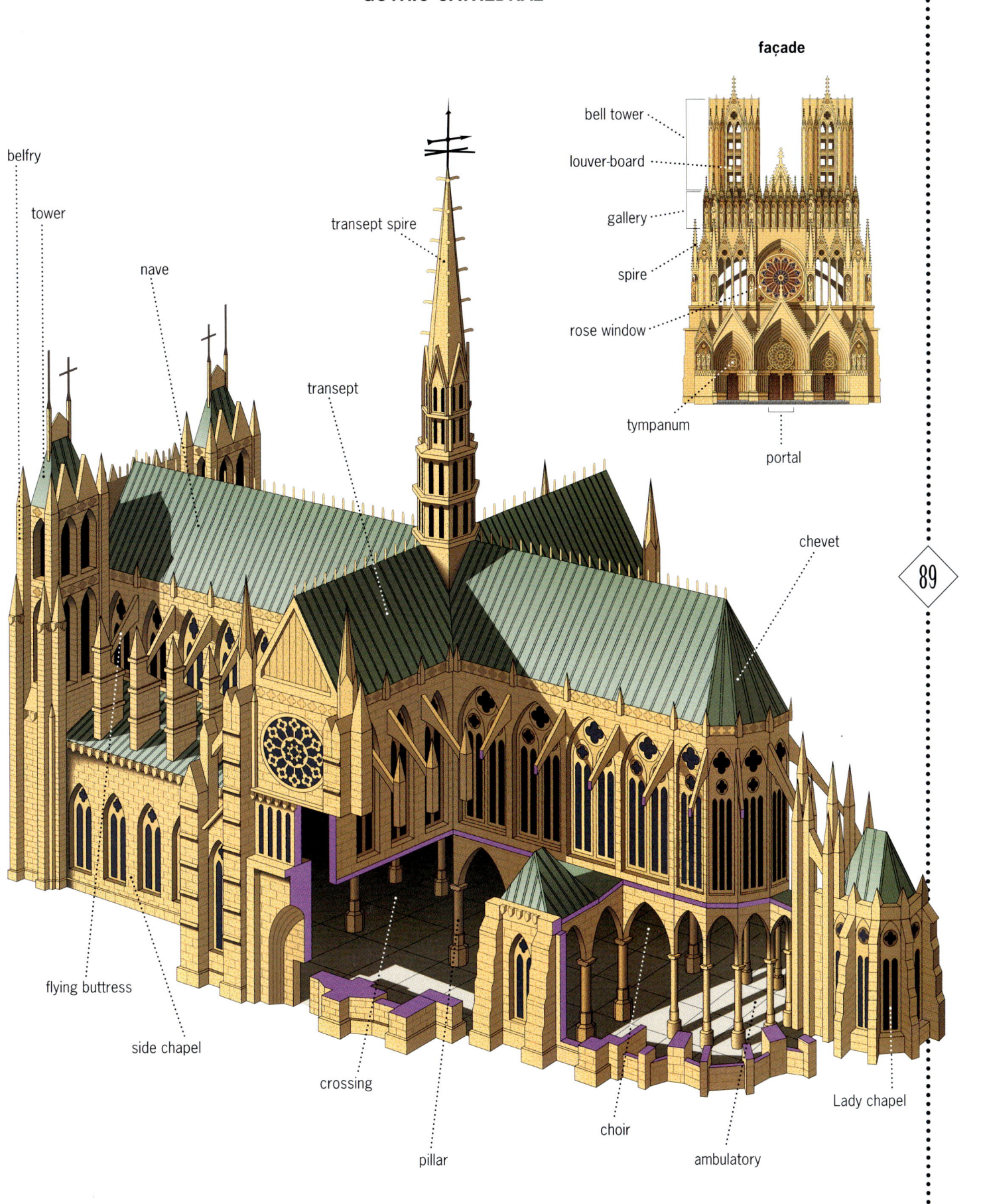

façade

- bell tower
- louver-board
- gallery
- spire
- rose window
- tympanum
- portal

- belfry
- tower
- nave
- transept spire
- transept
- chevet
- flying buttress
- side chapel
- crossing
- pillar
- choir
- ambulatory
- Lady chapel

ARCHITECTURE

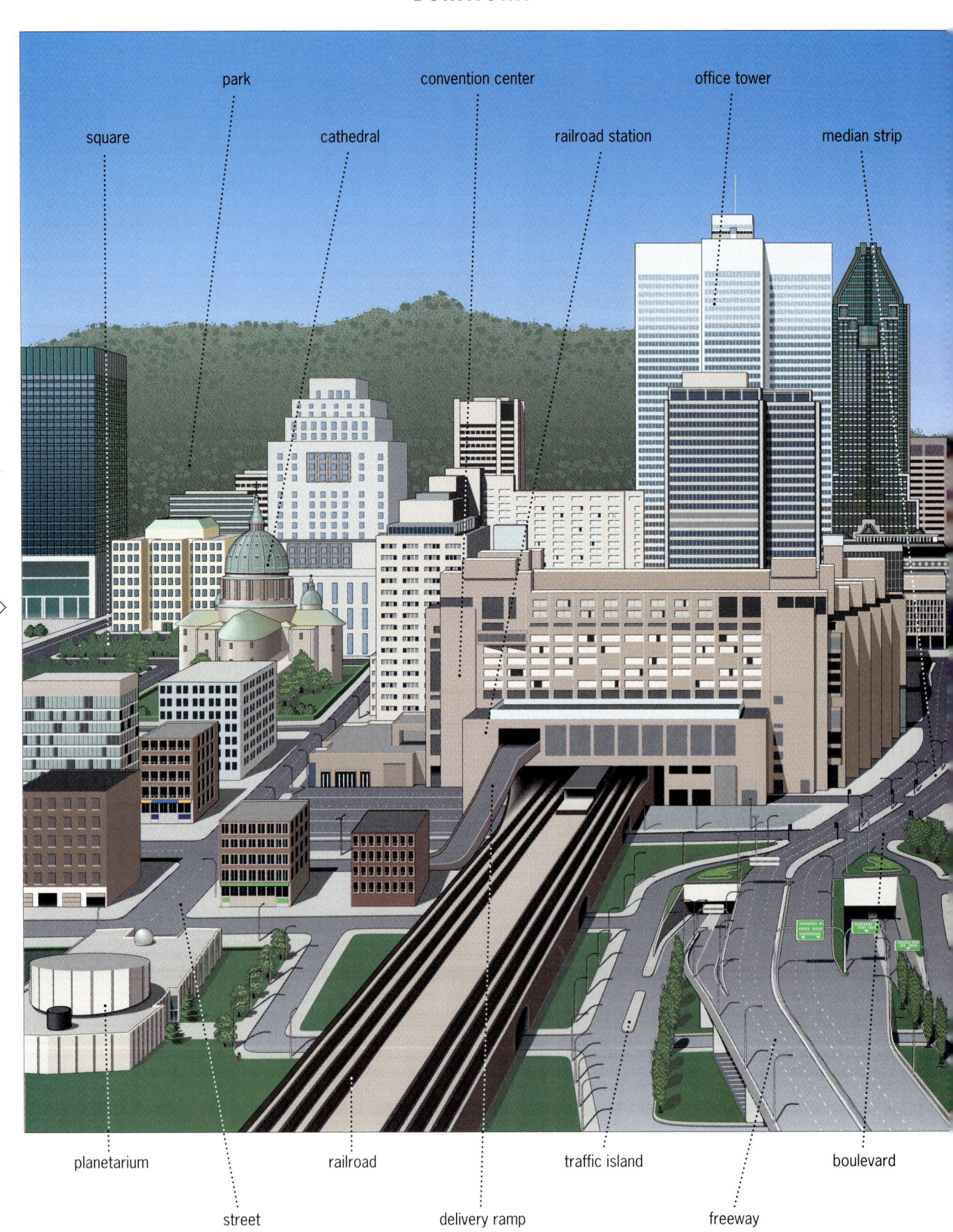

DOWNTOWN

square · park · cathedral · convention center · railroad station · office tower · median strip

planetarium · street · railroad · delivery ramp · traffic island · freeway · boulevard

DOWNTOWN

ARCHITECTURE

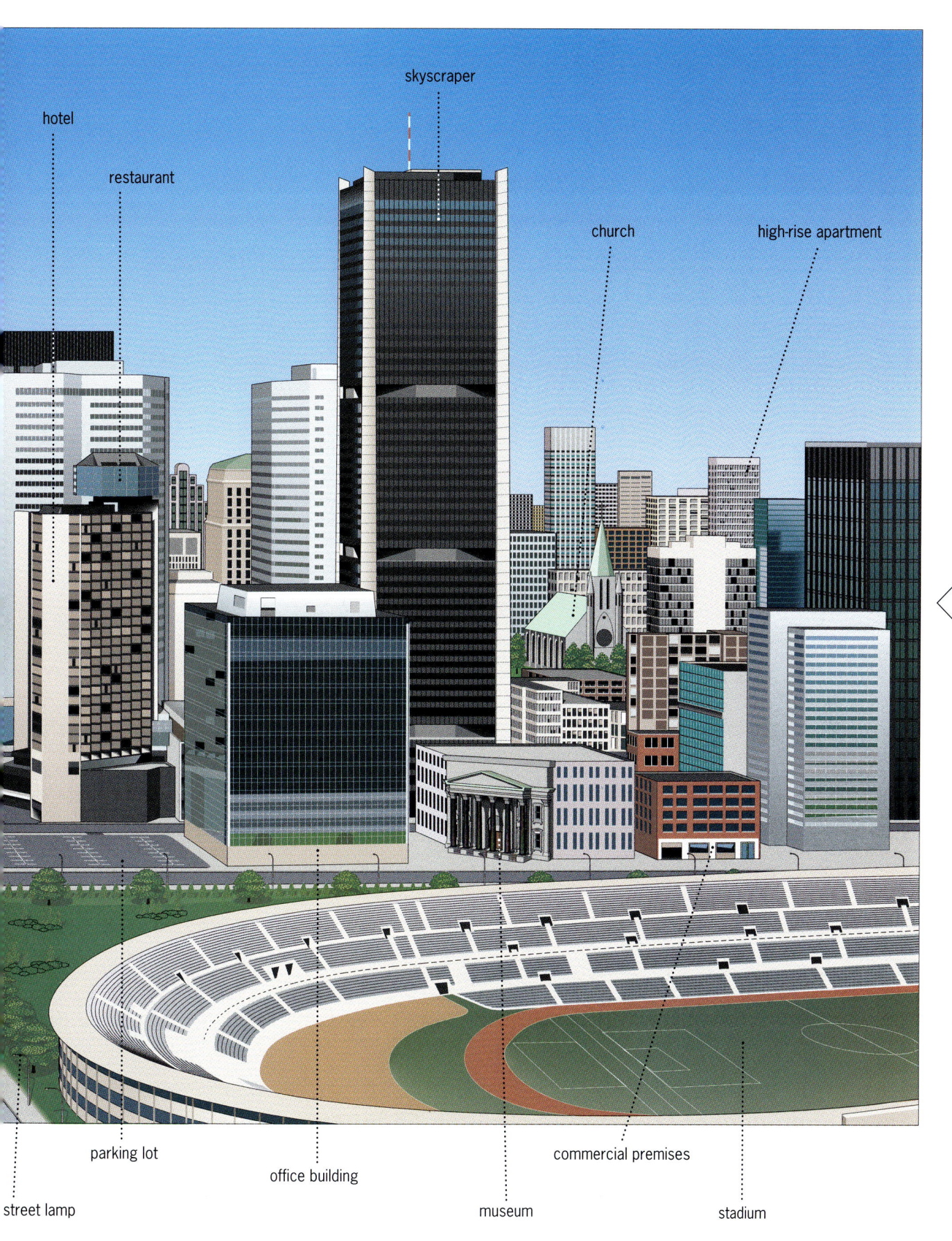

- hotel
- restaurant
- skyscraper
- church
- high-rise apartment
- street lamp
- parking lot
- office building
- museum
- commercial premises
- stadium

91

HOUSE

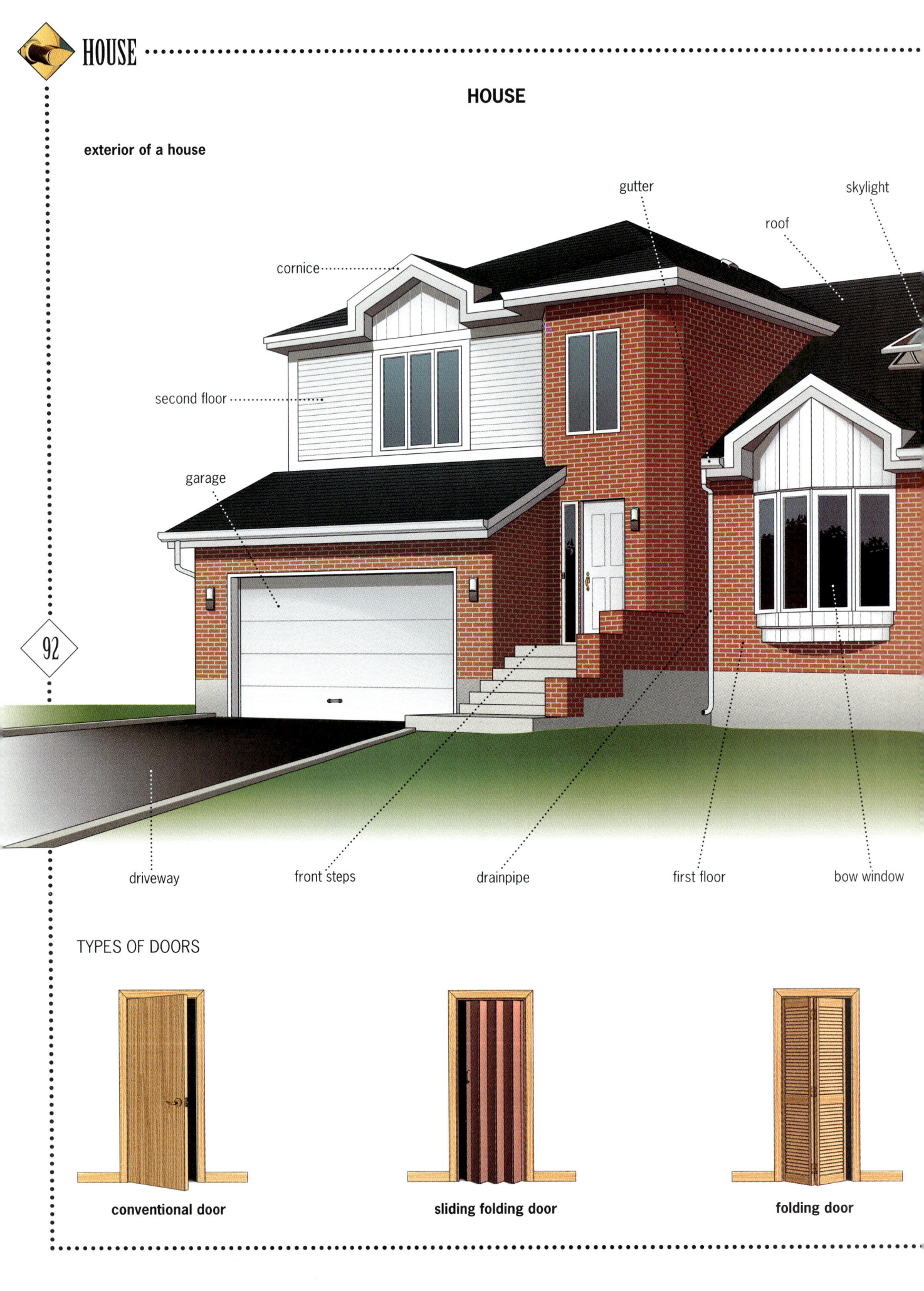

HOUSE

exterior of a house

- gutter
- skylight
- roof
- cornice
- second floor
- garage
- driveway
- front steps
- drainpipe
- first floor
- bow window

TYPES OF DOORS

conventional door

sliding folding door

folding door

HOUSE

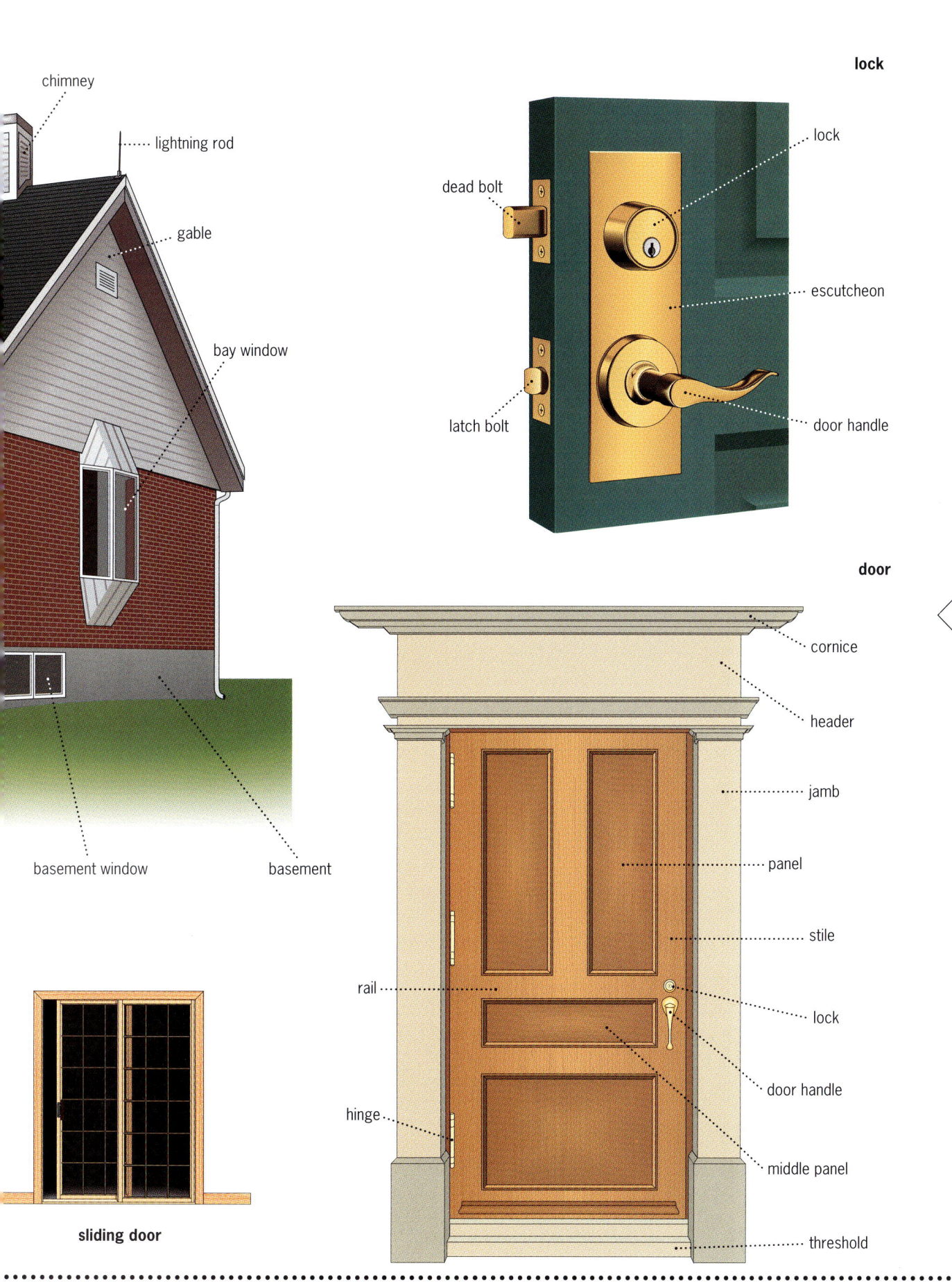

- chimney
- lightning rod
- gable
- bay window
- basement window
- basement

sliding door

lock
- dead bolt
- lock
- escutcheon
- latch bolt
- door handle

door
- cornice
- header
- jamb
- panel
- stile
- rail
- lock
- hinge
- door handle
- middle panel
- threshold

93

HOUSE

WINDOW

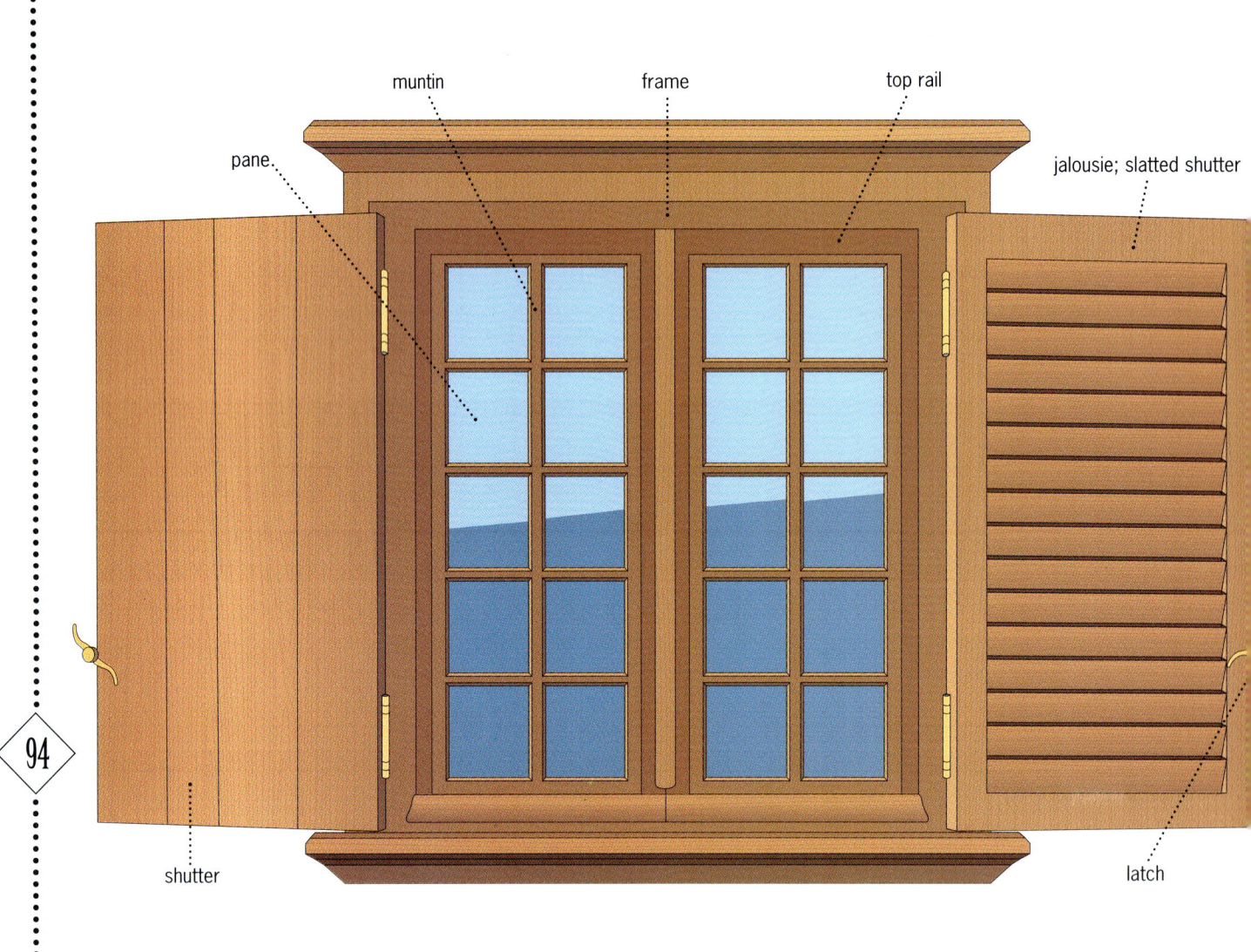

- muntin
- frame
- top rail
- pane
- jalousie; slatted shutter
- shutter
- latch

TYPES OF WINDOWS

casement window (inward opening)

casement window (outward opening)

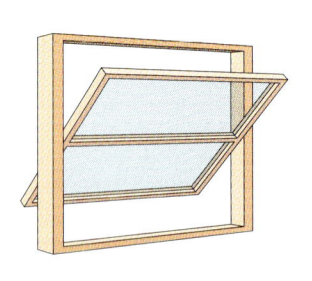

horizontal pivoting window

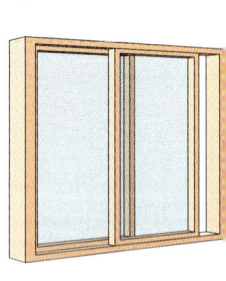

sliding window

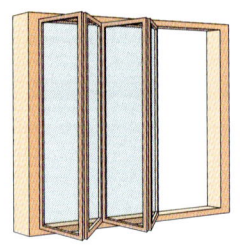

sliding folding window

vertical pivoting window

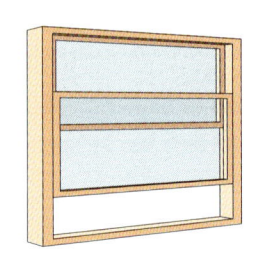

sash window

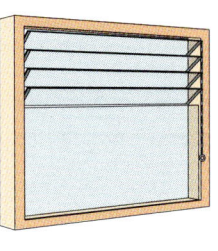

louvred window

HOUSE

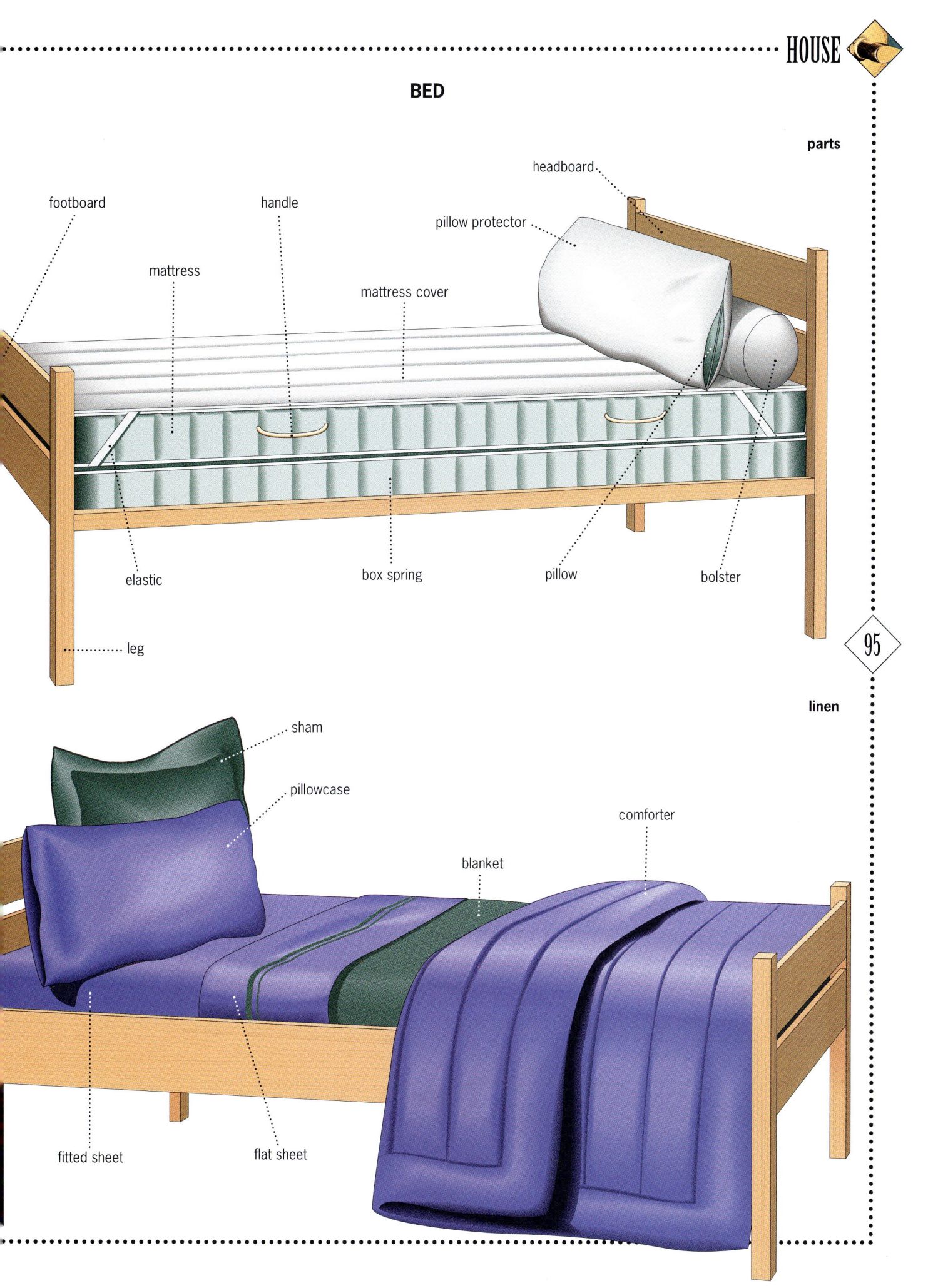

BED

parts

footboard, handle, mattress, headboard, pillow protector, mattress cover, elastic, box spring, pillow, bolster, leg

linen

sham, pillowcase, comforter, blanket, fitted sheet, flat sheet

95

HOUSE

SEATS

sofa

loveseat

armchair

footstool

bench

bar stool

stool

chaise longue

stacking chairs

folding chair

rocking chair

TABLE AND CHAIRS

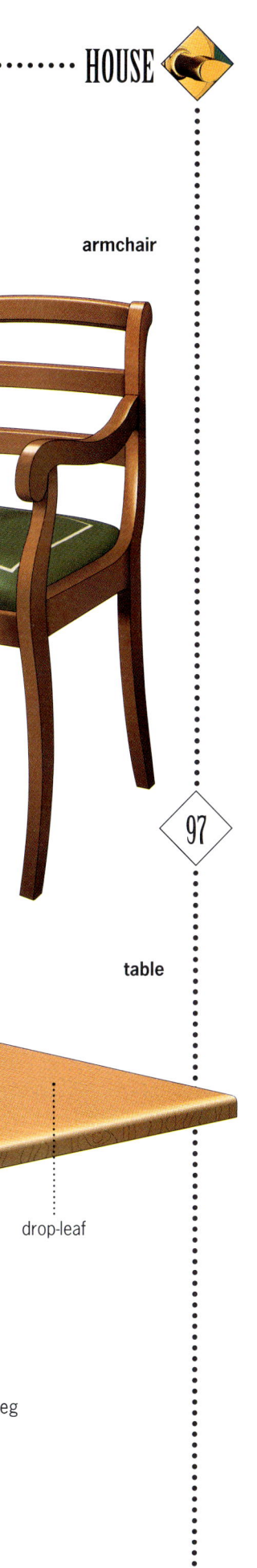

side chair

- ear
- rail
- back
- stile
- seat
- apron
- spindle
- support
- leg

armchair

- arm

table

- knob
- drawer
- top
- drop-leaf
- leg
- crosspiece

HOUSE

97

HOUSE

LIGHTS

track lighting

track

transformer

floor lamp

ceiling fixture

table lamp

shade

stand

hanging pendant

wall fixture

LIGHTING

incandescent lamp
- inert gas
- filament
- lead-in wire
- base
- contact

bulb

screw base

bayonet base

energy saving bulb
- bulb
- fluorescent tube
- housing
- base

tungsten-halogen lamp
- pin
- base

fluorescent tube
- pin base
- gas
- phosphorescent coating
- pin
- bulb

switch

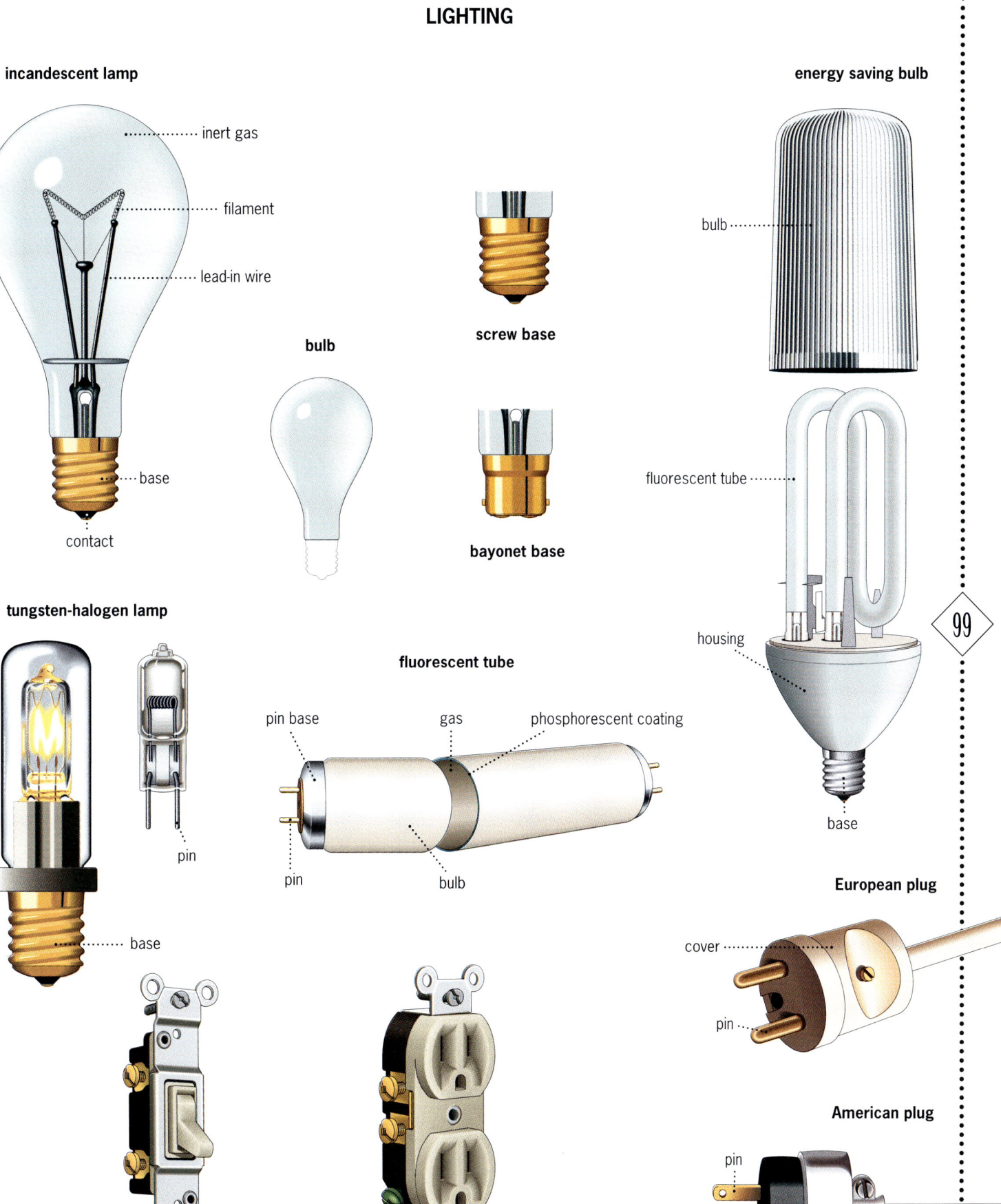

outlet

European plug
- cover
- pin

American plug
- pin
- grounding terminal

HOUSE

99

HOUSE

GLASSWARE

- champagne glass
- white wine glass
- red wine glass
- champagne flute
- tumbler; glass
- beer mug
- carafe
- decanter

DINNERWARE

- coffee cup
- cup
- mug
- creamer
- sugar bowl
- pepper shaker
- salt shaker
- butter dish
- cereal bowl
- soup bowl
- dinner plate
- salad plate
- bread and butter plate; side plate
- salad dish
- salad bowl
- teapot
- coffee plunger
- soup tureen
- water pitcher

SILVERWARE

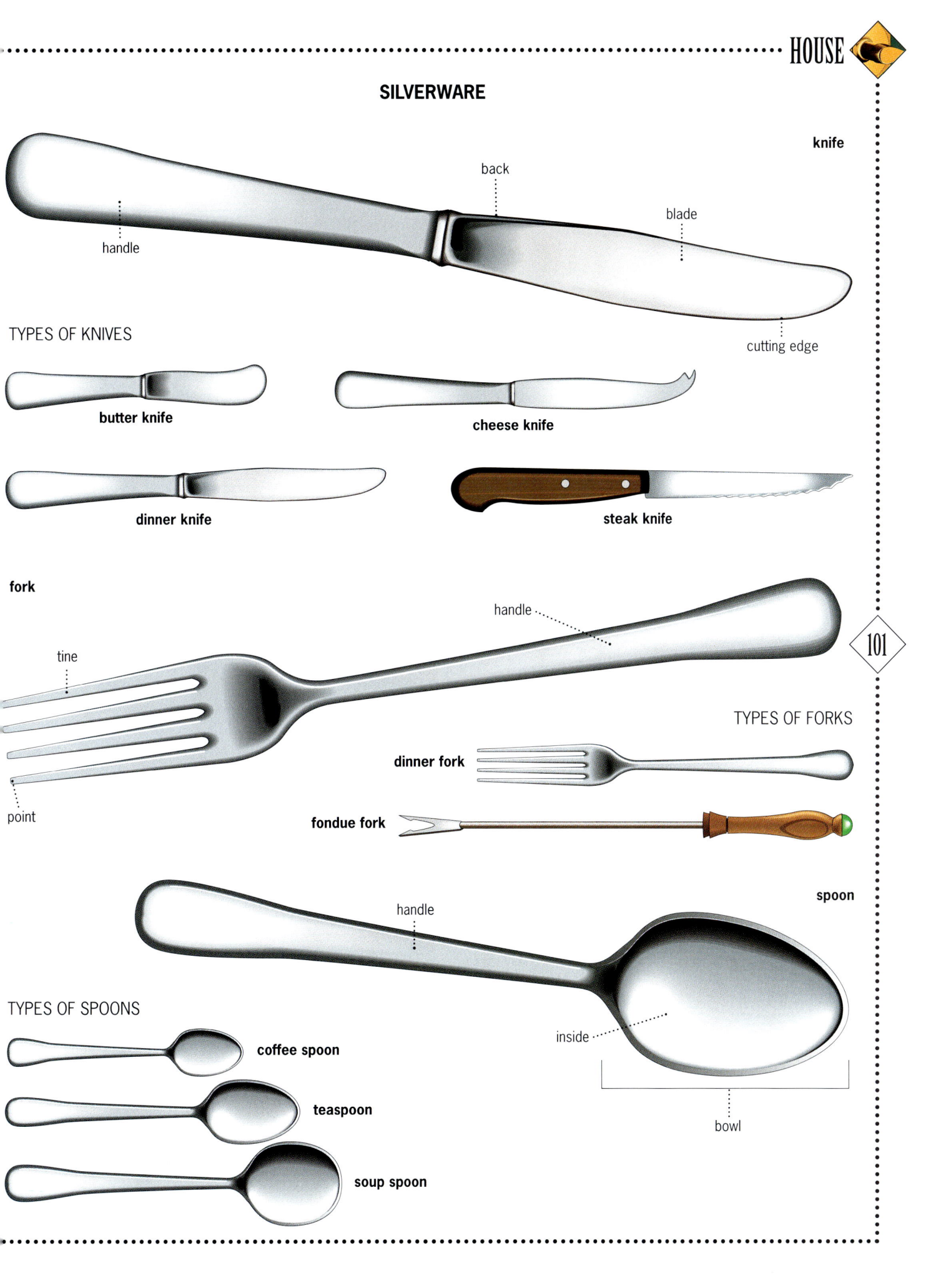

HOUSE

knife

- back
- blade
- handle
- cutting edge

TYPES OF KNIVES

- **butter knife**
- **cheese knife**
- **dinner knife**
- **steak knife**

fork

- handle
- tine
- point

TYPES OF FORKS

- **dinner fork**
- **fondue fork**

spoon

- handle
- inside
- bowl

TYPES OF SPOONS

- **coffee spoon**
- **teaspoon**
- **soup spoon**

101

HOUSE

KITCHEN UTENSILS

ladle

potato masher

spatula

whisk

egg beater

measuring spoons

nutcracker

lever corkscrew

bottle opener

peeler

rolling pin

can opener

HOUSE

spaghetti tongs

funnel

ice-cream scoop

colander

lemon squeezer

103

salad spinner

strainer

grater

HOUSE

COOKING UTENSILS

frying pan

sauté pan

stockpot; casserole

fondue set

wok

fondue pot

burner

double boiler

saucepan

vegetable steamer

roasting pans

pressure cooker

pressure regulator

safety valve

KITCHEN APPLIANCES

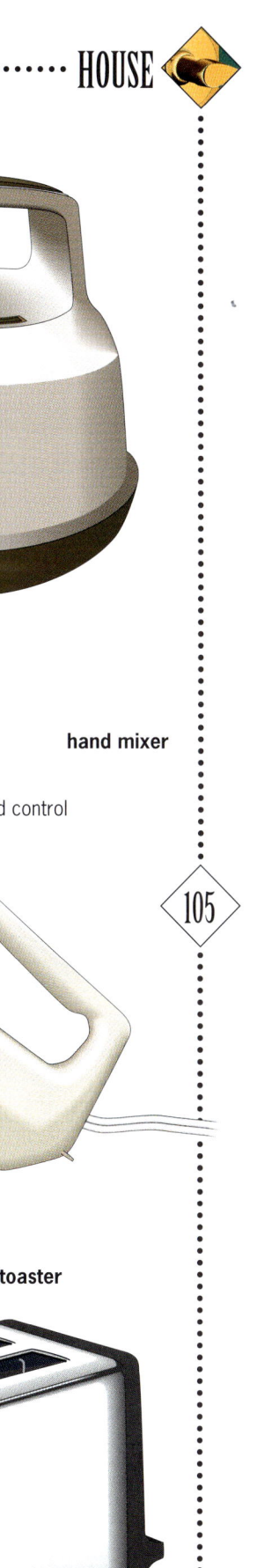

automatic drip coffee maker
- reservoir
- basket
- carafe
- warming plate
- on-off switch

kettle

hand mixer
- beater ejector
- speed control
- beater

blender
- container
- cutting blade
- push button

hand blender

toaster
- slot
- lever
- temperature control

HOUSE

105

HOUSE

REFRIGERATOR

- freezer compartment
- ice cube tray
- thermostat control
- egg tray
- butter compartment
- dairy compartment
- meat tray
- crisper
- glass cover
- refrigerator compartment
- shelf
- guard rail
- storage door

COOKING APPLIANCES

microwave oven

- sensor probe
- window
- door
- clock timer
- latch
- control panel

electric range

- oven control knob
- signal lamp
- control knob
- clock timer
- backguard
- cooktop
- ring
- oven
- rack
- window
- drawer

HOUSE

107

DO-IT-YOURSELF

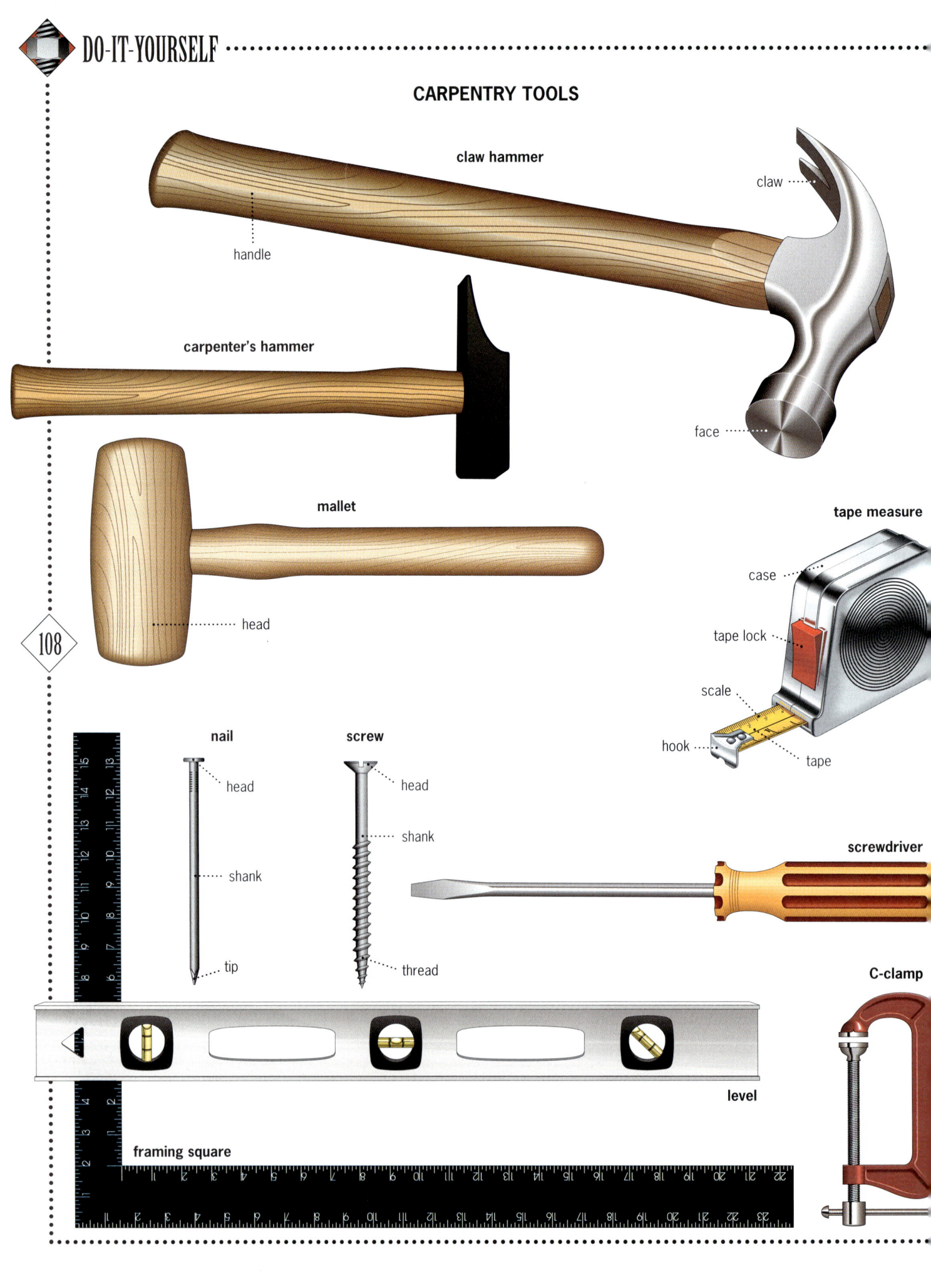

CARPENTRY TOOLS

claw hammer
- handle
- claw
- face

carpenter's hammer

mallet
- head

tape measure
- case
- tape lock
- scale
- hook
- tape

nail
- head
- shank
- tip

screw
- head
- shank
- thread

screwdriver

C-clamp

level

framing square

108

DO-IT-YOURSELF

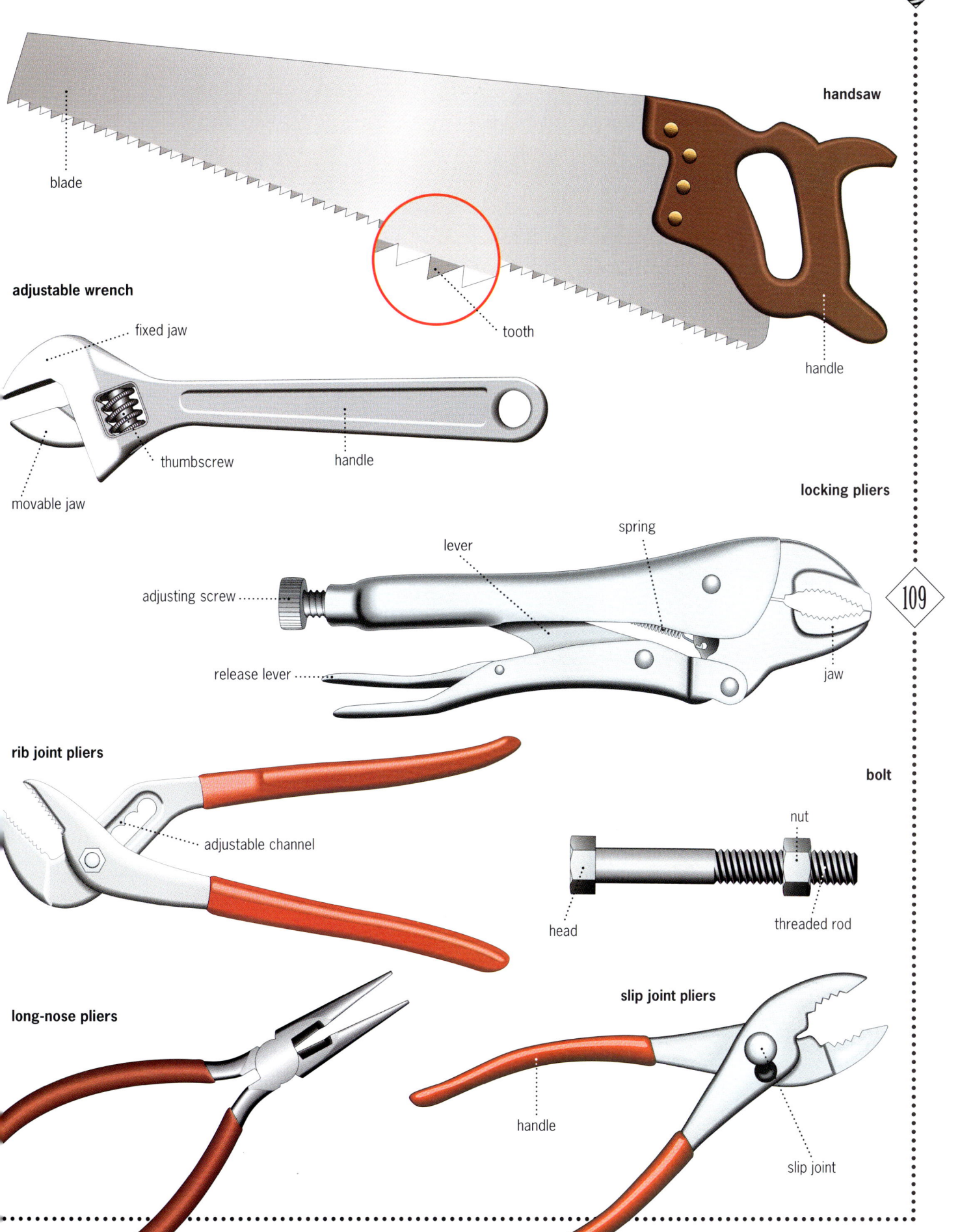

handsaw
- blade
- tooth
- handle

adjustable wrench
- fixed jaw
- thumbscrew
- handle
- movable jaw

locking pliers
- lever
- spring
- adjusting screw
- release lever
- jaw

rib joint pliers
- adjustable channel

bolt
- nut
- head
- threaded rod

long-nose pliers

slip joint pliers
- handle
- slip joint

109

DO-IT-YOURSELF

ELECTRIC TOOLS

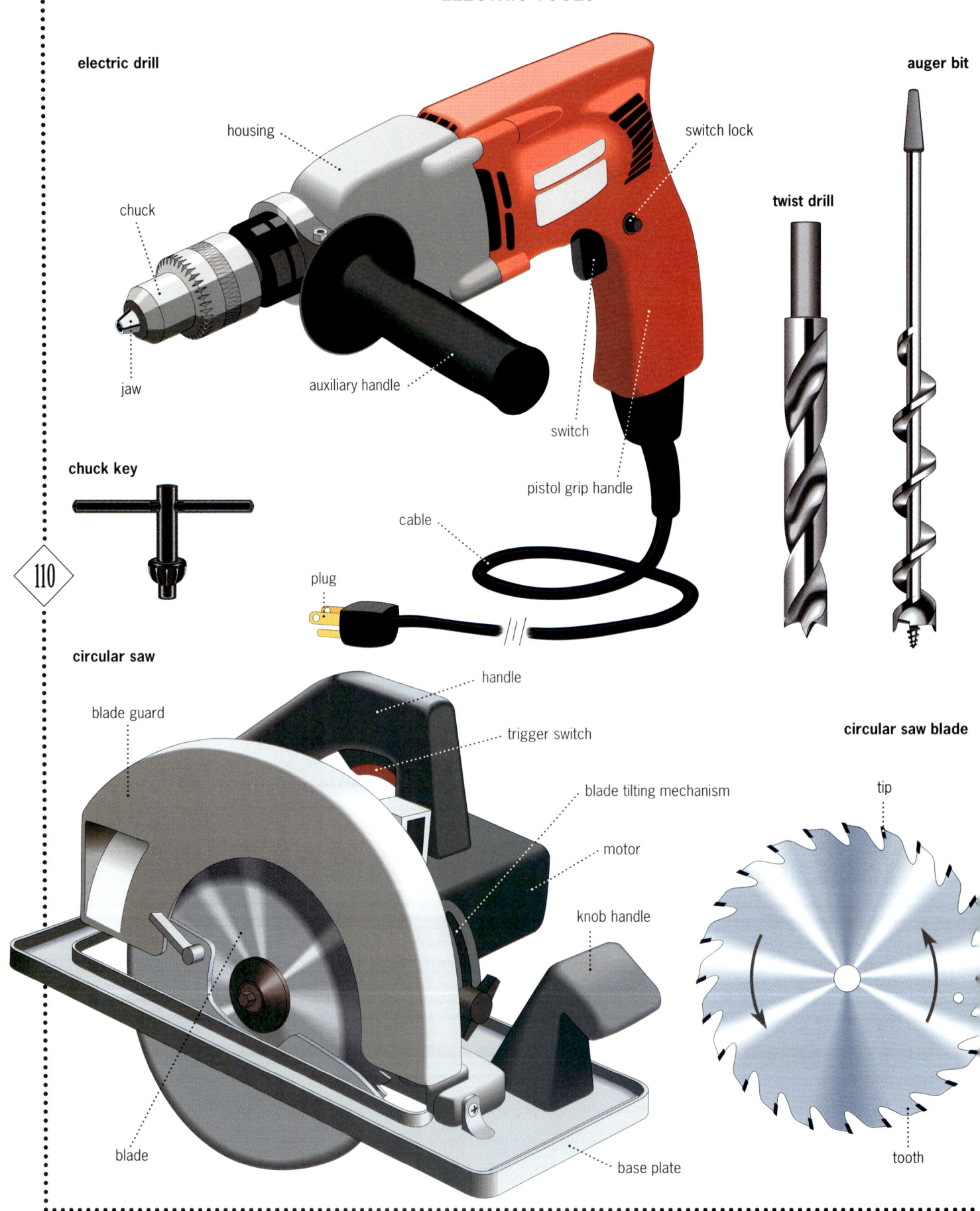

electric drill
- housing
- chuck
- jaw
- auxiliary handle
- switch lock
- switch
- pistol grip handle
- cable
- plug

chuck key

twist drill

auger bit

110

circular saw
- blade guard
- handle
- trigger switch
- blade tilting mechanism
- motor
- knob handle
- blade
- base plate

circular saw blade
- tip
- tooth

DO-IT-YOURSELF

PAINTING UPKEEP

paint roller

tray

scraper

blade

roller frame

extension ladder

roller cover

brush

handle

bristles

stepladder

side rail

pulley

locking device

rung

platform ladder

hoisting rope

anti-slip shoe

111

CLOTHING

MEN'S CLOTHING

shirt
- collar
- collar point
- placket
- breast pocket
- front
- button
- shirttail
- cuff

suspenders
- adjustment slide
- button loop
- leather end

suspender clip

tie
- rear apron
- neck end
- loop
- front apron

belt
- frame
- punch hole
- belt carrier
- tongue

pants
- waistband
- pocket
- fly
- crease
- cuff

boxer shorts

tank top; undershirt

briefs
- fly
- crotch
- waistband

112

CLOTHING

double-breasted jacket
- collar
- lining
- breast welt pocket
- sleeve
- flap
- patch pocket
- concealed pocket

duffle coat
- hood
- frog
- toggle fastening

cap
- crown
- peak

stocking cap

hunting cap
- ear flap

jacket
- snap fastener
- elastic waistband

windbreacker
- waistband
- drawstring

CLOTHING

WOMEN'S CLOTHING

toque

knitted hat

balaclava
peak

beret

blouse

double-breasted jacket

suit
jacket
skirt

overcoat

poncho

dress

114

CLOTHING

jeans

ski pants

shorts

Bermuda shorts

footstrap

115

straight skirt

culottes

pleated skirt

CLOTHING

WOMEN'S CLOTHING

pajamas

bra
- shoulder strap
- cup

pants

bathrobe

half-slip

CLOTHING

SWEATERS

cardigan

crew neck sweater

turtleneck

polo shirt

slipover

V-neck cardigan

- hanger loop
- sleeve
- V-neck
- button
- pocket
- ribbing

117

CLOTHING

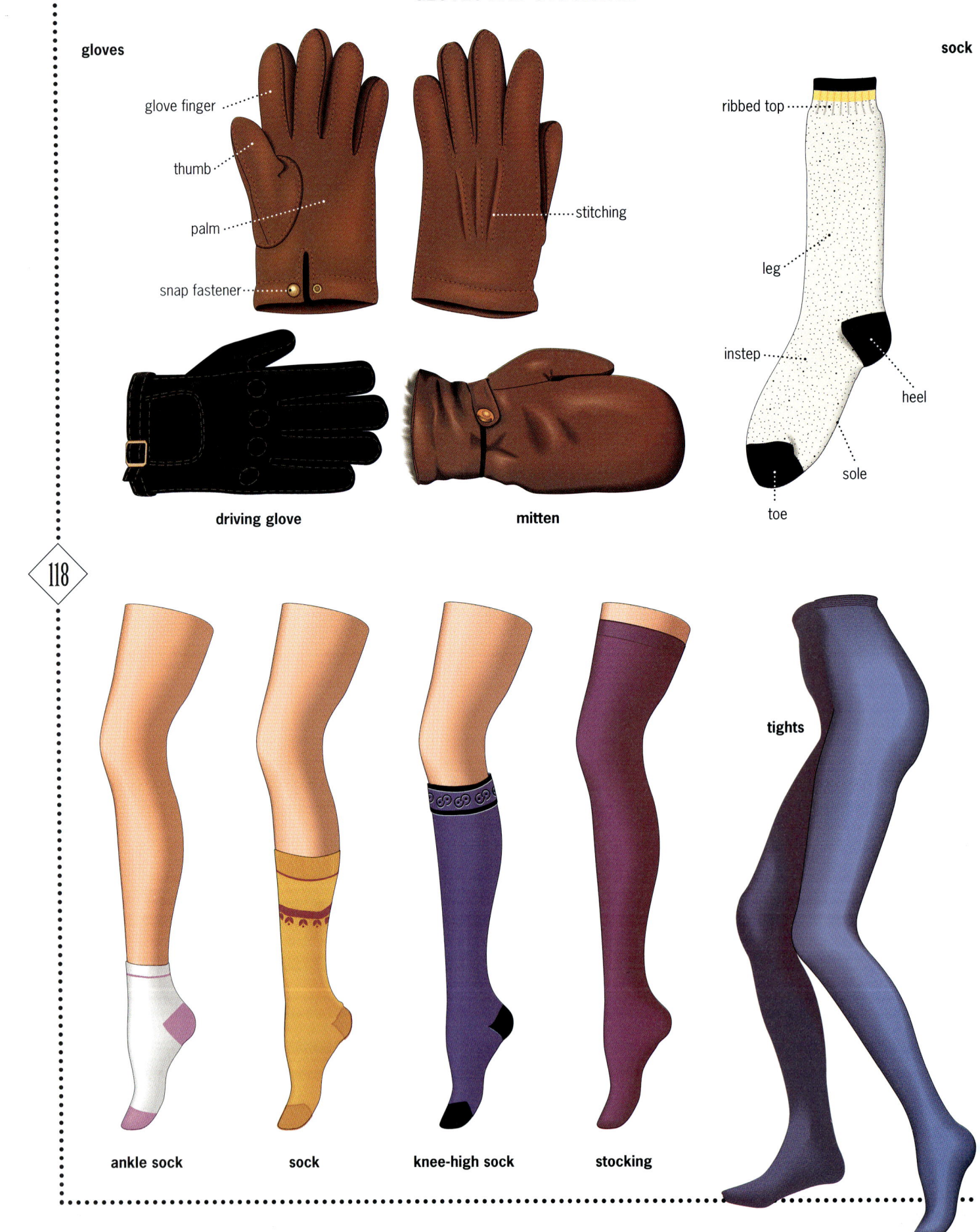

GLOVES AND STOCKINGS

gloves

- glove finger
- thumb
- palm
- snap fastener
- stitching

driving glove

mitten

sock

- ribbed top
- leg
- instep
- heel
- sole
- toe

118

ankle sock

sock

knee-high sock

stocking

tights

GLOVES AND STOCKINGS

CLOTHING

SHOES

heavy duty boot

slingback

ballerina

thigh-boot

pump

tennis shoe

espadrille

loafer

clog

moccasin

boot

ankle boot

119

CLOTHING

SPORTSWEAR

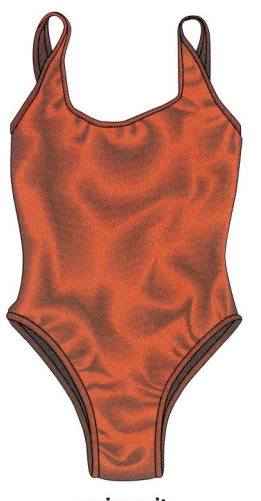

EXERCISE WEAR

tank top

swimsuit

leotard

TRACK SUIT

sweatshirt

hooded sweatshirt

windbreaker

pants

sweatpants

SPORTSWEAR

CLOTHING

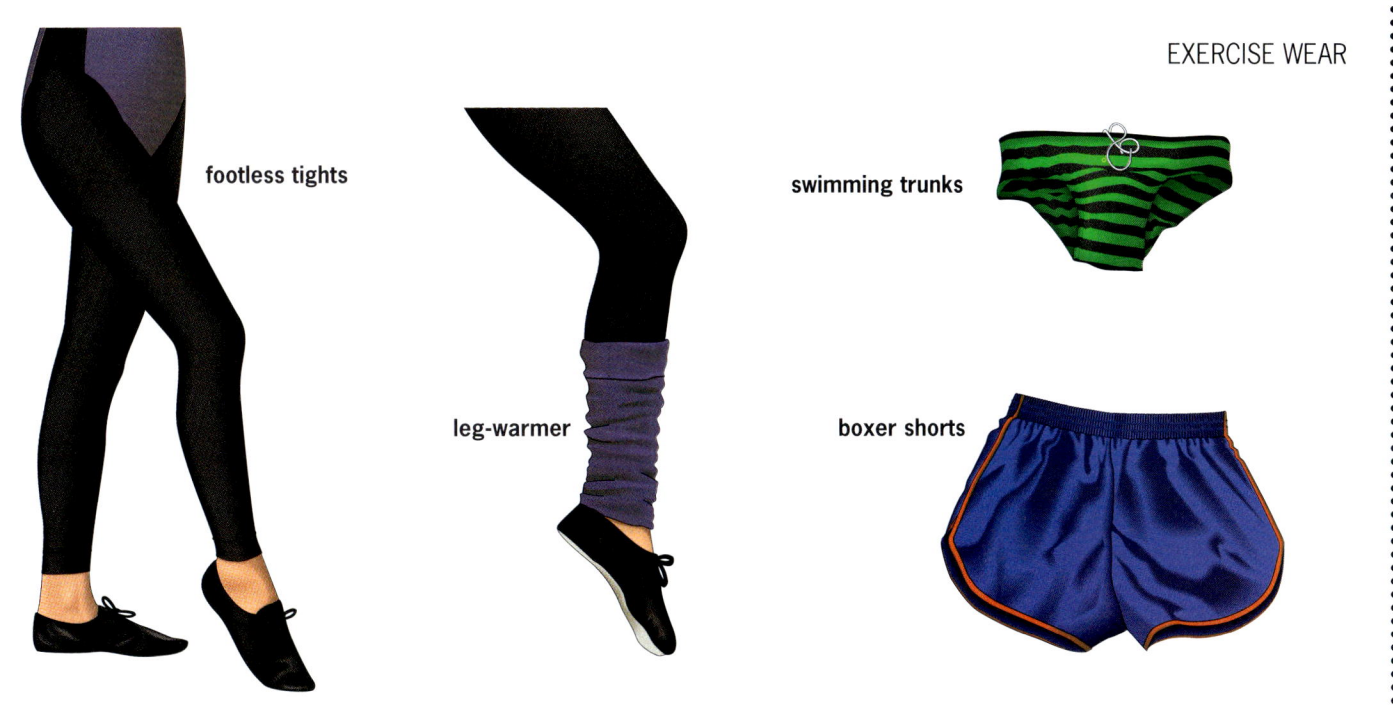

EXERCISE WEAR

footless tights

leg-warmer

swimming trunks

boxer shorts

running shoe

121

- counter
- collar
- quarter
- lining
- tongue
- nose of the quarter
- eyelet
- vamp
- heel
- stitching
- midsole
- air unit
- tag
- shoelace
- outsole
- stud

PERSONAL ARTICLES

DENTAL CARE

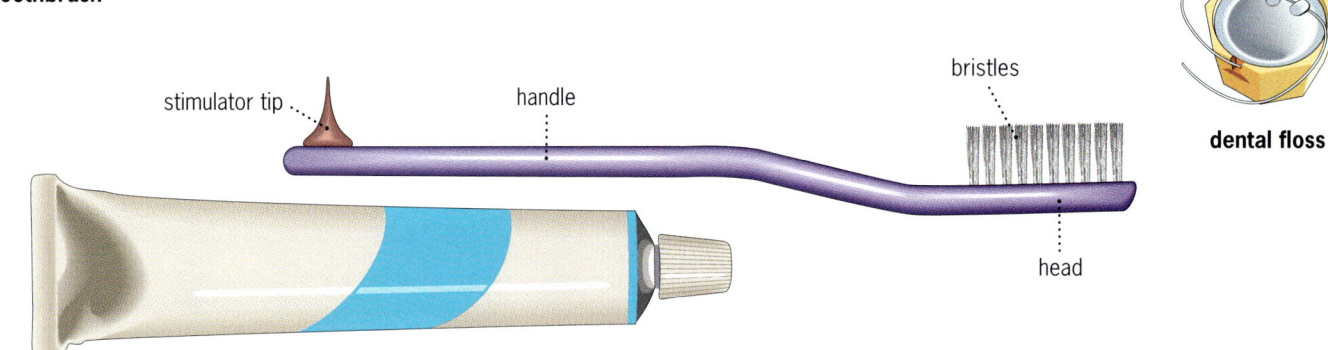

toothbrush

stimulator tip · handle · bristles

dental floss

head

toothpaste

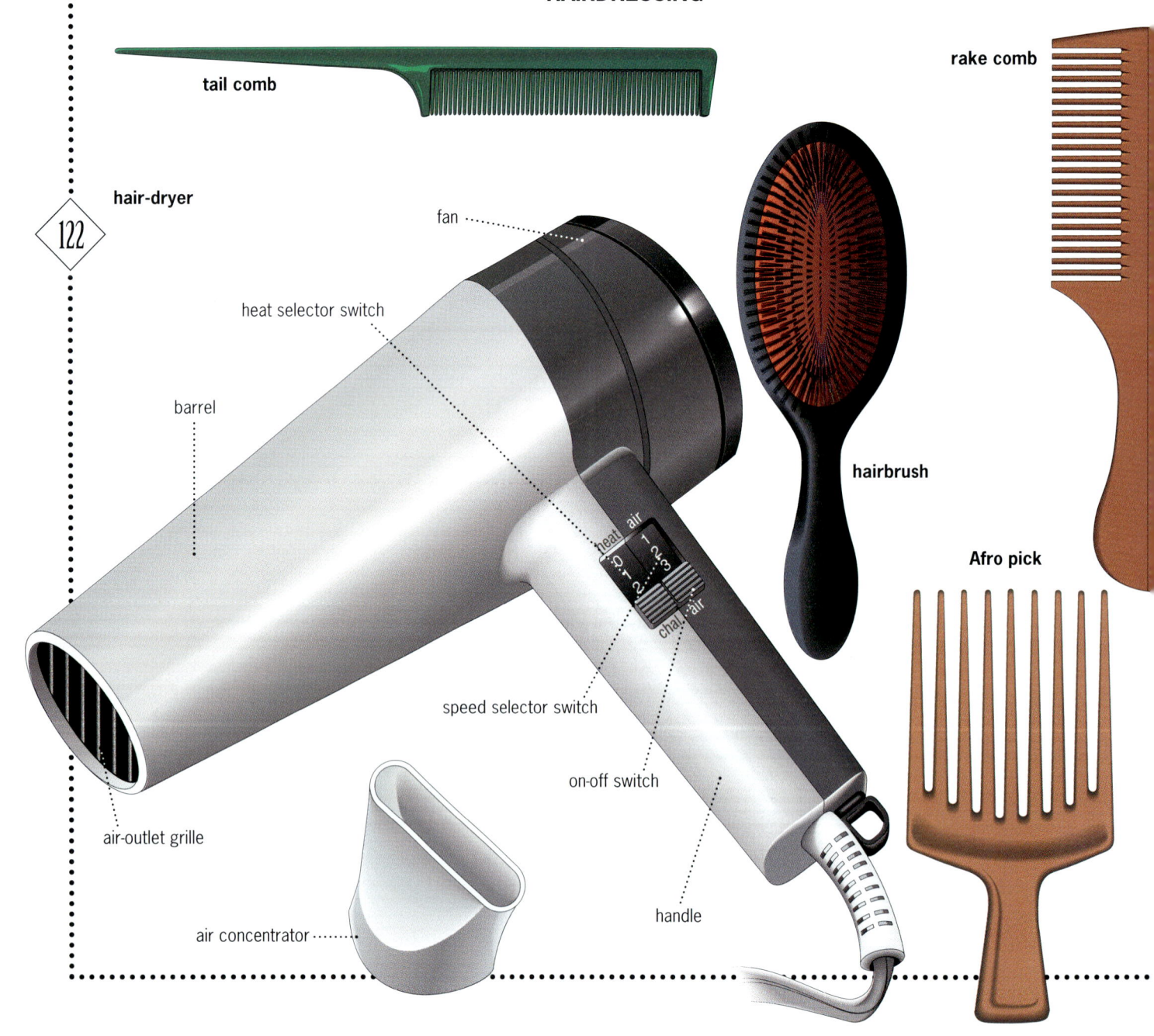

HAIRDRESSING

tail comb

rake comb

hair-dryer

fan

heat selector switch

barrel

hairbrush

Afro pick

speed selector switch

on-off switch

air-outlet grille

air concentrator

handle

PERSONAL ARTICLES

LEATHER GOODS

drawstring bag

- drawstring
- shoulder strap
- front pocket

knapsack

key case

wallet

purse

GLASSES

- glass lens
- bridge
- bar
- rim
- nose pad
- temple

UMBRELLA

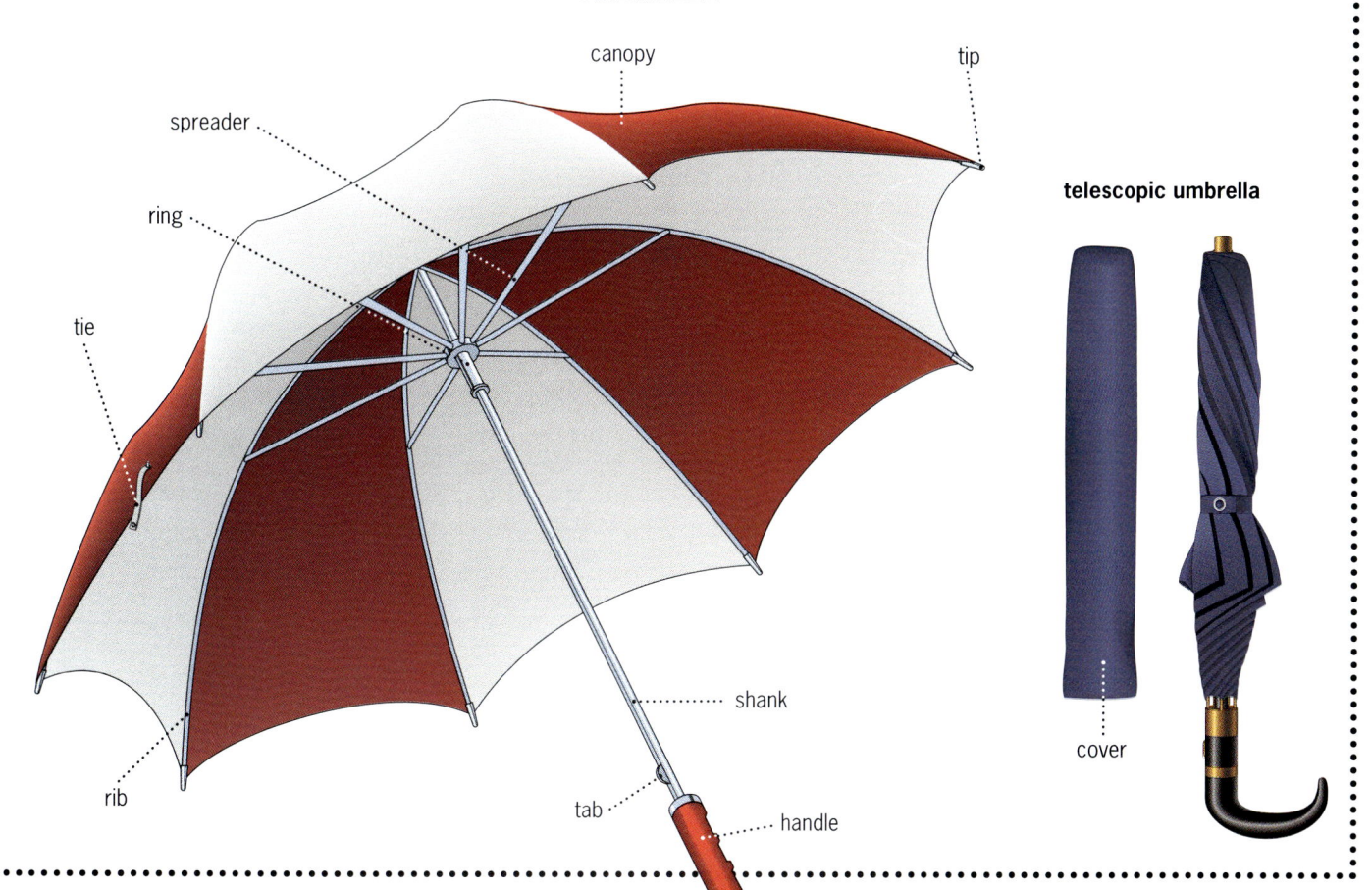

- canopy
- tip
- spreader
- ring
- tie
- shank
- rib
- tab
- handle

telescopic umbrella

- cover

COMMUNICATIONS

COMMUNICATION BY TELEPHONE

telephone set

- handset
- earpiece
- display
- mouthpiece
- function selectors
- automatic dialer
- push buttons
- telephone index
- handset cord

telephone answering machine

- outgoing announcement cassette
- incoming message cassette
- speaker
- listen button
- record announcement button
- volume control
- cassette player controls

pay phone

- coin slot
- display
- push buttons
- handset
- card reader
- coin return tray

push-button telephone

cordless telephone

portable cellular telephone

COMMUNICATIONS

PHOTOGRAPHY

single lens reflex (slr) camera

- accessory shoe
- film rewind button
- hot-shoe contact
- control panel
- film advance button
- control dial
- exposure button
- film speed
- remote control terminal
- camera body
- focus setting ring
- shutter release button
- objective lens

electronic flash
- flashtube
- photoelectric cell
- mounting foot

compact camera

cassette film
- perforation
- film leader

Polaroid® Land camera

pocket camera

cartridge film

film pack

125

COMMUNICATIONS

TELEVISION

television set

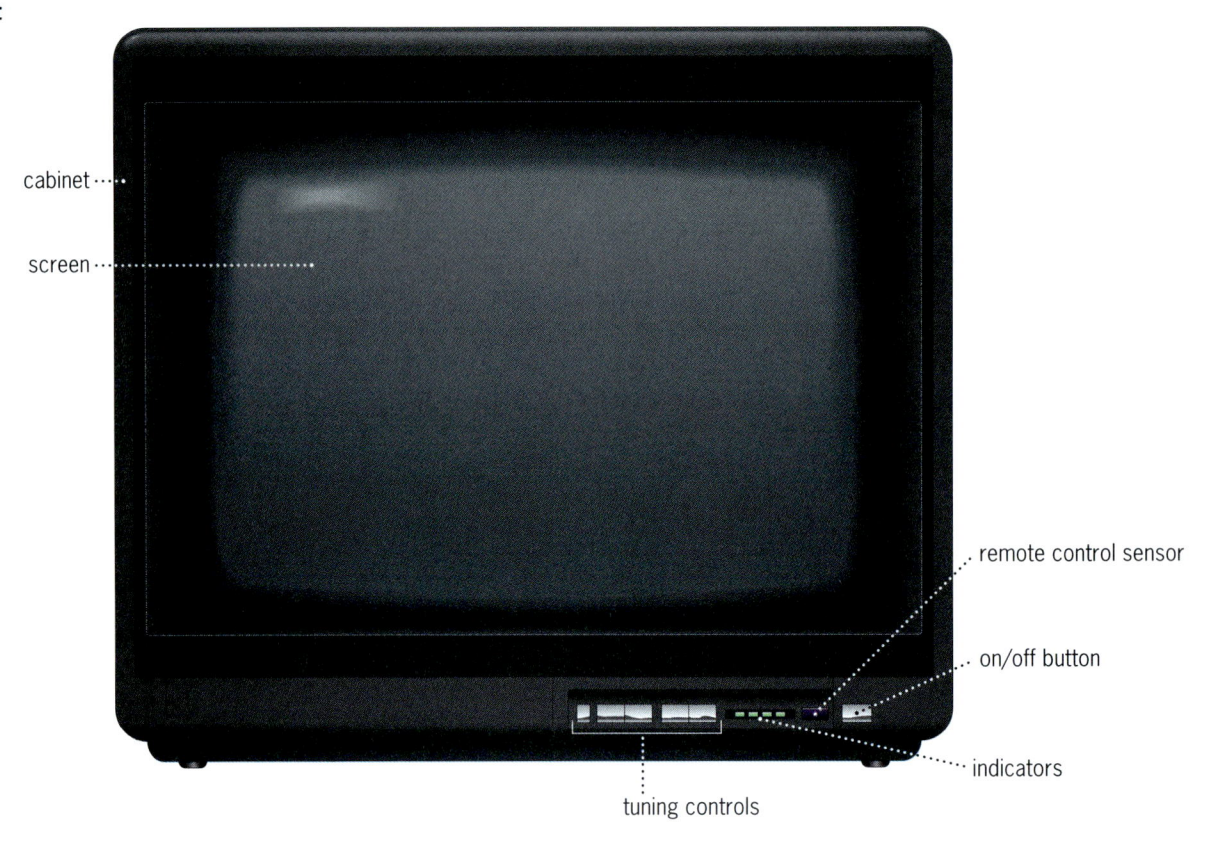

- cabinet
- screen
- remote control sensor
- on/off button
- indicators
- tuning controls

remote control

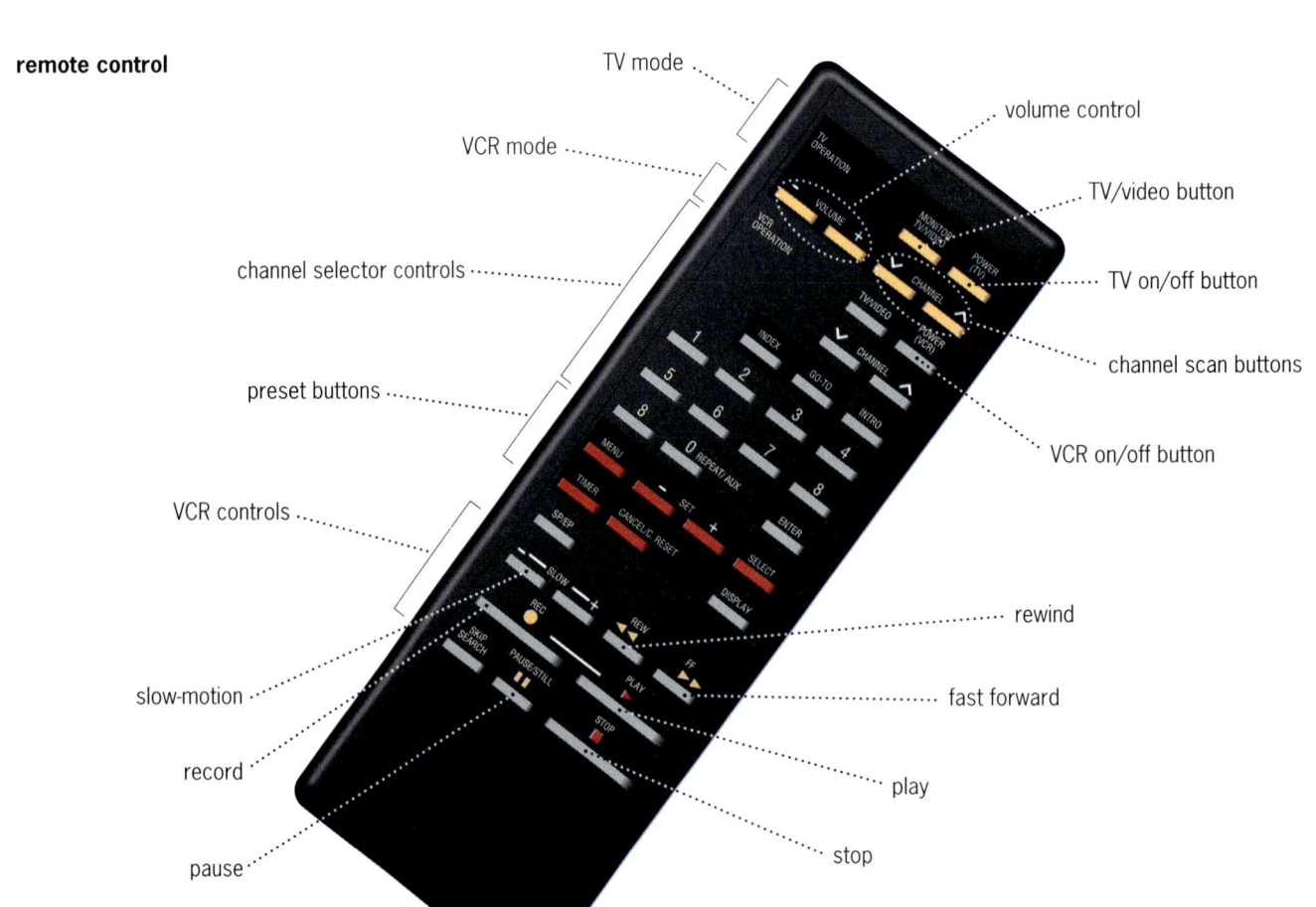

- TV mode
- VCR mode
- channel selector controls
- preset buttons
- VCR controls
- slow-motion
- record
- pause
- volume control
- TV/video button
- TV on/off button
- channel scan buttons
- VCR on/off button
- rewind
- fast forward
- play
- stop

TELEVISION

COMMUNICATIONS

VIDEO

videocassette recorder

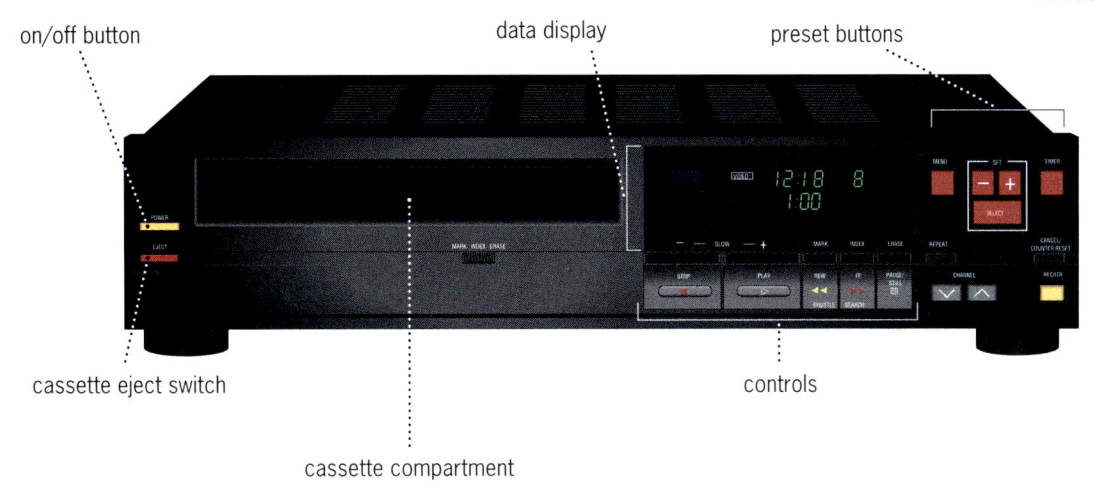

- on/off button
- data display
- preset buttons
- cassette eject switch
- cassette compartment
- controls

video camera

- accessory shoe
- eyepiece
- power zoom button
- electronic viewfinder
- cassette eject switch
- videotape operation controls
- viewfinder adjustment keys
- built-in microphone
- battery
- zoom lens
- battery eject switch
- data display
- shooting adjustment keys
- cassette compartment
- edit/search buttons

127

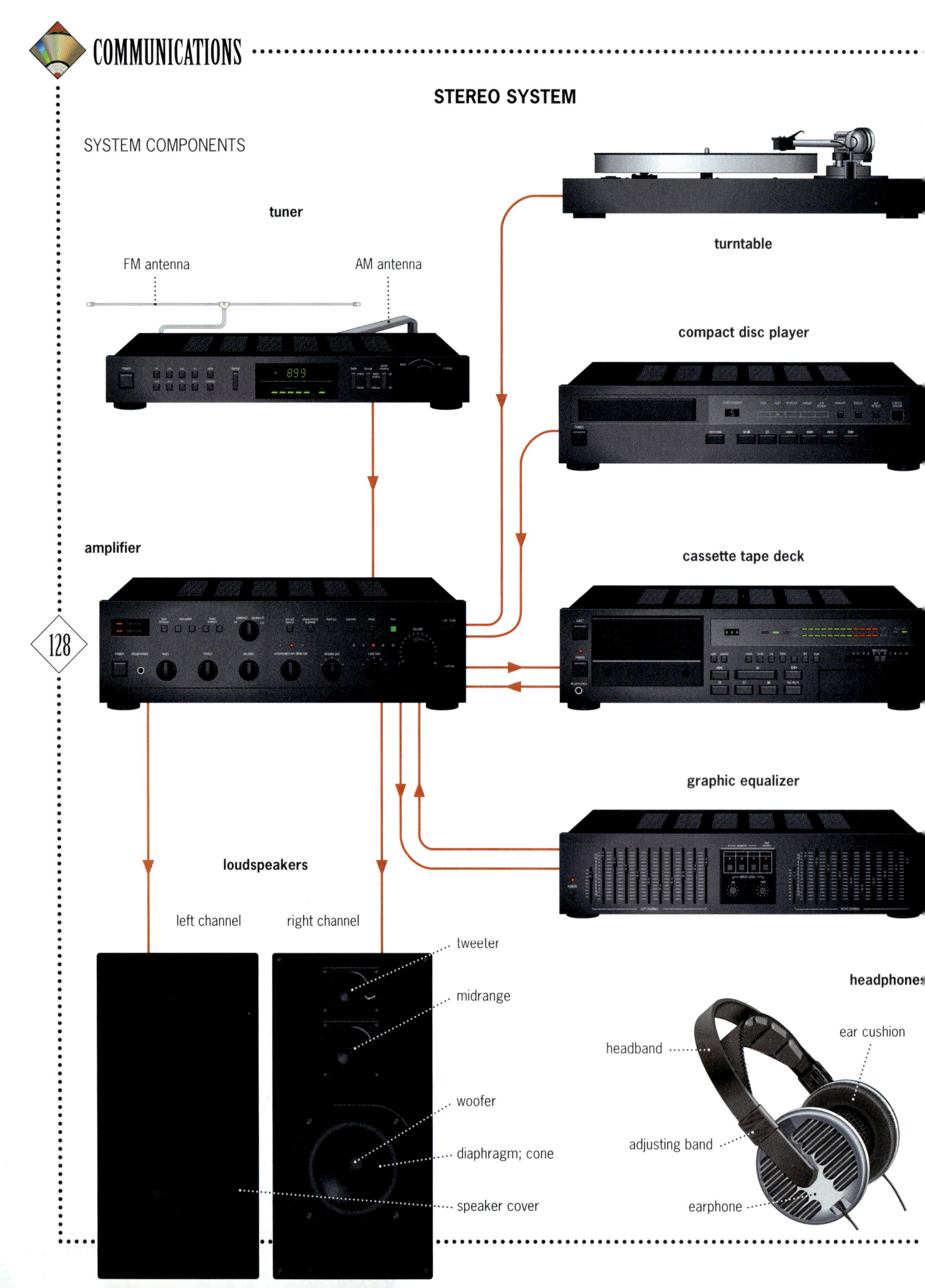

COMMUNICATIONS

STEREO SYSTEM

SYSTEM COMPONENTS

tuner

FM antenna

AM antenna

turntable

compact disc player

amplifier

cassette tape deck

graphic equalizer

loudspeakers

left channel

right channel

tweeter

midrange

woofer

diaphragm; cone

speaker cover

headphones

headband

ear cushion

adjusting band

earphone

COMMUNICATIONS

PORTABLE SOUND SYSTEMS

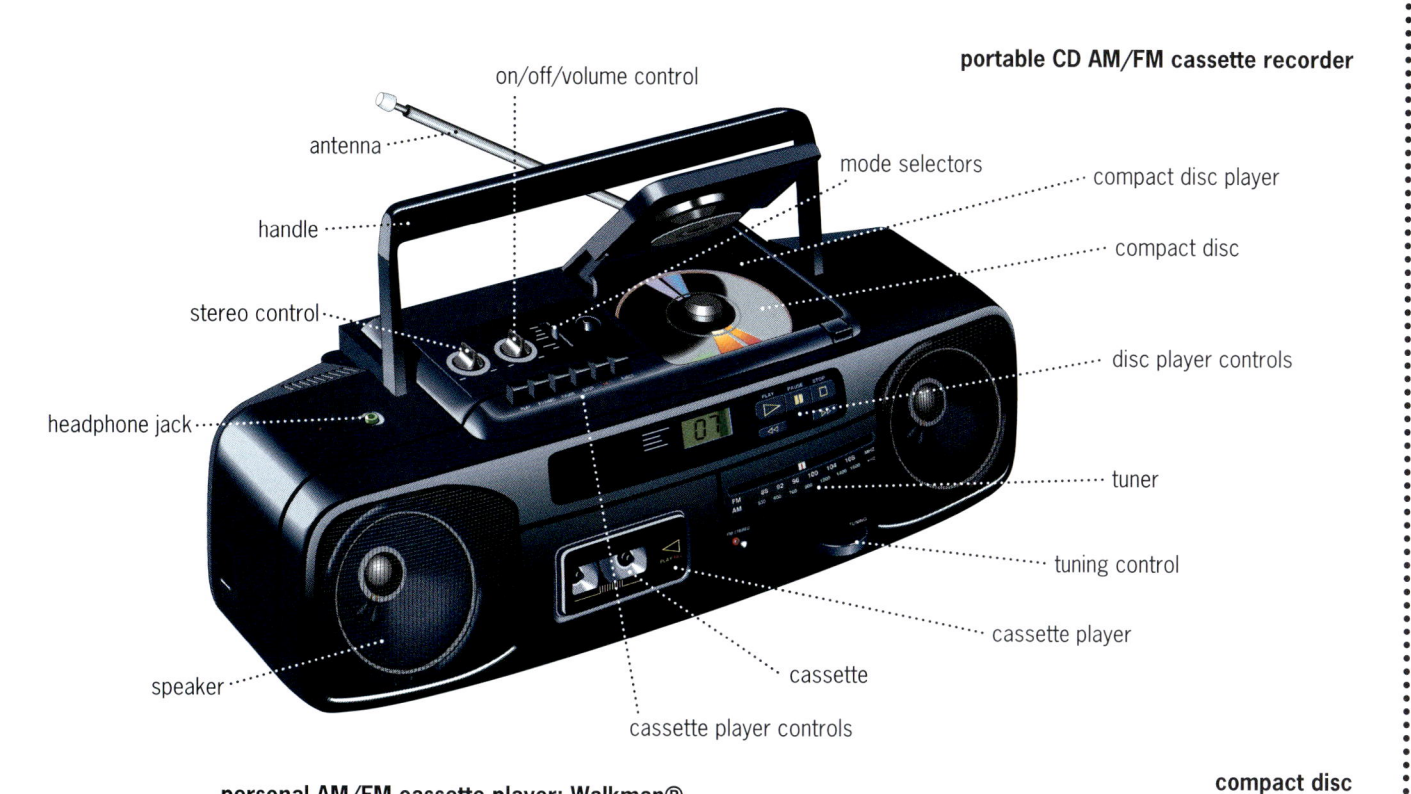

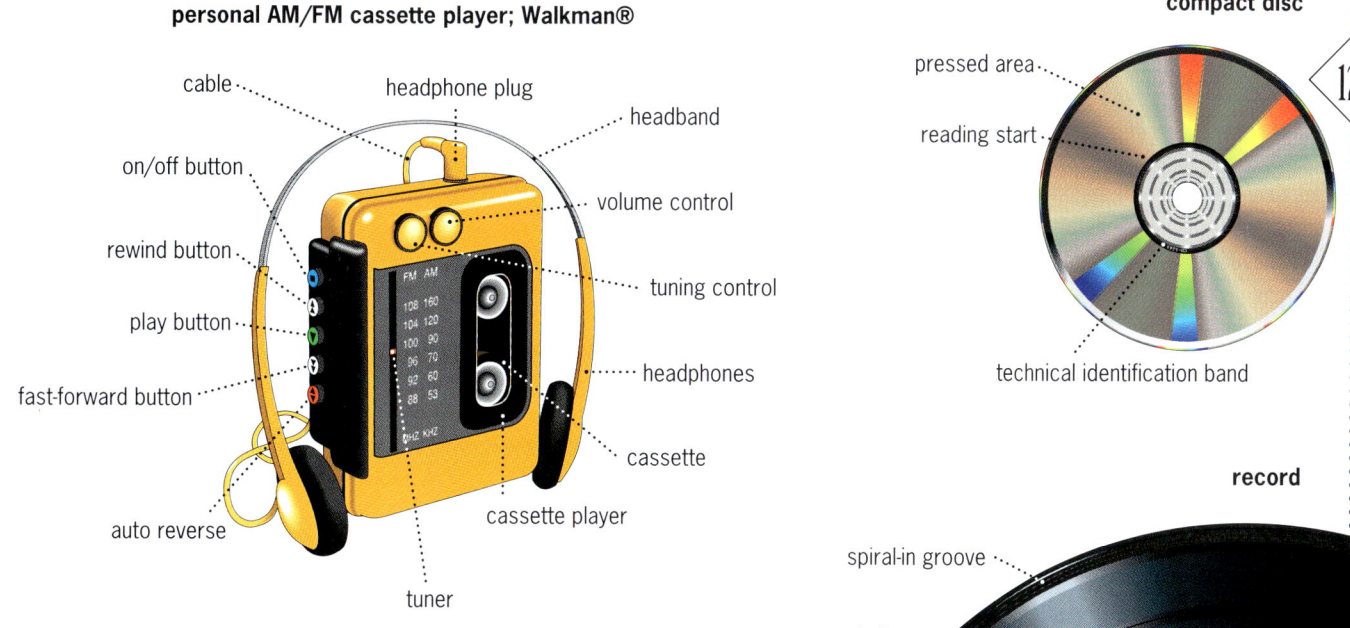

portable CD AM/FM cassette recorder

- on/off/volume control
- antenna
- handle
- mode selectors
- compact disc player
- compact disc
- stereo control
- disc player controls
- headphone jack
- tuner
- tuning control
- cassette player
- speaker
- cassette
- cassette player controls

personal AM/FM cassette player; Walkman®

- cable
- headphone plug
- headband
- on/off button
- volume control
- rewind button
- tuning control
- play button
- fast-forward button
- headphones
- cassette
- auto reverse
- cassette player
- tuner

compact disc

- pressed area
- reading start
- technical identification band

129

record

- spiral-in groove
- spiral
- band
- tail-out groove
- label
- center hole

cassette

- housing
- take-up reel
- recording tape
- tape guide
- guide roller
- playing window

ROAD TRANSPORT

CAR

body

- windshield
- windshield wiper
- outside mirror
- washer nozzle
- hood
- headlight
- grille
- bumper
- fender

130

CAR

ROAD TRANSPORT

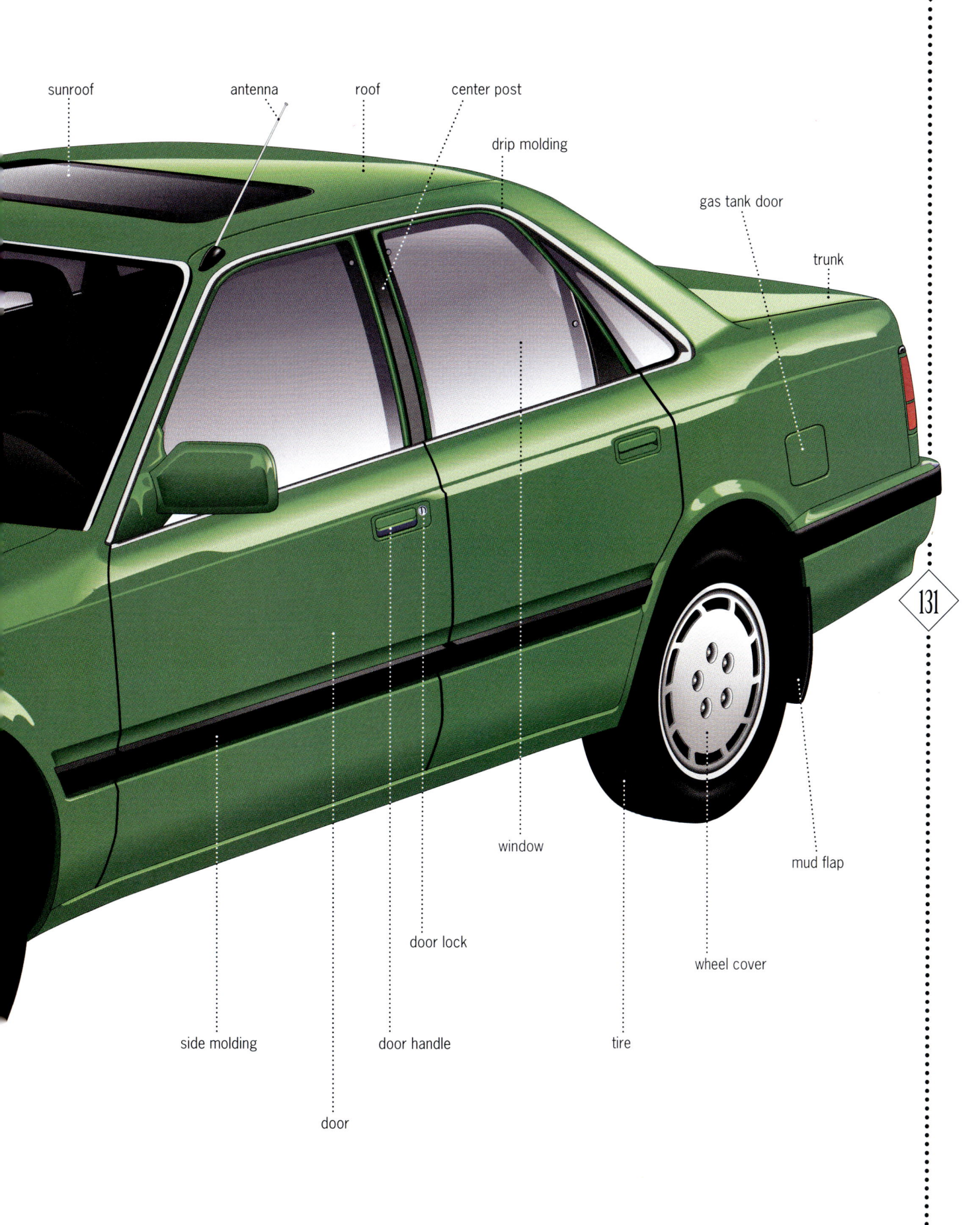

sunroof antenna roof center post
drip molding
gas tank door
trunk
window
door lock
side molding door handle tire wheel cover
mud flap
door

131

ROAD TRANSPORT

CAR

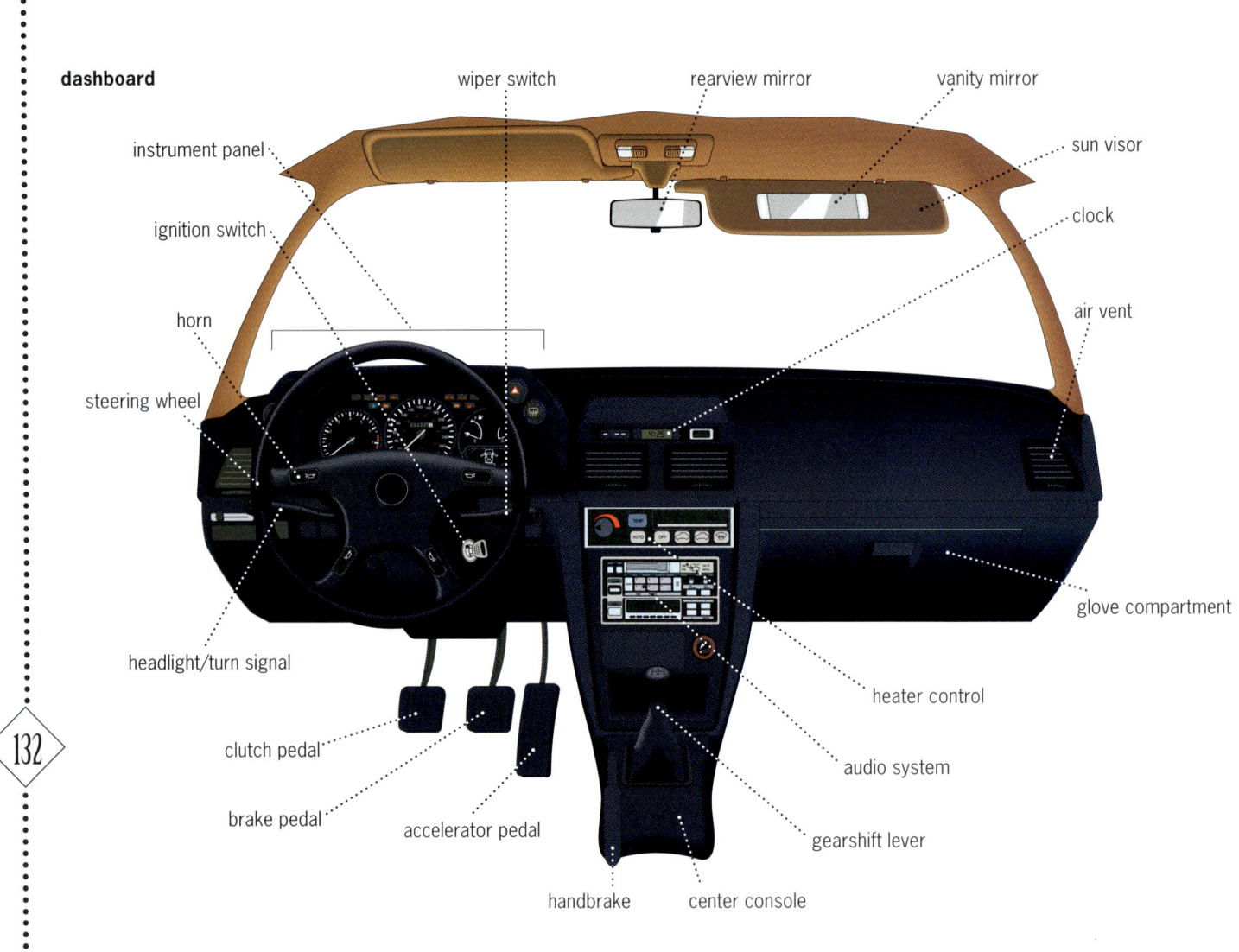

dashboard

- wiper switch
- rearview mirror
- vanity mirror
- instrument panel
- sun visor
- ignition switch
- clock
- horn
- air vent
- steering wheel
- glove compartment
- headlight/turn signal
- heater control
- clutch pedal
- audio system
- brake pedal
- accelerator pedal
- gearshift lever
- handbrake
- center console

instrument panel

- warning lights
- turn signal indicator
- fuel gauge
- high beam indicator light
- temperature gauge
- rev(olution) counter
- odometer
- trip odometer
- speedometer

ROAD TRANSPORT

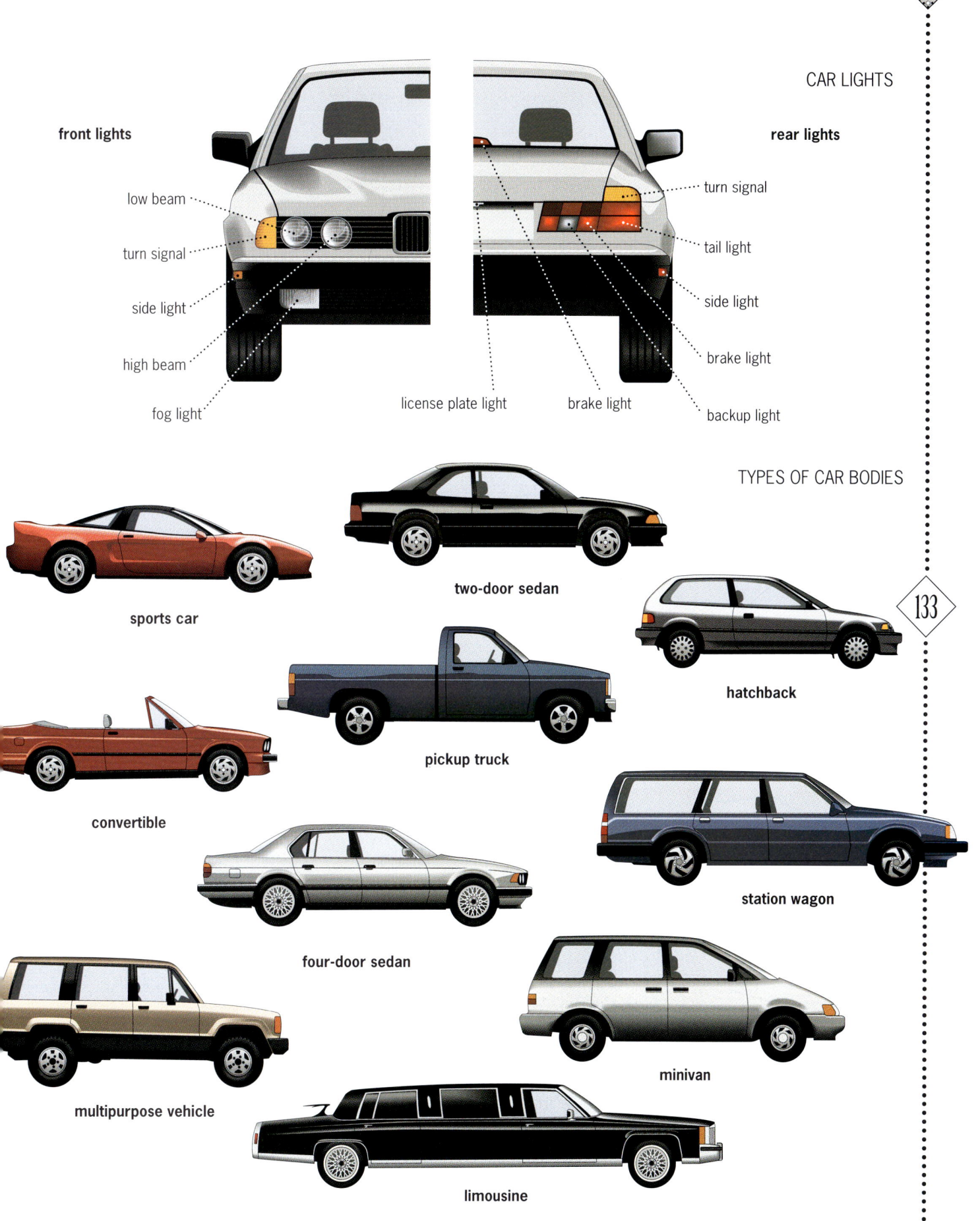

CAR LIGHTS

front lights
- low beam
- turn signal
- side light
- high beam
- fog light

rear lights
- turn signal
- tail light
- side light
- brake light
- backup light

license plate light
brake light

TYPES OF CAR BODIES

- sports car
- two-door sedan
- hatchback
- convertible
- pickup truck
- station wagon
- four-door sedan
- multipurpose vehicle
- minivan
- limousine

133

ROAD TRANSPORT

TRUCKING

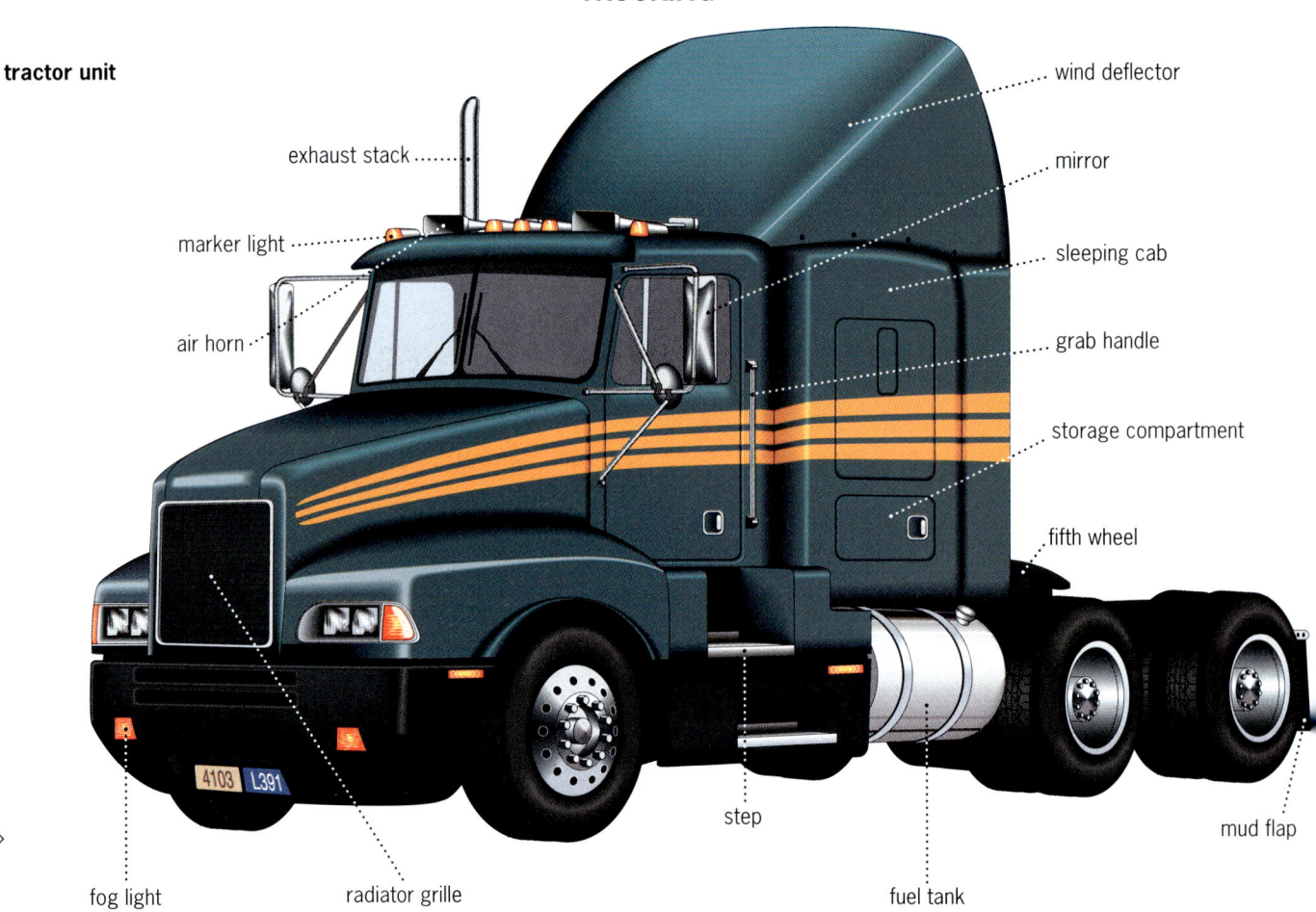

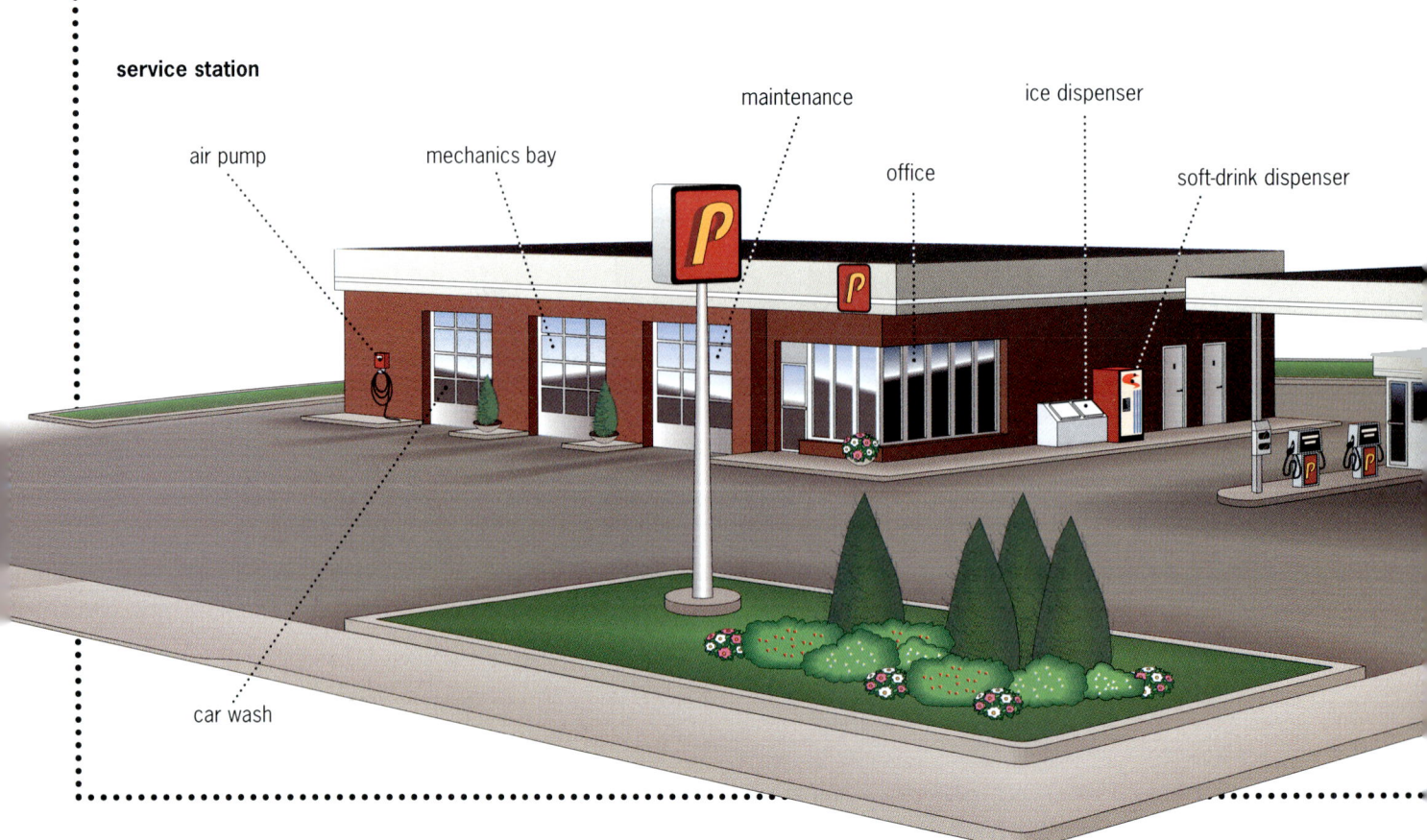

tractor unit

- exhaust stack
- marker light
- air horn
- fog light
- radiator grille
- step
- fuel tank
- wind deflector
- mirror
- sleeping cab
- grab handle
- storage compartment
- fifth wheel
- mud flap

service station

- air pump
- mechanics bay
- maintenance
- office
- ice dispenser
- soft-drink dispenser
- car wash

134

ROAD TRANSPORT

MOTORCYCLE

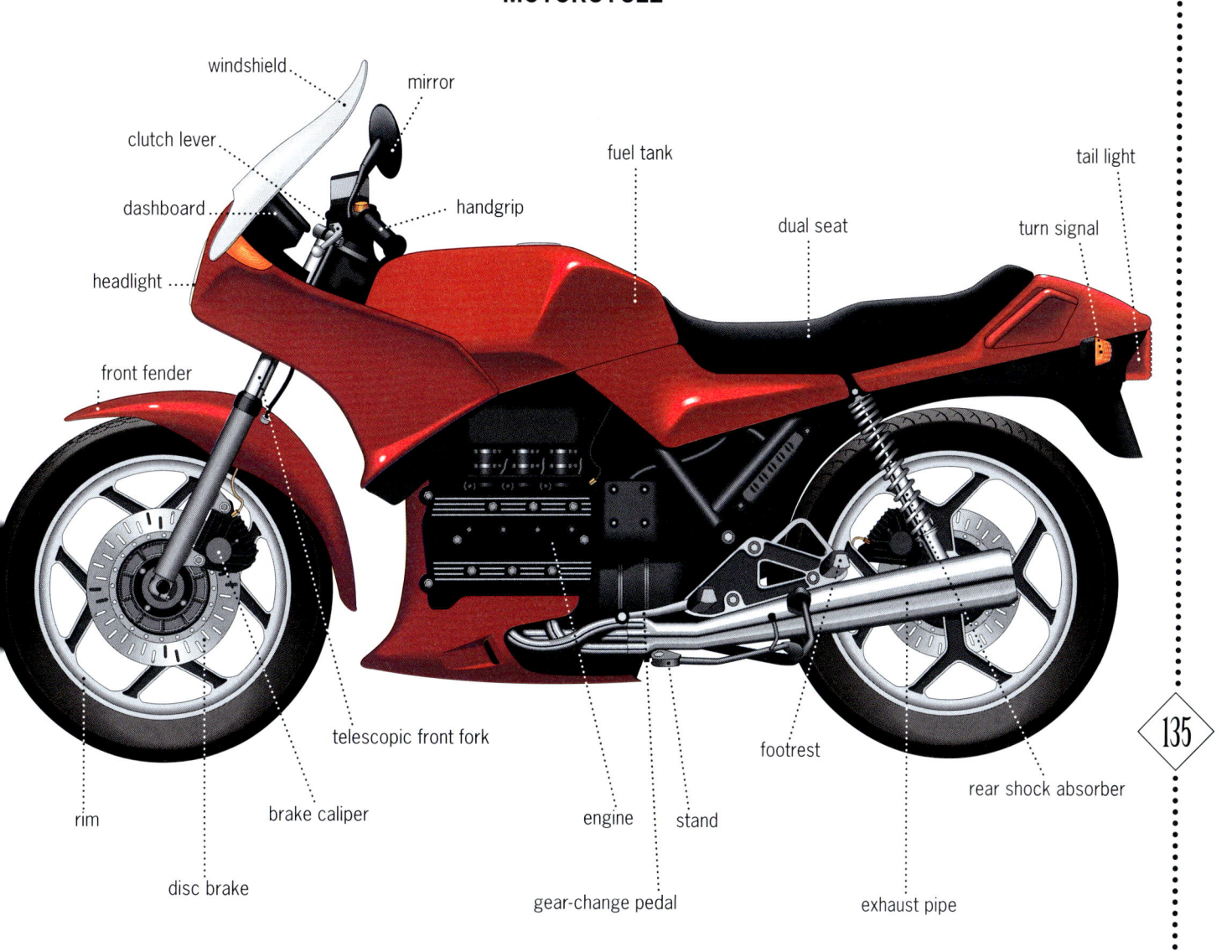

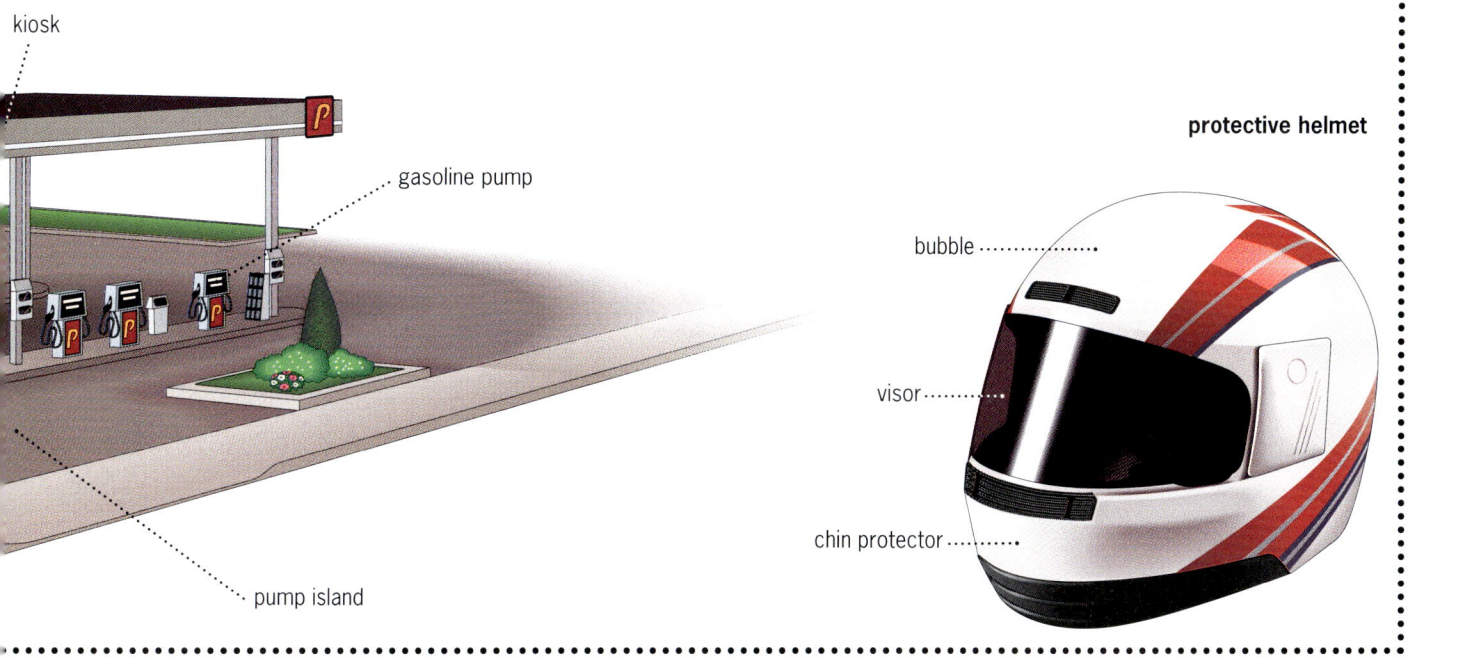

- windshield
- mirror
- clutch lever
- handgrip
- dashboard
- fuel tank
- headlight
- dual seat
- tail light
- turn signal
- front fender
- telescopic front fork
- brake caliper
- engine
- stand
- footrest
- rear shock absorber
- rim
- disc brake
- gear-change pedal
- exhaust pipe

- kiosk
- gasoline pump
- pump island

protective helmet
- bubble
- visor
- chin protector

135

ROAD TRANSPORT

BICYCLE

- saddle
- seat post
- carrier
- rear brake
- generator
- tire pump
- crossbar
- reflector
- water bottle clip
- rear light
- front derailleur
- water bottle
- mudguard
- chain wheel
- crank
- chain guide
- toe clip
- pedal
- rear derailleur
- drive chain

bicycle bag

lock

136

ROAD TRANSPORT

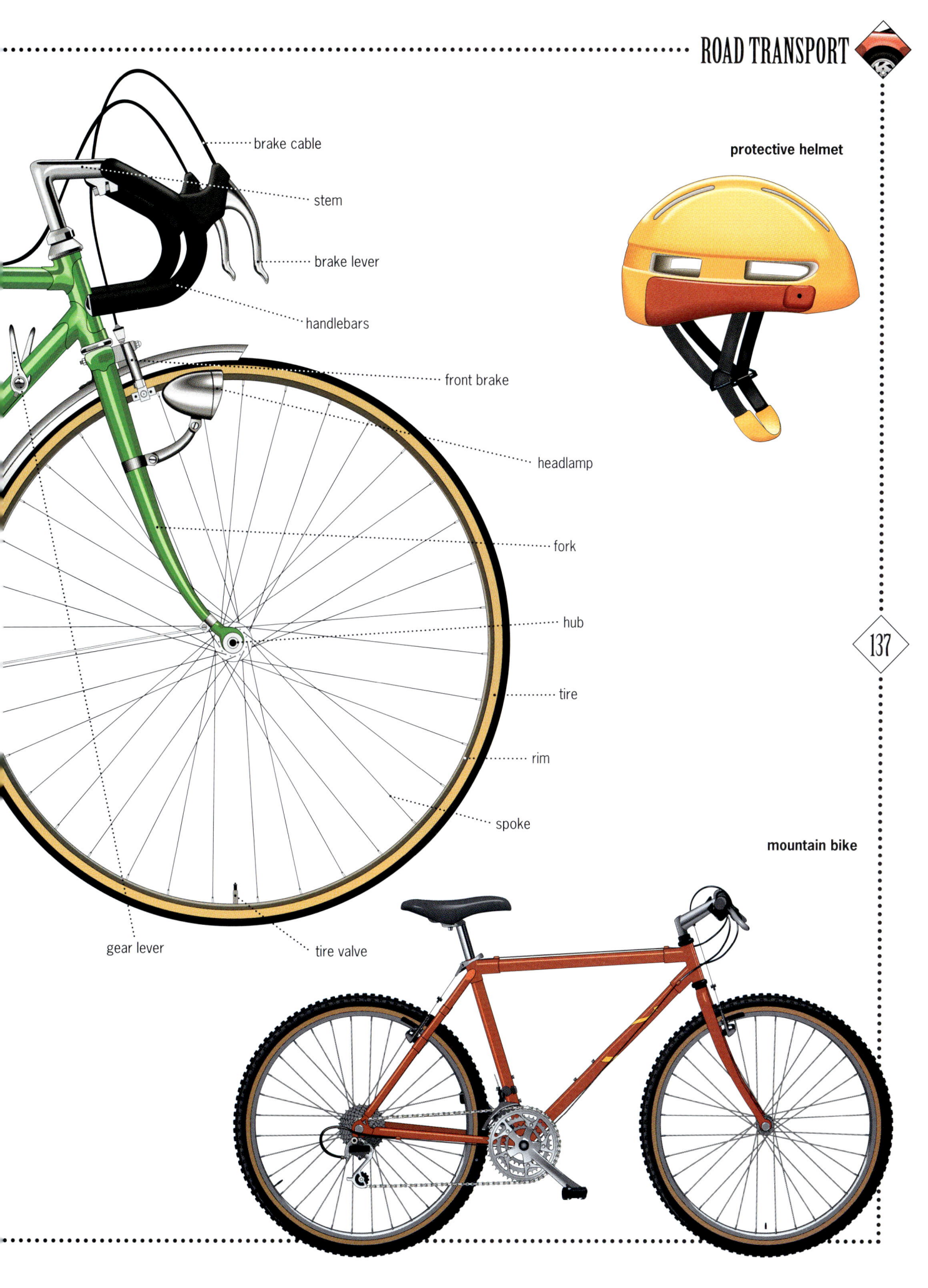

brake cable
stem
brake lever
handlebars
front brake
headlamp
fork
hub
tire
rim
spoke
gear lever
tire valve

protective helmet

137

mountain bike

RAIL TRANSPORT

DIESEL-ELECTRIC LOCOMOTIVE

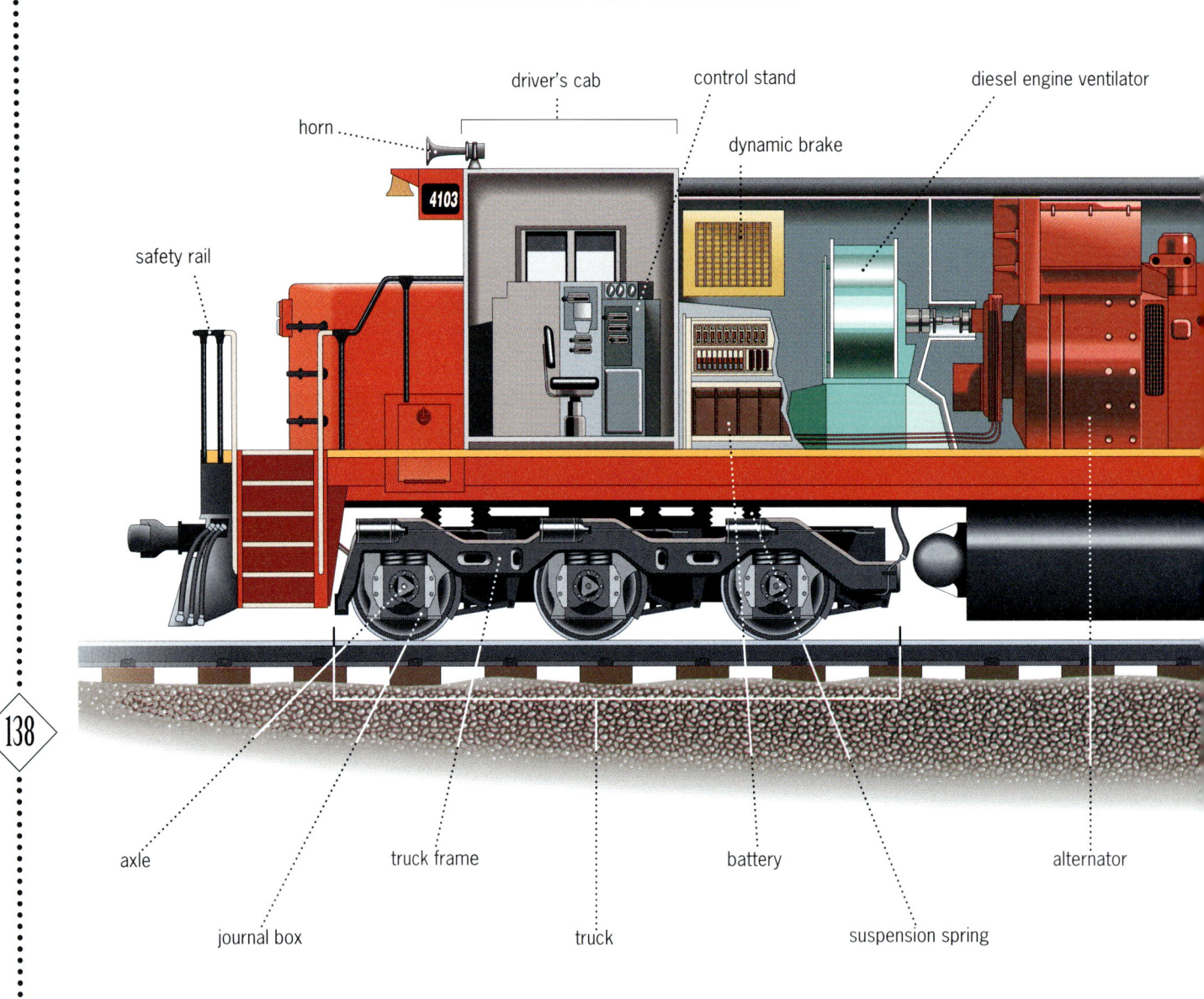

- horn
- driver's cab
- control stand
- diesel engine ventilator
- dynamic brake
- safety rail
- axle
- journal box
- truck frame
- truck
- battery
- suspension spring
- alternator

TYPES OF FREIGHT CARS

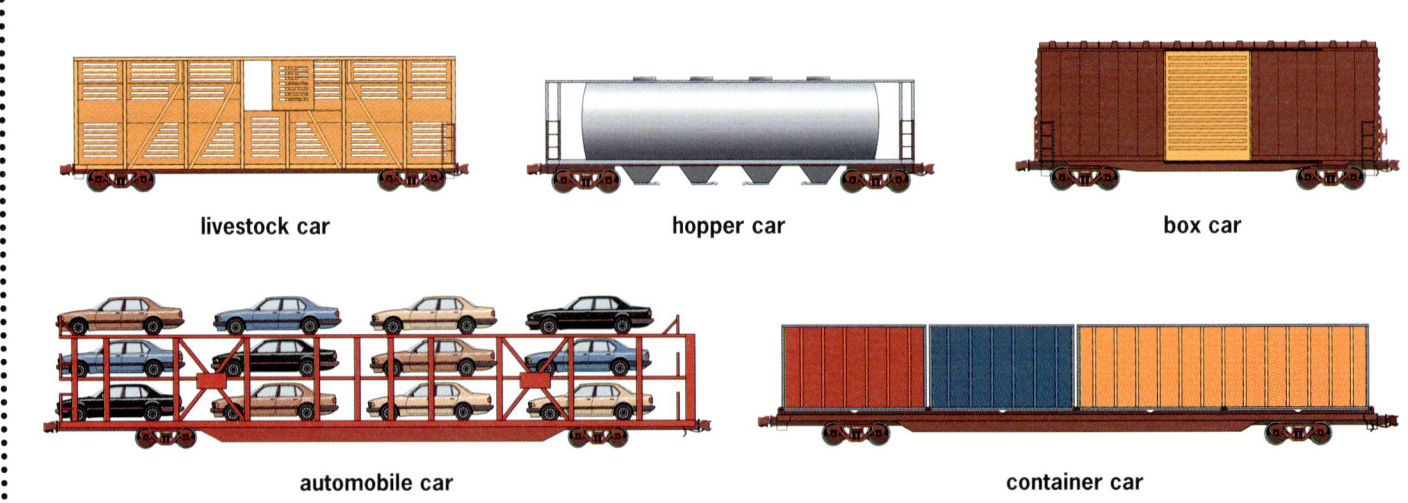

livestock car

hopper car

box car

automobile car

container car

RAIL TRANSPORT

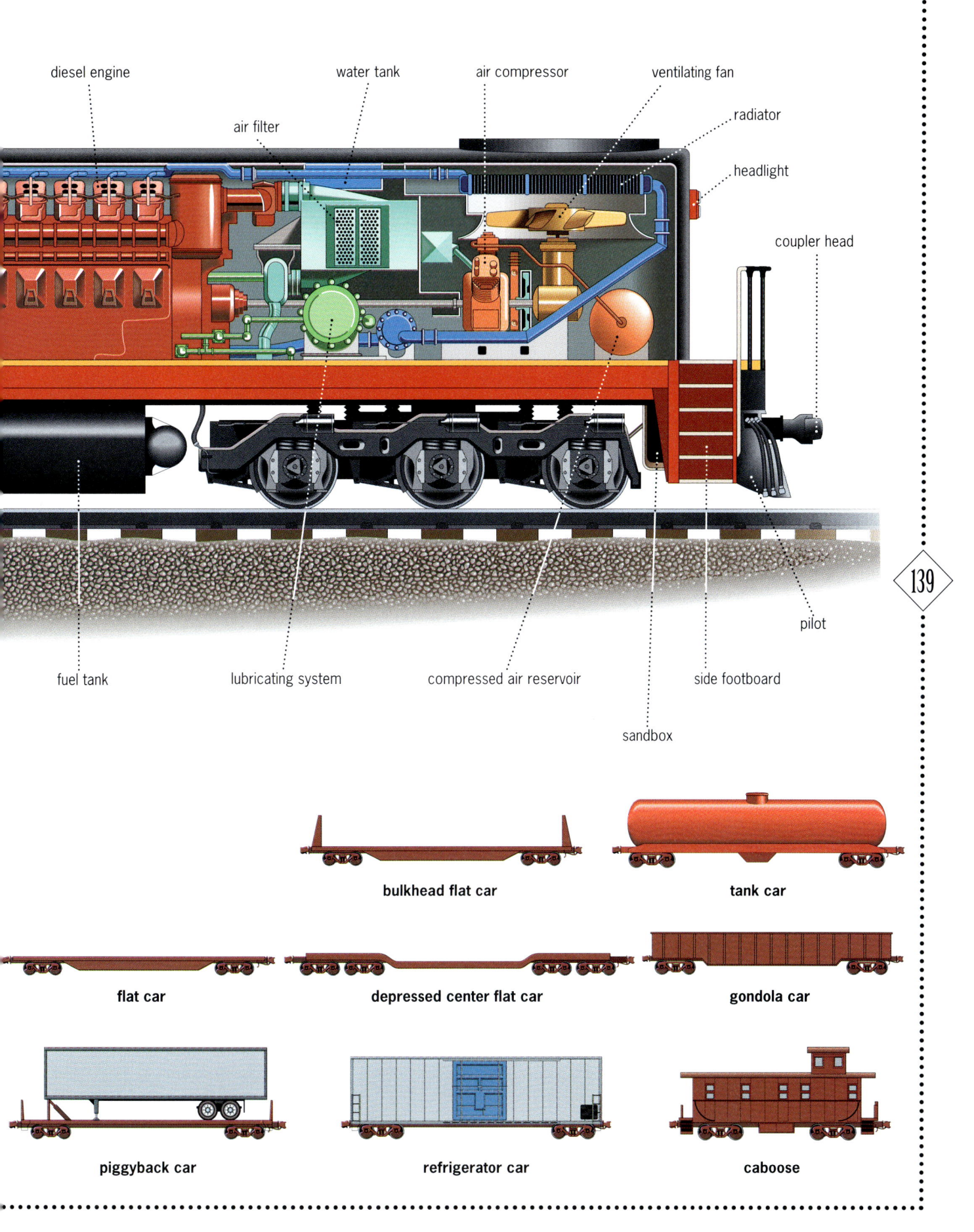

diesel engine · water tank · air compressor · ventilating fan · air filter · radiator · headlight · coupler head · fuel tank · lubricating system · compressed air reservoir · sandbox · side footboard · pilot

bulkhead flat car

tank car

flat car

depressed center flat car

gondola car

piggyback car

refrigerator car

caboose

RAIL TRANSPORT

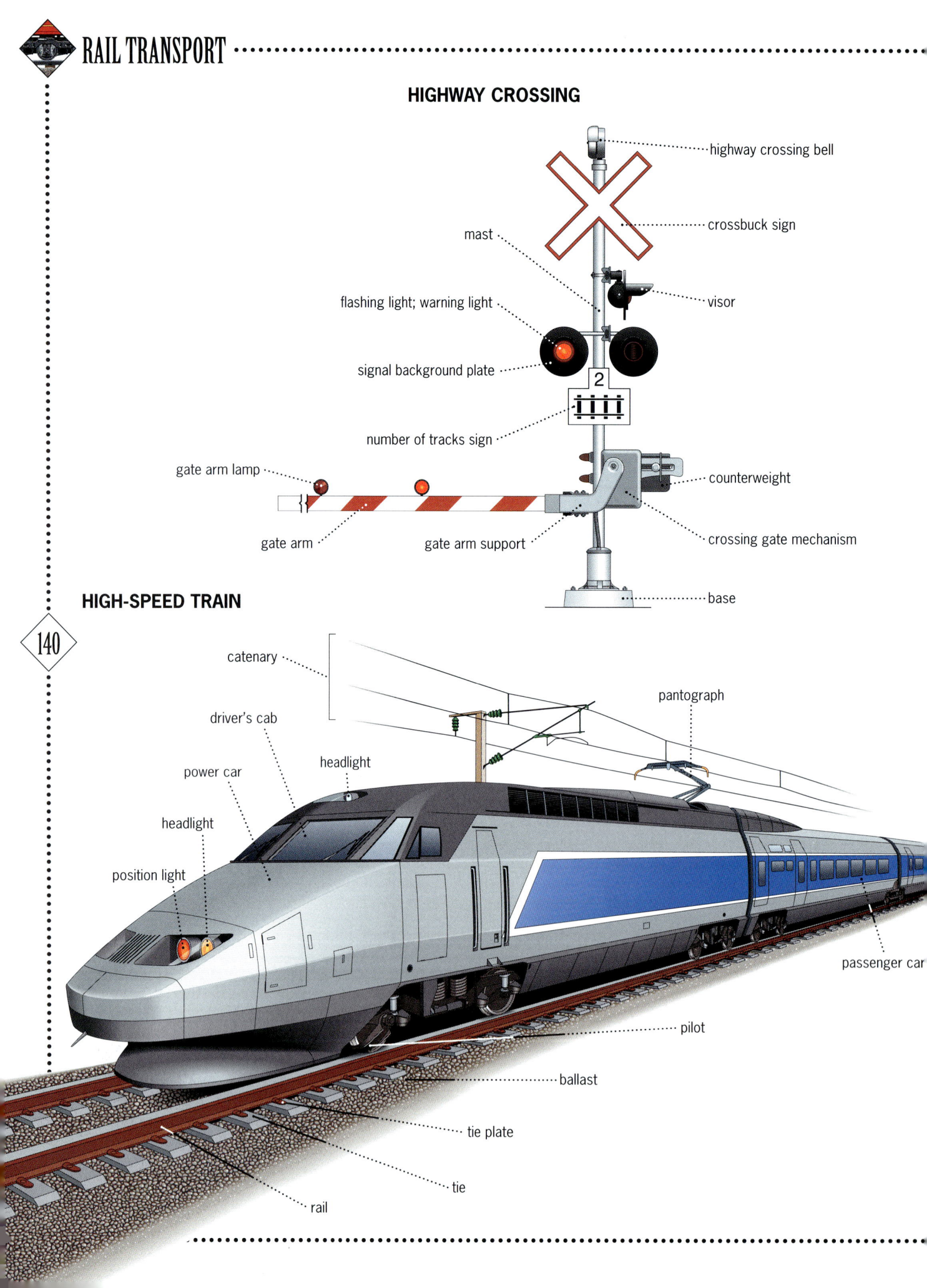

HIGHWAY CROSSING

- highway crossing bell
- crossbuck sign
- mast
- visor
- flashing light; warning light
- signal background plate
- number of tracks sign
- gate arm lamp
- counterweight
- gate arm
- gate arm support
- crossing gate mechanism
- base

HIGH-SPEED TRAIN

- catenary
- pantograph
- driver's cab
- power car
- headlight
- headlight
- position light
- passenger car
- pilot
- ballast
- tie plate
- tie
- rail

MARITIME TRANSPORT

FOUR-MASTED BARK

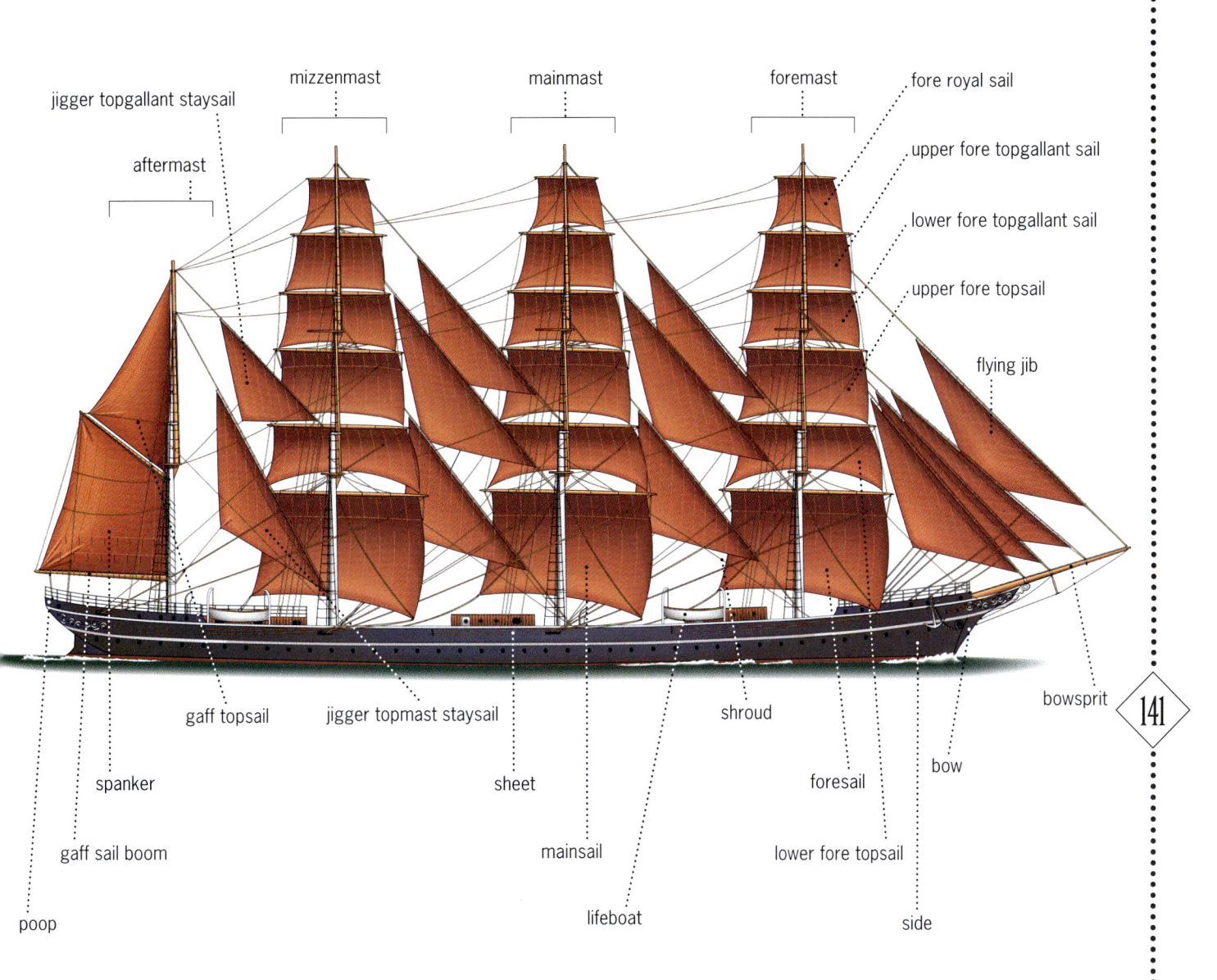

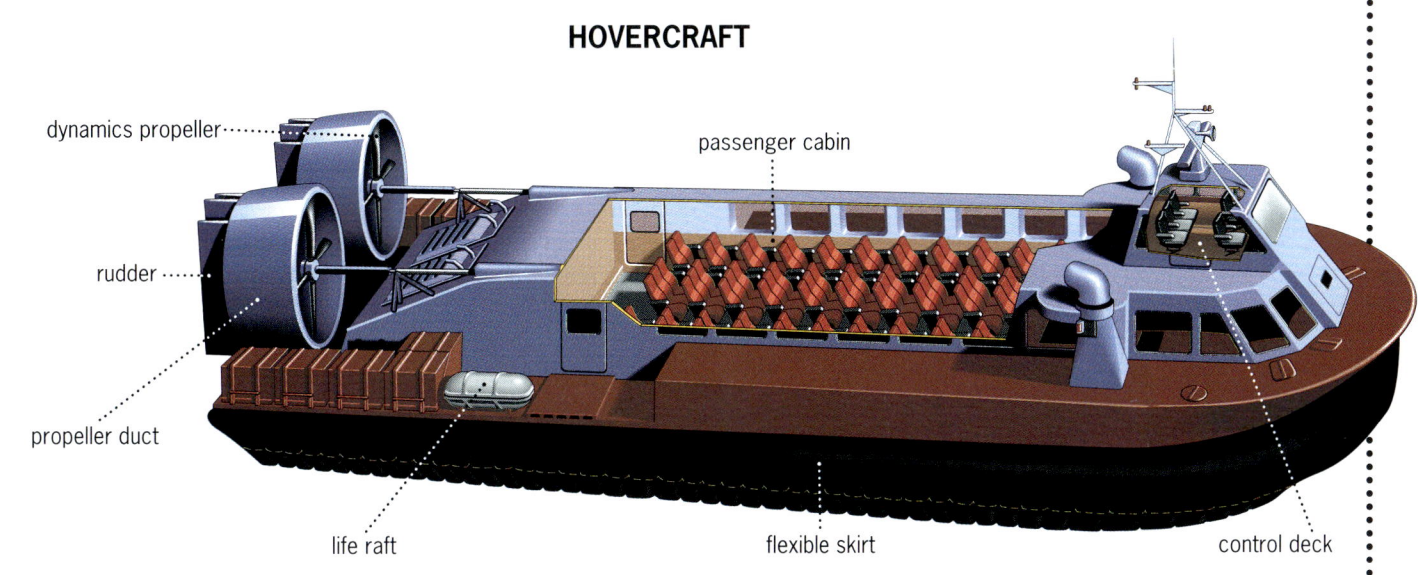

- jigger topgallant staysail
- aftermast
- mizzenmast
- mainmast
- foremast
- fore royal sail
- upper fore topgallant sail
- lower fore topgallant sail
- upper fore topsail
- flying jib
- gaff topsail
- jigger topmast staysail
- shroud
- bowsprit
- spanker
- sheet
- foresail
- bow
- gaff sail boom
- mainsail
- lower fore topsail
- poop
- lifeboat
- side

HOVERCRAFT

- dynamics propeller
- passenger cabin
- rudder
- propeller duct
- life raft
- flexible skirt
- control deck

141

MARITIME TRANSPORT

CRUISE LINER

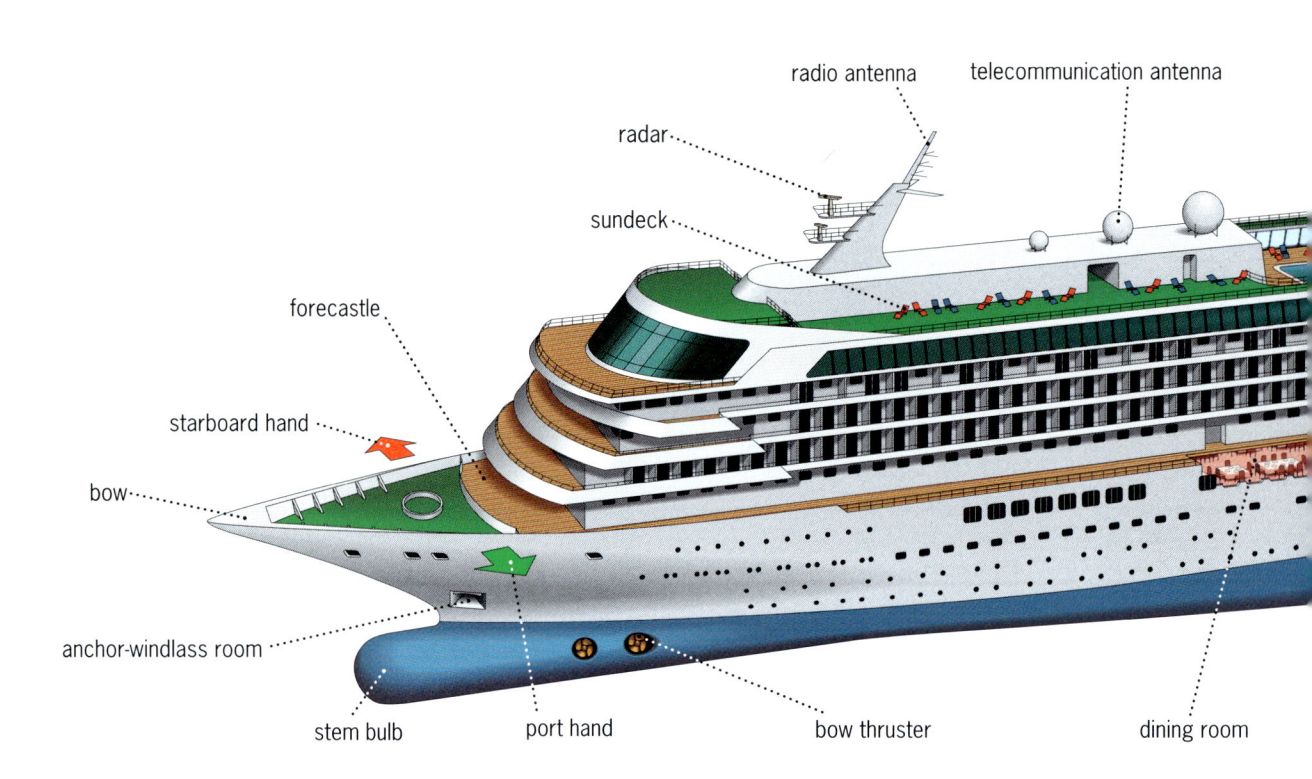

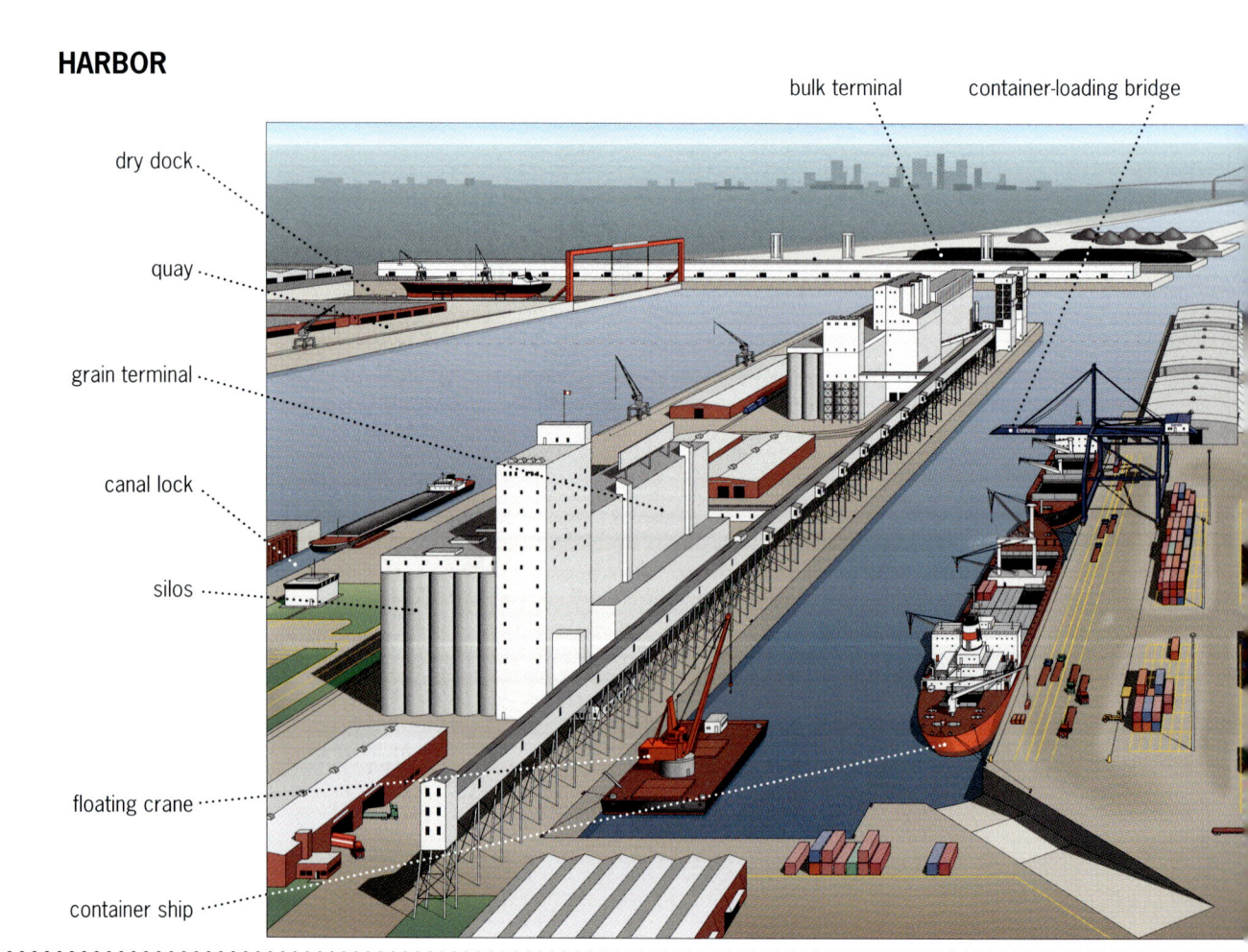

- radio antenna
- telecommunication antenna
- radar
- sundeck
- forecastle
- starboard hand
- bow
- anchor-windlass room
- stem bulb
- port hand
- bow thruster
- dining room

HARBOR

- bulk terminal
- container-loading bridge
- dry dock
- quay
- grain terminal
- canal lock
- silos
- floating crane
- container ship

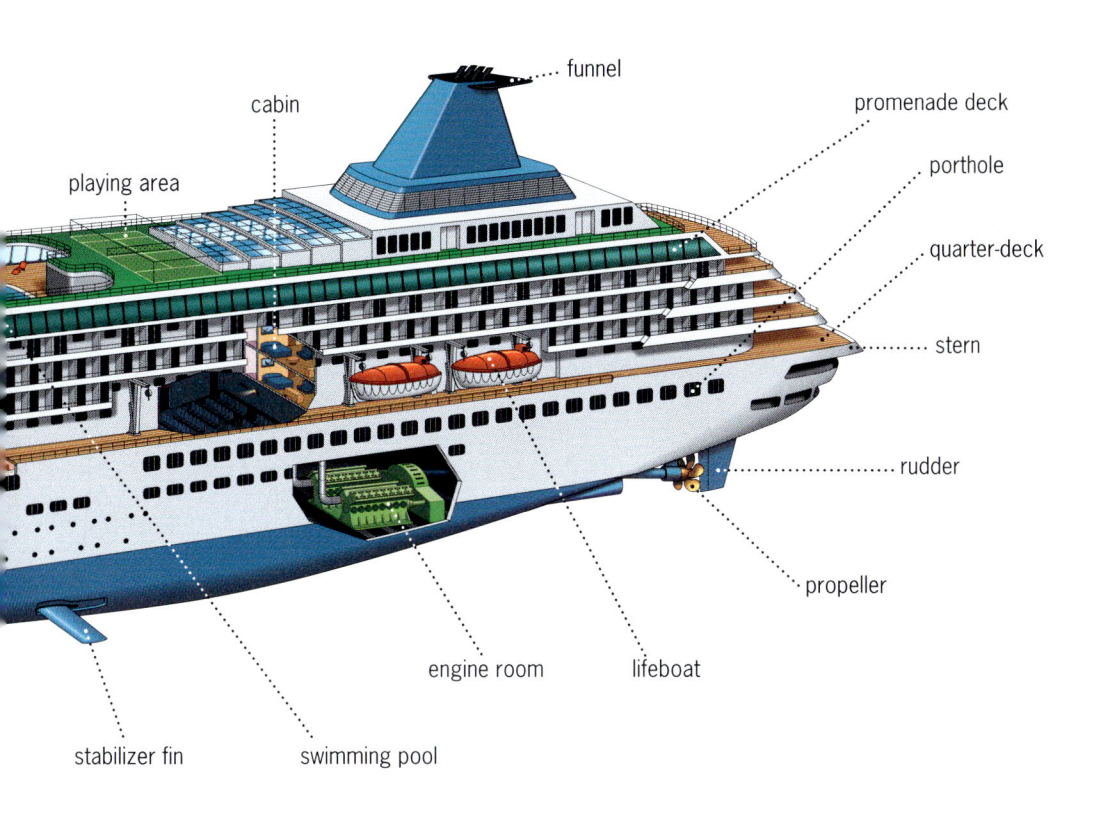

MARITIME TRANSPORT

- funnel
- cabin
- playing area
- promenade deck
- porthole
- quarter-deck
- stern
- rudder
- propeller
- lifeboat
- engine room
- swimming pool
- stabilizer fin

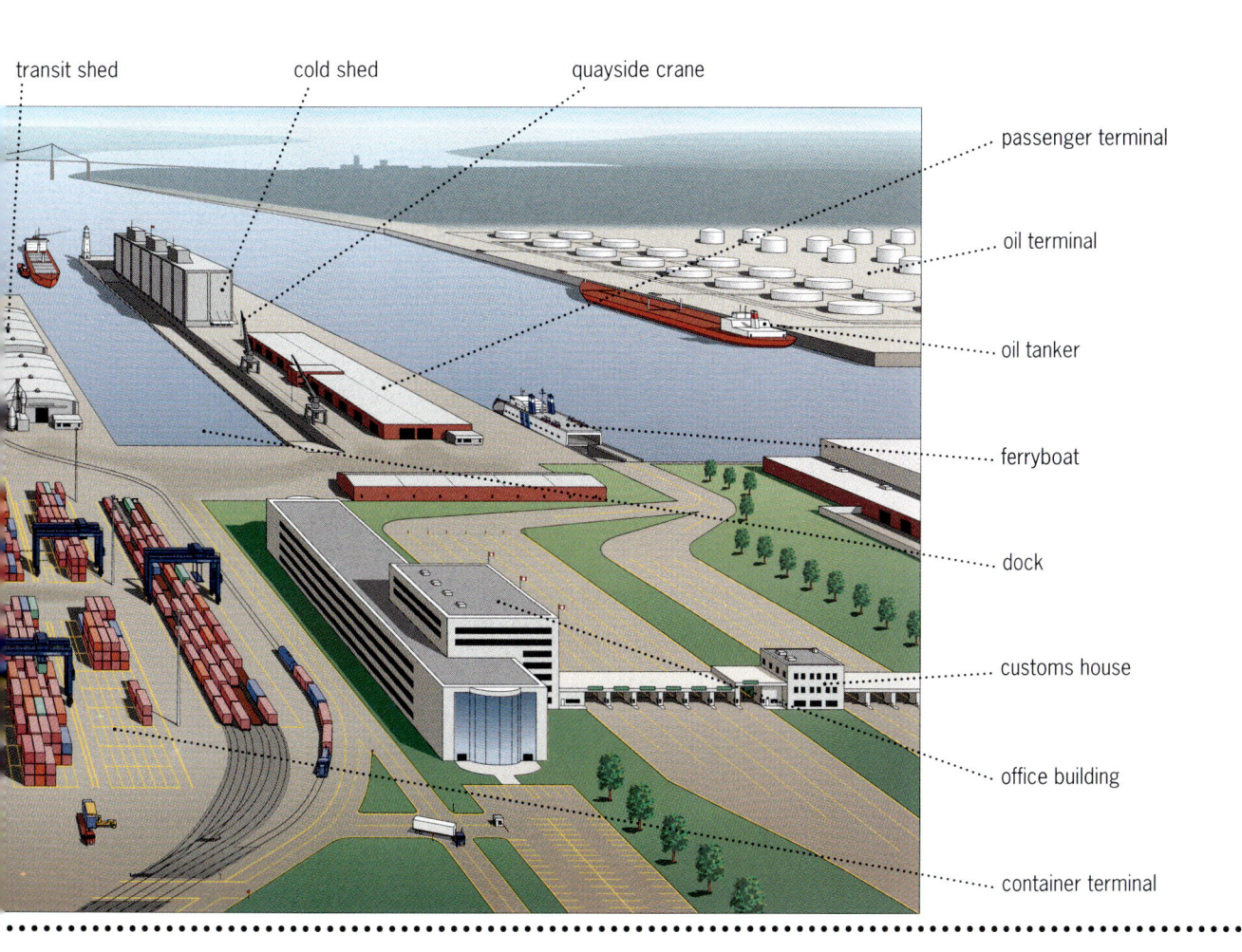

- transit shed
- cold shed
- quayside crane
- passenger terminal
- oil terminal
- oil tanker
- ferryboat
- dock
- customs house
- office building
- container terminal

143

AIR TRANSPORT

PLANE

TYPES OF WING SHAPES

straight wing

variable geometry wing

swept-back wing

tapered wing

delta wing

long-range jet

- fin
- rudder
- tail assembly
- tail
- fuselage
- horizontal stabilizer
- elevator
- aileron
- trailing edge
- spoiler
- trailing edge flap
- winglet
- wing
- main landing gear
- navigation light
- wing slat
- leading edge
- turbojet engine

144

AIR TRANSPORT

HELICOPTER

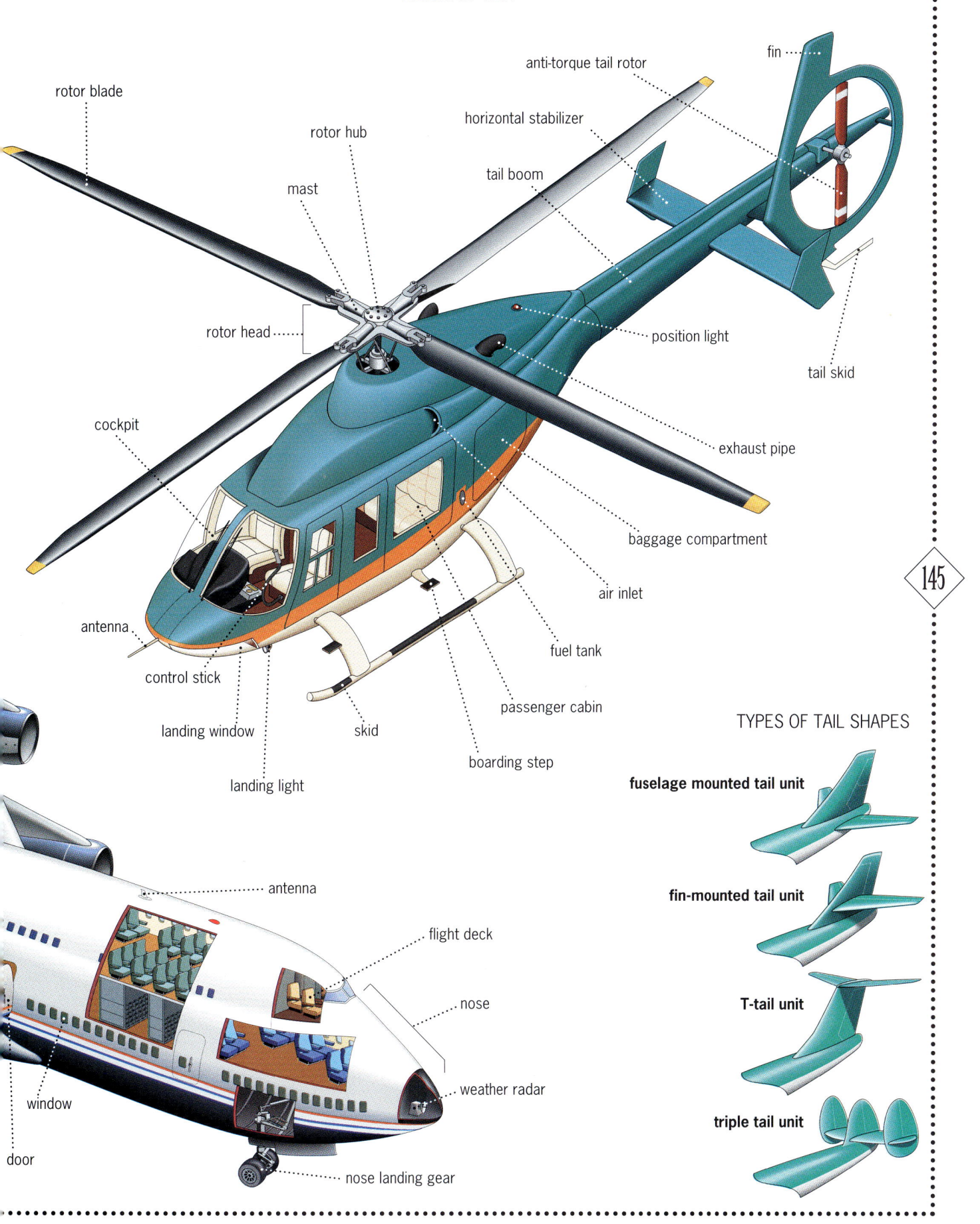

- rotor blade
- rotor hub
- mast
- anti-torque tail rotor
- horizontal stabilizer
- fin
- tail boom
- rotor head
- position light
- tail skid
- exhaust pipe
- cockpit
- baggage compartment
- air inlet
- fuel tank
- antenna
- passenger cabin
- control stick
- landing window
- skid
- boarding step
- landing light

- antenna
- flight deck
- nose
- weather radar
- window
- door
- nose landing gear

TYPES OF TAIL SHAPES

fuselage mounted tail unit

fin-mounted tail unit

T-tail unit

triple tail unit

145

AIR TRANSPORT

AIRPORT

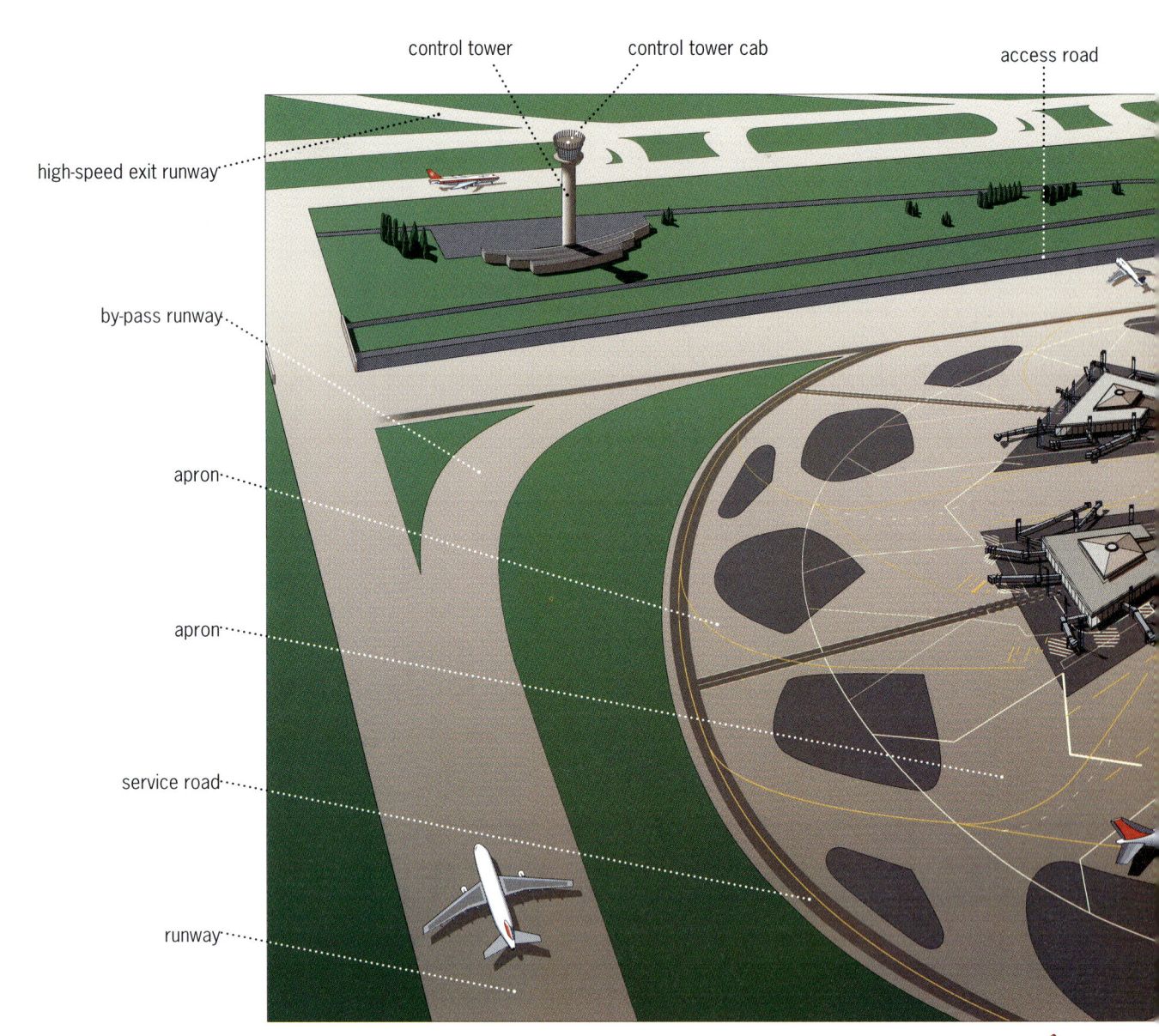

- control tower
- control tower cab
- access road
- high-speed exit runway
- by-pass runway
- apron
- apron
- service road
- runway

AIRPORT GROUND EQUIPMENT

- tow bar
- tow tractor 
- container/pallet loader 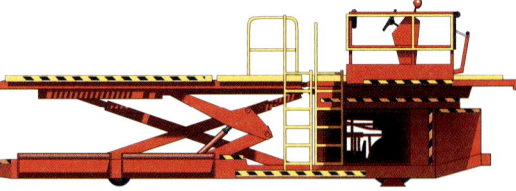
- universal step 
- baggage conveyor 
- wheel chock 

146

AIR TRANSPORT

- maintenance hangar
- parking area
- passenger terminal
- boarding walkway
- radial passenger loading area
- telescopic corridor
- service area
- runway line

baggage trailer

tow tractor

catering vehicle

passenger transfer vehicle

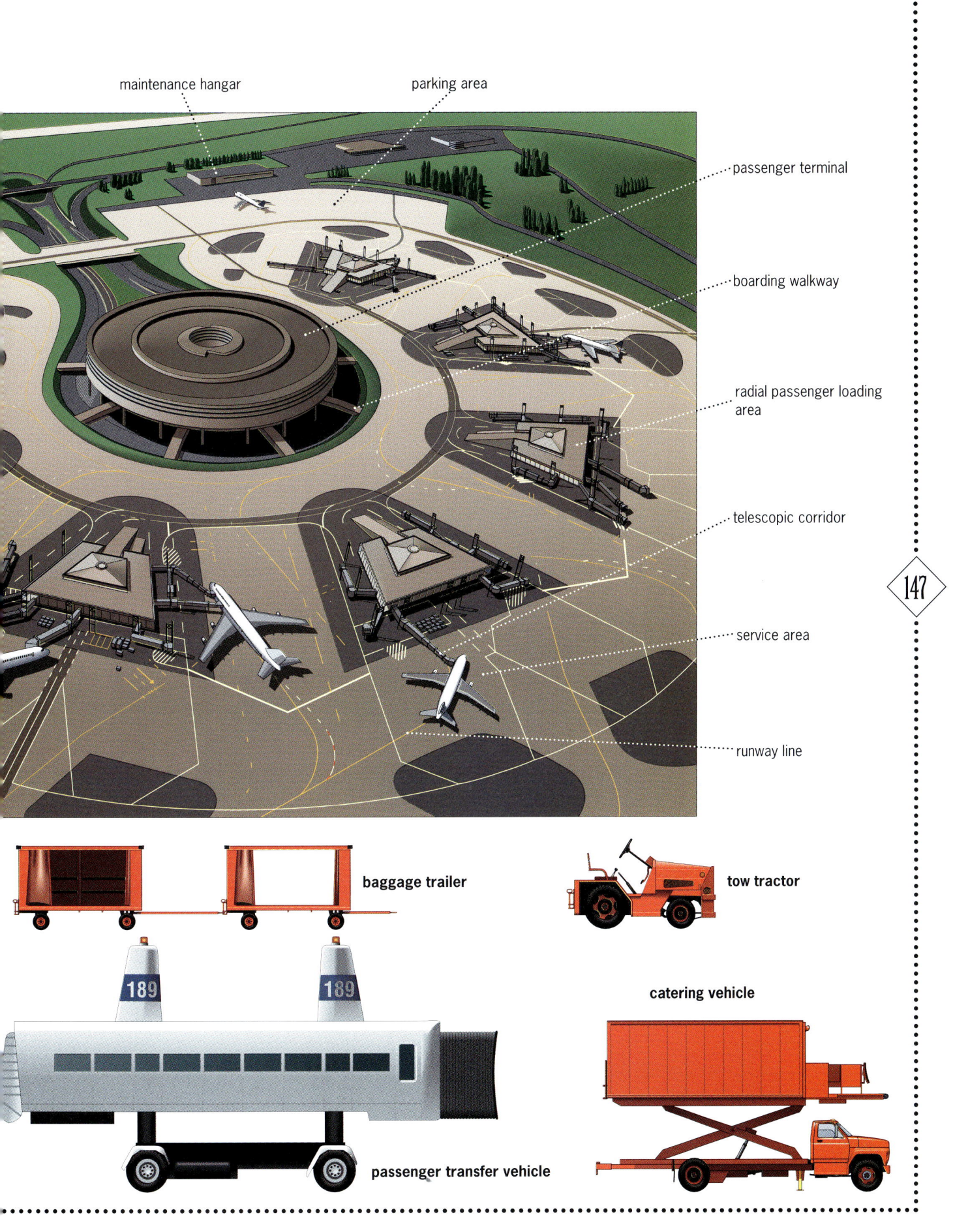

147

SPACE TRANSPORT

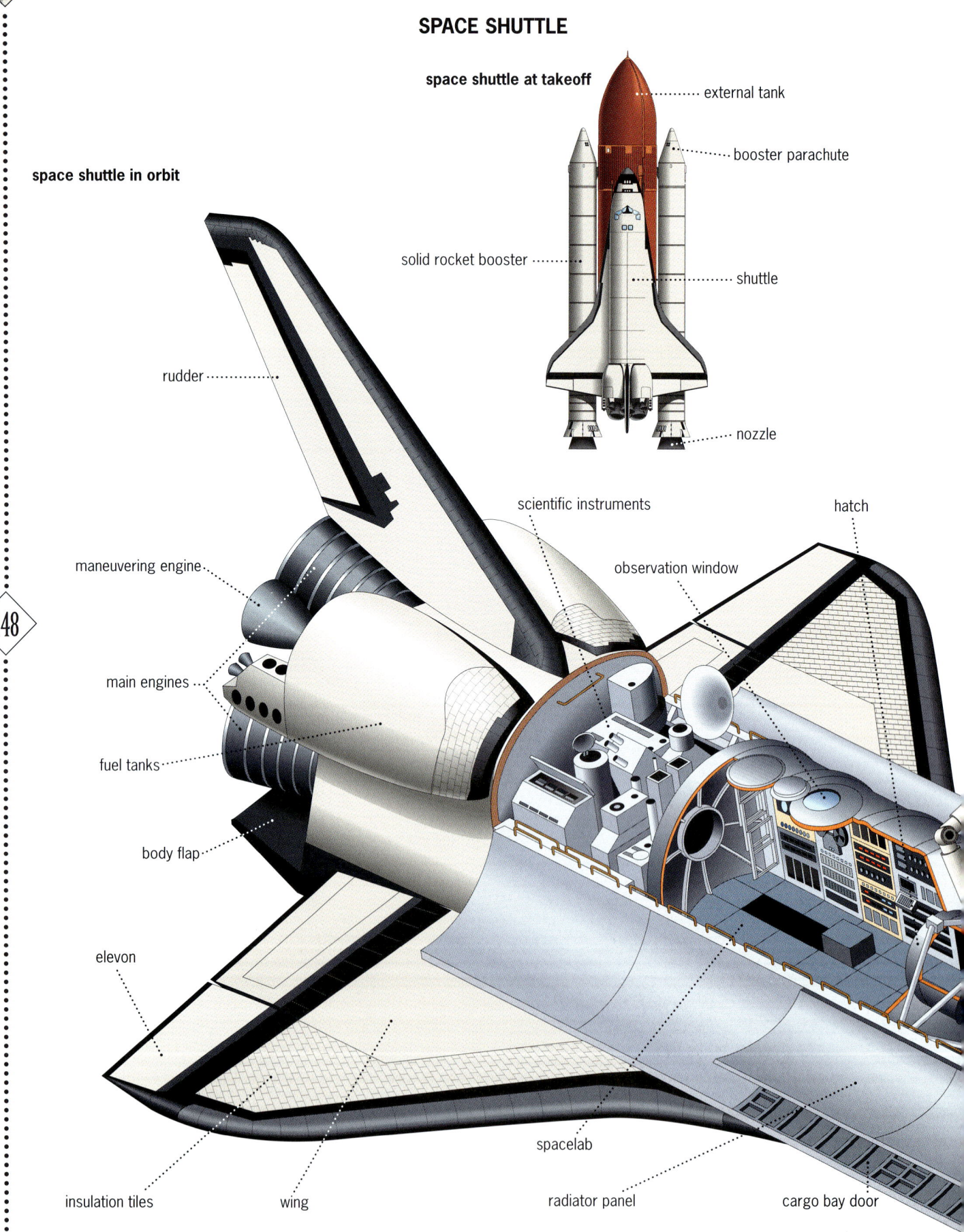

SPACE SHUTTLE

space shuttle at takeoff

- external tank
- booster parachute
- solid rocket booster
- shuttle
- nozzle

space shuttle in orbit

- rudder
- maneuvering engine
- main engines
- fuel tanks
- body flap
- elevon
- insulation tiles
- wing
- scientific instruments
- observation window
- hatch
- spacelab
- radiator panel
- cargo bay door

SPACE TRANSPORT

SPACESUIT

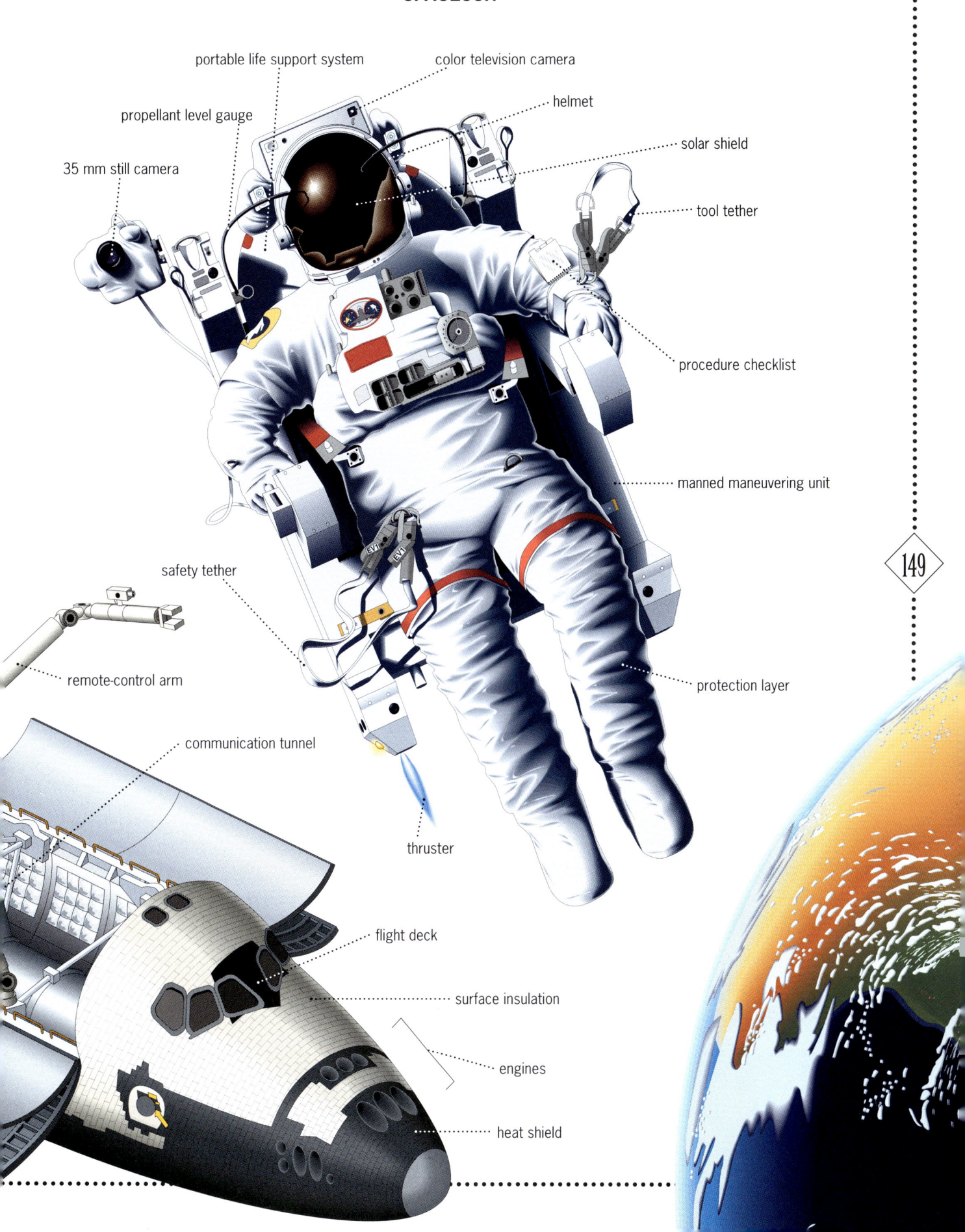

- portable life support system
- color television camera
- helmet
- propellant level gauge
- solar shield
- 35 mm still camera
- tool tether
- procedure checklist
- manned maneuvering unit
- protection layer
- safety tether
- remote-control arm
- communication tunnel
- thruster
- flight deck
- surface insulation
- engines
- heat shield

149

SCHOOL

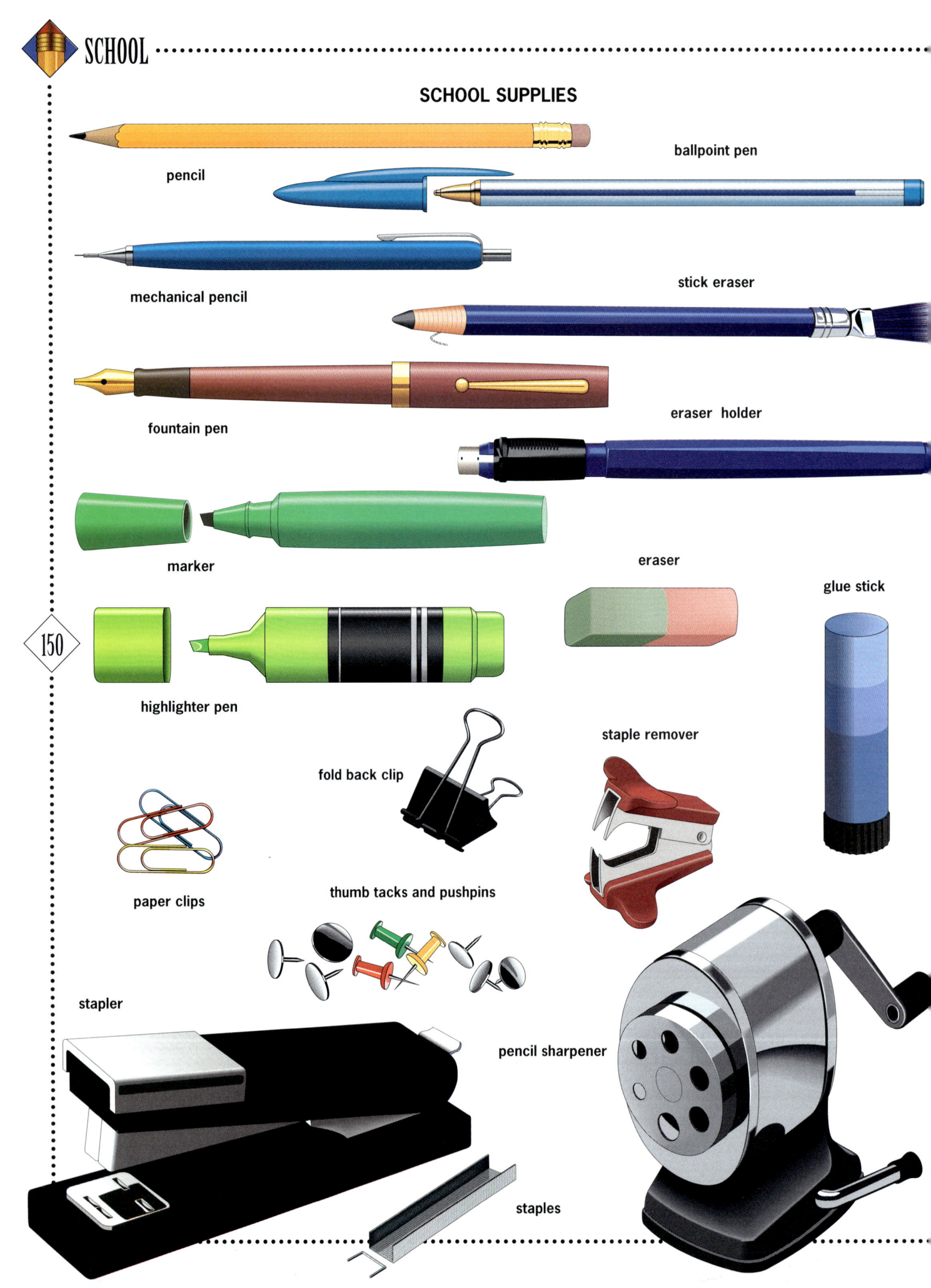

SCHOOL SUPPLIES

pencil

ballpoint pen

mechanical pencil

stick eraser

fountain pen

eraser holder

marker

eraser

glue stick

highlighter pen

staple remover

fold back clip

paper clips

thumb tacks and pushpins

stapler

pencil sharpener

staples

SCHOOL

ruler

protractor

set square

tape dispenser

ring binder

spiral bound notebook

loose-leaf paper

notebook

notepad

backpack

briefcase

151

SCHOOL

SCHOOL EQUIPMENT

blackboard

overhead projector
- mirror
- projection head
- optical lens
- optical stage

globe of Earth
- meridian band
- globe
- base
- axis of rotation

152

SCHOOL

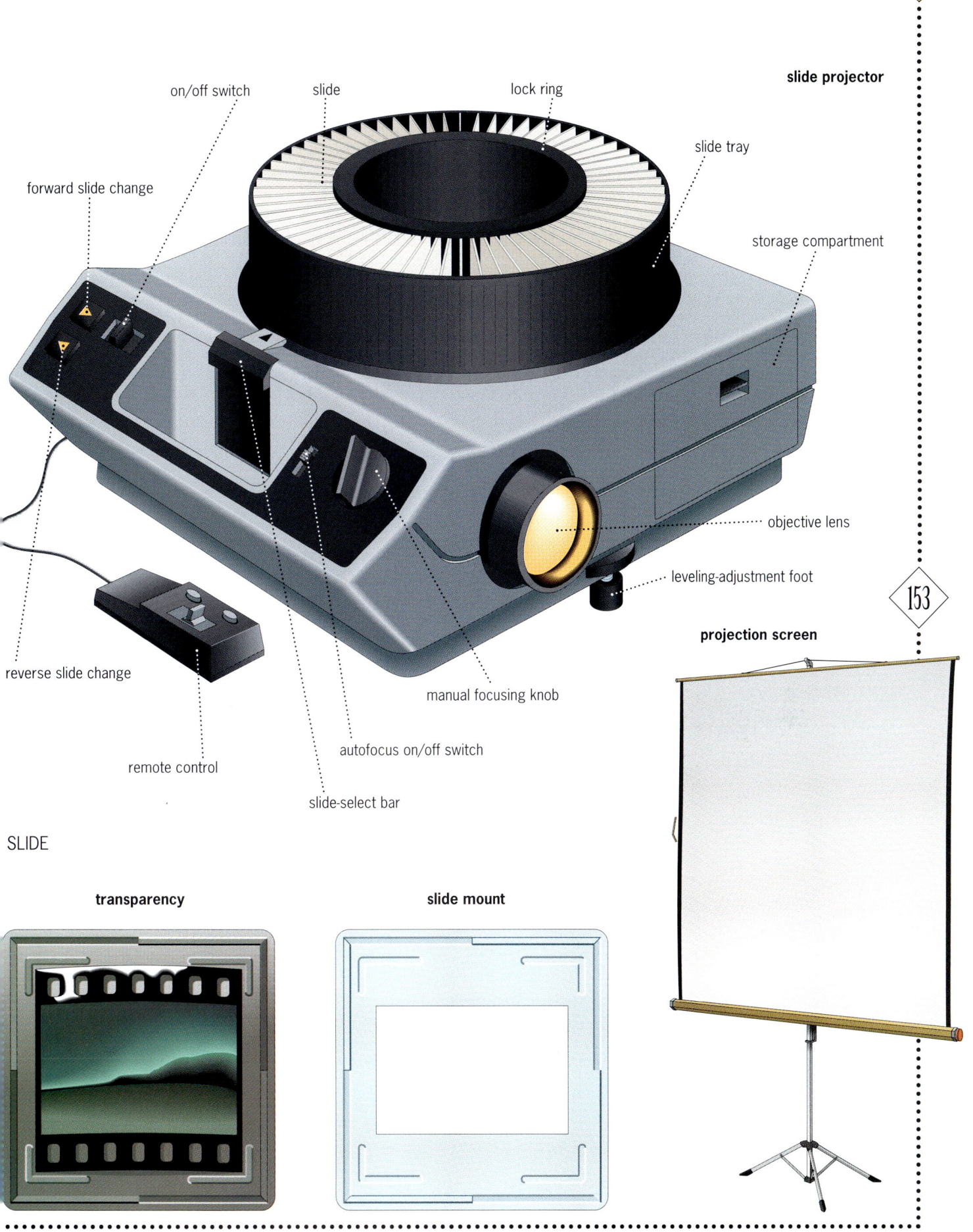

slide projector

- on/off switch
- slide
- lock ring
- slide tray
- forward slide change
- storage compartment
- objective lens
- leveling-adjustment foot
- reverse slide change
- remote control
- manual focusing knob
- autofocus on/off switch
- slide-select bar

SLIDE

transparency

slide mount

projection screen

153

SCHOOL

SCHOOL EQUIPMENT

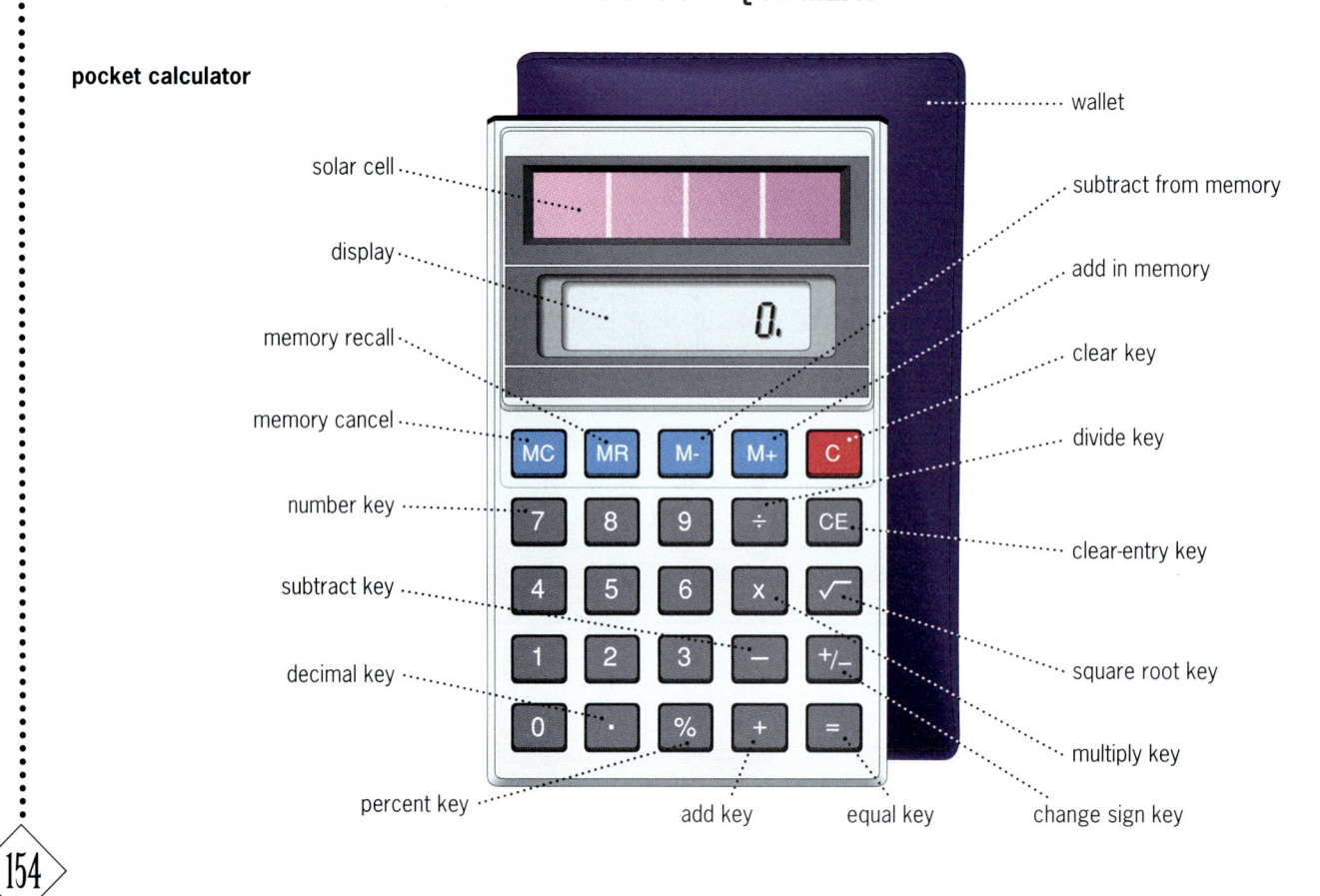

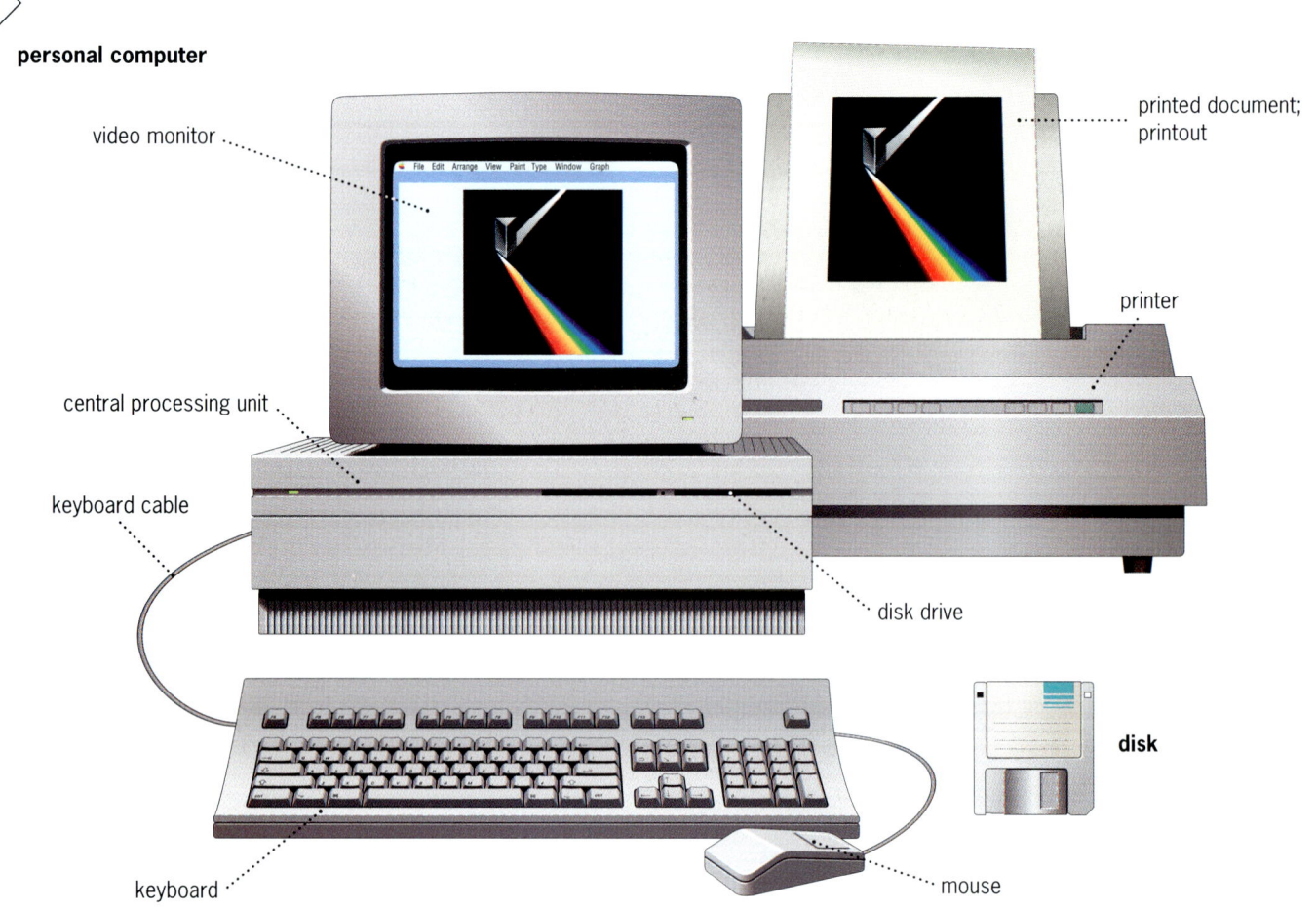

pocket calculator

- solar cell
- display
- memory recall
- memory cancel
- number key
- subtract key
- decimal key
- percent key
- add key
- equal key
- wallet
- subtract from memory
- add in memory
- clear key
- divide key
- clear-entry key
- square root key
- multiply key
- change sign key

personal computer

- video monitor
- central processing unit
- keyboard cable
- keyboard
- printed document; printout
- printer
- disk drive
- disk
- mouse

SCHOOL

magnifying glass

microscope

- eyepiece
- draw tube
- coarse adjustment knob
- fine adjustment knob
- revolving nosepiece
- objective
- arm
- stage clip
- glass slide
- stage
- condenser
- mirror
- base

test tube

155

SCHOOL

GEOMETRY

PLANE SURFACES

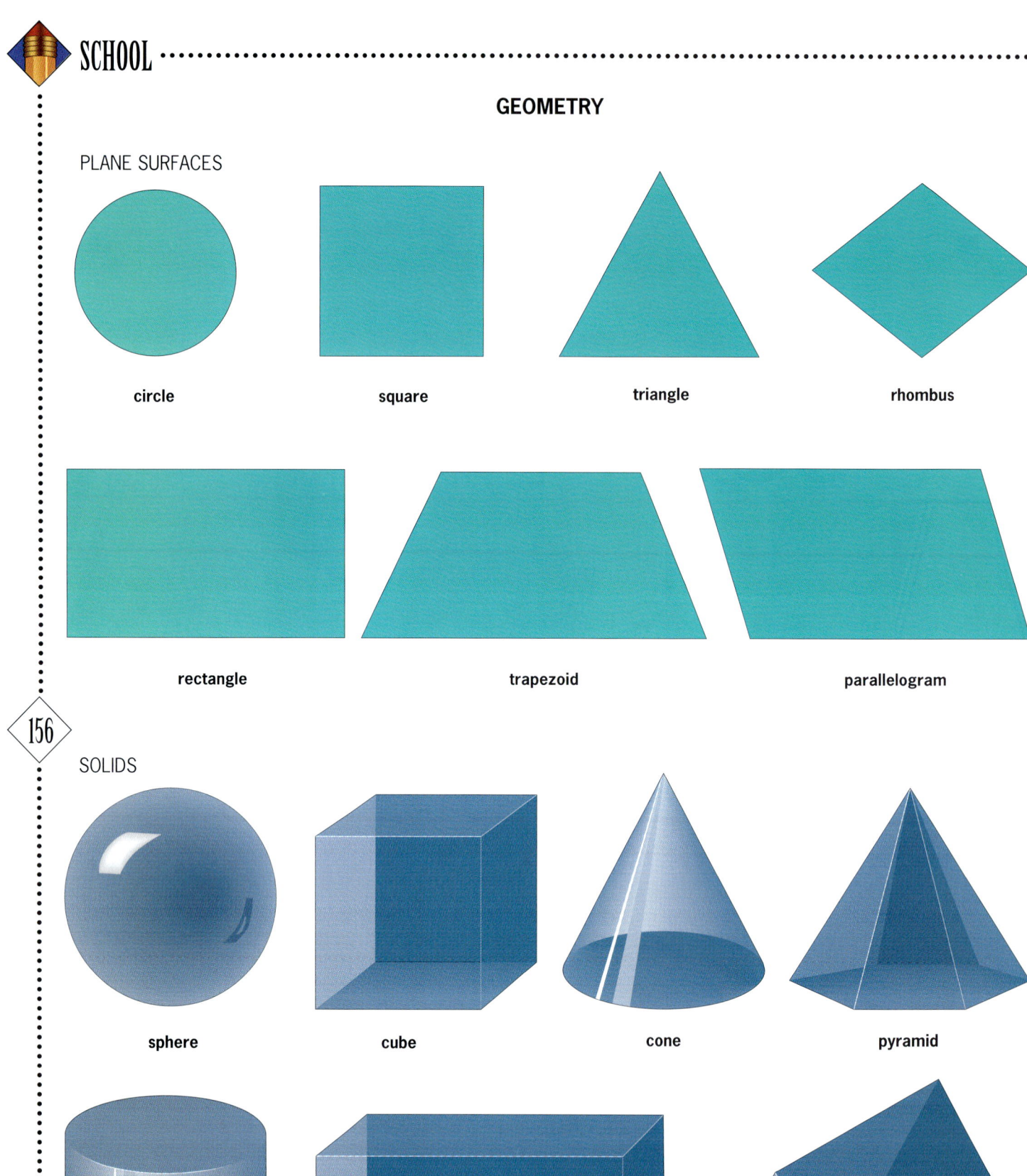

| circle | square | triangle | rhombus |

| rectangle | trapezoid | parallelogram |

SOLIDS

| sphere | cube | cone | pyramid |

| cylinder | parallelepiped | prism |

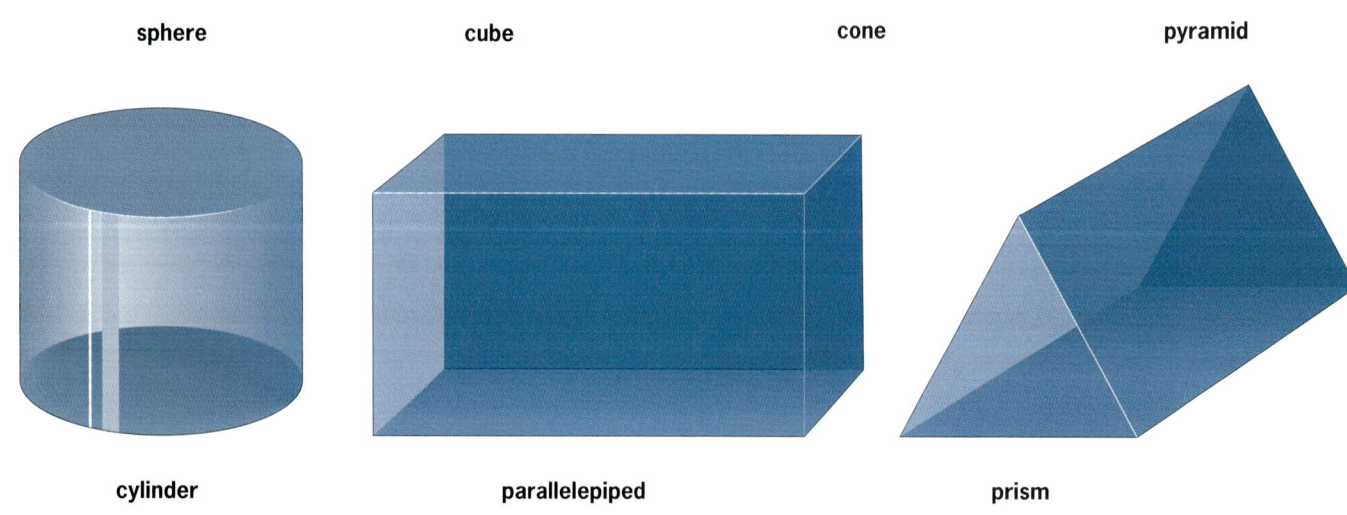

GEOMETRY

SCHOOL

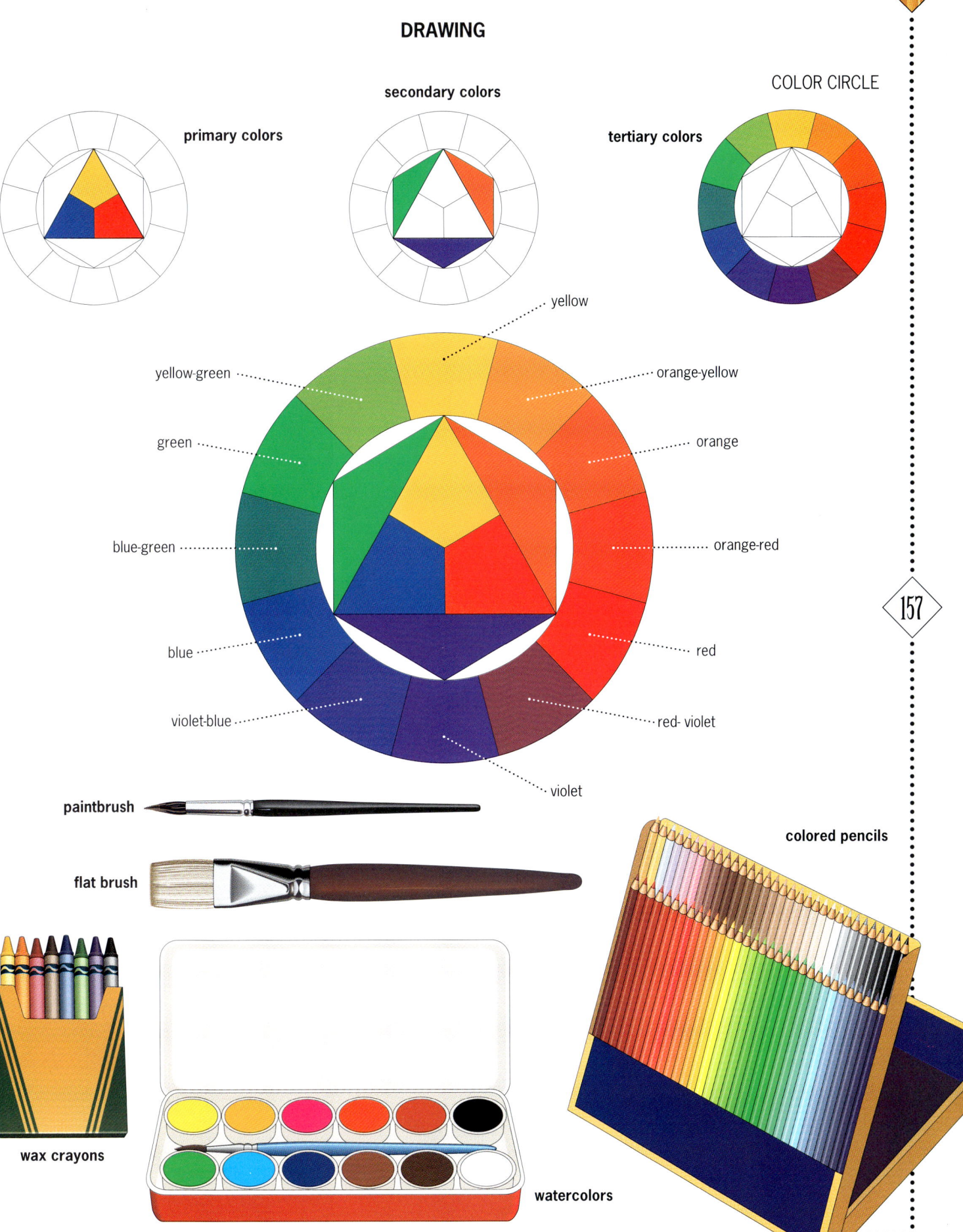

DRAWING

primary colors

secondary colors

tertiary colors

COLOR CIRCLE

- yellow
- yellow-green
- orange-yellow
- green
- orange
- blue-green
- orange-red
- blue
- red
- violet-blue
- red-violet
- violet

paintbrush

flat brush

colored pencils

wax crayons

watercolors

MUSIC

TRADITIONAL MUSICAL INSTRUMENTS

balalaika
- triangular body

mandolin
- pear-shaped body

zither
- soundboard
- open strings
- melody strings

lyre

banjo
- circular body

panpipes

harmonica

bagpipes
- drone pipe
- blowpipe; mouthpipe
- windbag
- chanter

accordion
- bellows
- treble keyboard
- treble register
- bass keyboard
- bass register

158

KEYBOARD INSTRUMENTS

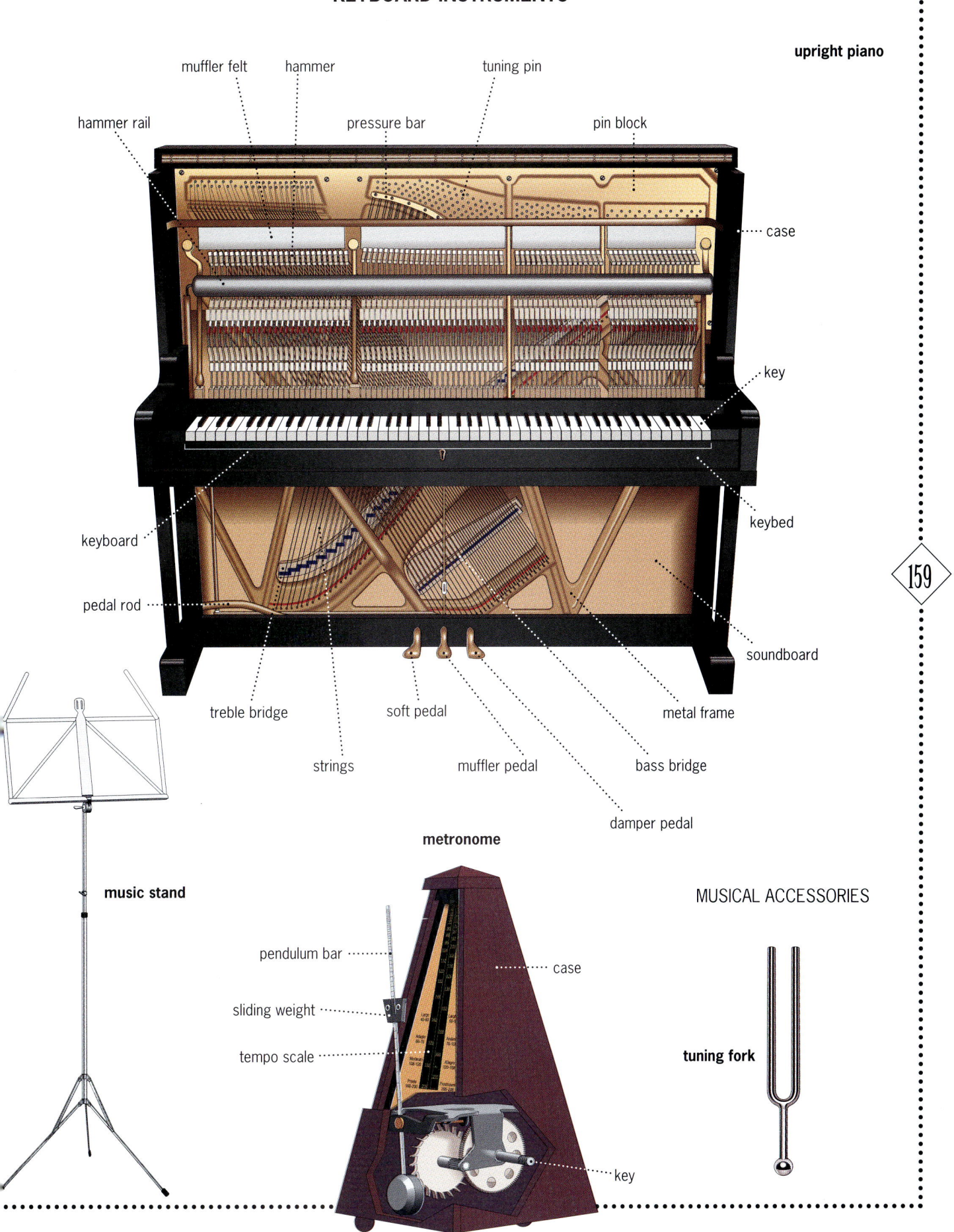

upright piano

- muffler felt
- hammer
- tuning pin
- hammer rail
- pressure bar
- pin block
- case
- key
- keybed
- keyboard
- soundboard
- pedal rod
- metal frame
- treble bridge
- soft pedal
- bass bridge
- strings
- muffler pedal
- damper pedal

metronome

- pendulum bar
- sliding weight
- tempo scale
- case
- key

music stand

MUSICAL ACCESSORIES

tuning fork

MUSIC

MUSICAL NOTATION

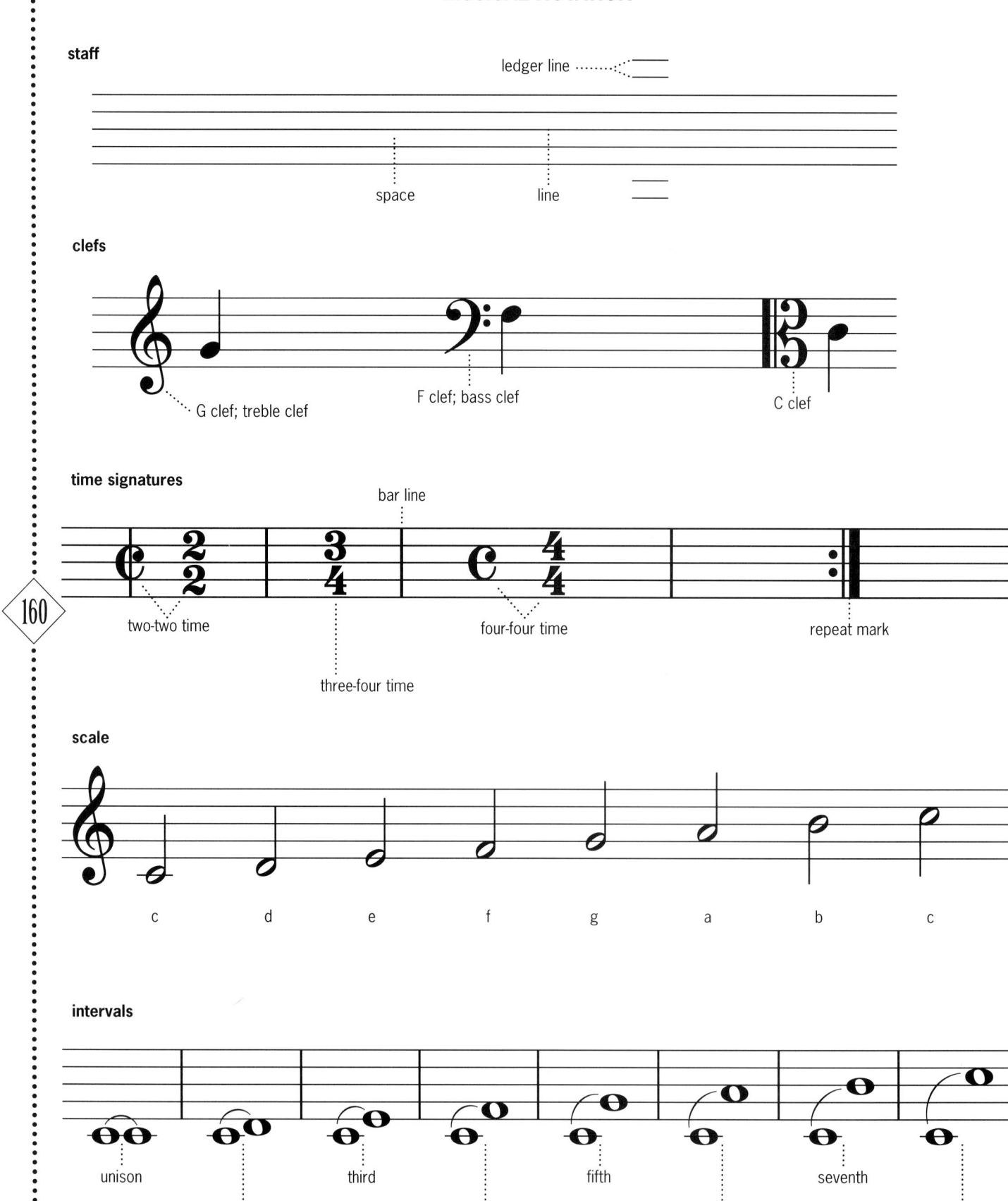

staff

ledger line

space　　　line

clefs

G clef; treble clef　　　F clef; bass clef　　　C clef

time signatures

bar line

two-two time　　　four-four time　　　repeat mark

three-four time

scale

c　d　e　f　g　a　b　c

intervals

unison　　　third　　　fifth　　　seventh

second　　　fourth　　　sixth　　　octave

MUSIC

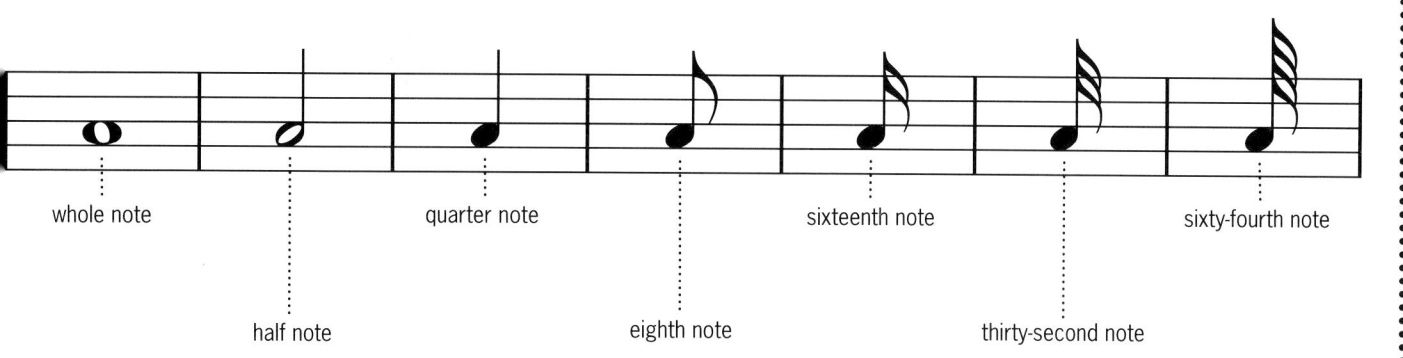

note symbols

whole note — half note — quarter note — eighth note — sixteenth note — thirty-second note — sixty-fourth note

rest symbols

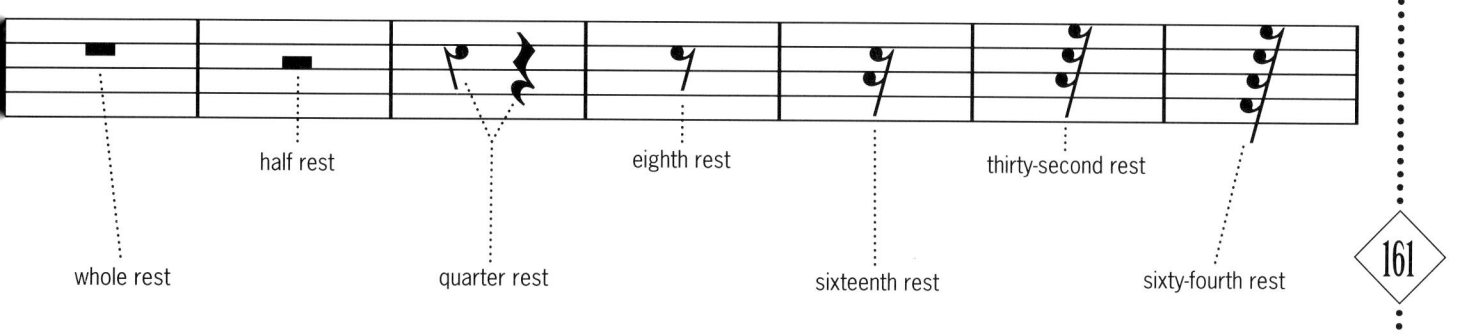

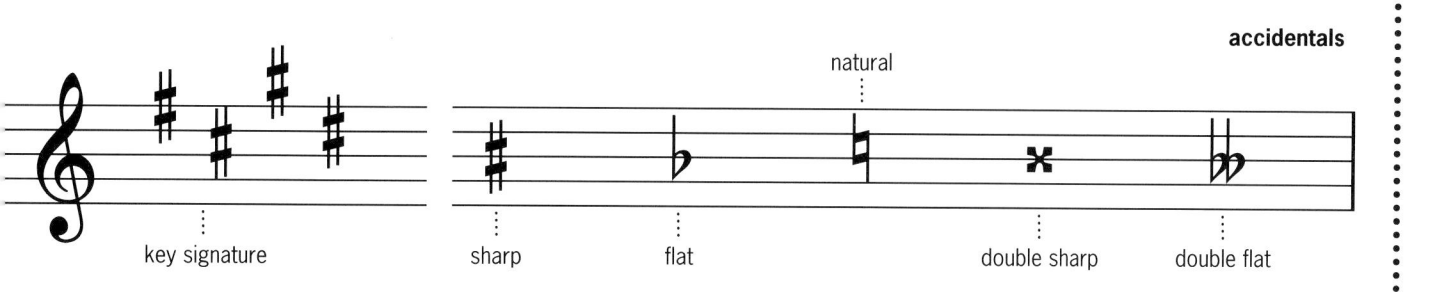

whole rest — half rest — quarter rest — eighth rest — sixteenth rest — thirty-second rest — sixty-fourth rest

accidentals

key signature — sharp — flat — natural — double sharp — double flat

ornaments

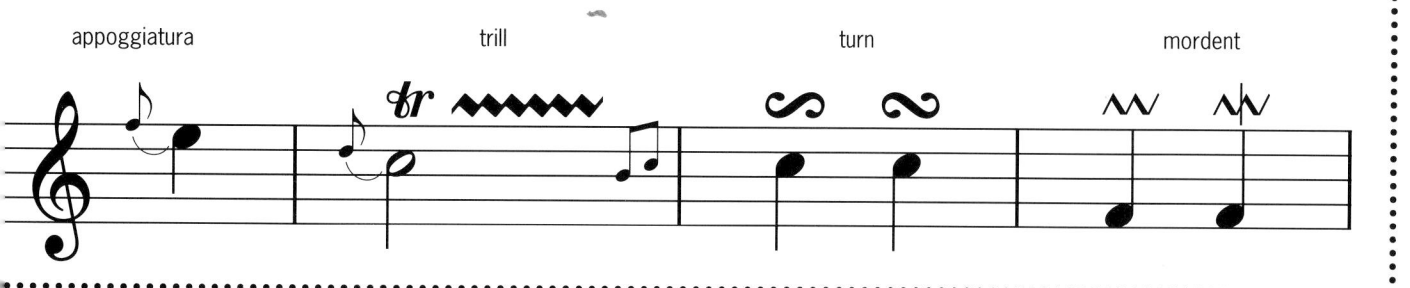

appoggiatura — trill — turn — mordent

MUSIC

STRINGED INSTRUMENTS

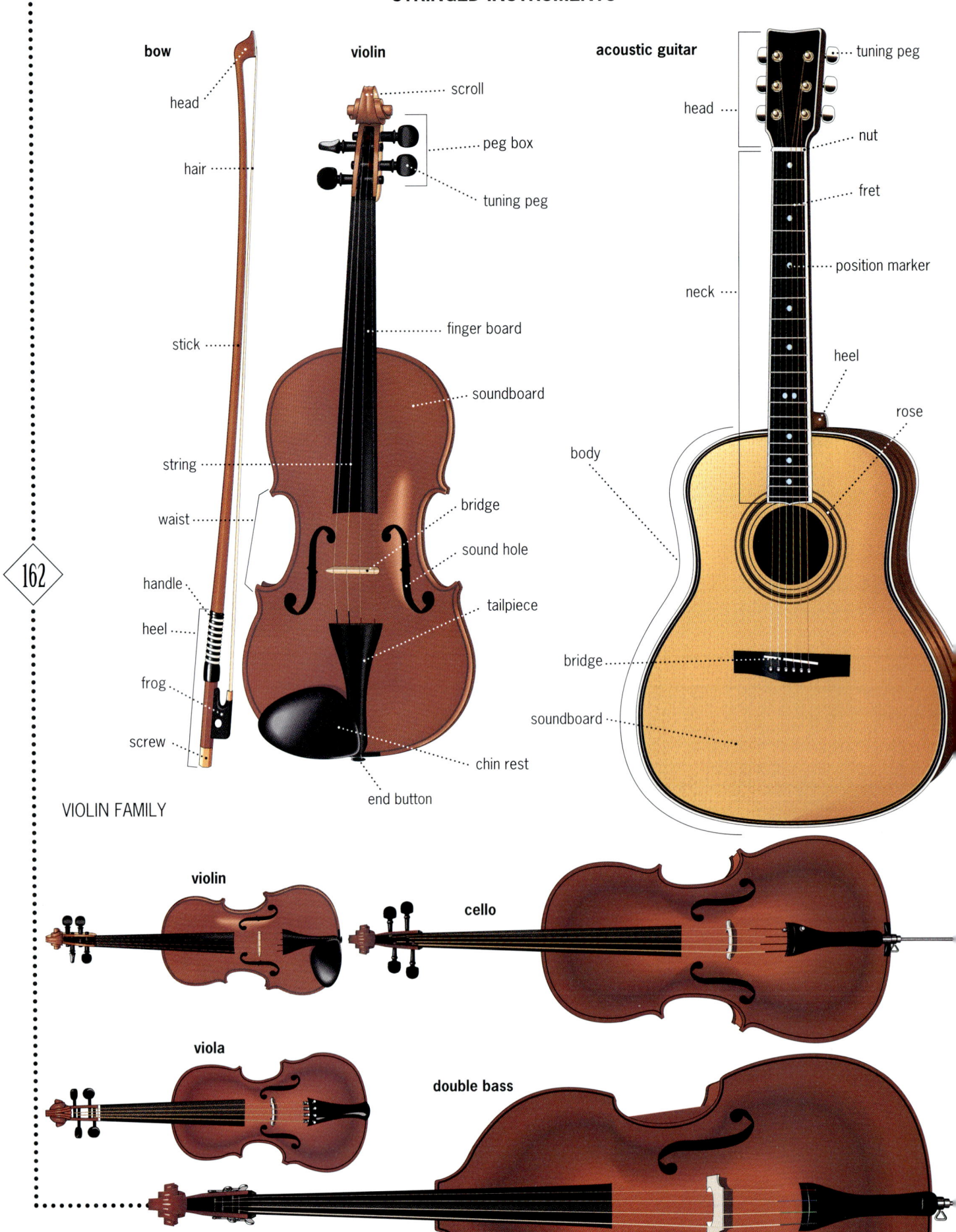

bow
- head
- hair
- stick
- handle
- heel
- frog
- screw

violin
- scroll
- peg box
- tuning peg
- finger board
- soundboard
- bridge
- sound hole
- tailpiece
- chin rest
- end button
- string
- waist

acoustic guitar
- tuning peg
- head
- nut
- fret
- position marker
- neck
- heel
- rose
- body
- bridge
- soundboard

VIOLIN FAMILY

- violin
- viola
- cello
- double bass

162

MUSIC

electric guitar

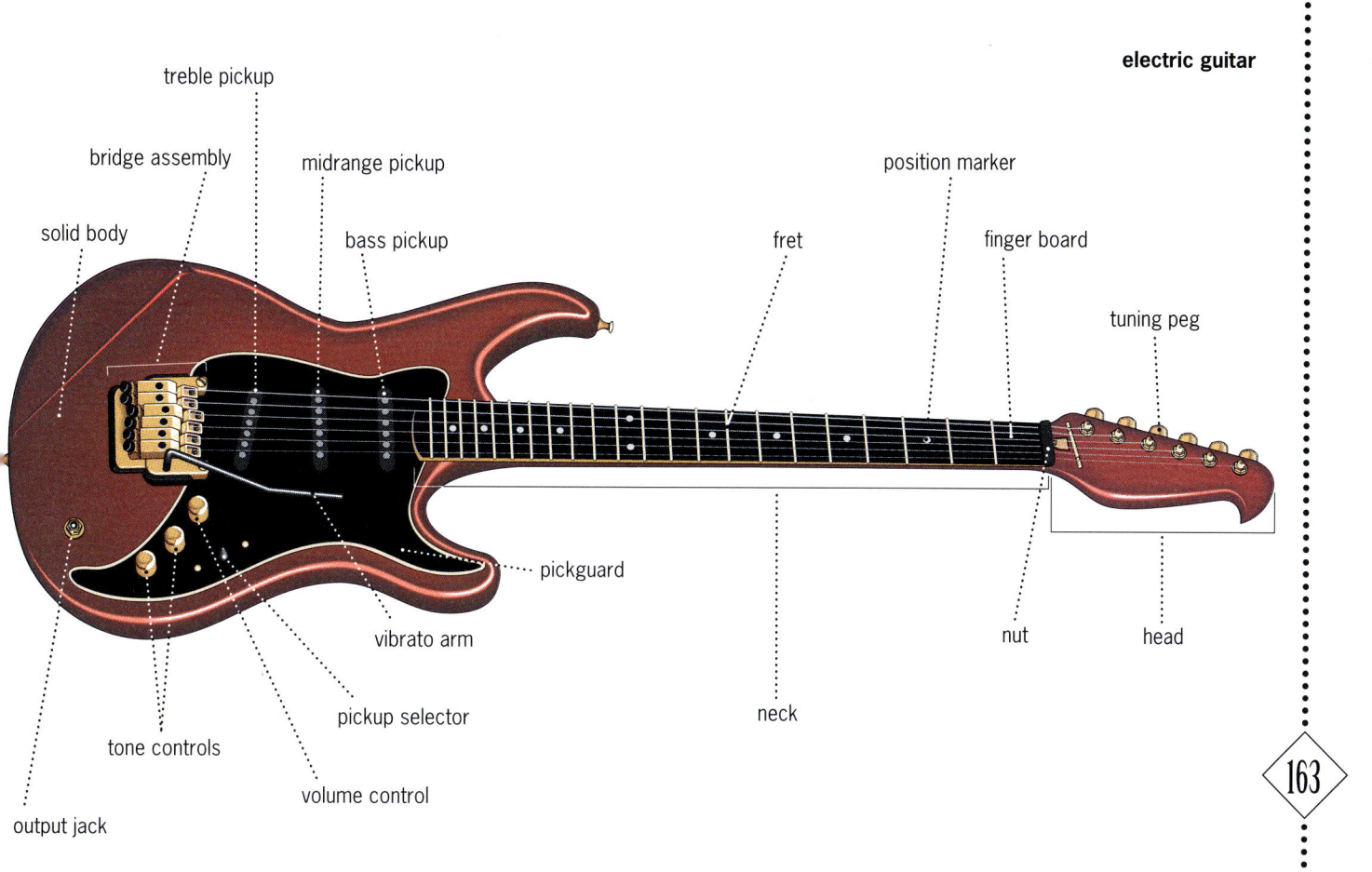

- treble pickup
- bridge assembly
- midrange pickup
- bass pickup
- solid body
- position marker
- fret
- finger board
- tuning peg
- pickguard
- vibrato arm
- nut
- head
- pickup selector
- neck
- tone controls
- volume control
- output jack

bass guitar

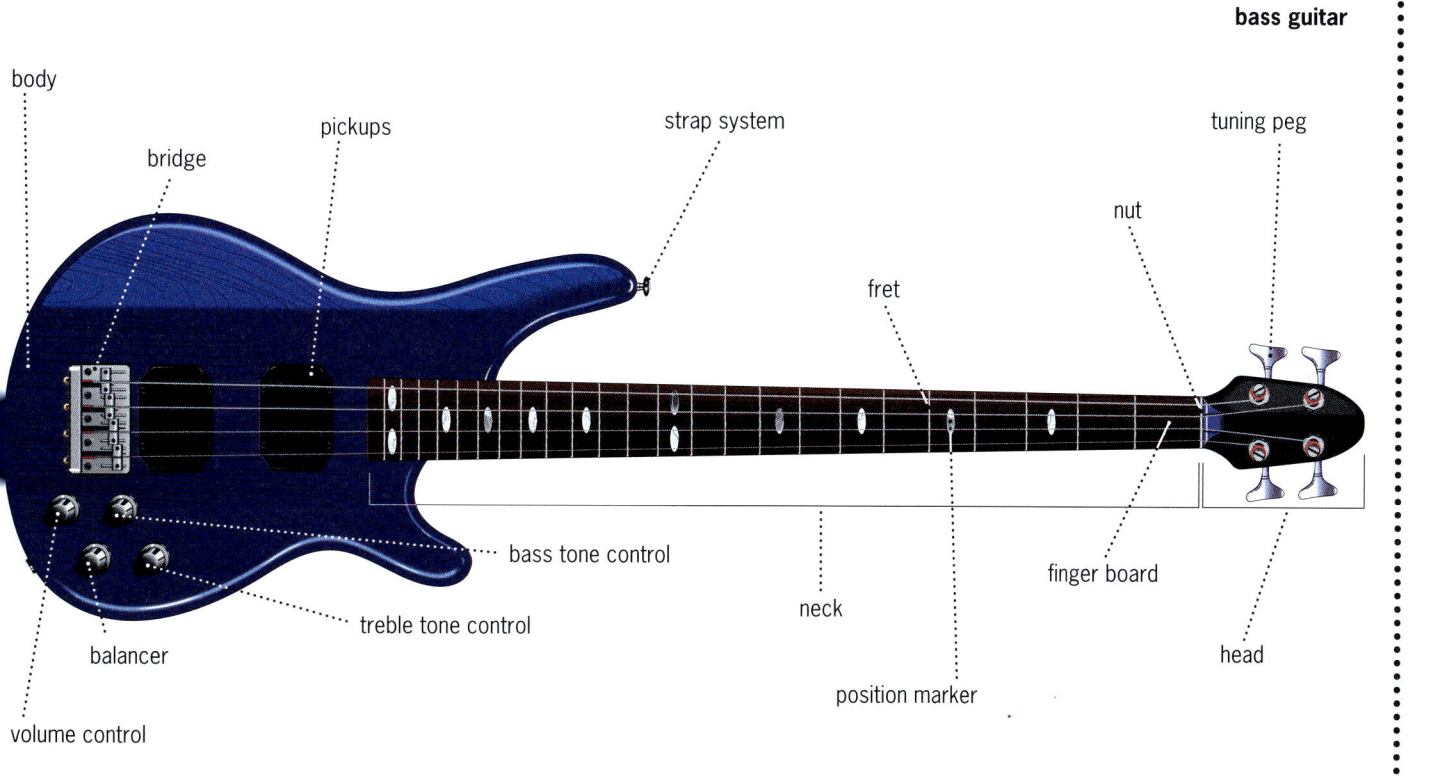

- body
- bridge
- pickups
- strap system
- tuning peg
- nut
- fret
- bass tone control
- treble tone control
- neck
- finger board
- balancer
- position marker
- head
- volume control

MUSIC

WIND INSTRUMENTS

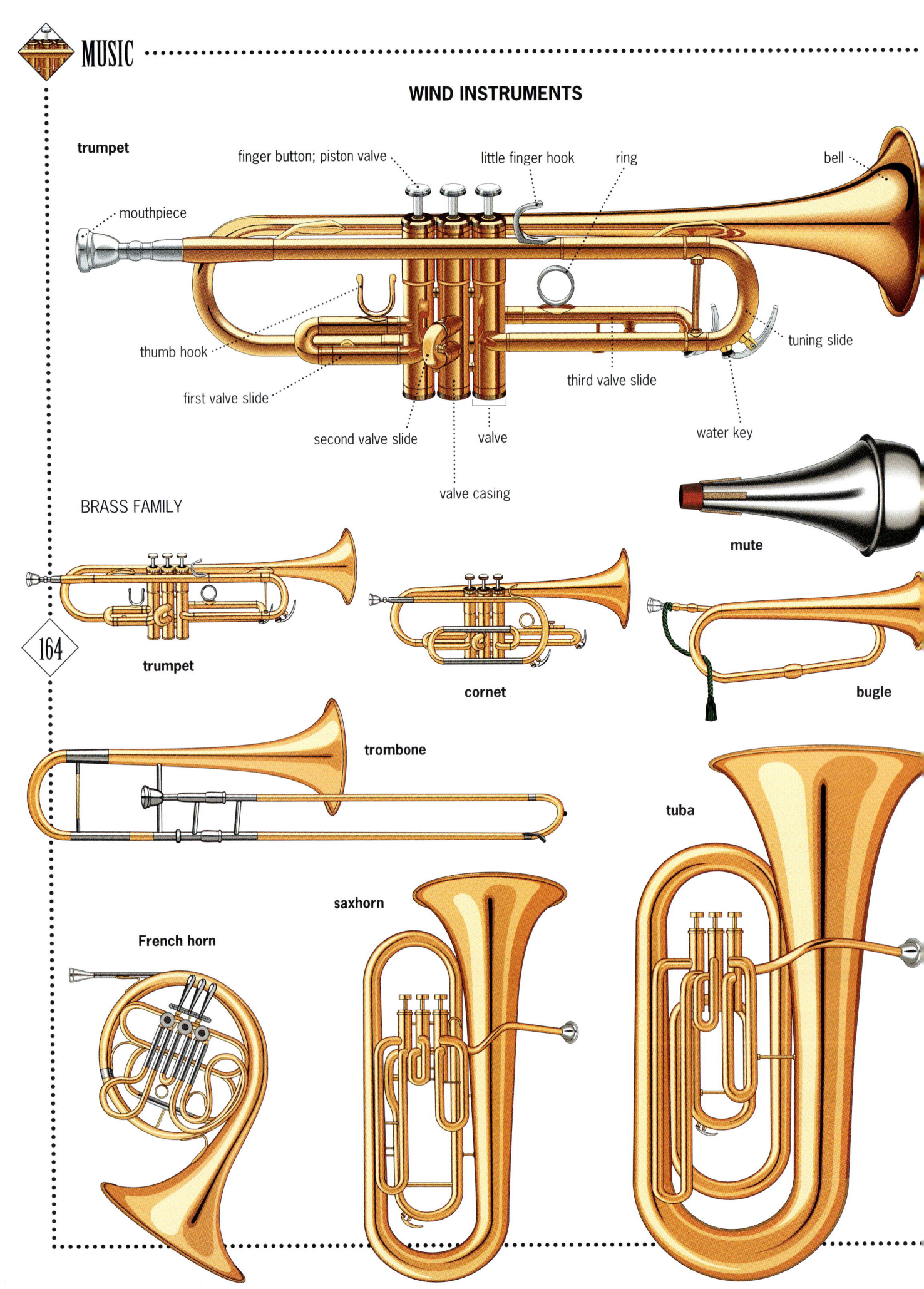

trumpet

- finger button; piston valve
- little finger hook
- ring
- bell
- mouthpiece
- tuning slide
- thumb hook
- first valve slide
- second valve slide
- valve
- valve casing
- third valve slide
- water key

BRASS FAMILY

trumpet

cornet

mute

bugle

trombone

tuba

French horn

saxhorn

MUSIC

reed
ligature
mouthpiece
crook
octave mechanism

REEDS

single reed
double reed

WOODWIND FAMILY

saxophone
piccolo
flute
recorder
oboe
clarinet
English horn
bassoon

saxophone

bell
bell brace
body
thumb rest
key

165

MUSIC

PERCUSSION INSTRUMENTS

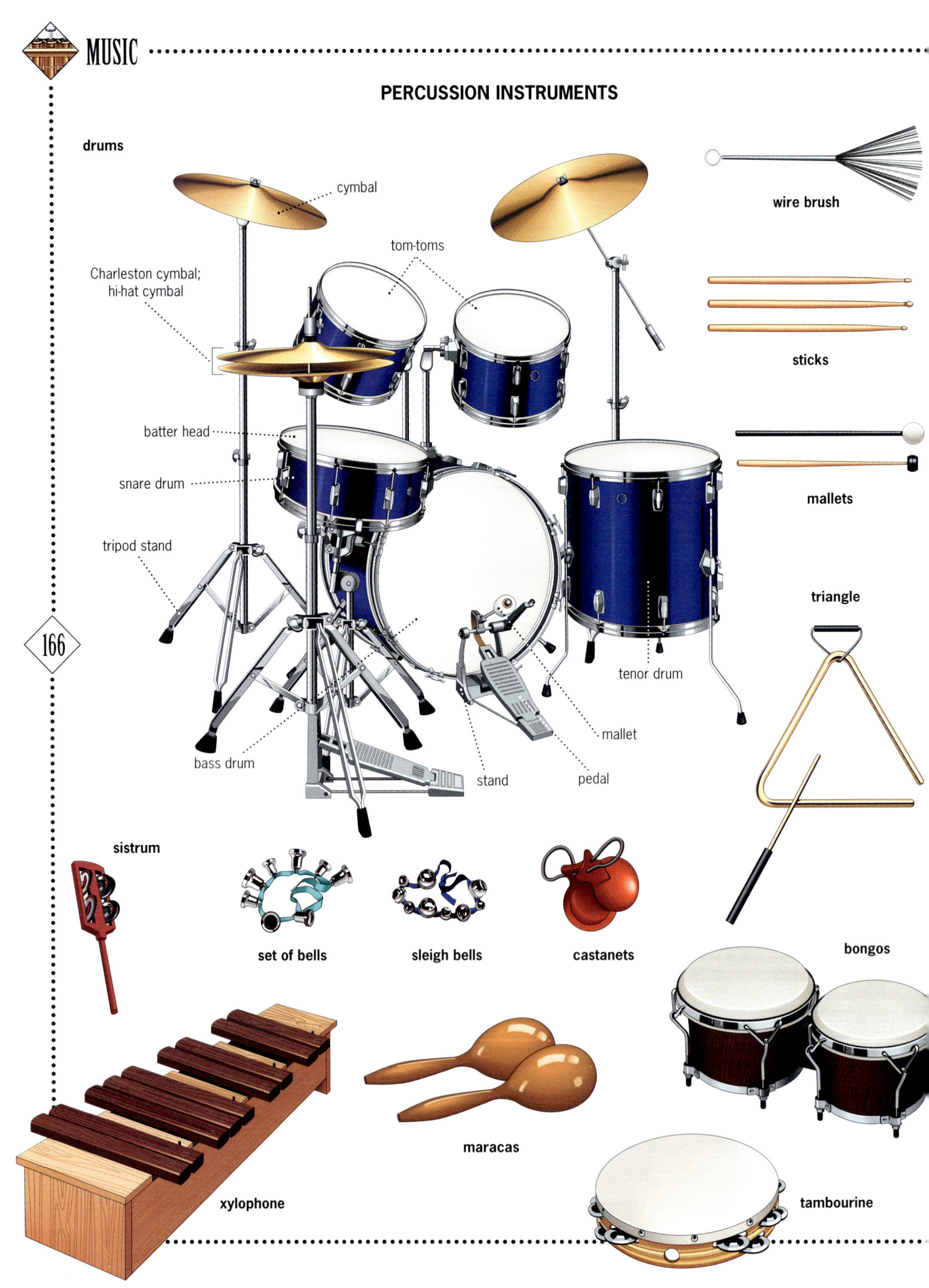

drums

- cymbal
- tom-toms
- Charleston cymbal; hi-hat cymbal
- batter head
- snare drum
- tripod stand
- bass drum
- stand
- pedal
- mallet
- tenor drum

wire brush

sticks

mallets

triangle

sistrum

set of bells

sleigh bells

castanets

bongos

xylophone

maracas

tambourine

166

MUSIC

SYMPHONY ORCHESTRA

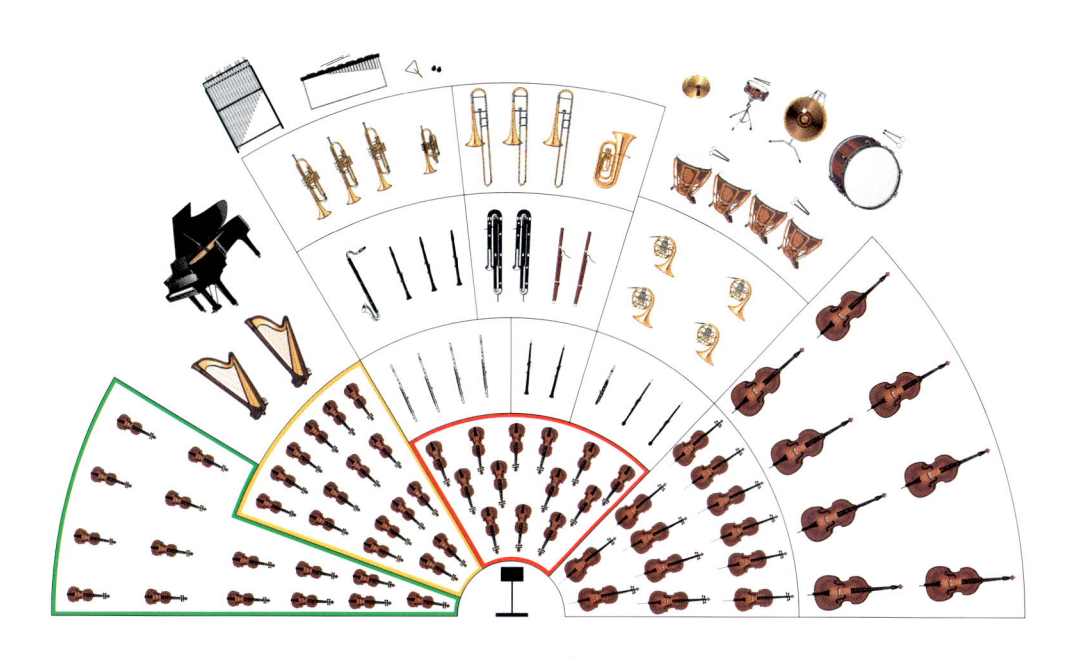

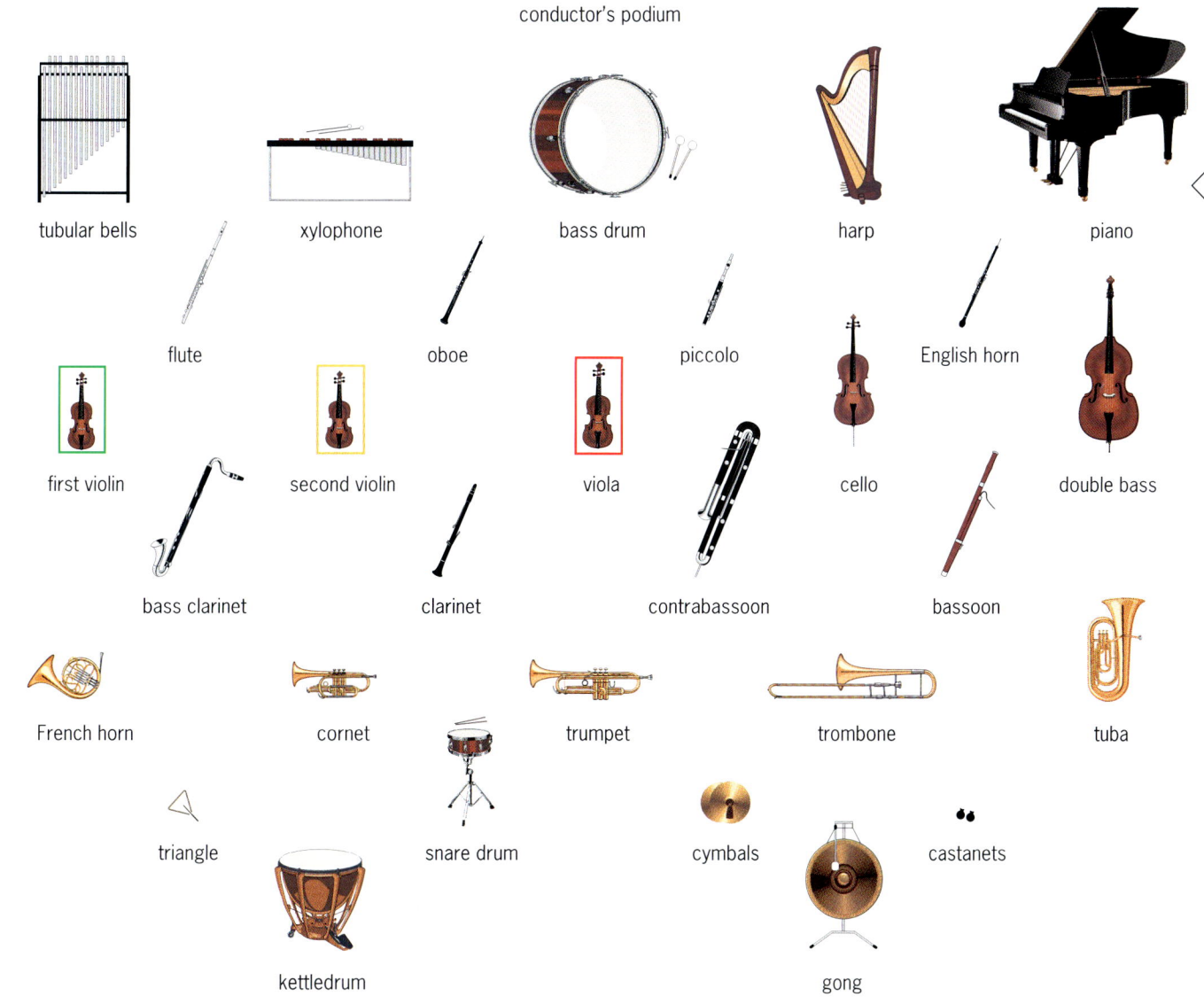

conductor's podium

| tubular bells | xylophone | bass drum | harp | piano |

| flute | oboe | piccolo | English horn |

| first violin | second violin | viola | cello | double bass |

| bass clarinet | clarinet | contrabassoon | bassoon |

| French horn | cornet | trumpet | trombone | tuba |

| triangle | snare drum | cymbals | castanets |

| kettledrum | | gong |

167

TEAM GAMES

BASEBALL

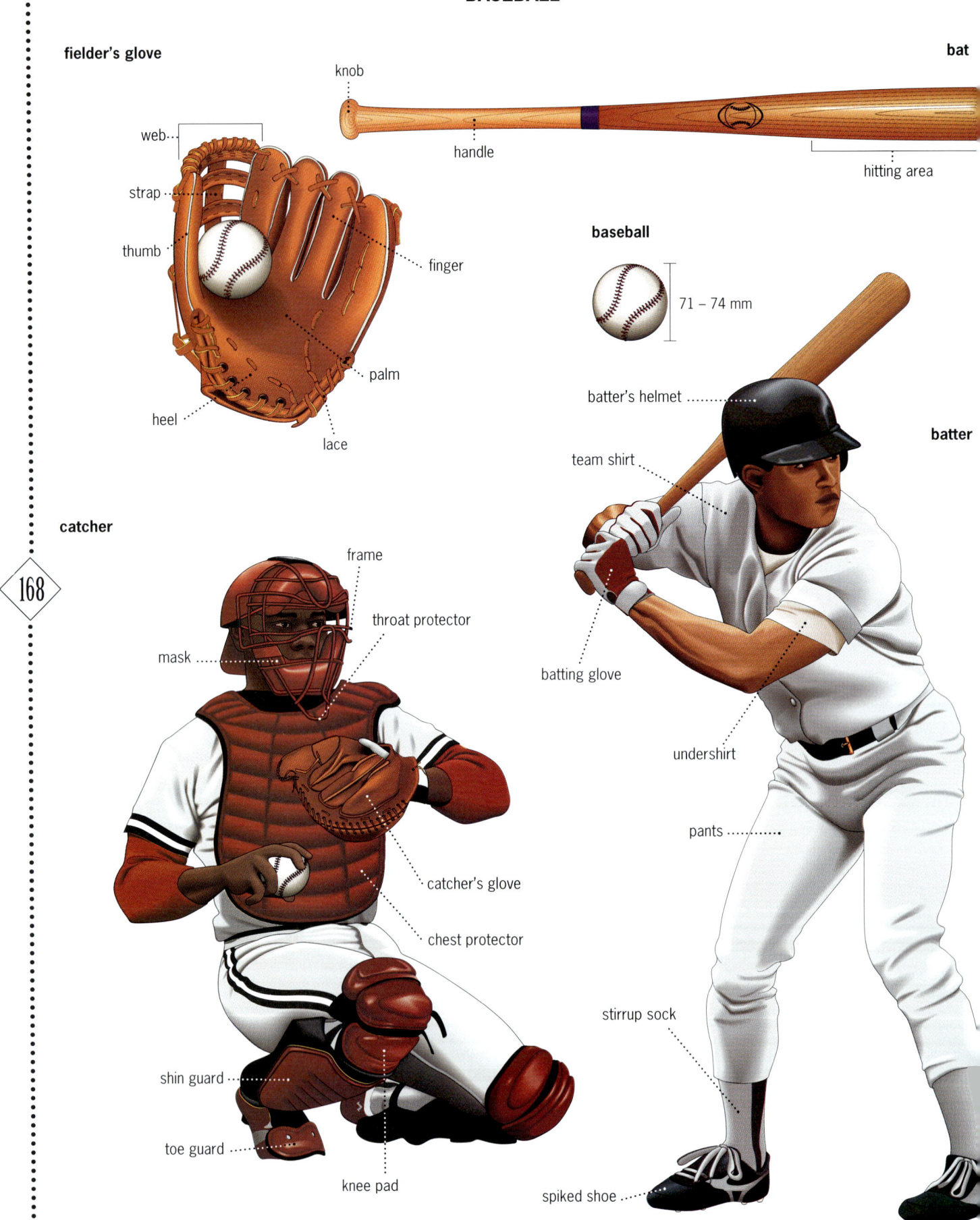

fielder's glove
- web
- strap
- thumb
- finger
- palm
- heel
- lace

bat
- knob
- handle
- hitting area

baseball
71 – 74 mm

catcher
- mask
- frame
- throat protector
- catcher's glove
- chest protector
- shin guard
- toe guard
- knee pad

batter
- batter's helmet
- team shirt
- batting glove
- undershirt
- pants
- stirrup sock
- spiked shoe

168

TEAM GAMES

field

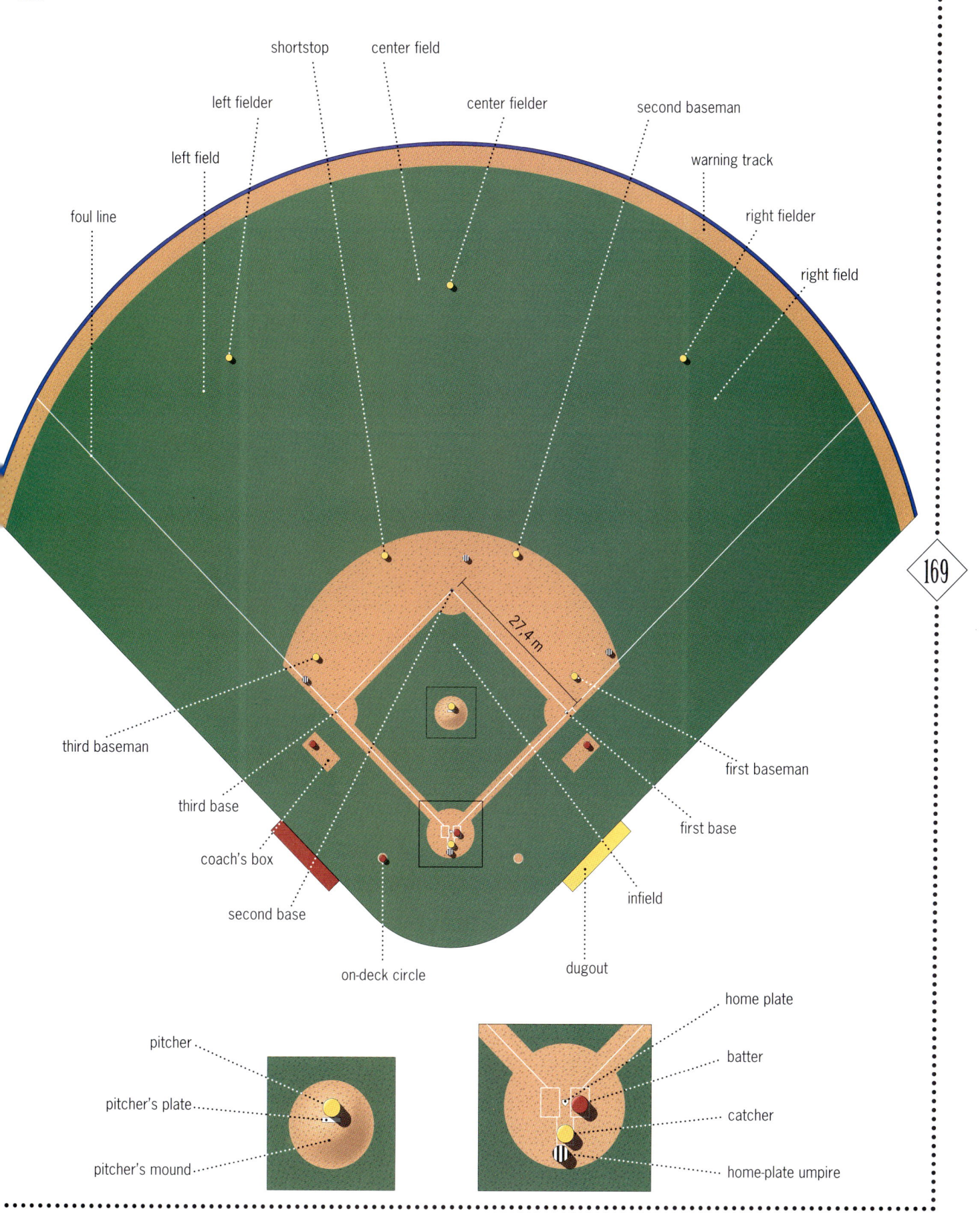

- foul line
- left field
- left fielder
- shortstop
- center field
- center fielder
- second baseman
- warning track
- right fielder
- right field
- third baseman
- third base
- coach's box
- second base
- on-deck circle
- first baseman
- first base
- infield
- dugout
- 27.4 m

- pitcher
- pitcher's plate
- pitcher's mound

- home plate
- batter
- catcher
- home-plate umpire

169

TEAM GAMES

FOOTBALL

American football player

- helmet
- chin strap
- player's number
- team shirt
- wristband
- pants
- sock
- cleated shoe

football

279 – 286 mm

protective equipment

- helmet
- face mask
- shoulder pad
- chest protector
- arm guard
- rib pad
- elbow pad
- hip pad
- lumbar pad
- protective cup
- thigh pad
- knee pad

170

TEAM GAMES

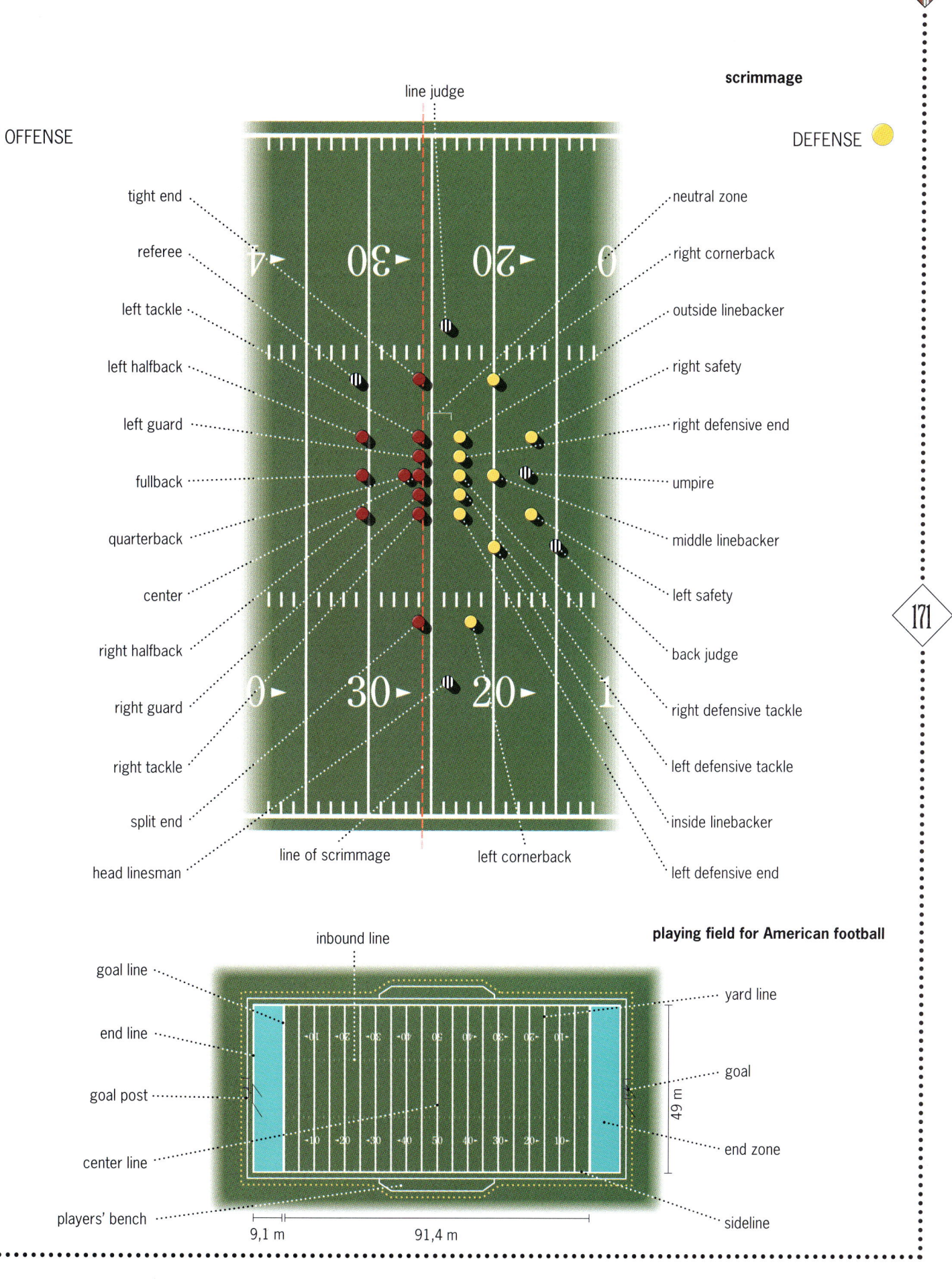

scrimmage

OFFENSE DEFENSE

- tight end
- referee
- left tackle
- left halfback
- left guard
- fullback
- quarterback
- center
- right halfback
- right guard
- right tackle
- split end
- head linesman

- line judge
- line of scrimmage
- left cornerback

- neutral zone
- right cornerback
- outside linebacker
- right safety
- right defensive end
- umpire
- middle linebacker
- left safety
- back judge
- right defensive tackle
- left defensive tackle
- inside linebacker
- left defensive end

playing field for American football

- inbound line
- goal line
- end line
- goal post
- center line
- players' bench
- yard line
- goal
- end zone
- sideline

9,1 m   91,4 m   49 m

TEAM GAMES

SOCCER

soccer player

- team shirt
- shorts
- shin guard
- soccer shoe
- interchangeable studs

soccer ball

218 mm

TEAM GAMES

playing field

- corner arc
- referee
- goal
- 45 – 90 m
- corner flag
- goal area
- penalty area
- penalty area marking
- penalty spot
- penalty arc
- 90 – 120 m
- center flag
- outside right
- center spot
- center forward
- inside right
- right half
- touch line
- linesman
- right back
- center circle
- center back
- goalkeeper
- inside left
- left back
- left half
- midfield line
- outside left

173

TEAM GAMES

CRICKET

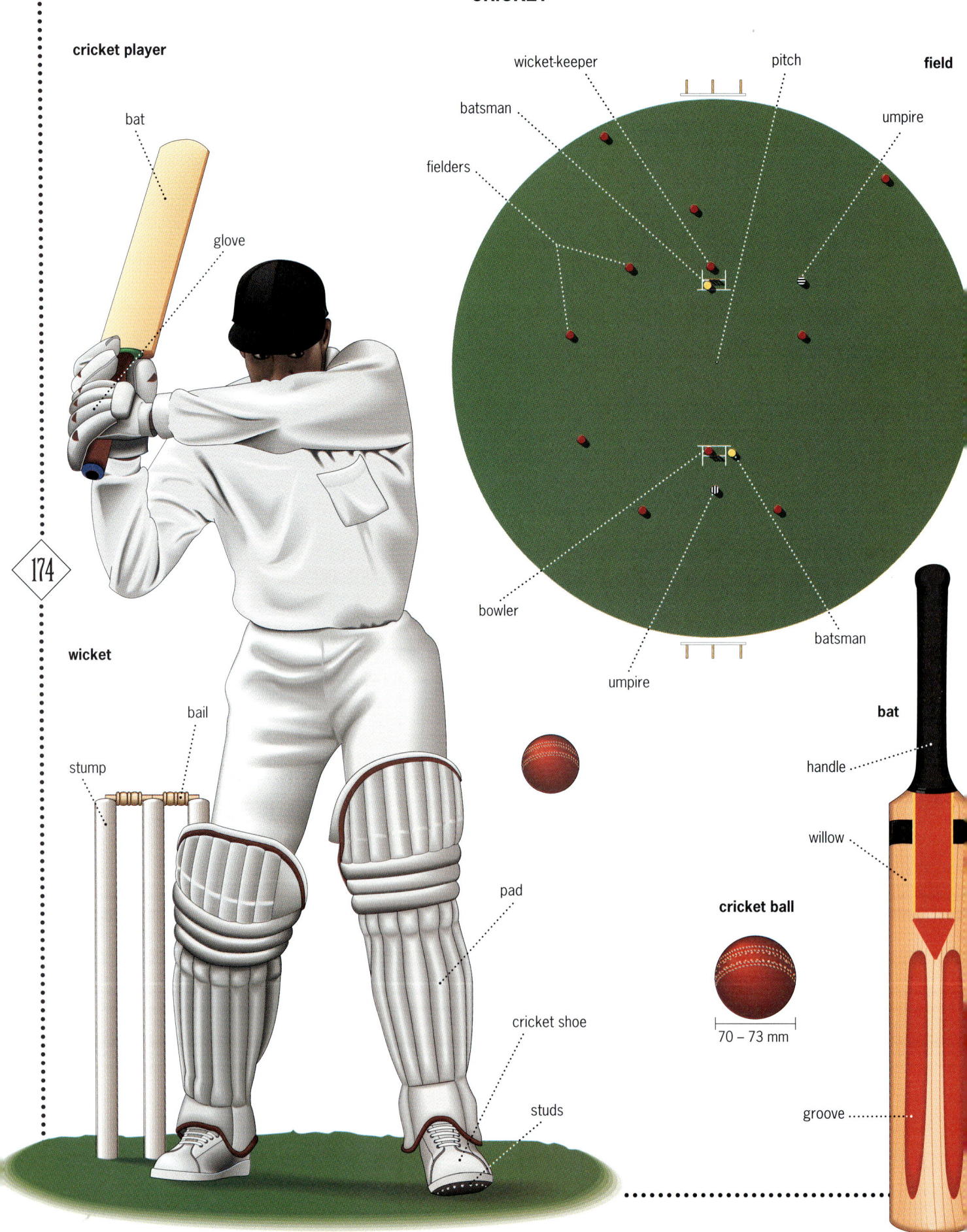

cricket player
- bat
- glove

wicket
- stump
- bail
- pad
- cricket shoe
- studs

field
- wicket-keeper
- batsman
- fielders
- pitch
- umpire
- bowler
- batsman
- umpire

cricket ball
70 – 73 mm

bat
- handle
- willow
- groove

174

TEAM GAMES

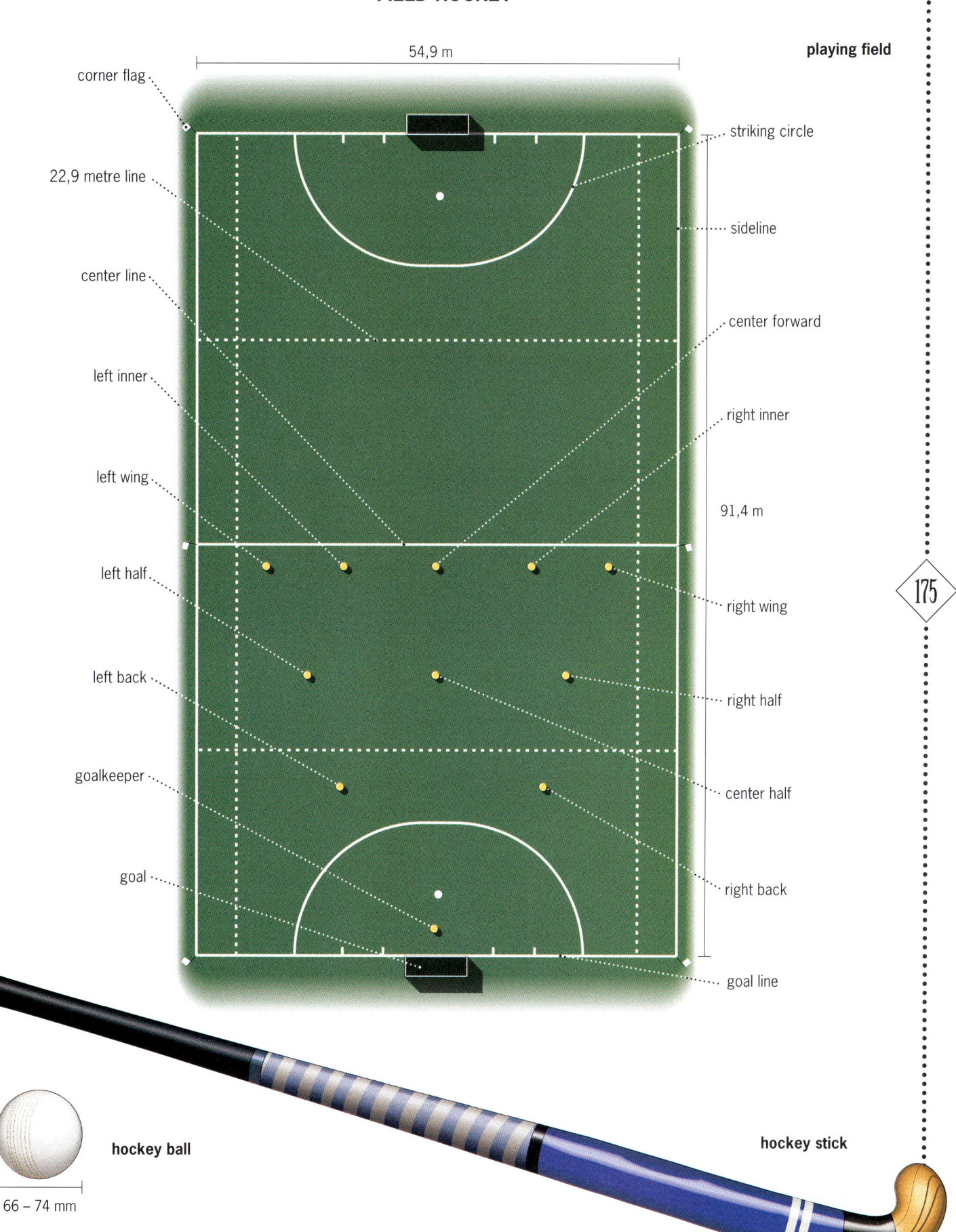

FIELD HOCKEY

playing field

- corner flag
- 22,9 metre line
- center line
- left inner
- left wing
- left half
- left back
- goalkeeper
- goal
- 54,9 m
- striking circle
- sideline
- center forward
- right inner
- 91,4 m
- right wing
- right half
- center half
- right back
- goal line

hockey ball

66 – 74 mm

hockey stick

FIELD HOCKEY

TEAM GAMES

ICE HOCKEY

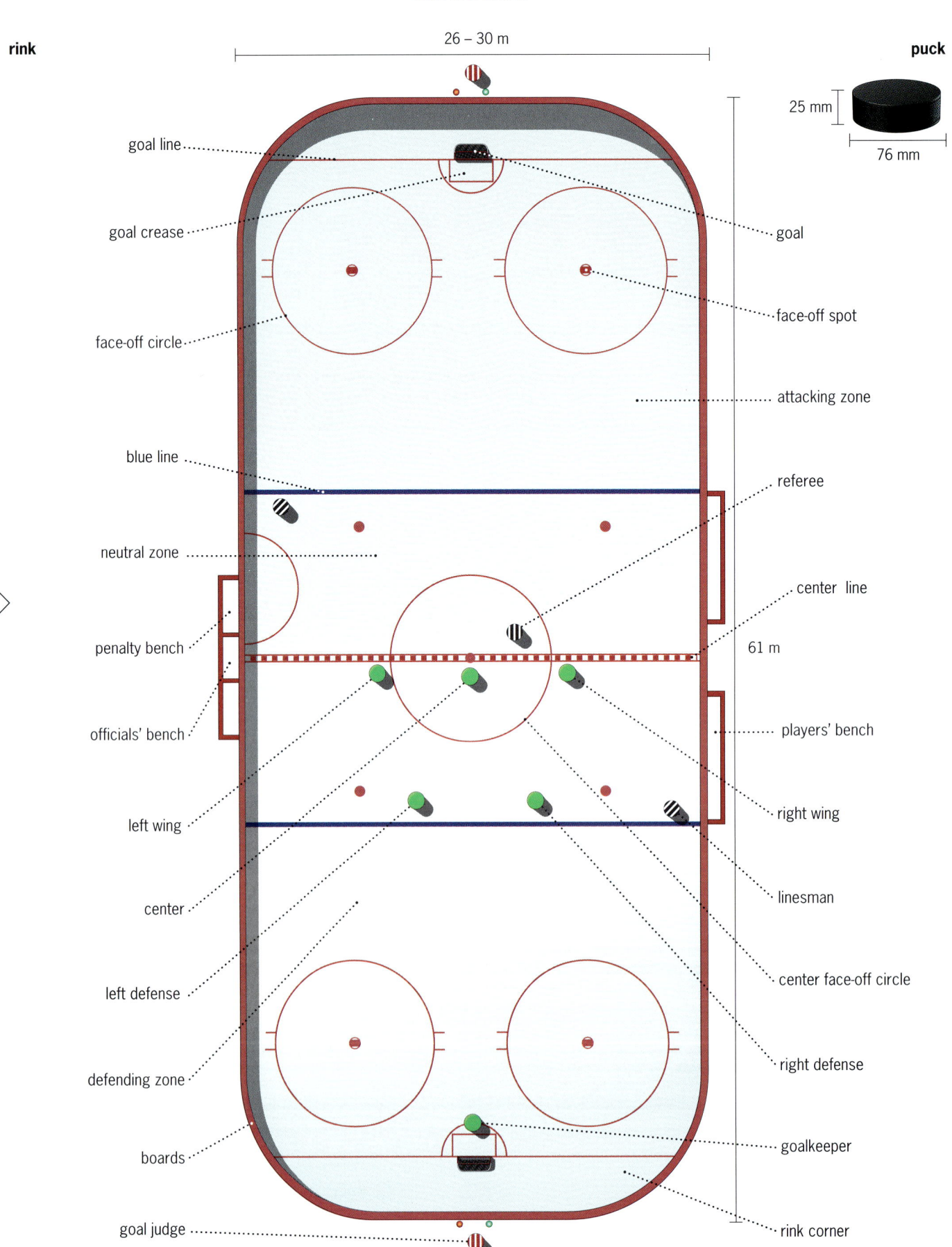

rink

- 26 – 30 m
- goal line
- goal crease
- face-off circle
- blue line
- neutral zone
- penalty bench
- officials' bench
- left wing
- center
- left defense
- defending zone
- boards
- goal judge
- goal
- face-off spot
- attacking zone
- referee
- center line
- 61 m
- players' bench
- right wing
- linesman
- center face-off circle
- right defense
- goalkeeper
- rink corner

puck

- 25 mm
- 76 mm

TEAM GAMES

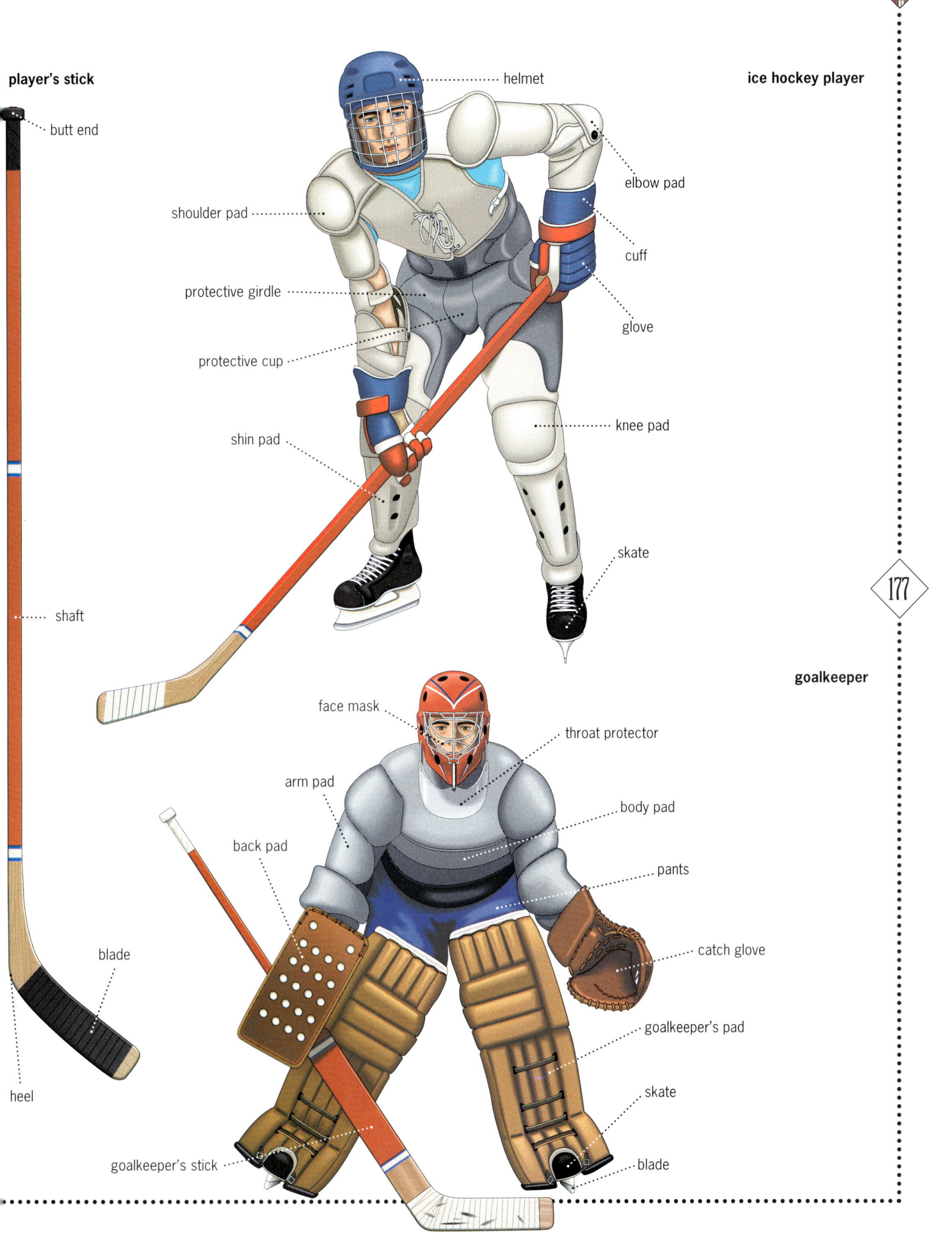

player's stick

- butt end
- shaft
- blade
- heel

ice hockey player

- helmet
- elbow pad
- cuff
- shoulder pad
- glove
- protective girdle
- protective cup
- knee pad
- shin pad
- skate

goalkeeper

- face mask
- throat protector
- arm pad
- body pad
- back pad
- pants
- catch glove
- goalkeeper's pad
- skate
- goalkeeper's stick
- blade

177

TEAM GAMES

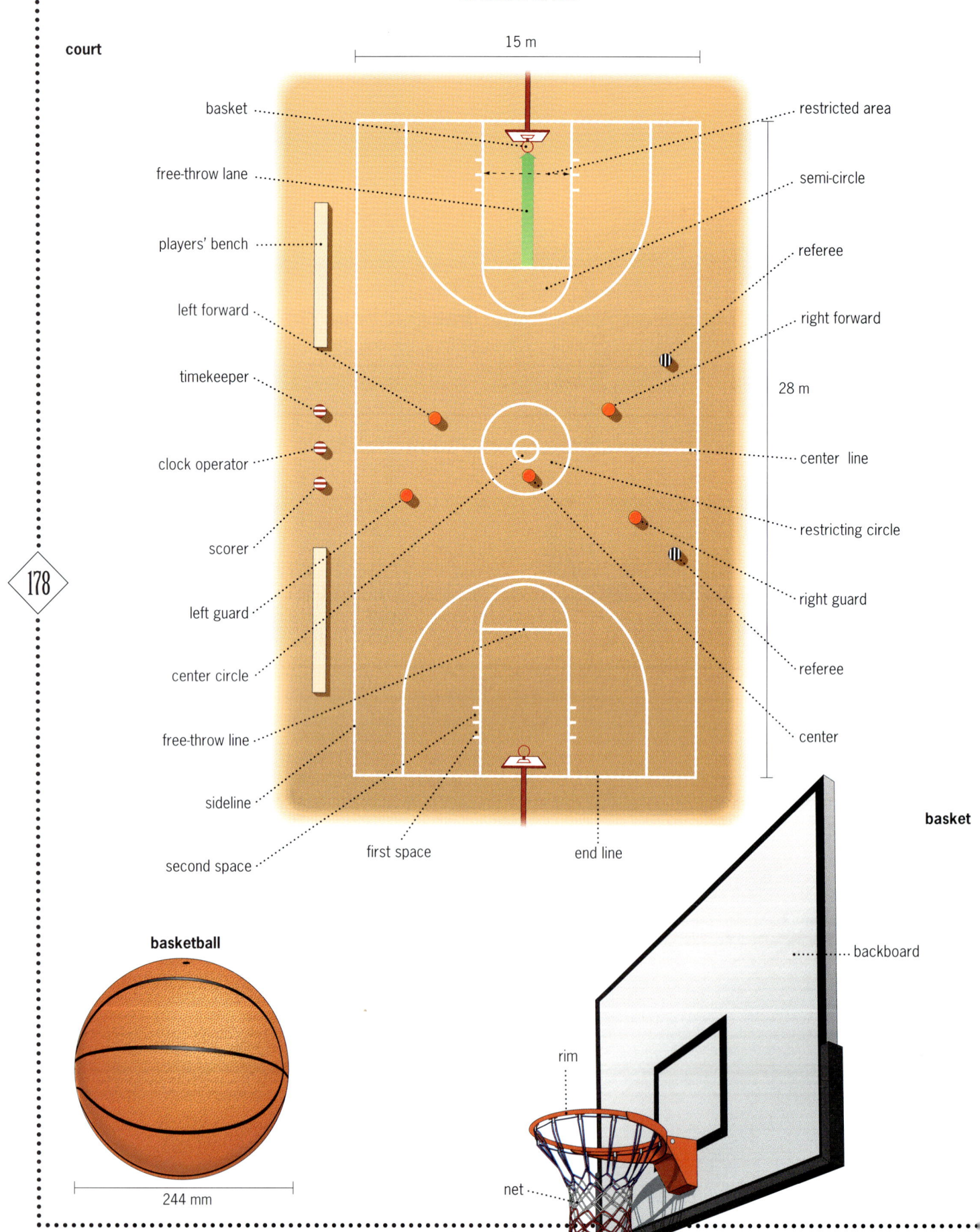

BASKETBALL

court

15 m

basket
free-throw lane
players' bench
left forward
timekeeper
clock operator
scorer
left guard
center circle
free-throw line
sideline
second space

first space
end line

restricted area
semi-circle
referee
right forward
28 m
center line
restricting circle
right guard
referee
center

basketball

244 mm

basket

backboard
rim
net

178

TEAM GAMES

VOLLEYBALL

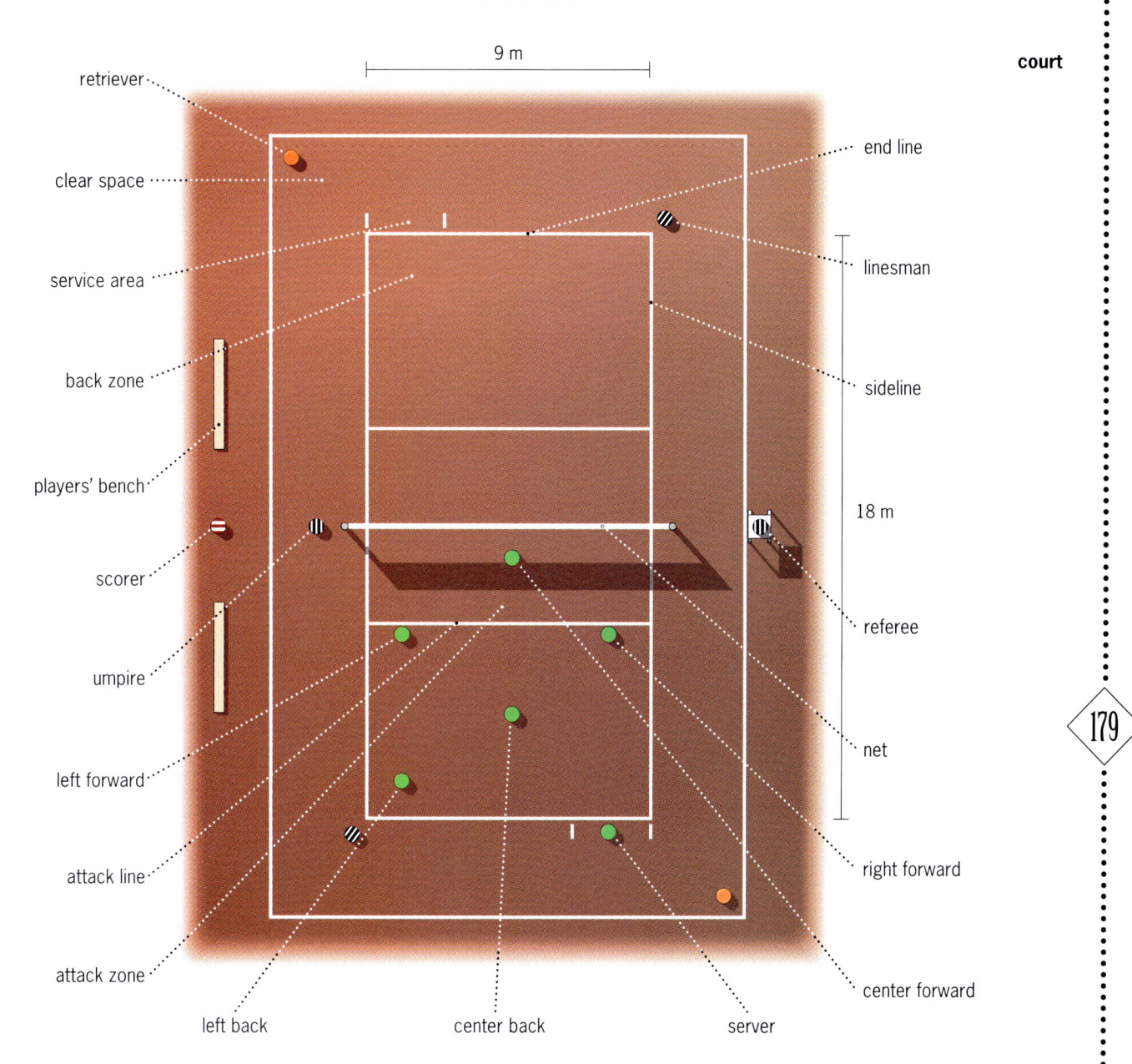

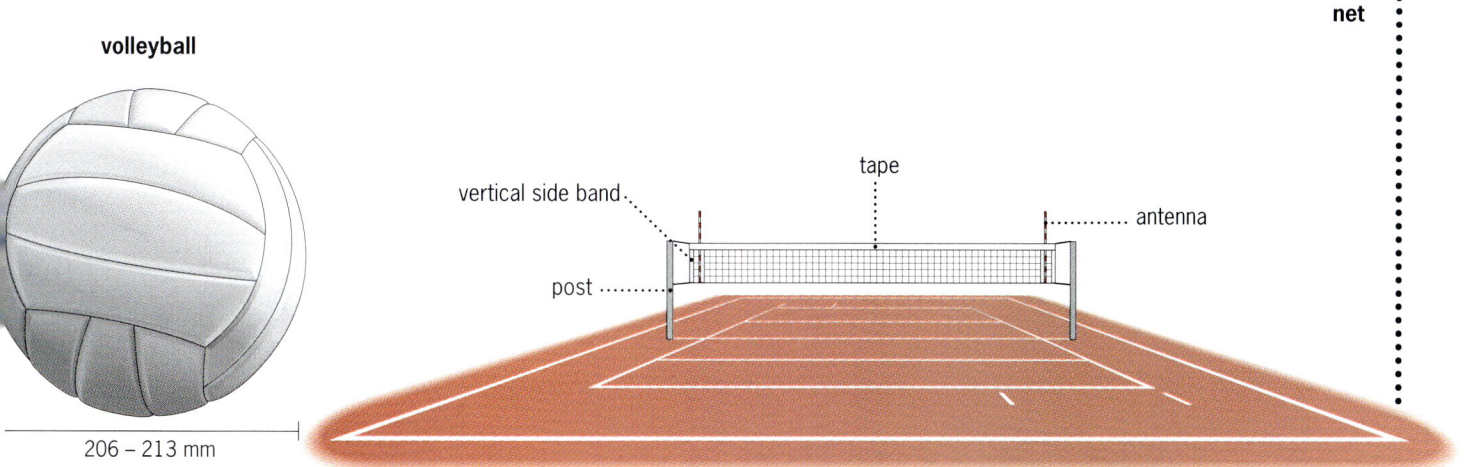

9 m

retriever
clear space
service area
back zone
players' bench
scorer
umpire
left forward
attack line
attack zone
end line
linesman
sideline
18 m
referee
net
right forward
center forward
left back
center back
server

court

net

volleyball

206 – 213 mm

vertical side band
post
tape
antenna

VOLLEYBALL

TEAM GAMES

TENNIS

court

- 8,23 m
- linesman
- center mark
- receiver
- baseline
- backcourt
- service line
- forecourt
- service judge
- singles sideline
- center service line
- umpire
- 23,8 m
- left service court
- net judge
- alley
- net
- server
- right service court
- foot fault judge
- ball boy
- doubles sideline
- 11 m

net

- net band
- center strap
- singles pole
- doubles pole

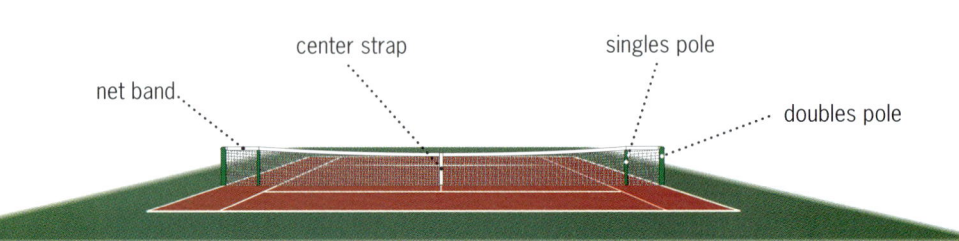

TEAM GAMES

tennis ball

64 – 68 mm

tennis player

- headband
- polo shirt
- wristband
- skirt
- sock
- tennis shoe

tennis racket

- butt
- handle
- shaft
- throat
- shoulder
- head
- frame
- strings

181

WATER SPORTS

SWIMMING

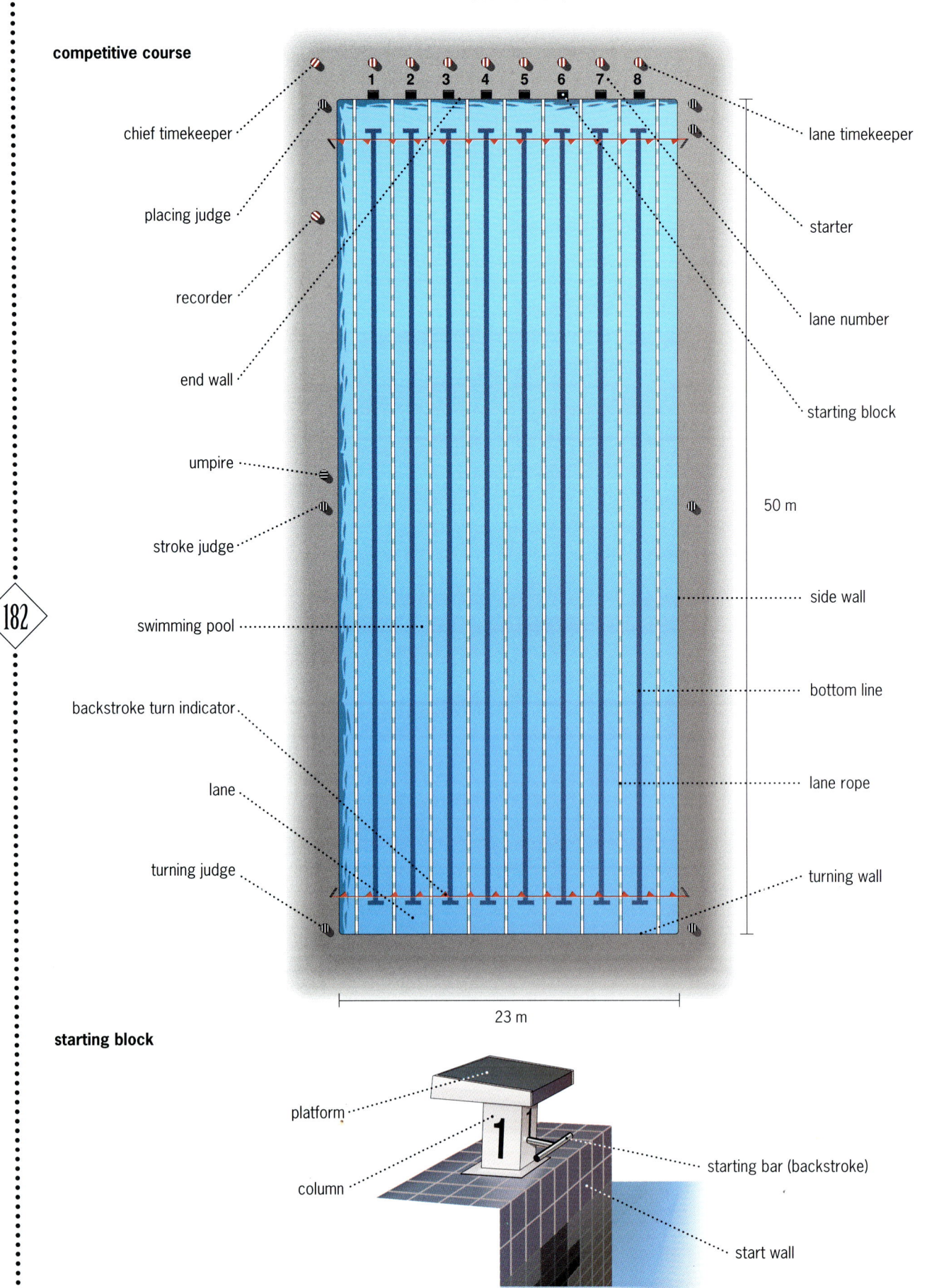

competitive course

- chief timekeeper
- placing judge
- recorder
- end wall
- umpire
- stroke judge
- swimming pool
- backstroke turn indicator
- lane
- turning judge
- lane timekeeper
- starter
- lane number
- starting block
- side wall
- bottom line
- lane rope
- turning wall

50 m

23 m

starting block

- platform
- column
- starting bar (backstroke)
- start wall

WATER SPORTS

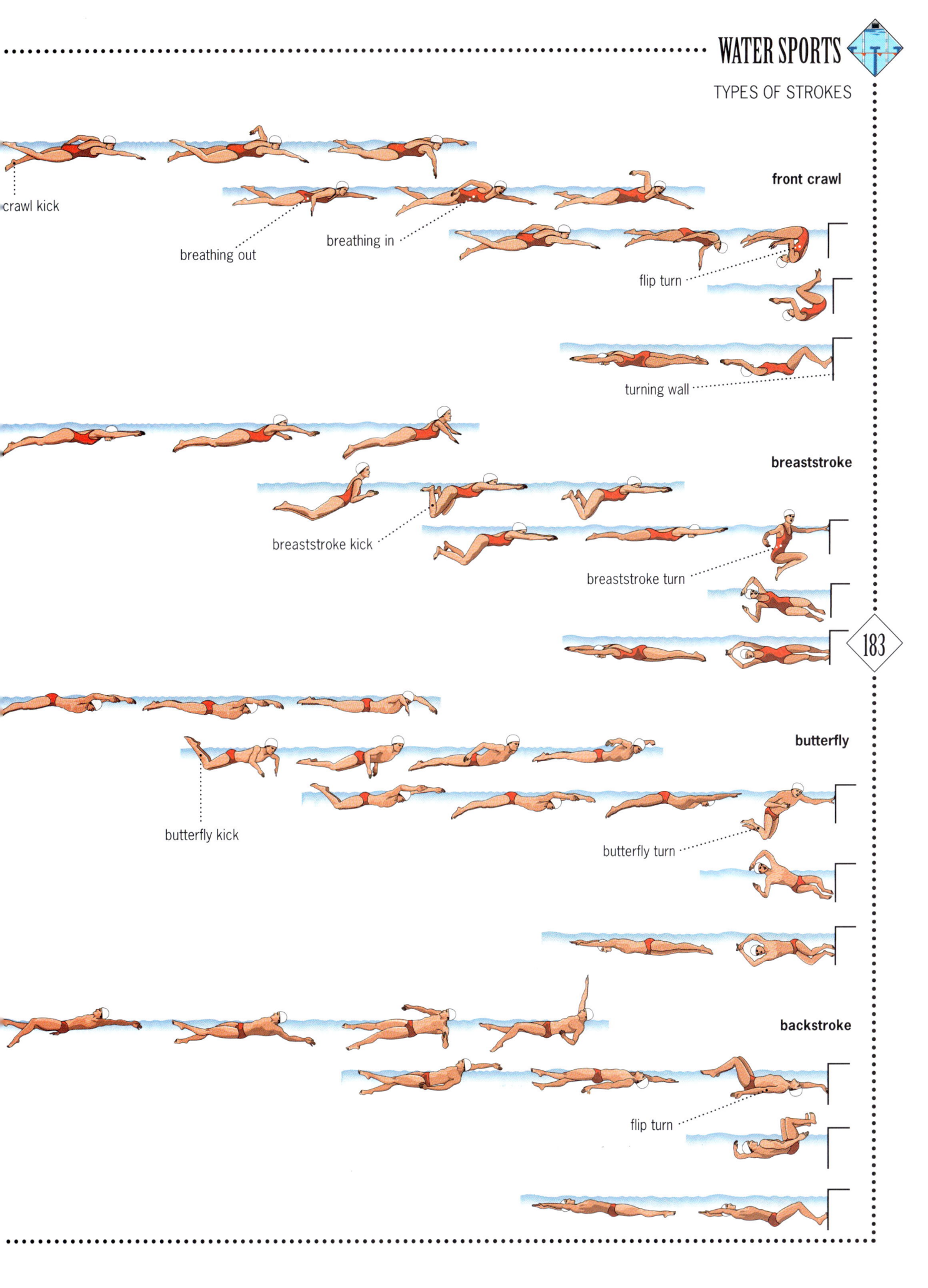

TYPES OF STROKES

front crawl

crawl kick
breathing out
breathing in
flip turn
turning wall

breaststroke

breaststroke kick
breaststroke turn

butterfly

butterfly kick
butterfly turn

backstroke

flip turn

183

WATER SPORTS

SAILBOARD

sail

masthead
mast sleeve
luff
batten pocket
window
wishbone boom
mast
uphaul
tack
mast foot
board
bow
batten
clew
foot strap
daggerboard
skeg
stern

184

WINTER SPORTS

SKATING

in-line skate
- inner boot
- upper shell
- adjusting buckle
- boot
- axle
- wheel
- truck
- heel stop

speed skate

hockey skate
- tendon guard
- boot
- toe box
- point
- blade

figure skate
- tongue
- hook
- backstay
- eyelet
- boot
- stanchion
- edge
- blade
- lace
- sole
- toe pick

skate guard

185

WINTER SPORTS

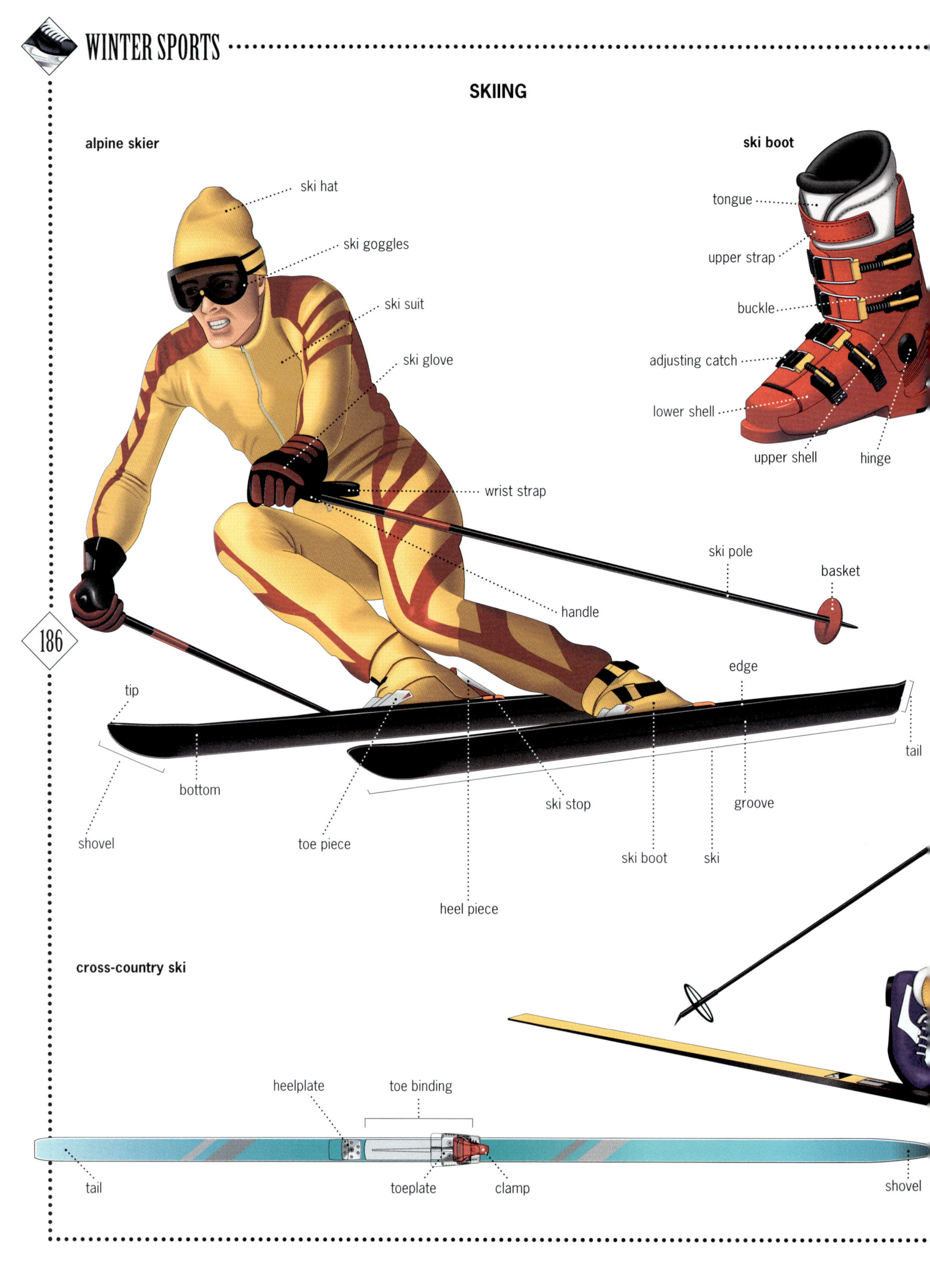

SKIING

alpine skier
- ski hat
- ski goggles
- ski suit
- ski glove
- wrist strap
- ski pole
- basket
- handle
- edge
- tail
- groove
- ski
- ski boot
- ski stop
- heel piece
- toe piece
- bottom
- tip
- shovel

ski boot
- tongue
- upper strap
- buckle
- adjusting catch
- lower shell
- upper shell
- hinge

cross-country ski
- tail
- heelplate
- toe binding
- toeplate
- clamp
- shovel

186

WINTER SPORTS

safety binding

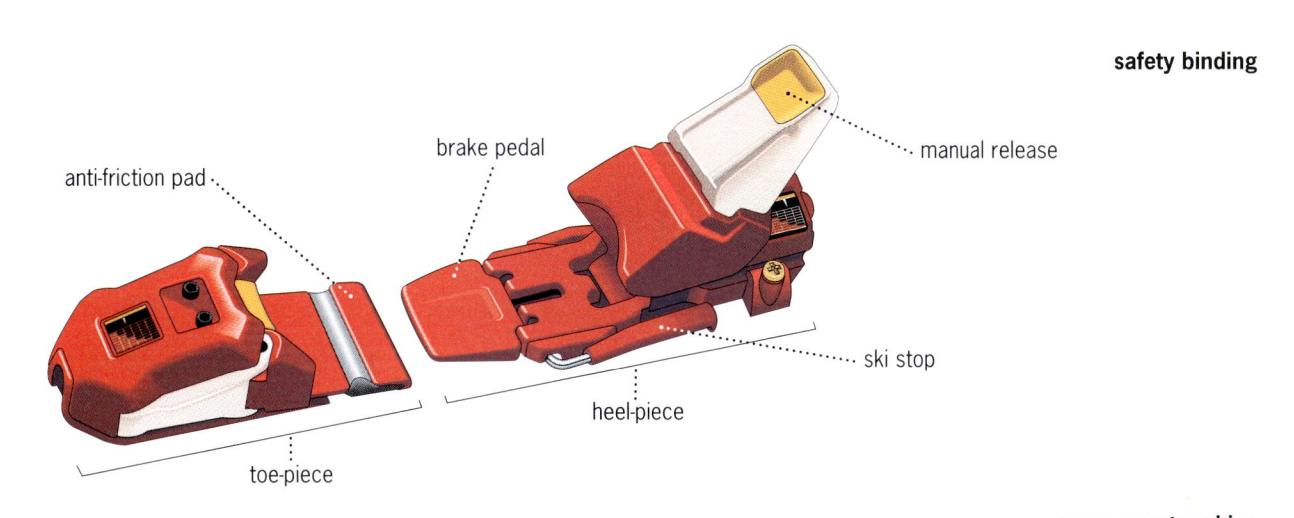

- anti-friction pad
- brake pedal
- manual release
- ski stop
- heel-piece
- toe-piece

cross-country skier

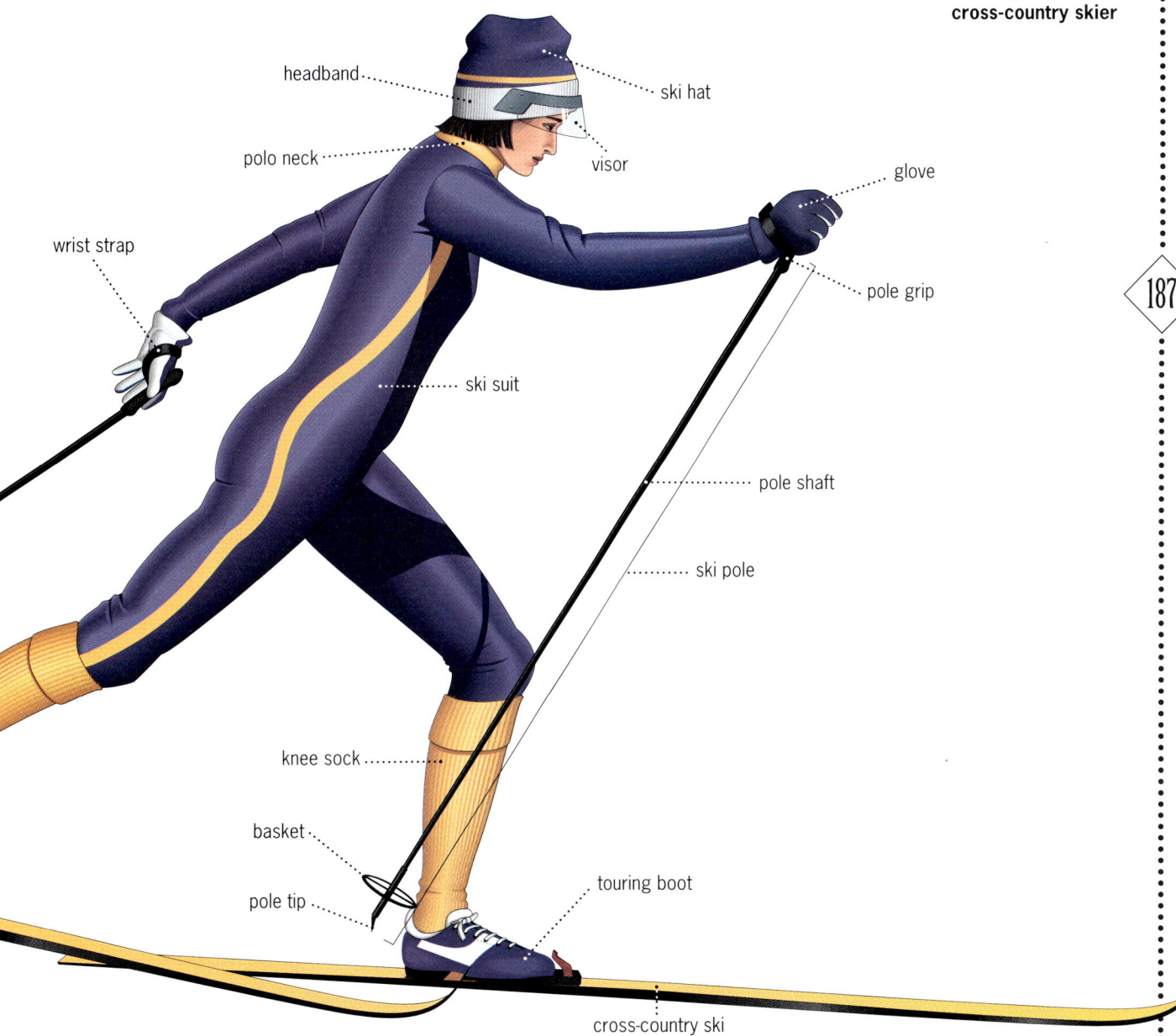

- headband
- ski hat
- polo neck
- visor
- glove
- wrist strap
- pole grip
- ski suit
- pole shaft
- ski pole
- knee sock
- basket
- touring boot
- pole tip
- cross-country ski

187

ATHLETICS

GYMNASTICS

pommel horse

horse

base

neck — saddle — croup — pommel

fastening system

vaulting horse

balance beam

springboard

trampoline

safety pad — bed

leg — spring — frame

ATHLETICS

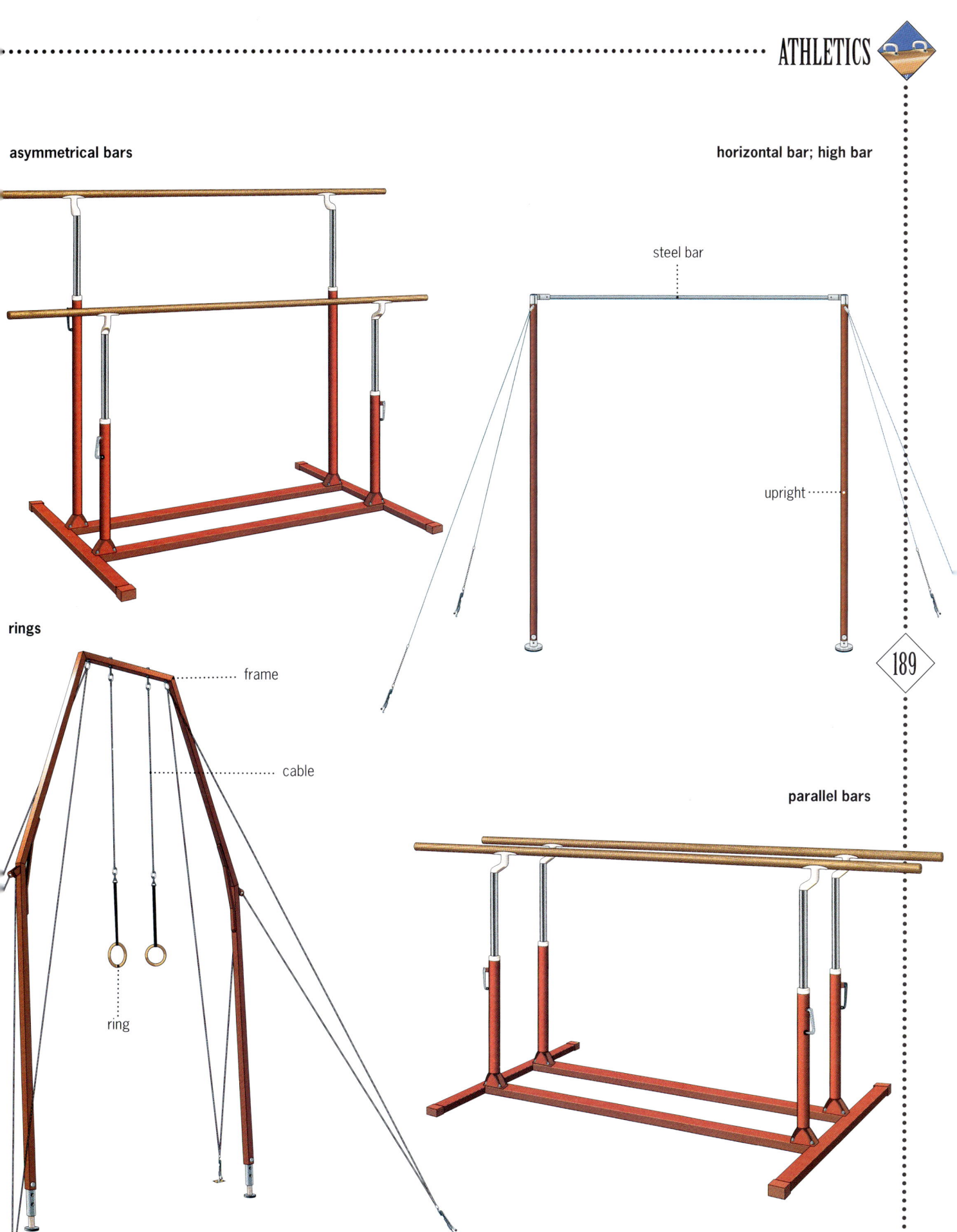

asymmetrical bars

horizontal bar; high bar

steel bar

upright

189

rings

frame

cable

ring

parallel bars

CAMPING

TENTS

two-person tent

- rainfly
- door
- awning
- guy line
- strainer
- zipper
- inner tent
- stake

MAJOR TYPES OF TENTS

wagon tent

wall tent

pup tent

dome tent

pop-up tent

family tent

one-person tent

CAMPING

SLEEPING EQUIPMENT

BEDS AND MATTRESSES

foam pad

self-inflating mattress

inflator

inflator-deflator

folding cot

air mattress

SLEEPING BAGS

mummy

semi-mummy

rectangular

191

CAMPING

CAMPING EQUIPMENT

Swiss army knife

- scissors
- ruler
- fish scaler
- file
- cross-tip screwdriver
- magnifier
- small blade
- bottle opener
- screwdriver
- nail nick
- awl
- corkscrew
- can opener
- large blade
- screwdriver

hatchet

leather sheath

knife

sheath

flashlight

COOKING SET

canteen

coffee pot

frying pan

handle

plate

cup

saucepan

CAMPING

backpack

- top flap
- shoulder strap
- side compression strap
- internal frame
- waist belt
- tightening buckle
- strap loop
- front compression strap

193

magnetic compass

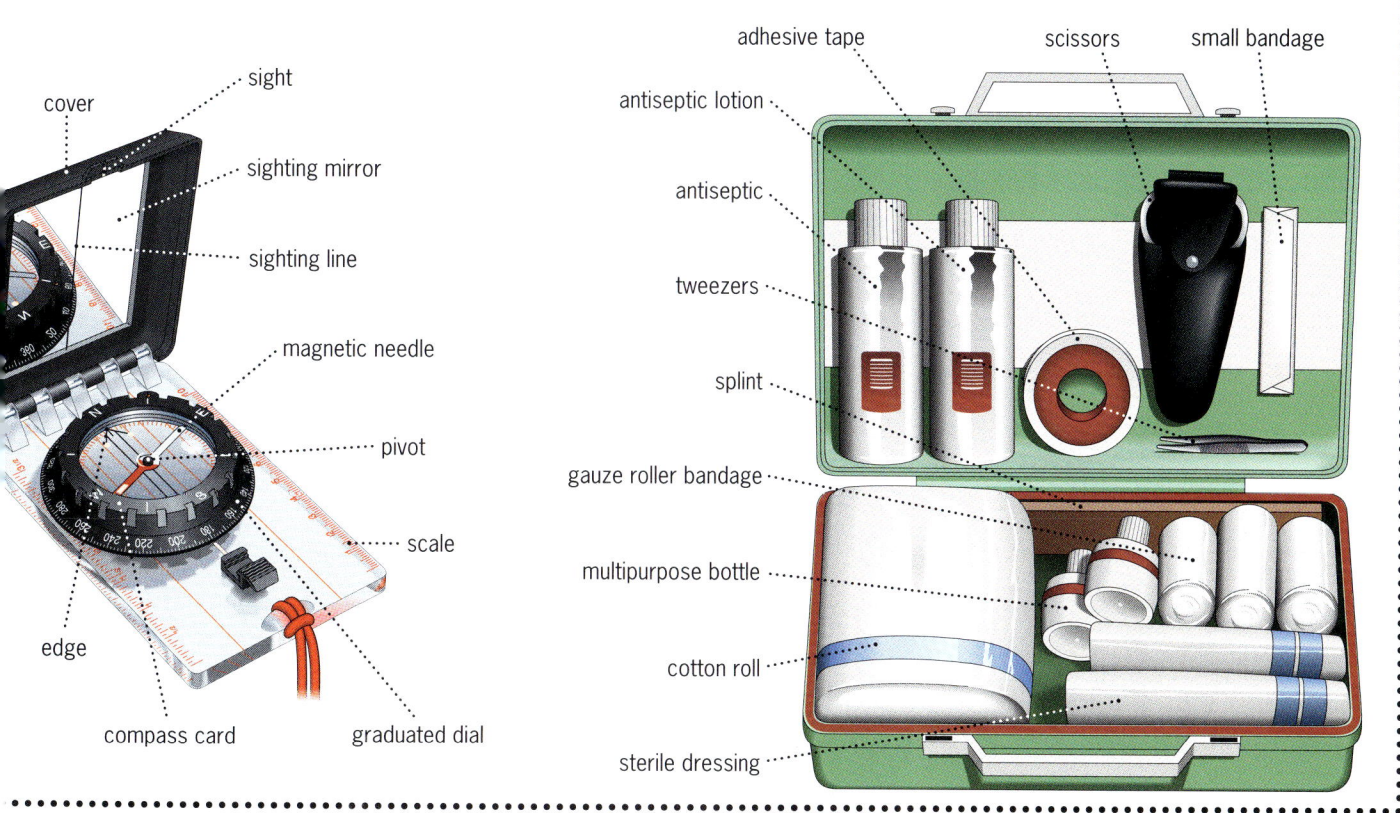

- cover
- sight
- sighting mirror
- sighting line
- magnetic needle
- pivot
- scale
- edge
- compass card
- graduated dial

first aid kit

- adhesive tape
- scissors
- small bandage
- antiseptic lotion
- antiseptic
- tweezers
- splint
- gauze roller bandage
- multipurpose bottle
- cotton roll
- sterile dressing

INDOOR GAMES

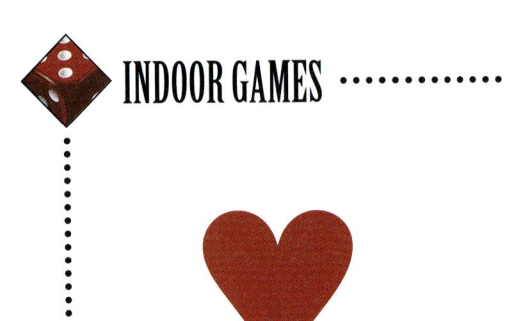

CARD GAMES

heart

diamond

club

spade

Joker

Ace

King

Queen

Jack

DICE

poker die

ordinary die

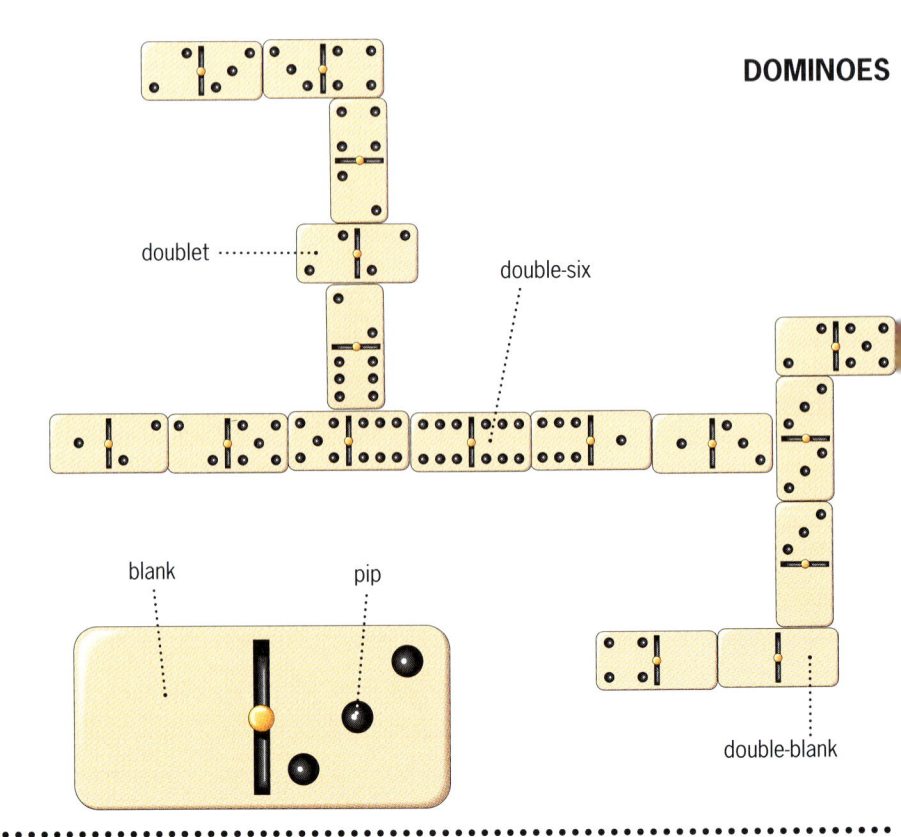

DOMINOES

doublet

double-six

blank

pip

double-blank

INDOOR GAMES

CHESS

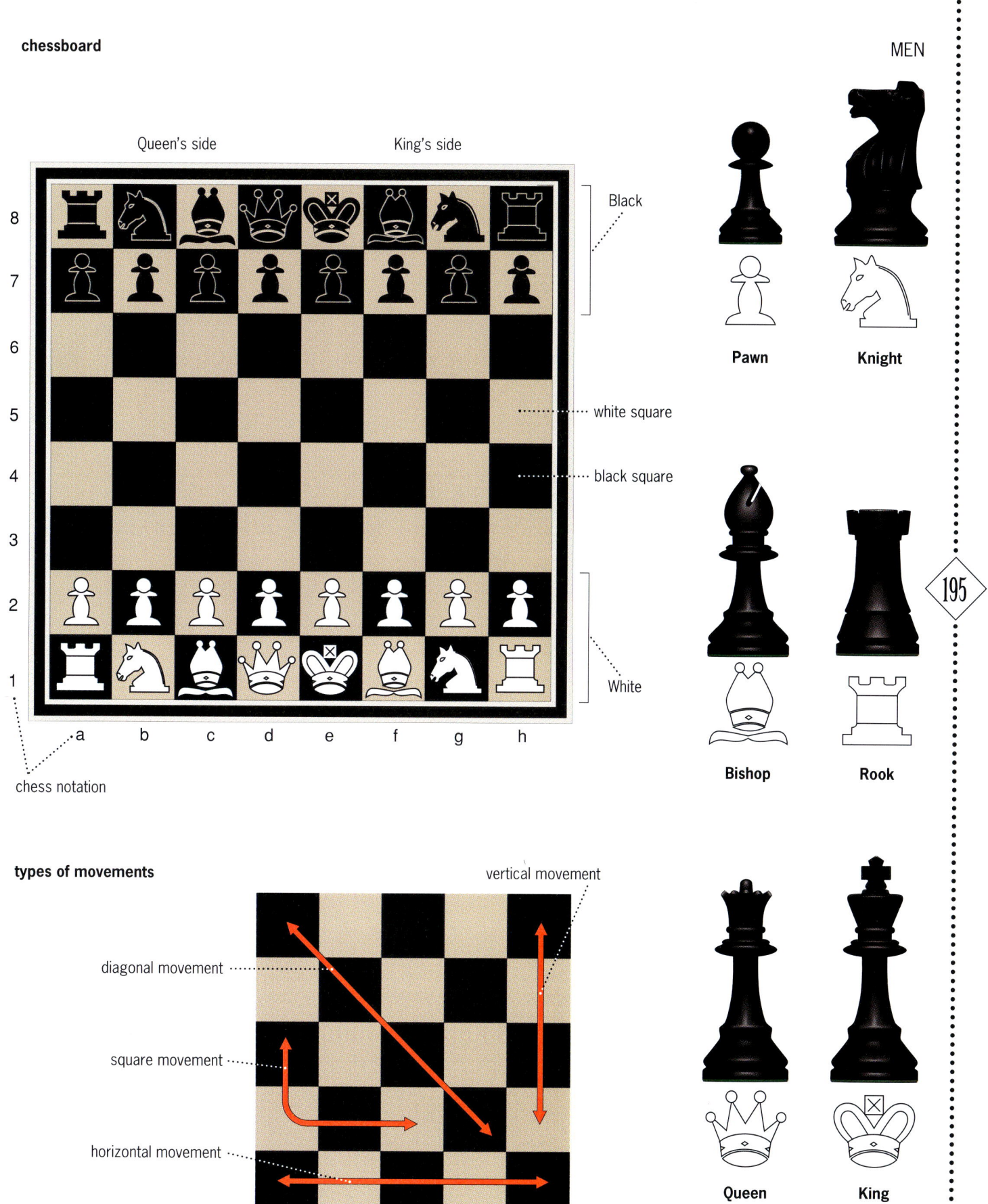

chessboard

Queen's side   King's side

Black

white square

black square

White

a b c d e f g h

chess notation

types of movements

vertical movement

diagonal movement

square movement

horizontal movement

MEN

Pawn   **Knight**

Bishop   **Rook**

Queen   **King**

195

INDOOR GAMES

BACKGAMMON

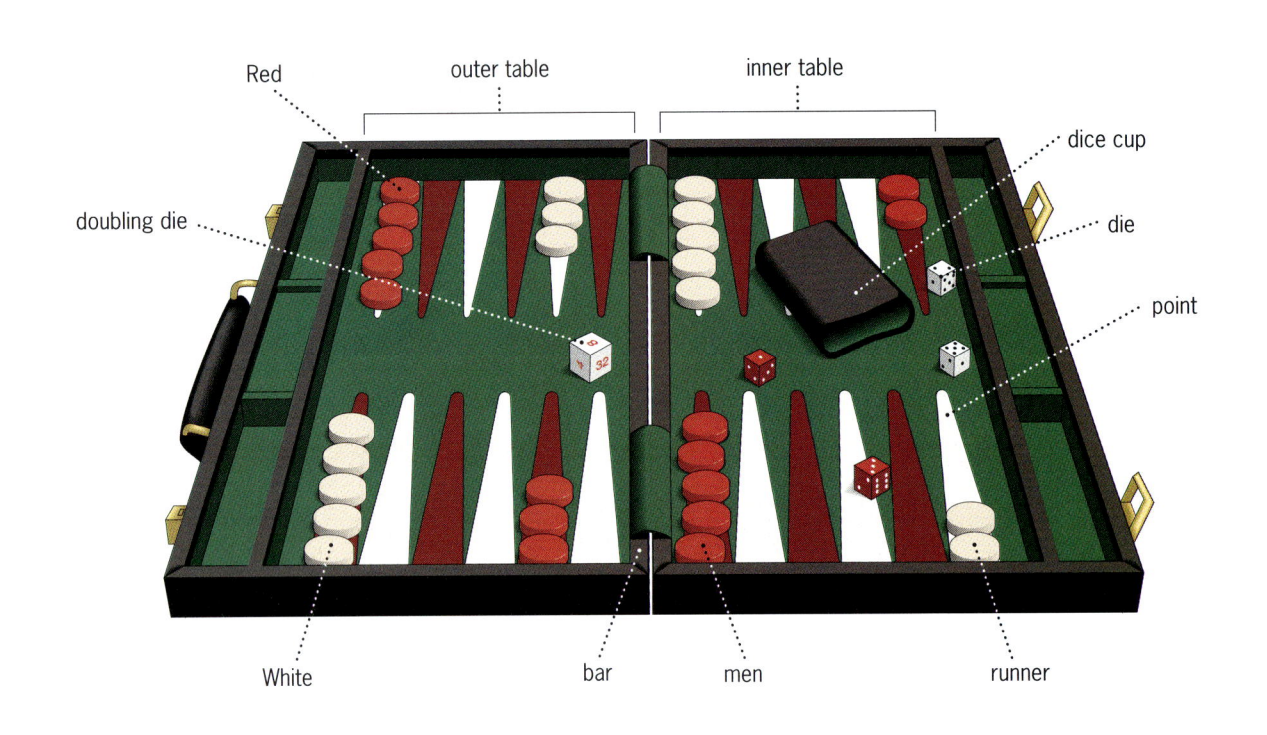

- Red
- outer table
- inner table
- dice cup
- doubling die
- die
- point
- White
- bar
- men
- runner

CHECKERS

- checker
- checkerboard

INDOOR GAMES

VIDEO ENTERTAINMENT SYSTEM

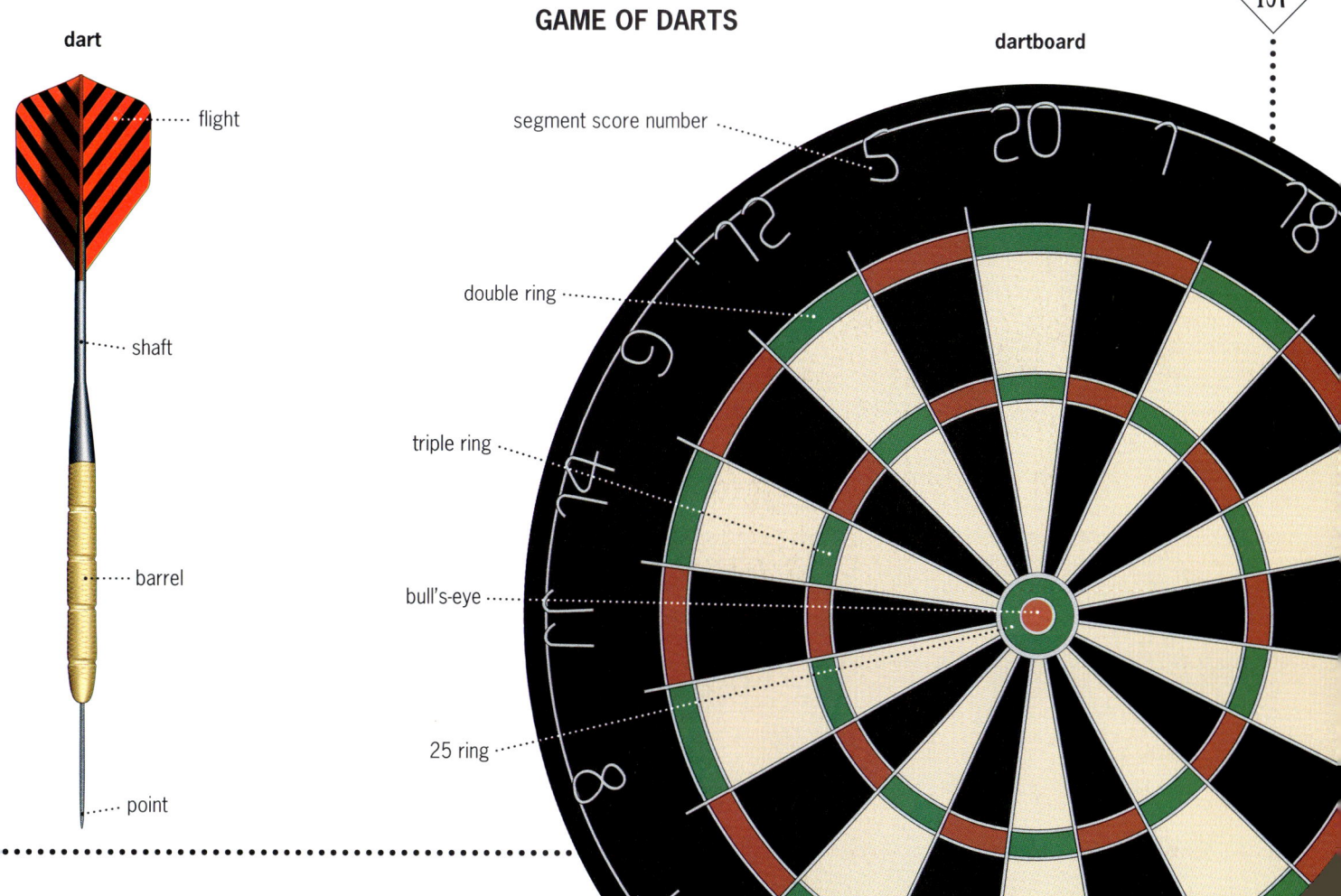

- visual display
- game cartridge
- control deck
- control pad
- function button

GAME OF DARTS

dart
- flight
- shaft
- barrel
- point

dartboard
- segment score number
- double ring
- triple ring
- bull's-eye
- 25 ring

MEASURING DEVICES

MEASURE OF TIME

stopwatch

- ring
- start button
- reset button
- stop button
- second hand
- minute hand
- 1/10th second hand
- case

analog watch
- dial

kitchen timer

egg timer

digital watch
- liquid crystal display

sundial
- gnomon
- shadow
- dial

MEASURING DEVICES

MEASURE OF TEMPERATURE

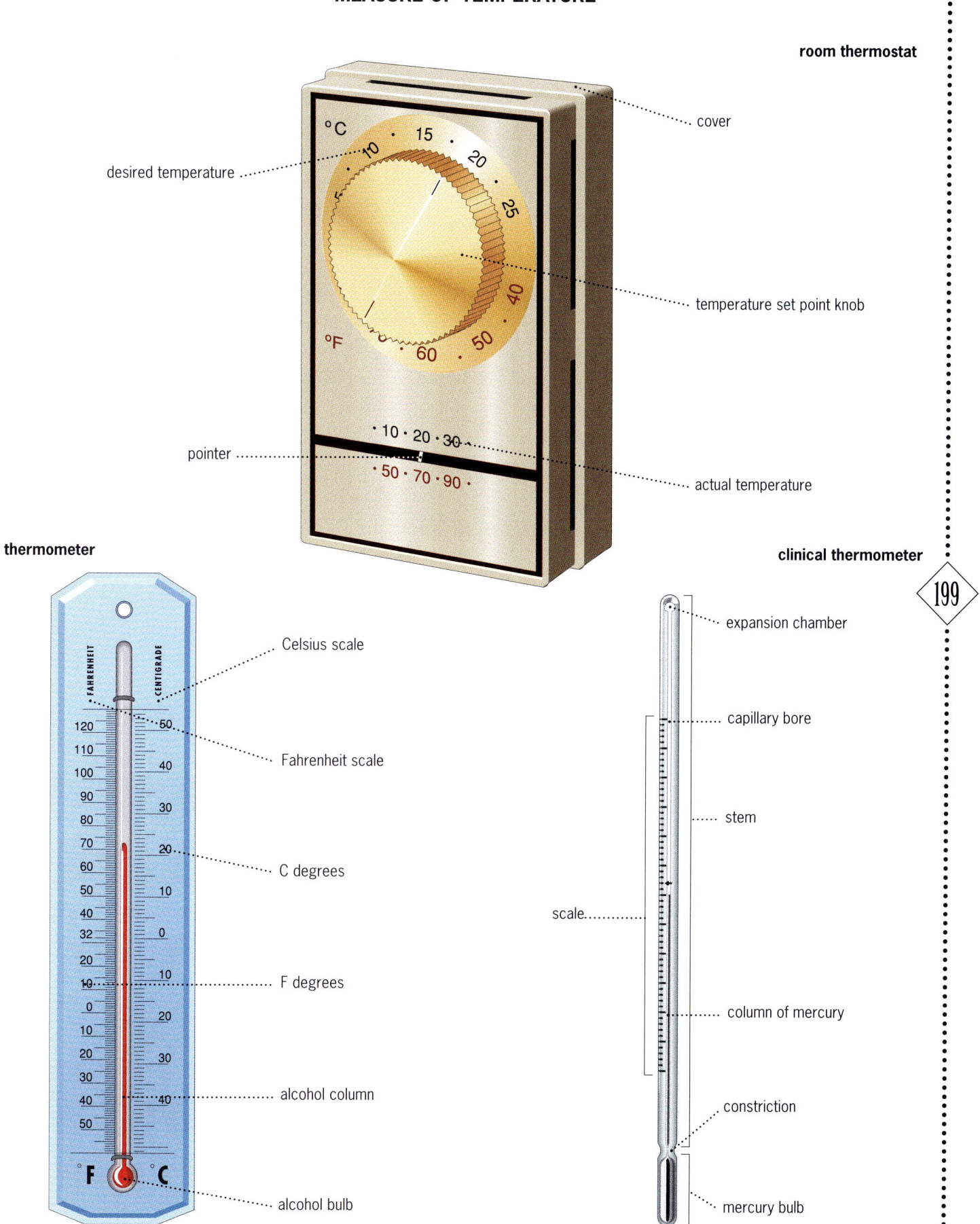

room thermostat

- cover
- desired temperature
- temperature set point knob
- pointer
- actual temperature

thermometer

- Celsius scale
- Fahrenheit scale
- C degrees
- F degrees
- alcohol column
- alcohol bulb

clinical thermometer

- expansion chamber
- capillary bore
- stem
- scale
- column of mercury
- constriction
- mercury bulb

199

MEASURING DEVICES

MEASURE OF WEIGHT

balance

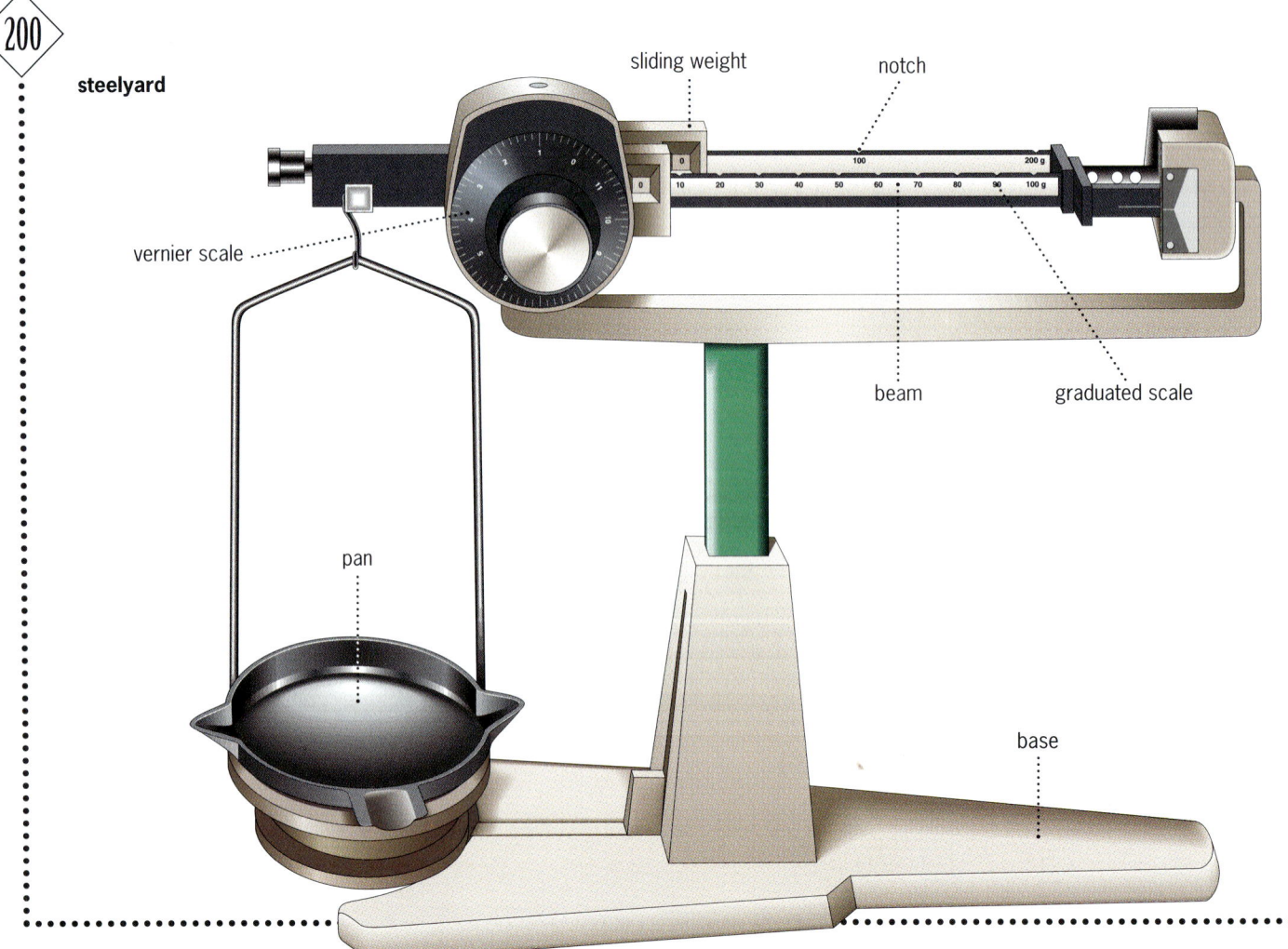

dial — pointer — weight — pan — base — beam

steelyard

sliding weight — notch — vernier scale — pan — beam — graduated scale — base

MEASURING DEVICES

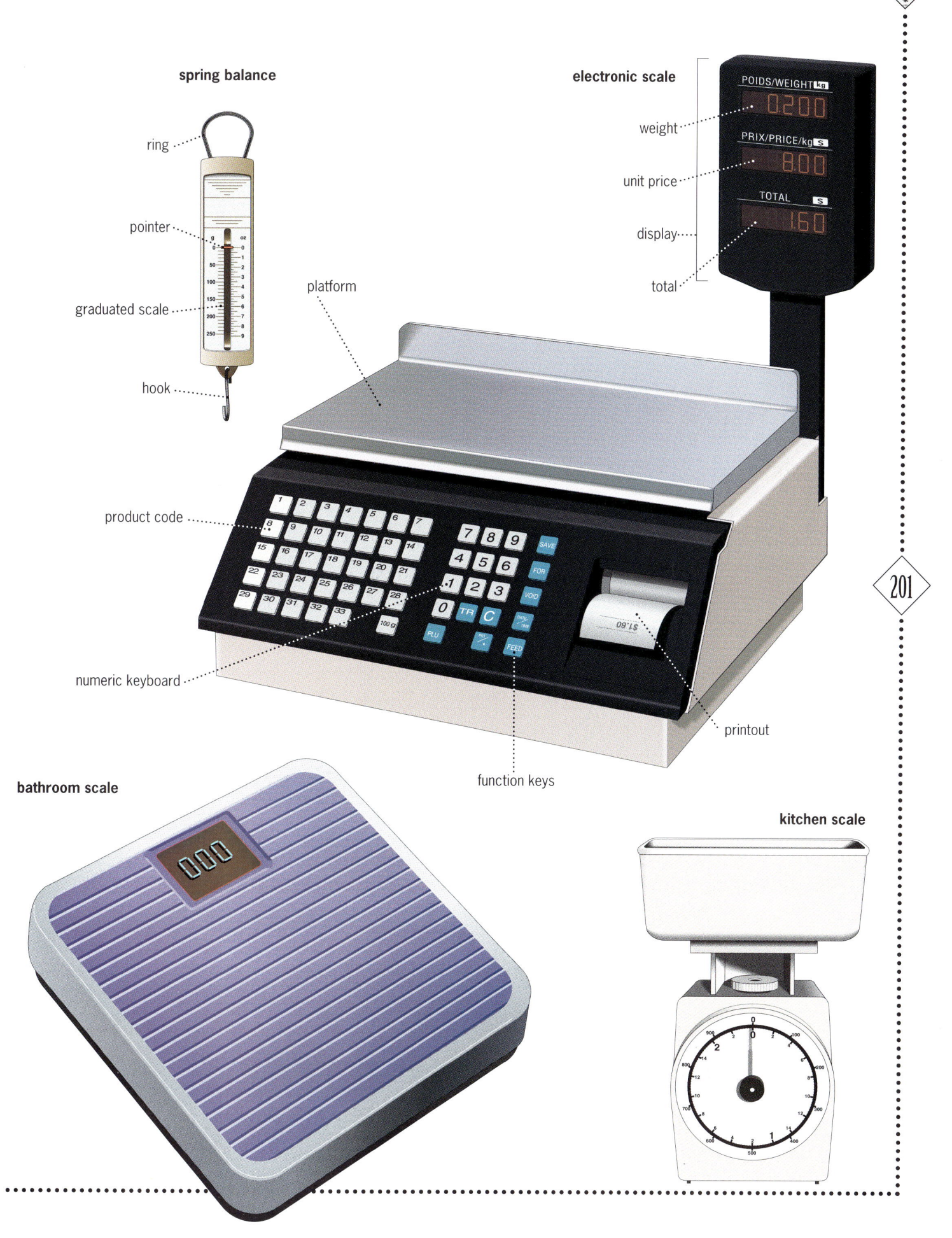

spring balance
- ring
- pointer
- graduated scale
- hook

electronic scale
- weight
- unit price
- display
- total
- platform
- product code
- numeric keyboard
- function keys
- printout

bathroom scale

kitchen scale

201

ENERGY

OIL

PROSPECTING

surface prospecting

DRILLING

drilling rig

GROUND TRANSPORT

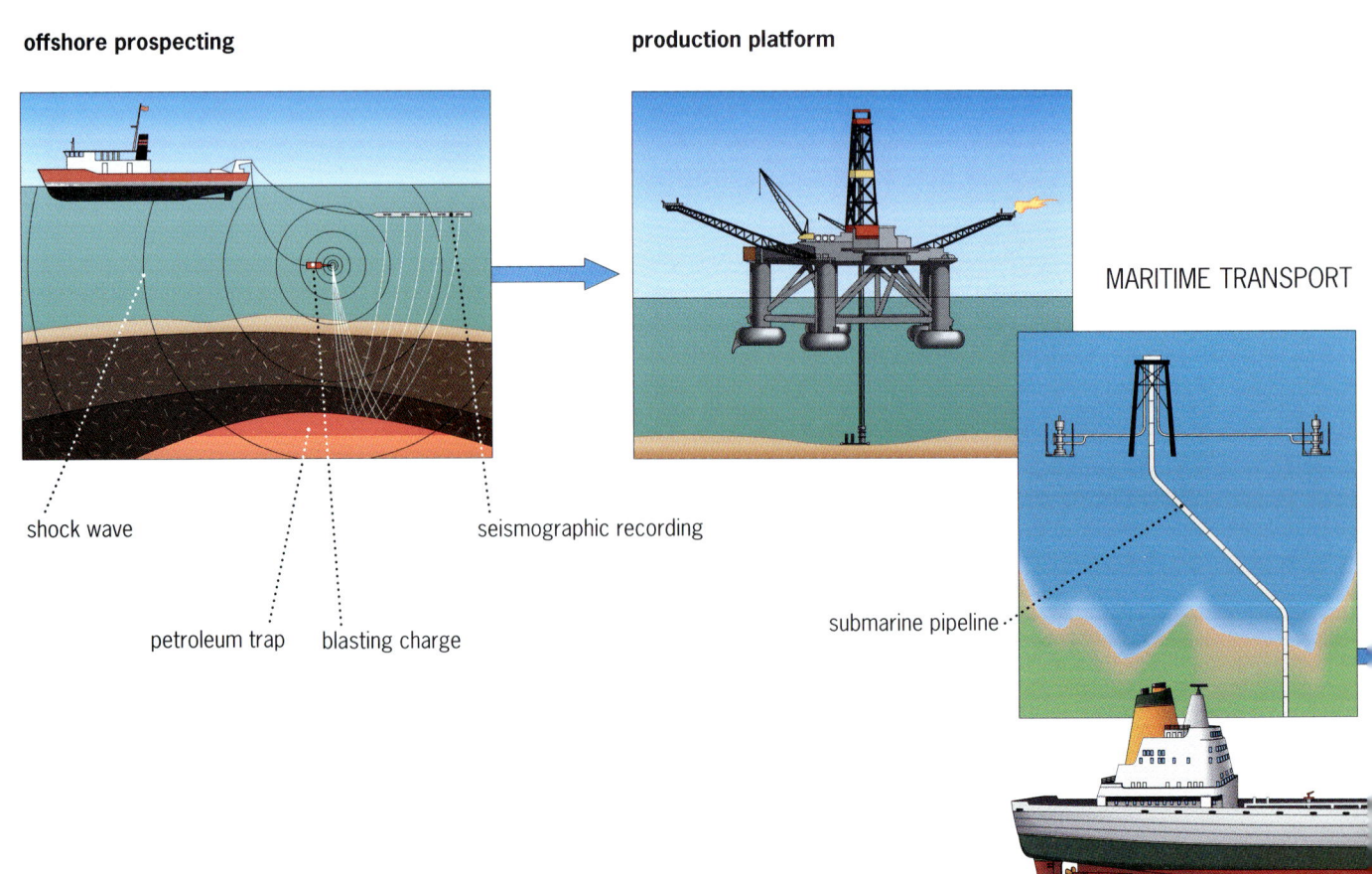

pipeline

tank trailer

offshore prospecting

shock wave

petroleum trap   blasting charge

seismographic recording

production platform

MARITIME TRANSPORT

submarine pipeline

ENERGY

REFINERY PRODUCTS

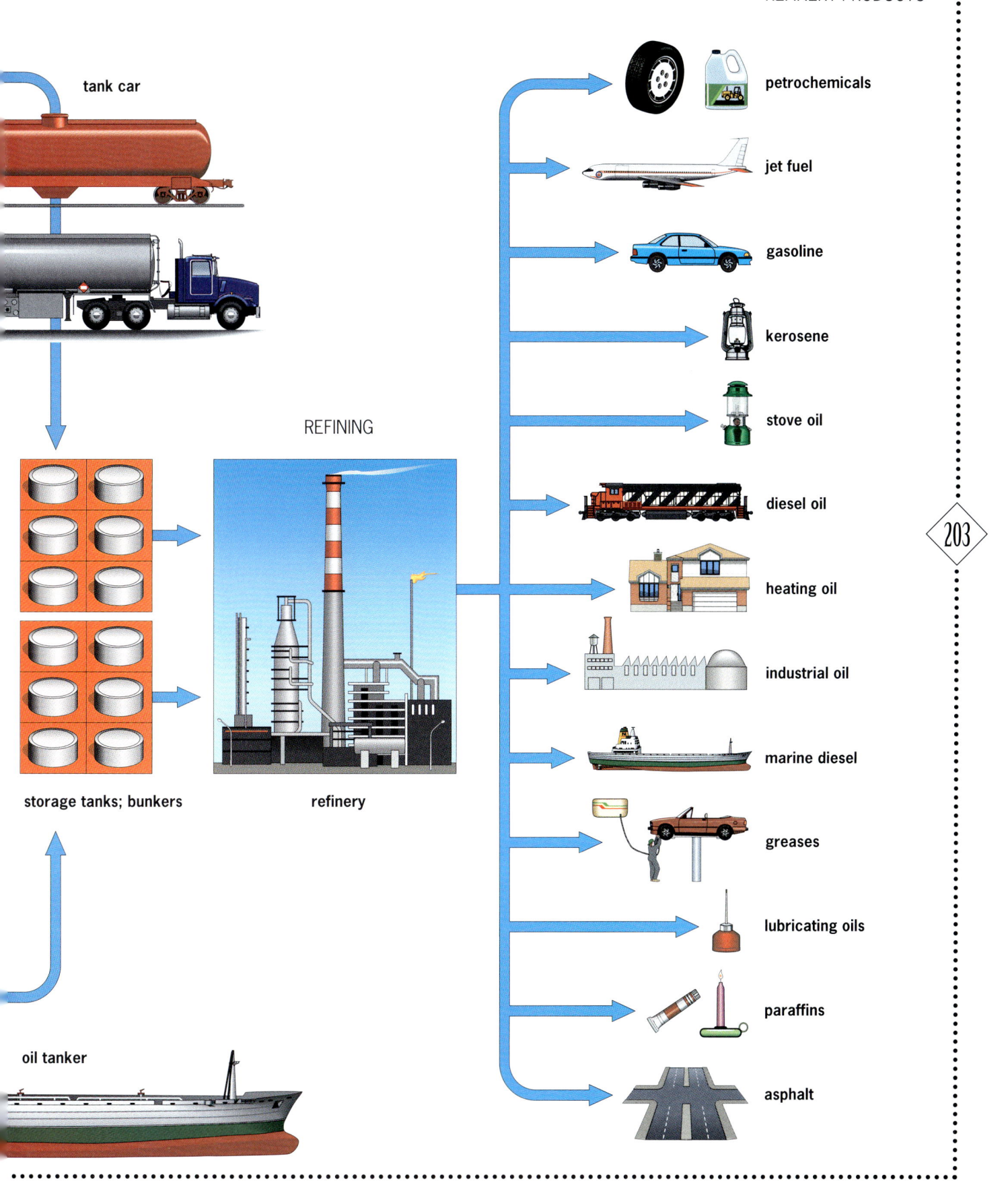

tank car

REFINING

storage tanks; bunkers

refinery

oil tanker

petrochemicals

jet fuel

gasoline

kerosene

stove oil

diesel oil

heating oil

industrial oil

marine diesel

greases

lubricating oils

paraffins

asphalt

203

ENERGY

HYDROELECTRIC ENERGY

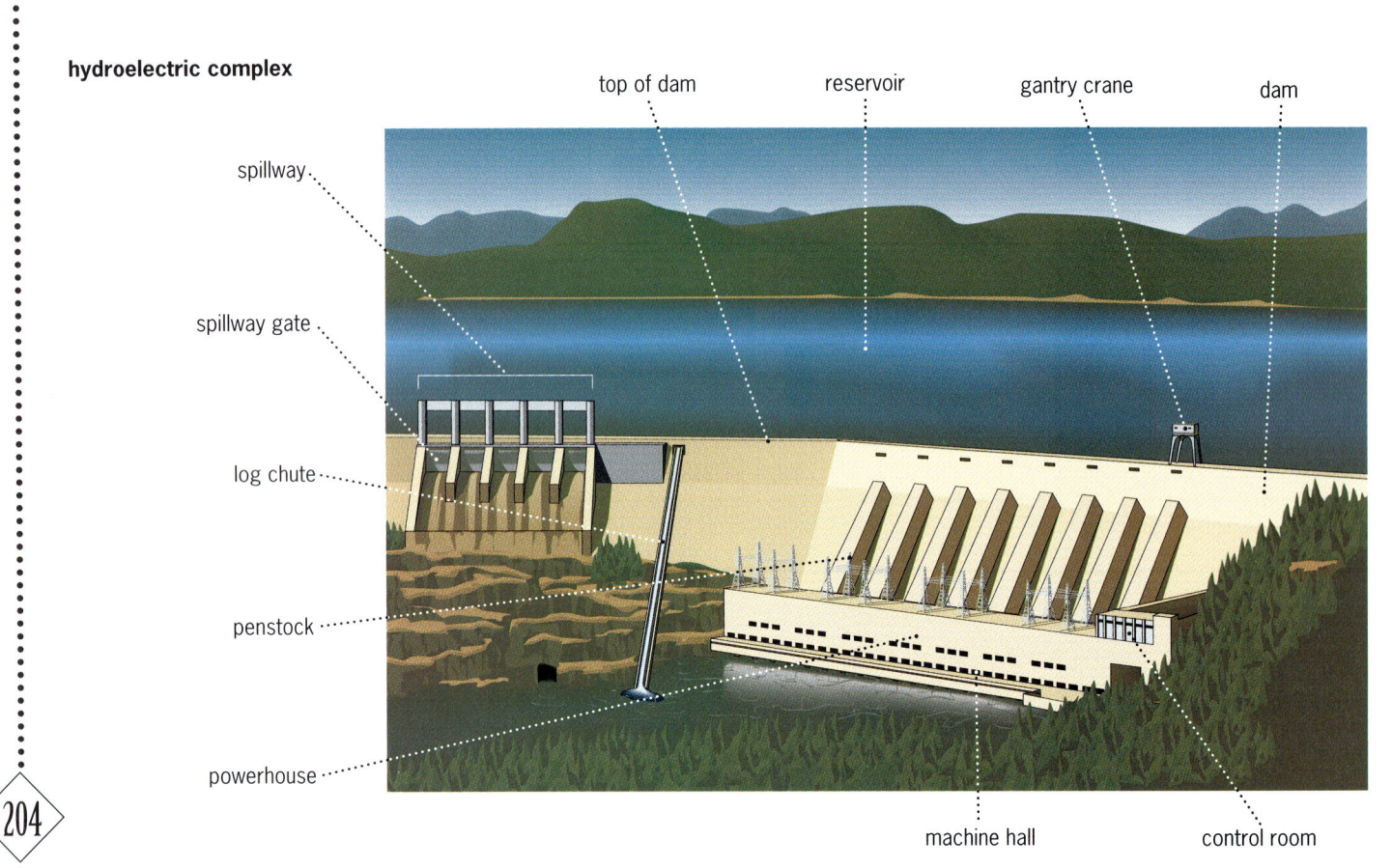

hydroelectric complex

- spillway
- top of dam
- reservoir
- gantry crane
- dam
- spillway gate
- log chute
- penstock
- powerhouse
- machine hall
- control room

cross section of hydroelectric power station

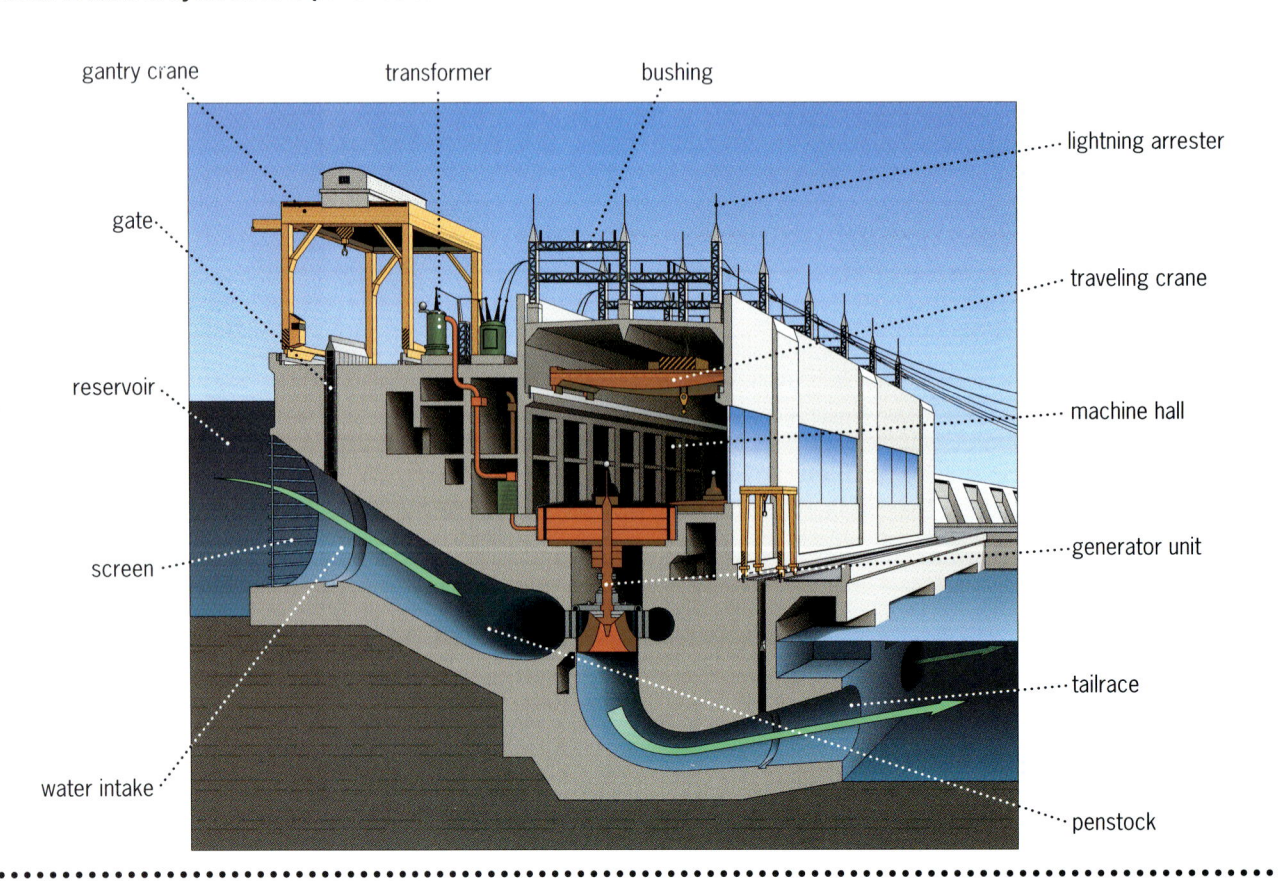

- gantry crane
- transformer
- bushing
- lightning arrester
- gate
- traveling crane
- reservoir
- machine hall
- screen
- generator unit
- tailrace
- water intake
- penstock

ENERGY

electric circuit

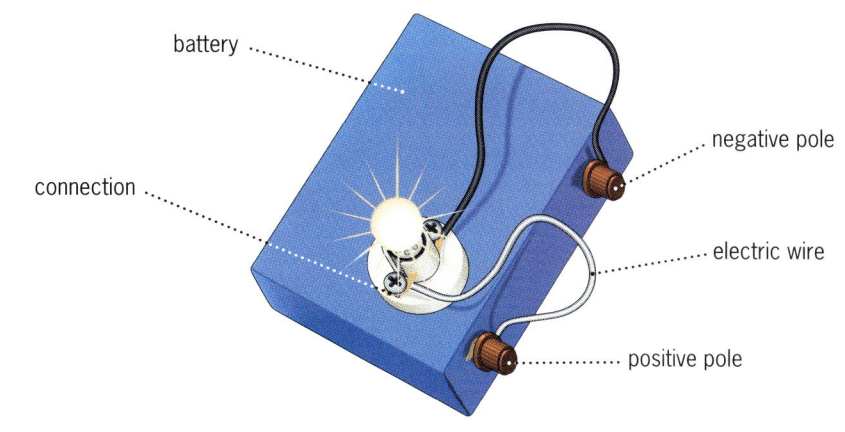

- battery
- connection
- negative pole
- electric wire
- positive pole

steps in production of electricity

- supply of water
- energy integration to the transmission network
- voltage increase
- production of electricity by the generator
- high-tension electricity transmission
- voltage decrease
- transmission to consumers
- head of water
- water under pressure
- transmission of the rotative movement to the rotor
- turbined water draining
- transformation of mechanical work into electricity
- rotation of the turbine

205

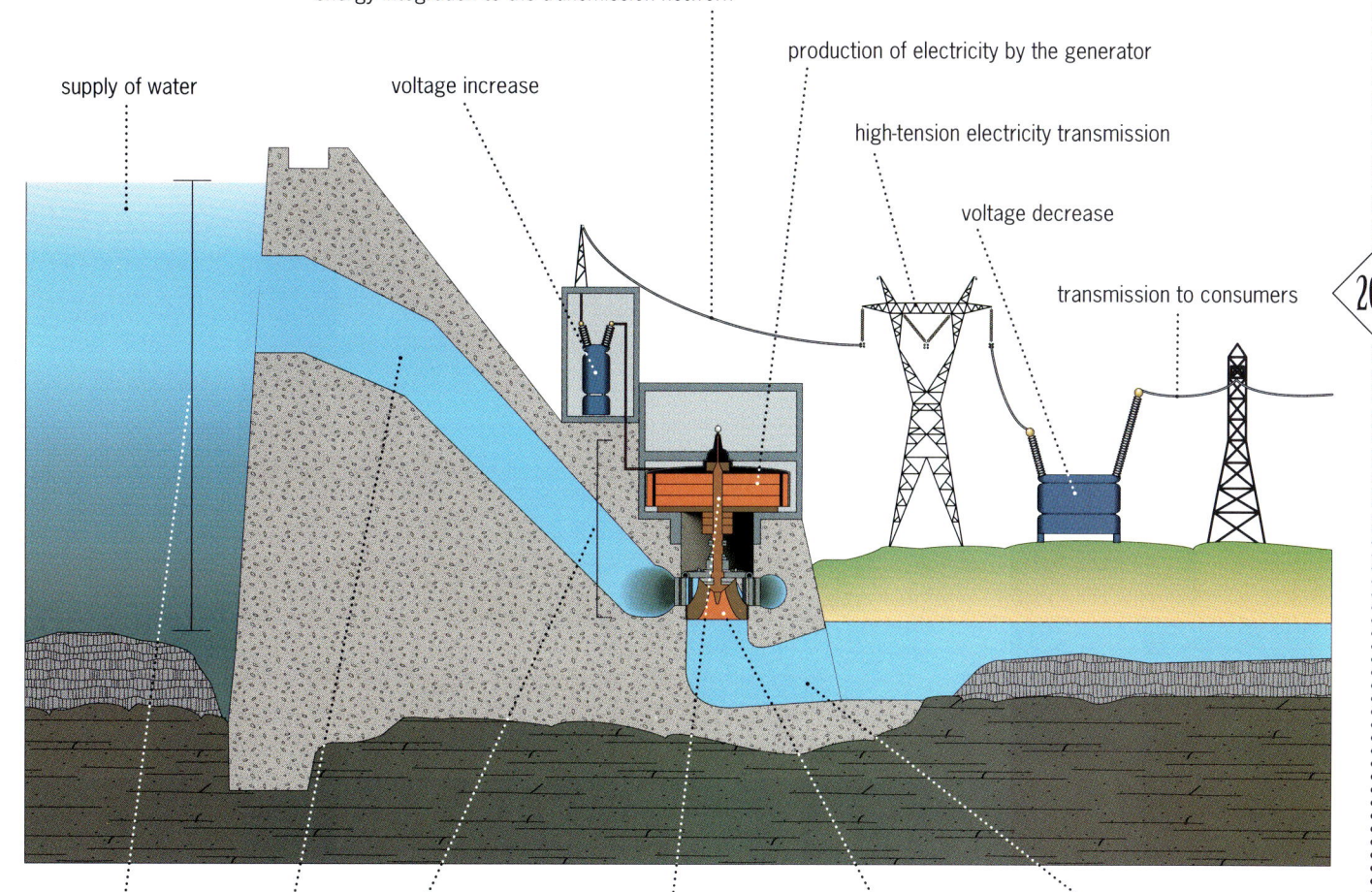

ENERGY

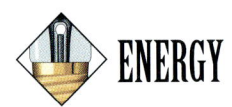

NUCLEAR ENERGY

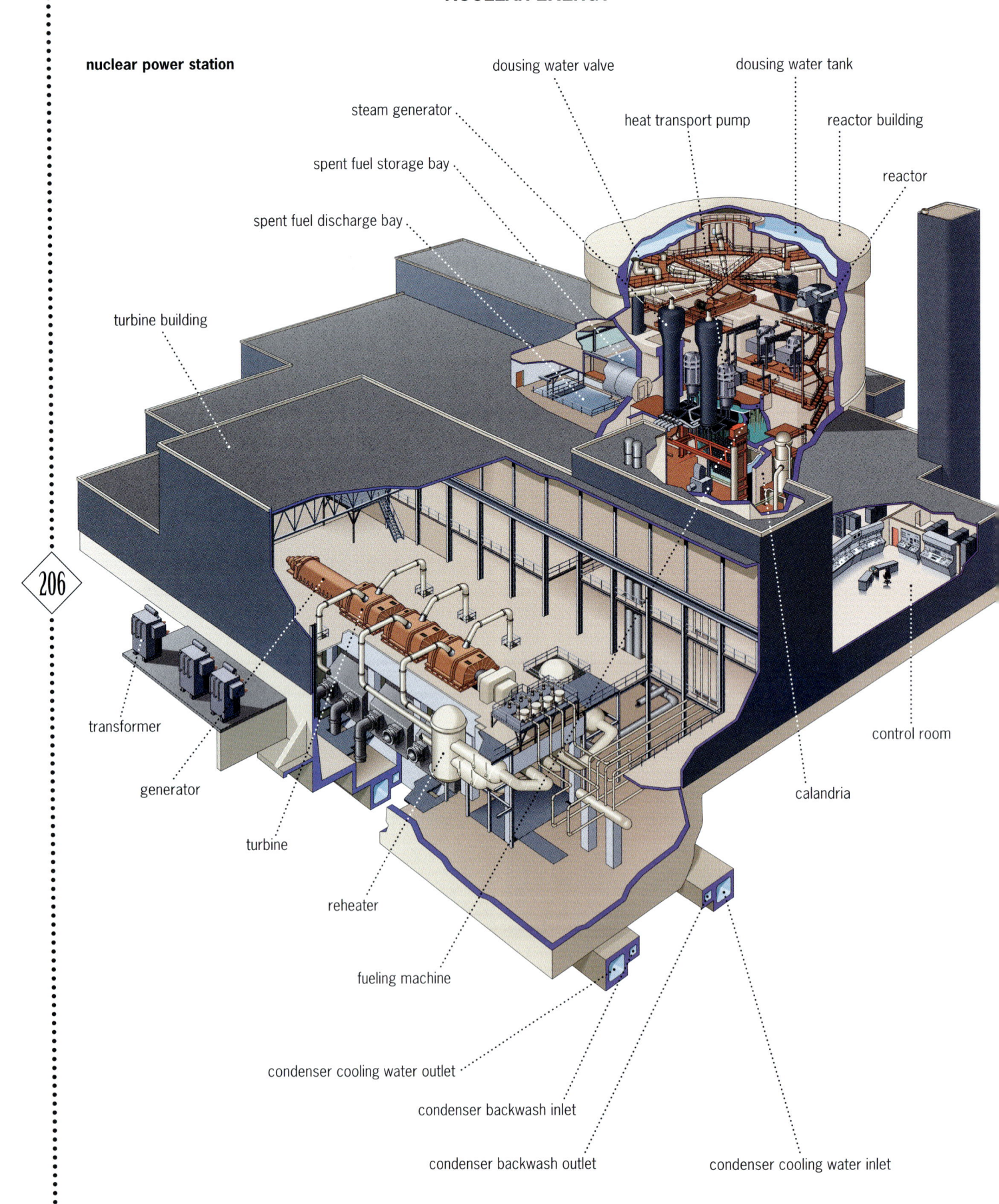

nuclear power station

- dousing water valve
- dousing water tank
- steam generator
- heat transport pump
- reactor building
- spent fuel storage bay
- reactor
- spent fuel discharge bay
- turbine building
- transformer
- generator
- turbine
- reheater
- fueling machine
- control room
- calandria
- condenser cooling water outlet
- condenser backwash inlet
- condenser backwash outlet
- condenser cooling water inlet

ENERGY

production of electricity from nuclear energy

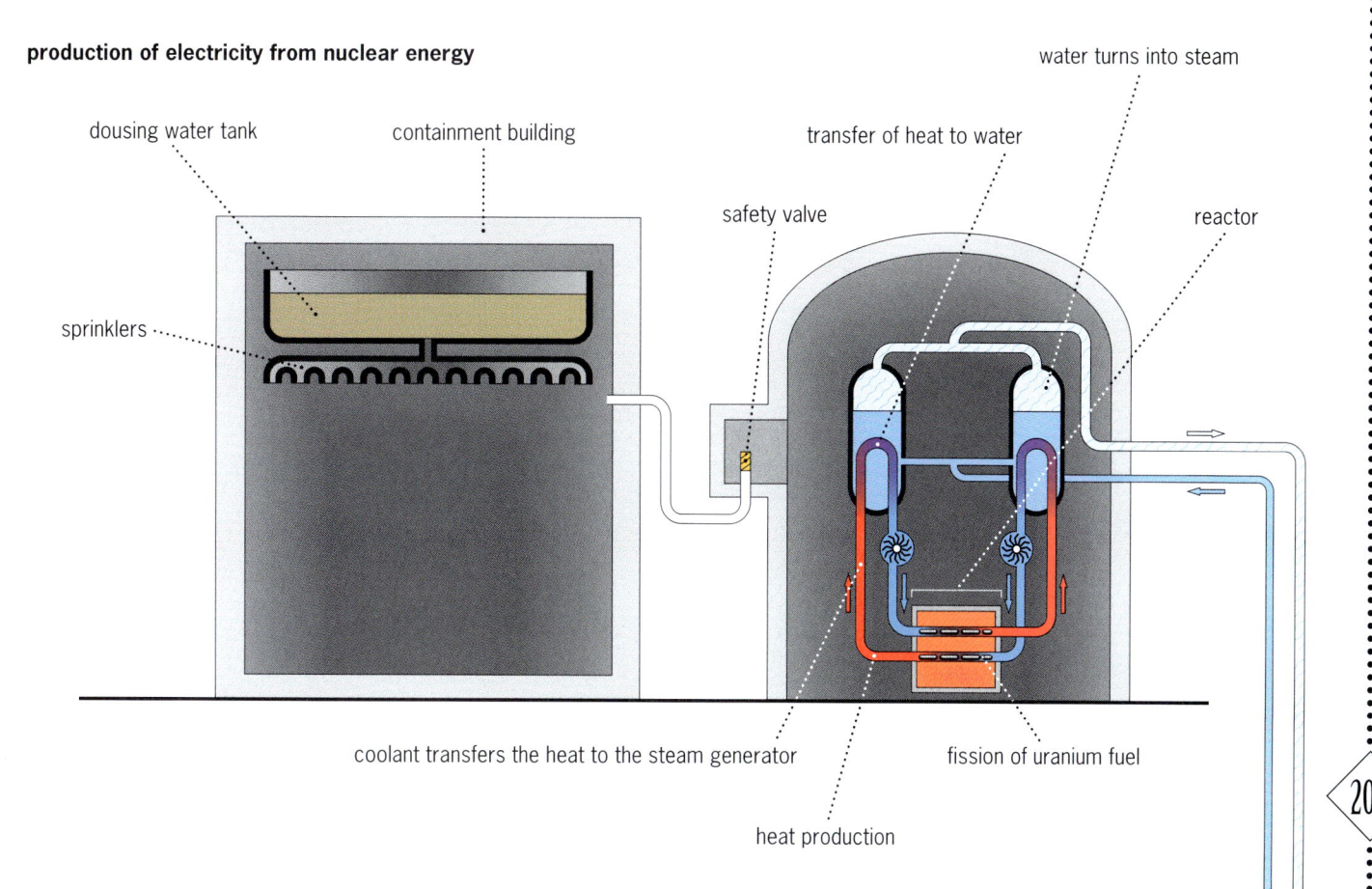

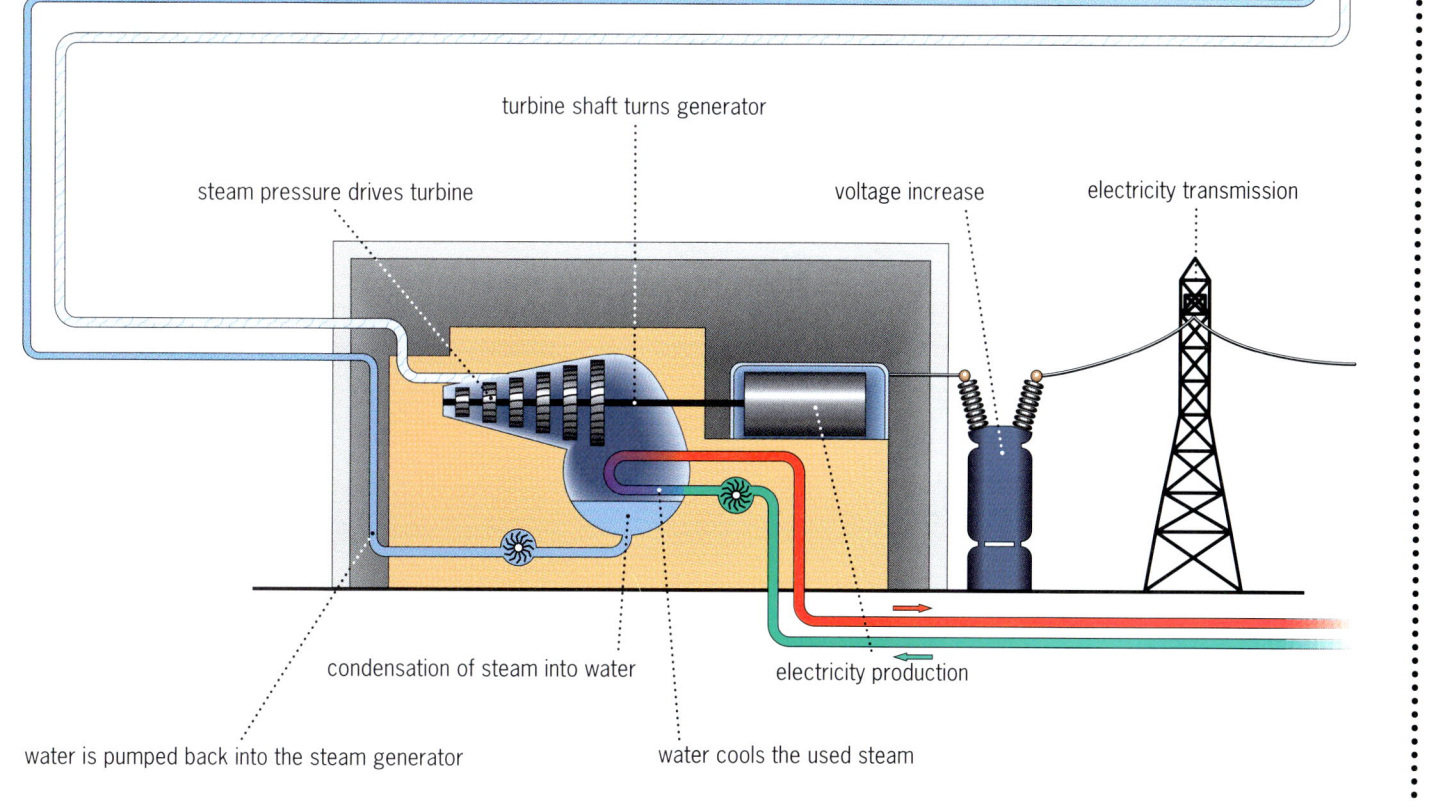

- dousing water tank
- containment building
- safety valve
- transfer of heat to water
- water turns into steam
- reactor
- sprinklers
- coolant transfers the heat to the steam generator
- fission of uranium fuel
- heat production
- steam pressure drives turbine
- turbine shaft turns generator
- voltage increase
- electricity transmission
- condensation of steam into water
- electricity production
- water is pumped back into the steam generator
- water cools the used steam

207

ENERGY

SOLAR ENERGY

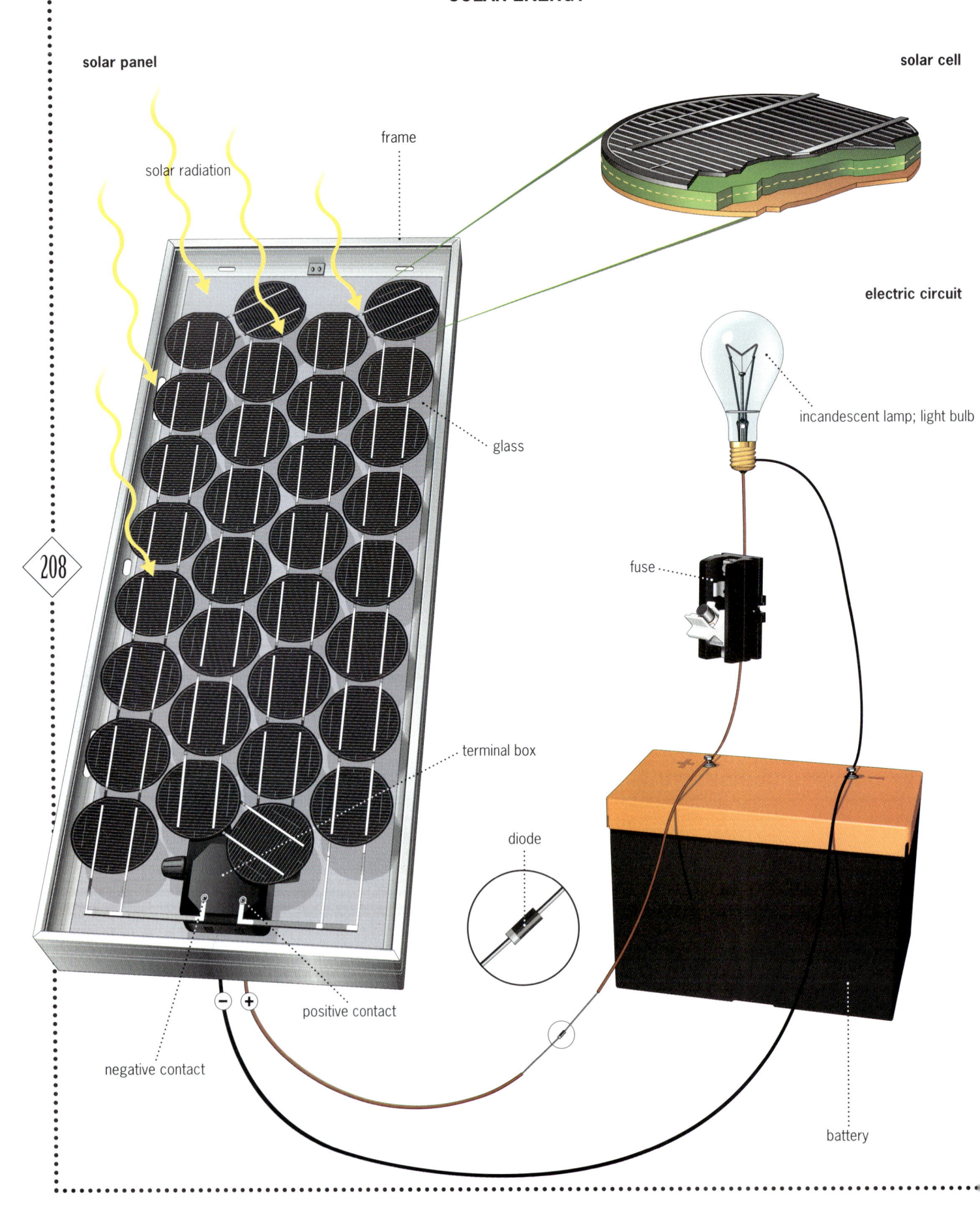

solar panel

solar radiation

frame

solar cell

glass

electric circuit

incandescent lamp; light bulb

fuse

terminal box

diode

negative contact

positive contact

battery

ENERGY

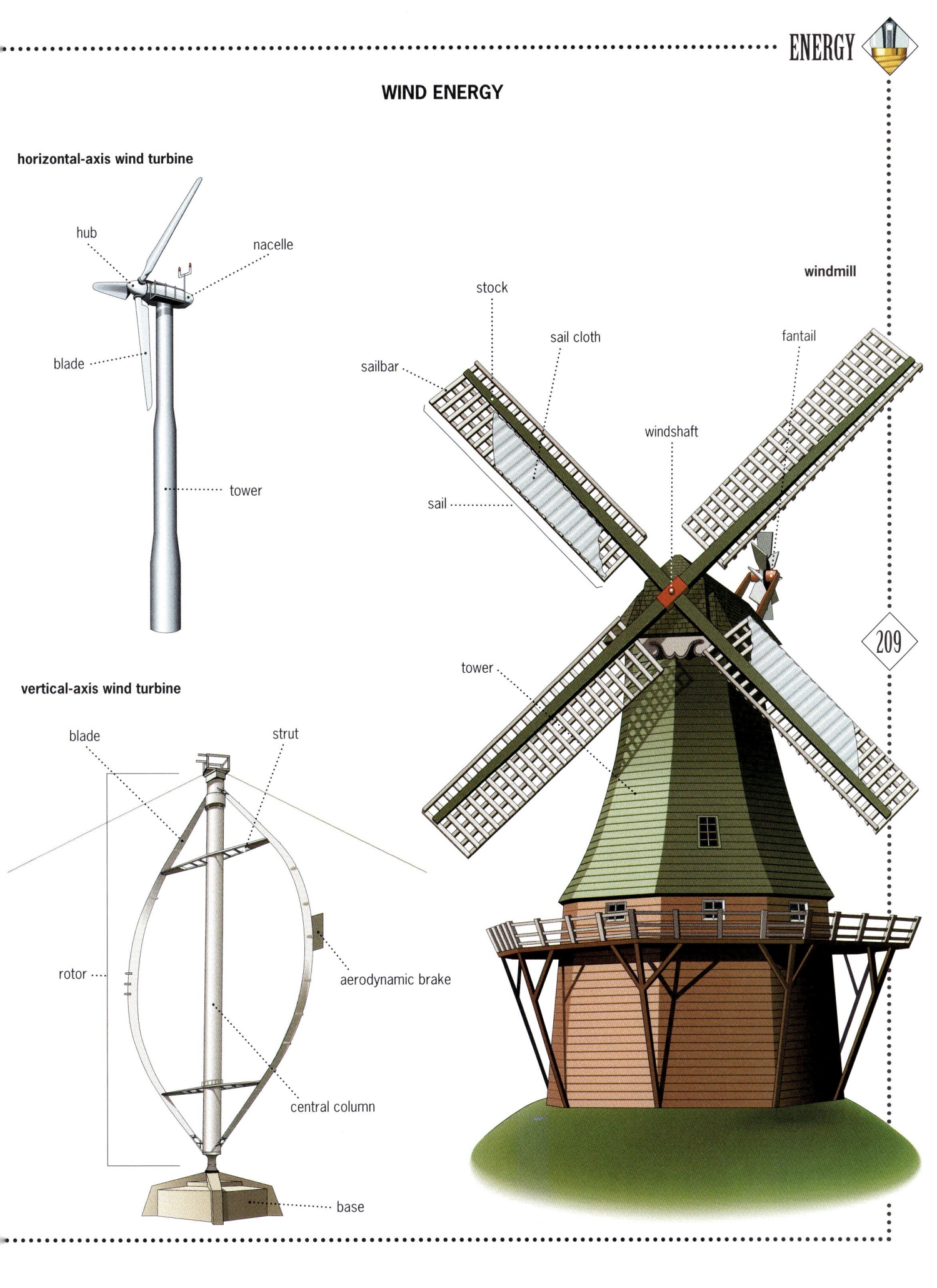

WIND ENERGY

horizontal-axis wind turbine

- hub
- nacelle
- blade
- tower

vertical-axis wind turbine

- blade
- strut
- rotor
- aerodynamic brake
- central column
- base

windmill

- stock
- sail cloth
- fantail
- sailbar
- windshaft
- sail
- tower

WIND ENERGY

HEAVY MACHINERY

FIRE PREVENTION

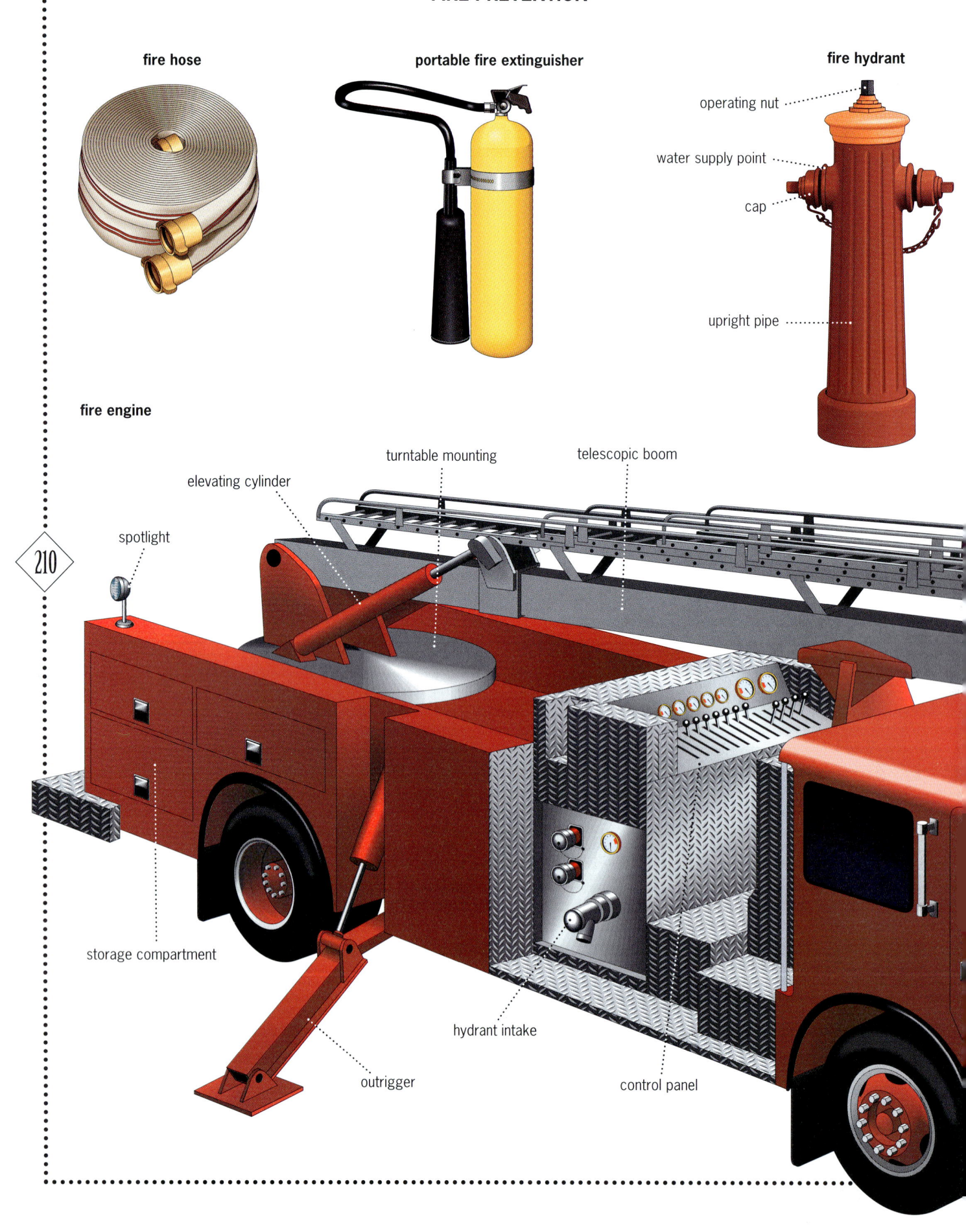

fire hose

portable fire extinguisher

fire hydrant
- operating nut
- water supply point
- cap
- upright pipe

fire engine
- spotlight
- elevating cylinder
- turntable mounting
- telescopic boom
- storage compartment
- outrigger
- hydrant intake
- control panel

HEAVY MACHINERY

pike pole

fire-fighter's hatchet

fire-fighter

compressed-air cylinder

helmet

full face mask

self-contained breathing apparatus

air-supply tube

tower ladder

flashing light

top ladder

warning device

ladder pipe nozzle

fireproof and waterproof garment

rubber boot

211

HEAVY MACHINERY

HEAVY VEHICLES

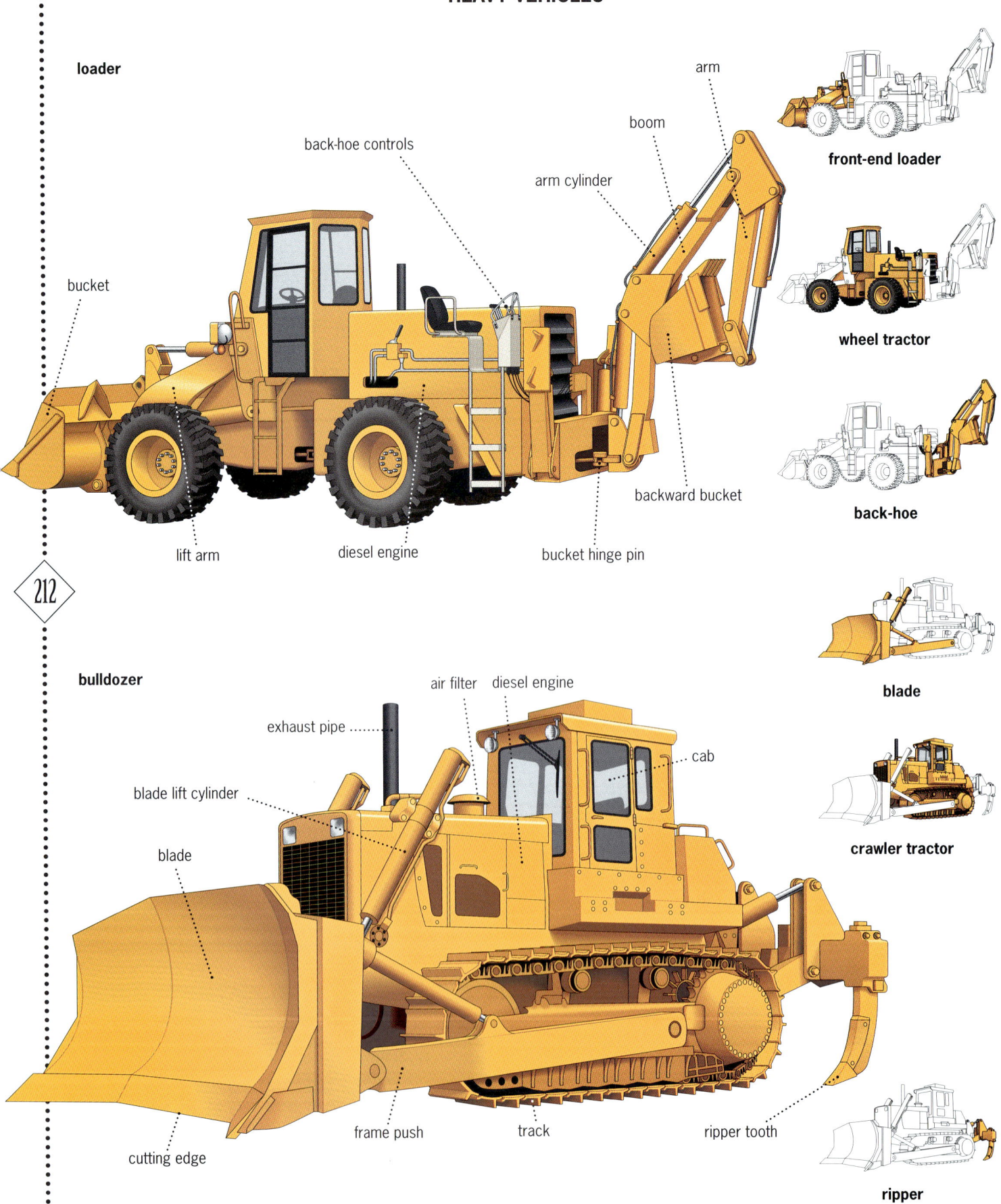

loader

- bucket
- lift arm
- diesel engine
- back-hoe controls
- arm cylinder
- boom
- arm
- backward bucket
- bucket hinge pin

front-end loader

wheel tractor

back-hoe

bulldozer

- blade
- cutting edge
- blade lift cylinder
- exhaust pipe
- air filter
- diesel engine
- cab
- frame push
- track
- ripper tooth

blade

crawler tractor

ripper

212

HEAVY MACHINERY

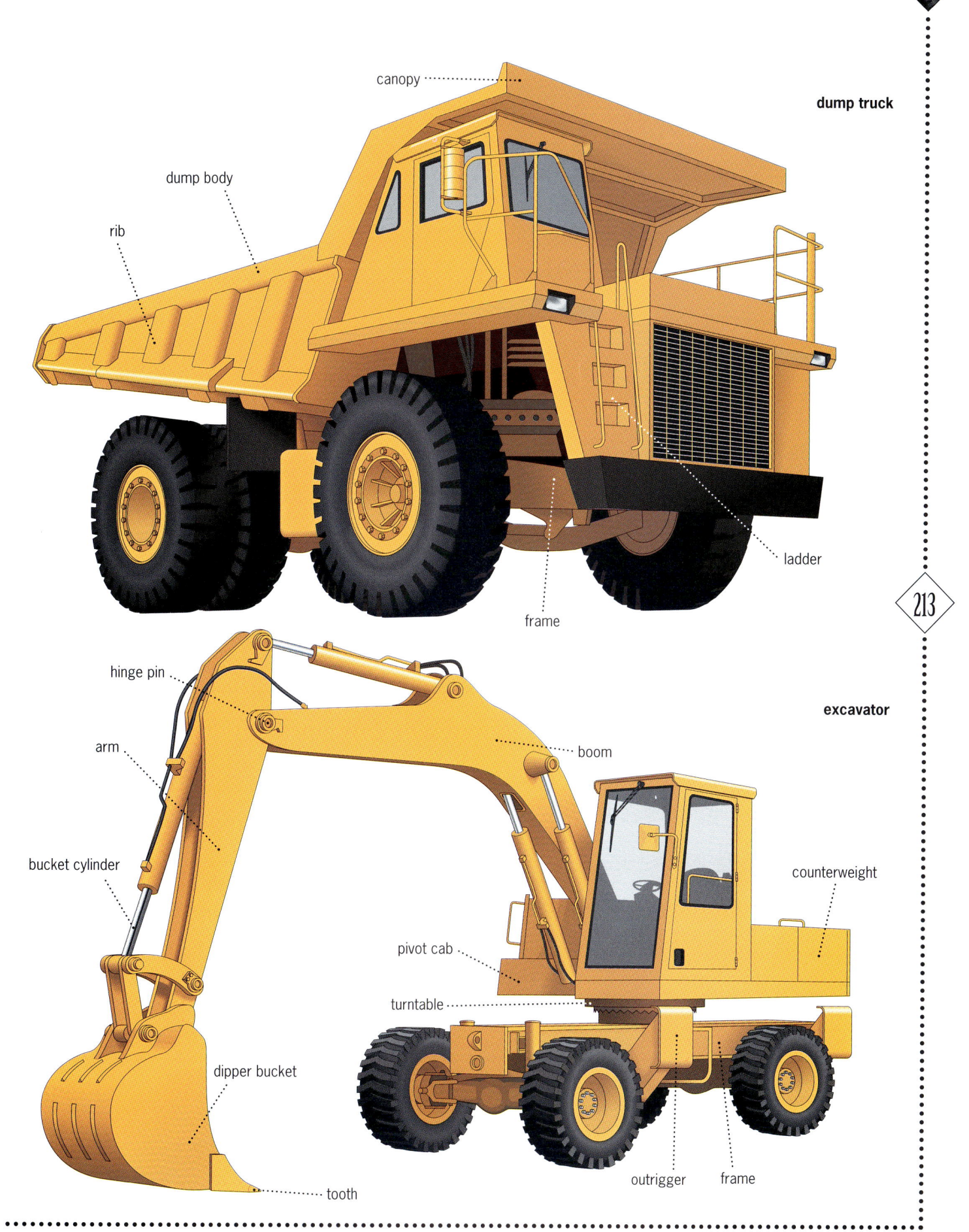

dump truck

canopy
dump body
rib
ladder
frame

excavator

hinge pin
arm
bucket cylinder
boom
counterweight
pivot cab
turntable
dipper bucket
tooth
outrigger
frame

213

HEAVY MACHINERY

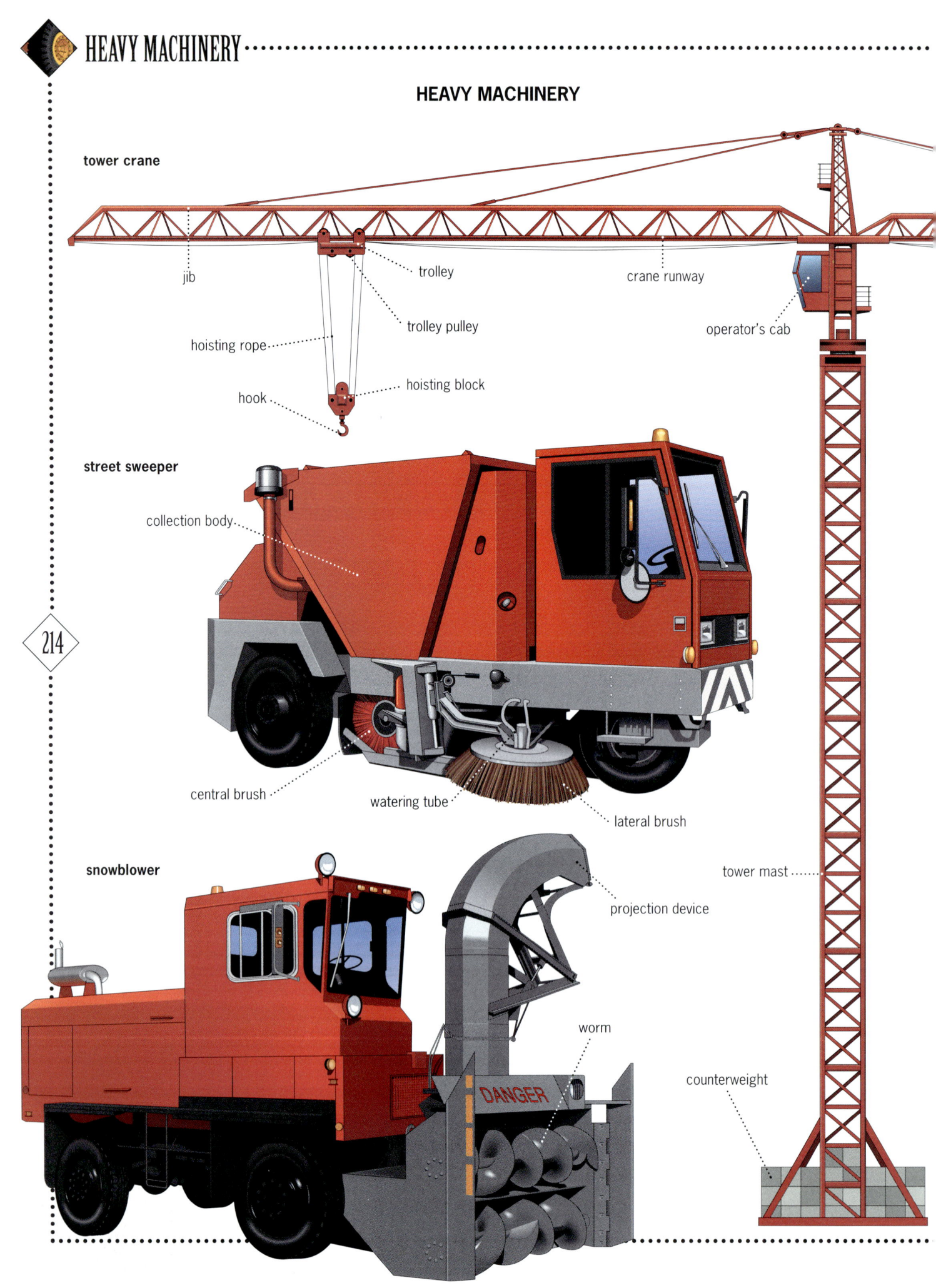

HEAVY MACHINERY

tower crane

- jib
- trolley
- crane runway
- trolley pulley
- operator's cab
- hoisting rope
- hoisting block
- hook
- tower mast
- counterweight

street sweeper

- collection body
- central brush
- watering tube
- lateral brush

snowblower

- projection device
- worm

214

HEAVY MACHINERY

sanitation truck

jib tie
counterjib ballast
counterjib
packer body
loading hopper

truck crane

telescopic boom
elevating cylinder
outrigger

tow truck

boom
elevating cylinder
winch
cable
hook
towing device
winch controls

215

SYMBOLS

COMMON SYMBOLS

women's rest room	 men's rest room	 wheelchair access	 hospital	 telephone
 no smoking	 camping (tent)	 camping prohibited		stop at intersection

SAFETY SYMBOLS

- corrosive
- electrical hazard 
- explosive 
- flammable 
- radioactive 
- poisonous 

PROTECTION

- eye protection
- ear protection 
- head protection 
- hand protection 
- foot protection 
- respiratory system protection 

216

INDEX

1/10th second hand 198.
22,9 metre line, field hockey 175.
25 ring, dartboard 197.
35 mm still camera 149.

A

a 160.
abdomen 61.
abdomen 57, 59, 74, 78.
ablutions fountain 87.
absorbed heat 28.
accelerator pedal 132.
access road 146.
accessory shoe 125, 127.
accidentals, musical notation 161.
accordion 158.
Ace 194.
achene 44.
acid precipitation 31.
acid rain 32, 33.
acoustic guitar 162.
action of wind 31.
actual temperature 199.
Adam's apple 78.
add in memory 154.
add key 154.
adhesive tape 193.
adjustable channel 109.
adjustable wrench 109.
adjusting band 128.
adjusting buckle 185.
adjusting catch 186.
adjusting screw 109.
adjustment slide 112.
aerodynamic brake 209.
aerosol 29.
Africa 19.
Afro pick 122.
aftermast 141.
aileron 144.
air compressor 139.
air concentrator 122.
air conditioner 29.
air filter 139, 212.
air horn 134.
air inlet 145.
air mattress 191.
air pressure, measure 23.
air pump 134.
air space 75.
air unit 121.
air vent 132.
air-outlet grille 122.
air-supply tube 211.
AIRPORT 146.
airport 27.
airport ground equipment 146.
ala 84.
albumen 75.
alcohol bulb 199.
alcohol column 199.
alighting board 59.
alley 180.
alpine skier 186.
alternator 138.
altitude clamp 11.
altitude fine adjustment 11.
AM antenna 128.
ambulatory 89.
American football, playing field 171.
AMPHIBIANS 60.
amphibians 60.
amplifier 128.
anal fin 63.
analog watch 198.
anchor-windlass room 142.
anemometer 23.
ankle 78.
ankle boot 119.
ankle sock 118.
annual ring 40.
annular eclipse 10.
ant 56.
Antarctic Circle 12.
Antarctica 18.
antenna 57, 58, 61, 129, 131, 145, 179.
antennule 61.
anther 38.
anti-friction pad 187.
anti-slip shoe 111.
anti-torque tail rotor 145.
antiseptic 193.

The terms in **bold type** correspond to an illustration; those in CAPITALS indicate a title.

antiseptic lotion 193.
aortic arch 81.
appendix 81.
apple 46.
appoggiatura, musical notation 161.
apricot 45.
apron 97, 146.
aquatic bird 74.
Arabian camel 73.
archipelago 26.
Arctic 18.
Arctic Circle 12, 24.
Arctic Ocean 19.
arm 67, 79, 97, 155, 212, 213.
arm guard 170.
arm pad 177.
armchair 96, 97.
armpit 78.
arterial blood 81.
artery, anterior tibial 81.
artery, common carotid 81.
artery, femoral 81.
artichoke 49.
artichoke, Jerusalem 51.
ash layer 15.
Asia 19.
asparagus 52.
asphalt 203.
asteroid belt 6.
asymmetrical bars 189.
Atlantic Ocean 18.
atmosphere 12, 20.
atmospheric pollution 30.
attack line 179.
attack on human beings 31.
attack on nature 31.
attack zone 179.
attacking zone 176.
audio system 131.
auditory canal 83.
auditory nerve 83.
auditory ossicles 83.
auger bit 110.
auricle 83.
Australia 19.
auto reverse 129.
autofocus on/off switch 153.
automatic dialer 124.
automatic drip coffee maker 105.
automobile car 138.
autumn 20.
autumn squash 49.
autumnal equinox 20.
auxiliary handle 110.
avocado 48.
awl 192.
awning 190.
axillary bud 36.
axis of rotation 152.
axle 138, 185.
azimuth clamp 11.
azimuth fine adjustment 11.

B

b 160.
back 66, 67, 75, 79, 97, 101.
back judge 171.
back pad 177.
back zone 179.
back, left 175.
back, right 175.
back-hoe 212.
back-hoe controls 212.
backboard 178.
backcourt 180.
BACKGAMMON 196.
backguard 107.
backpack 151, 193.
backstay 185.
backstroke 183.
backstroke turn indicator 182.
backup light 133.
backward bucket 212.
bag, drawstring 123.
baggage compartment 145.
baggage conveyor 146.
baggage trailer 147.
bagpipes 158.
bail 174.
bailey 88.
balaclava 114.
balalaika 158.
balance 200.

balance beam 188.
balancer 163.
ball boy 180.
ballast 140.
ballerina 119.
ballpoint pen 150.
banana 48.
band 129.
banjo 158.
bar 123, 196.
bar line 160.
bar stool 96.
BARK, FOUR-MASTED 141.
bark, inner 40.
bark, outer 40.
barograph 23.
barrel 122, 197.
base 99, 140, 152, 155, 188, 200, 209.
base plate 110.
BASEBALL 168.
baseball 168.
baseball, field 169.
baseline 180.
baseman, first 169.
baseman, second 169.
baseman, third 169.
basement 93.
basement window 93.
basic source of food 28.
basket 178.
basket 105, 178, 186, 187.
BASKETBALL 178.
basketball 178.
basketball, court 178.
bass bridge 159.
bass clarinet 167.
bass drum 166, 167.
bass guitar 163.
bass keyboard 158.
bass pickup 163.
bass register 158.
bass tone control 163.
bassoon 165.
bassoon 167.
bat 168, 174.
bat 174.
bathrobe 116.
bathroom scales 201.
batsman 174.
batter 168.
batter 169.
batter head 166.
batter's helmet 168.
battery 127, 138, 205, 208.
battery eject switch 127.
batting glove 168.
battlement 88.
bay 9, 26.
bay window 93.
bayonet base 99.
beach 14.
beam 200.
bean sprouts 52.
beater 105.
beater ejector 105.
beaver 70.
BED 95.
bed 188, 191.
bedrock 34.
beer mug 100.
beet 51.
begonia 38.
belfry 89.
bell 164, 165.
bell brace 165.
bell tower 89.
bellows 158.
belly 67.
belt 112.
belt carrier 112.
belt highway 27.
bench 96.
beret 114.
Bering Sea 19.
Bermuda shorts 115.
berries, major types 44.
BERRY FRUITS 44.
berry, section 44.
BICYCLE 136.
bicycle bag 136.
bile duct 81.
bill 74.
bills, principal types 74.
birch 42.

BIRD 74.
bird feeder 75.
bird of prey 74.
bird's nest 75.
bird, morphology 74.
birdhouse 75.
BIRDS, EXAMPLES 76.
Bishop 195.
bitter taste 84.
Black 195.
black bass 63.
black currant 44.
Black Sea 19.
black square 195.
blackboard 152.
bladder 81.
blade 212.
blade 36, 101, 109, 110, 111, 177, 185, 209, 212.
blade guard 110.
blade tilting mechanism 110.
blank 194.
blanket 95.
blasting charge 202.
blastodisc 75.
blender 105.
blouse 114.
blow pipe 158.
blue 157.
blue line 176.
blue-green 157.
blueberry 44.
board 184.
boarding step 145.
boarding walkway 147.
boards 176.
bodies, types 133.
body 130.
body 162, 163, 165.
body flap 148.
body pad 177.
bolster 95.
bolt 109.
bongos 166.
boom 212, 213, 215.
booster parachute 148.
boot 119.
boot 185.
bottle opener 102.
bottle opener 192.
bottom 186.
bottom line 182.
boulevard 90.
bow 162.
bow 142, 184.
bow thruster 142.
bow window 92.
bowl 101.
bowler 174.
bowsprit 141.
box car 138.
box spring 95.
boxer shorts 112, 121.
bra 116.
brake cable 137.
brake caliper 135.
brake lever 137.
brake light 133.
brake pedal 132, 187.
branch 43.
branch 40.
branches 40.
brass family 164.
brassiere cup 116.
brattice 88.
bread and butter plate 100.
breast 74, 78.
breast pocket 112.
breast welt pocket 113.
breaststroke 183.
breaststroke kick 183.
breaststroke turn 183.
breathing in 183.
breathing out 183.
bridge 123, 162, 163.
bridge assembly 163.
briefcase 151.
briefs 112.
bristles 111, 122.
broad beans 52.
broccoli 49.
brush 111.
Brussels sprouts 53.
bubble 135.
bucket 212.
bucket hinge pin 212.

buckle 186.
bud 50.
bud, flower 36.
bud, terminal 34, 36.
bugle 164.
built-in microphone 127.
bulb 99.
bulb 99.
bulb vegetables 50.
bulb, energy saving 97.
bulbil 50.
bulk terminal 142.
bulkhead flat car 139.
bull's-eye 197.
bulldozer 212.
bumper 130.
bunkers 203.
burner 104.
bushing 204.
butt 181.
butt end 177.
butter compartment 106.
butter dish 100.
butter knife 101.
BUTTERFLY 57.
butterfly kick 183.
butterfly stroke 183.
butterfly turn 183.
butterfly, hind leg 57, 59.
buttock 79.
button 112, 117.
button loop 112.
by-pass runway 146.

C

c 160.
C clef 160.
C-clamp 108.
cab 212.
cabbage lettuce 53.
cabin 143.
cabinet 126.
cable 110, 129, 189, 215.
caboose 139.
calandria 206.
calculator, pocket 154.
calf 68.
calf 79.
Callisto 6.
calyx 38.
cambium 40.
camera body 125.
camera, 35 mm still 149.
camera, pocket 125.
camera, single lens reflex 125.
camera, video 127.
camping (tent) 216.
CAMPING EQUIPMENT 192.
camping prohibited 216.
can opener 102.
can opener 192.
canal lock 142.
canine 70, 85.
cannon 67.
canopy 123, 213.
cantaloupe 49.
canteen 192.
cap 113.
cap 35, 210.
cape 26.
capillary bore 199.
capital 26.
CAR 130, 132.
car lights 133.
car wash 134.
carafe 100.
carafe 105.
carapace 61, 64.
carbon dioxide 33.
CARD GAMES 194.
card reader 124.
cardigan 117.
cardoon 52.
cargo bay door 148.
Caribbean Sea 18.
carnassial 70.
carnation 39.
carnivore's jaw 70.
carnivores 29, 33.
CARPENTRY TOOLS 108.
carpus 80.
carrier 136.

217

INDEX

carrot 51.
CARTOGRAPHY 24, 26.
cartridge film 125.
case 108, 159, 198.
casement window 94.
casement window (inward opening) 94.
casing 54.
Caspian Sea 19.
casserole 104.
cassette 129.
cassette 129.
cassette compartment 127.
cassette eject switch 127.
cassette film 125.
cassette player 129.
cassette player controls 124, 129.
cassette tape deck 128.
castanets 166.
castanets 167.
CASTLE 88.
castle 88.
CAT 66.
catch glove 177.
catcher 168.
catcher 169.
catcher's glove 168.
catenary 140.
catering vehicle 147.
caterpillar 57.
cathedral 90.
CATHEDRAL, GOTHIC 89.
caudal fin 63.
cauliflower 49.
CAVE 13.
cave 14.
ceiling fixture 98.
celeriac 51.
celery 52.
cell 57, 59.
cello 162.
cello 167.
Celsius scale 199.
center 171, 176, 178.
center back 173, 179.
center circle 173, 178.
center console 132.
center face-off circle 176.
center field 169.
center fielder 169.
center flag 173.
center forward 173, 175, 179.
center half 175.
center hole 129.
center line 171, 175, 176, 178.
center mark 180.
center post 131.
center service line 180.
center spot 173.
center strap 180.
Central America 18.
central brush 214.
central column 209.
central incisor 85.
central nave 87.
central processing unit 154.
cephalothorax 61.
cereal bowl 100.
chain guide 136.
chain wheel 136.
CHAIRS 97.
chaise longue 96.
chameleon 65.
champagne flute 100.
champagne glass 100.
change sign key 154.
channel scan buttons 126.
channel selector controls 126.
chanter 158.
chapel 88.
chapel, Lady 89.
chapel, side 89.
Charleston cymbal 166.
Charon 7.
checker 196.
checkerboard 196.
CHECKERS 196.
cheek 66, 78.
cheese knife 101.
cherimoya 48.
cherry 45.
CHESS 195.
chess notation 195.
chessboard 195.
chest 67, 78.
chest protector 168, 170.

chestnut 67.
chevet 89.
chick 68.
chick peas 52.
chicory 53.
chief timekeeper 182.
chilli 49.
chimney 93.
chin 74, 78.
chin protector 135.
chin rest 162.
chin strap 170.
China Sea 19.
Chinese cabbage 53.
chives 50.
choir 89.
chrysalis 57.
chrysalis 59.
chuck 110.
chuck key 110.
church 91.
ciliate 37.
circle 156.
circular body 158.
circular saw 110.
circular saw blade 110.
cirque 9.
cirque, glacial 16.
citrus fruit, section 47.
CITRUS FRUITS 47.
citrus fruits, major types 47.
city 26.
clamp 186.
clarinet 165.
clarinet 167.
clavicle 80.
claw 57, 61, 64, 66, 75, 108.
clear key 154.
clear space 179.
clear-entry key 154.
cleated shoe 170.
clefs 160.
clew 184.
cliff 9, 14, 17.
CLIMATES OF THE WORLD 21.
clinical thermometer 199.
clip 150.
clock 132.
clock operator 178.
clock timer 107.
clog 119.
cloud 22.
cloud of volcanic ash 15.
club 194.
clutch lever 135.
clutch pedal 132.
coach's box 169.
cobra 64.
coccyx 80.
cochlea 83.
cock 68.
cockpit 145.
cod 63.
coffee cup 100.
coffee plunger 100.
coffee pot 192.
coffee spoon 101.
coin return tray 124.
coin slot 124.
colander 103.
cold shed 143.
collar 36, 112, 113, 121.
collar point 112.
collecting funnel 23.
collecting vessel 23.
collection body 214.
color circle 157.
color television camera 149.
colored pencils 157.
column 13, 182.
column of mercury 199.
coma 10.
COMET 10.
comforter 95.
commercial premises 91.
commissure of lips 84.
COMMON SYMBOLS 216.
COMMUNICATION BY TELEPHONE 124.
communication tunnel 149.
compact camera 125.
compact disk 129.

compact disk player 128.
compact disk player 129.
COMPASS CARD 27.
compass card 193.
compass, magnetic 193.
compost bin 55.
compound eye 57, 58.
compound leaves 36.
compressed air reservoir 139.
compressed-air cylinder 211.
computer, personal 154.
concealed pocket 113.
concentration of gases 29.
condensation 31.
condensation of steam into water 207.
condenser 155.
condenser backwash inlet 206.
condenser backwash outlet 206.
condenser cooling water inlet 206.
condenser cooling water outlet 206.
conductor's podium 167.
cone 14, 43, 156.
cone 128.
CONFIGURATION OF THE CONTINENTS 18.
conical projection 25.
CONIFER 43.
coniferous forest 20.
connection 205.
constriction 199.
contact 99.
container 23, 105.
container car 138.
container ship 142.
container terminal 143.
container-loading bridge 142.
container/pallet loader 146.
containment building 207.
continental climates 21.
CONTINENTS, CONFIGURATION 18.
contrabassoon 167.
control deck 141, 197.
control dial 125.
control knob 107.
control pad 197.
control panel 107, 125, 210.
control room 204, 206.
control stand 138.
control stick 145.
control tower 146.
control tower cab 146.
controls 127.
convection zone 8.
convention center 90.
conventional door 92.
convertible 133.
COOKING APPLIANCES 107.
cooking set 192.
COOKING UTENSILS 104.
cooktop 107.
coolant transfers the heat to the steam generator 207.
cordless telephone 124.
corkscrew 192.
corkscrew, lever 102.
corn salad 53.
corner arc 173.
corner flag 173, 175.
corner tower 88.
cornet 164.
cornet 167.
cornice 92, 93.
corolla 38.
corona 8.
coronet 67.
corrosive 216.
cotton roll 193.
cotyledons 34.
counter 121.
counterjib 215.
counterjib ballast 215.
counterweight 11, 140, 213, 214.
country 26.
coupler head 139.
courtyard 87.
cover 99, 123, 193, 199.
covered parapet walk 88.
cow 68.
crab 61.
cradle 11.
cranberry 44.
crane runway 214.
crane, floating 142.

crane, gantry 204.
crane, quayside 143.
crane, tower 214.
crank 136.
crater 9, 15.
crawl kick 183.
crawler tractor 212.
crayfish 61.
creamer 100.
crease 112.
crenate 37.
crenel 88.
crest 17.
crevasse 16.
crew neck sweater 117.
CRICKET 174.
cricket ball 174.
cricket player 174.
cricket shoe 174.
cricket, field 174.
crisper 106.
crocodile 64.
crocus 39.
crook 165.
cross-country ski 186.
cross-country ski 187.
cross-country skier 187.
cross-tip screwdriver 192.
crossbuck sign 140.
crossing 89.
crossing gate mechanism 140.
crosspiece 97.
crotch 112.
croup 67, 188.
crow 76.
crown 40, 74, 85, 113.
CRUISE LINER 142.
CRUSTACEANS 61.
cube 156.
cucumber 49.
cuff 112, 177.
cultivated mushroom 35.
cup 100, 192.
curly endive 53.
curly kale 53.
curtain wall 88.
customs house 143.
cutting blade 105.
cutting edge 101, 212.
cylinder 156.
cylinder 75, 212, 213, 215.
cylindrical projection 25.
cymbal 166.
cymbals 167.
cypress scalelike leaves 43.

D

d 160.
daffodil 39.
daggerboard 184.
dairy compartment 106.
dairy products 33.
dam 204.
damper pedal 159.
dandelion 53.
dart 197.
dartboard 197.
dashboard 132.
dashboard 135.
data display 127.
date 45.
dead bolt 93.
deadly mushroom 35.
decanter 100.
deciduous forest 20.
decimal key 154.
declination setting scale 11.
decomposers 29.
deer, white-tailed 73.
defending zone 176.
defense 171.
deflector 54.
deforestation 29.
degrees, C 199.
degrees, F 199.
Deimos 6.
delivery ramp 90.
delta wing 144.
DENTAL CARE 122.
dental floss 122.
dentate 37.
dentin 85.

depressed center flat car 139.
depth of focus 13.
desert 21.
desired temperature 199.
destroying angel 35.
dew 22.
dew shield 11.
dewclaw 67.
diagonal movement 195.
dial 198, 200.
diamond 194.
diaphragm 81, 128.
diastema 70.
DICE 194.
dice cup 196.
die 196.
diesel engine 139, 212.
diesel engine ventilator 138.
diesel oil 203.
diesel, marine 203.
DIESEL-ELECTRIC LOCOMOTIVE 138.
digit 60.
digital pad 66.
digital watch 198.
dining room 142.
dinner fork 101.
dinner knife 101.
dinner plate 100.
DINNERWARE 100.
diode 157.
dipper bucket 213.
direct-reading rain gauge 23.
direction of Mecca 87.
disk 154.
disk brake 135.
disk drive 154.
disk player controls 129.
dispersed heat 29.
display 124, 154, 201.
divide key 154.
dock 143.
DOG 66.
dog's forepaw 66.
dog, morphology 66.
dolphin 72.
dome tent 190.
DOMINOES 194.
door 93.
door 87, 107, 131, 145, 190.
door handle 93, 131.
door lock 131.
doors, types 92.
dormant volcano 14.
dorsum of nose 84.
double bass 162.
double bass 167.
double boiler 104.
double flat, musical notation 161.
double reed 165.
double ring 197.
double sharp, musical notation 161.
double-blank 194.
double-breasted jacket 113, 114.
double-six 194.
doubles pole 180.
doubles sideline 180.
doublet 194.
doubling die 196.
dousing water tank 206, 207.
dousing water valve 206.
DOWNTOWN 90.
dragonfly 56.
drainpipe 92.
draw tube 155.
drawbridge 88.
drawer 97, 107.
DRAWING 157.
drawstring 113, 123.
drawstring bag 123.
dress 114.
drilling 202.
drilling rig 202.
drip molding 131.
drive chain 136.
driver's cab 138, 140.
driveway 92.
driving glove 118.
dromedary 73.
drone pipe 158.
drone, honey-bee 58.
drop-leaf 97.
drums 166.
drupelet 44.
dry continental - arid 21.
dry continental - semiarid 21.
dry dock 142.
dry gallery 13.

218

The terms in **bold type** correspond to an illustration; those in CAPITALS indicate a title.

INDEX

dry subtropical 21.
dual seat 135.
duck 68.
duffle coat 113.
dugout 169.
dump body 213.
dump truck 213.
dune 14.
duodenum 81.
dust 30, 31.
dust tail 10.
dynamic brake 138.
dynamics propeller 141.

E

e 160.
EAR 83.
ear 78, 97.
ear cushion 128.
ear drum 83.
ear flap 113.
ear protection 216.
ear, parts 83.
eardrum 60, 64.
earphone 128.
earpiece 124.
Earth 6, 10.
EARTH COORDINATE SYSTEM 12.
Earth's crust 12, 13.
EARTHQUAKE 13.
East 27.
East-northeast 27.
East-southeast 27.
Eastern hemisphere 24.
Eastern meridian 24.
eclipse, annular 10.
eclipse, partial 10.
ECLIPSE, SOLAR 10.
eclipse, total 10.
ECOLOGY 28, 30, 32.
edge 185, 186, 193.
edible crustaceans 61.
edible mushroom 35.
edit/search buttons 127.
eel 63.
egg 75.
egg 59.
egg beater 102.
egg timer 198.
egg tray 106.
eggplant 49.
eggs 60.
eighth note 161.
eighth rest 161.
elastic 95.
elastic waistband 113.
elbow 66, 67, 79.
elbow pad 170, 177.
electric circuit 205, 208.
electric drill 110.
electric guitar 163.
electric range 107.
ELECTRIC TOOLS 110.
electric wire 205.
electrical hazard 216.
electricity production 207.
electricity transmission 207.
electronic flash 125.
electronic scale 201.
electronic viewfinder 127.
elephant 73.
elevating cylinder 210, 215.
ELEVATION ZONES AND VEGETATION 20.
elevator 144.
elevon 148.
enamel 85.
end button 162.
end line 171, 178, 179.
end wall 182.
end zone 171.
endive, broad-leaved 53.
endocarp 45, 46.
energy integration to the transmission network 205.
ENERGY, HYDROELECTRIC 204.
ENERGY, NUCLEAR 206.
ENERGY, SOLAR 208.
energy, solar 28.
ENERGY, WIND 209.
engine 135.
engine room 143.
engines 149.

English horn 165.
English horn 167.
entire 37.
entrance 59.
entrance slide 59.
epicenter 13.
equal key 154.
Equator 12, 24.
equinox, autumnal 20.
eraser 150.
eraser holder 150.
espadrille 119.
escutcheon 93.
Eurasia 19.
Europa 6.
European robin 77.
Eustachian tube 83.
evaporation 30, 31.
excavator 213.
exercise wear 120, 121.
exhaust pipe 135, 145, 212.
exhaust stack 134.
exit cone 59.
exocarp 44, 45, 46.
expansion chamber 199.
explosive 216.
exposure button 125.
extension ladder 111.
exterior of a house 92.
external ear 83.
external gills 60.
external tank 148.
EYE 82.
eye 61, 64, 74, 78.
eye protection 216.
eye, compound 57, 58.
eye, simple 57.
eyeball 60.
eyebrow 82.
eyelash 82.
eyelashes 66.
eyelet 121, 185.
eyelid 64.
eyepiece 11, 127, 155.
eyepiece holder 11.

F

f 160.
f clef 160.
façade 89.
face 78, 108.
face mask 170, 177.
face-off circle 176.
face-off spot 176.
Fahrenheit scale 199.
fallout 31.
family tent 190.
fan 122.
fang 64.
fantail 209.
FARM ANIMALS 68.
farm animals 29.
farm pollution 32.
fast forward 126.
fast-forward button 129.
fastening system 188, 189.
fauces 84.
fault 13.
feet, principal types 74.
female cone 43.
femur 80.
fennel 52.
fender 130.
ferryboat 143.
fertilizers 29, 32.
fetlock 67.
fetlock joint 67.
fibula 80.
FIELD HOCKEY 175.
fielder's glove 168.
fielder, left 169.
fielder, right 169.
fielders 174.
fifth wheel 134.
fifth, musical interval 160.
fig 48.
figure skate 185.
filament 38, 99.
file 192.
film advance button 125.
film leader 125.
film pack 125.

film rewind button 125.
film speed 125.
fin 144, 145.
fin, anal 63.
fin, caudal 63.
fin, pectoral 62.
fin, pelvic 62.
fin, second dorsal 63.
fin-mounted tail unit 145.
finderscope 11.
fine adjustment knob 155.
finger 168.
finger board 162, 163.
finger button 164.
finger, little 82.
finger, middle 82.
finger, third 82.
fingernail 82.
fir needles 43.
fire engine 210.
fire extinguisher 210.
fire fighter 211.
fire fighter's hatchet 211.
fire hose 210.
fire hydrant 210.
FIRE PREVENTION 210.
fireproof and waterproof garment 211.
firn 16.
first aid kit 193.
first base 169.
first baseman 169.
first dorsal fin 62.
first floor 92.
first leaves 34.
first molar 85.
first premolar 85.
first quarter 9.
first space 178.
first valve slide 164.
first violin 167.
fish scaler 192.
FISHES 62.
fishes, morphology 62.
fission of uranium fuel 207.
fixed jaw 109.
flamingo 76.
flammable 216.
flank 67, 75.
flanking tower 88.
flap 113.
flare 8.
flashing light 140, 211.
flashlight 192.
flashtube 125.
flat brush 157.
flat car 139.
flat mirror 11.
flat, musical notation 161.
flesh 44, 45, 46.
FLESHY FRUITS 44, 47.
fleshy leaves 50.
FLESHY POME FRUITS 46.
FLESHY STONE FRUITS 45.
flews 66.
flexible skirt 141.
flight 197.
flight deck 145, 149.
flip turn 183.
floating crane 142.
floating rib 80.
floor lamp 98.
flounder 63.
flower 36.
flower bud 36.
FLOWERS 38.
flowers, examples 38.
fluorescent tube 99.
fluorescent tube 99.
flute 165.
flute 167.
fly 56.
fly 112.
fly agaric 35.
flying buttress 89.
flying jib 141.
FM antenna 128.
foam pad 191.
focus 13.
focus setting ring 125.
focusing knob 11.
fog 22.
fog light 133, 134.
folding chair 96.
folding cot 191.
folding door 92.
foliage 40.
fondue fork 101.

fondue pot 104.
fondue set 104.
food chain 28.
food pollution in water 32.
food pollution on ground 32.
foot 75, 78, 79.
foot fault judge 180.
foot protection 216.
foot strap 184.
FOOTBALL 170.
football 170.
football player 170.
footboard 95.
footbridge 88.
footless tights 121.
footrest 135.
footstool 96.
footstrap 115.
fore royal sail 141.
forearm 66, 79.
forecastle 142.
forecourt 180.
forehead 74, 78.
foreleg 57, 58.
forelimb 60.
forelock 67.
foremast 141.
foresail 141.
forest 17.
forest, coniferous 20.
forest, deciduous 20.
forest, tropical 20.
forewing 57.
fork 55, 101.
fork 11, 137.
forked tongue 64.
forks, types 101.
fortified wall 87.
forward slide change 153.
forward, left 178.
forward, right 178.
fossil fuels 28.
foul line 169.
fountain pen 150.
four-door sedan 133.
four-four time 160.
FOUR-MASTED BARK 141.
four-toed hoof 71.
fourth, musical interval 160.
frame 94, 112, 136, 168, 181, 188, 189, 208, 213.
framing square 108.
free-throw lane 178.
free-throw line 178.
freeway 90.
freezer compartment 106.
FREIGHT CARS, TYPES 138.
French horn 164.
French horn 167.
fret 162, 163.
frog 60.
frog 113, 162.
frog, life cycle 60.
front 112.
front apron 112.
front brake 137.
front compression strap 193.
front crawl 183.
front derailleur 136.
front fender 135.
front lights 133.
front pocket 123.
front steps 92.
front-end loader 212.
fruit vegetables 49.
frying pan 104, 192.
fuel gauge 132.
fuel tank 134, 135, 139, 145.
fuel tanks 148.
fueling machine 206.
full face mask 211.
full Moon 9.
fullback 171.
fumarole 14.
function button 197.
function keys 201.
function selectors 124.
funnel 103.
funnel 143.
fuse 208.
fuselage 144.
fuselage mounted tail unit 145.

G

g 160.
g clef 160.
gable 93.
gaff sail boom 141.
gaff topsail 141.
gall bladder 81.
gallery 89.
game cartridge 197.
GAME OF DARTS 197.
gantry crane 204.
Ganymede 6.
garage 92.
garden sorrel 53.
GARDENING 54.
garlic 50.
gas 30, 31, 99.
gas tail 10.
gas tank door 131.
gaskin 67.
gasoline 203.
gasoline pump 135.
gate 204.
gate arm 140.
gate arm lamp 140.
gate arm support 140.
gauze roller bandage 193.
gear lever 137.
gear-change pedal 135.
gearshift lever 132.
generator 136, 206.
generator unit 204.
GEOMETRY 156.
germ 34.
GERMINATION 34.
geyser 15.
gill 35.
gills 62.
gills, external 60.
giraffe 72.
glacial cirque 16.
GLACIER 16.
glacier 20.
glacier tongue 16.
glass 100.
glass 208.
glass cover 106.
glass lens 123.
glass slide 155.
GLASSES 123.
GLASSWARE 100.
glazed frost 22.
globe 152.
globe of Earth 152.
glottis 64.
glove 174, 177, 187.
glove compartment 132.
glove finger 118.
GLOVES 118.
gloves 118.
glue stick 150.
gnomon 198.
goal 171, 173, 175, 176.
goal area 173.
goal crease 176.
goal judge 176.
goal line 171, 175, 176.
goal post 171.
goalkeeper 177.
goalkeeper 173, 175, 176.
goalkeeper's pad 177.
goalkeeper's stick 177.
goat 69.
gondola car 139.
gong 167.
goose 68.
gooseberry 44.
gorge 13.
GOTHIC CATHEDRAL 89.
gour 13.
grab handle 134.
graduated dial 193.
graduated scale 200, 201.
grain terminal 142.
granivorous bird 74.
grape 44.
grapefruit 47.
graphic equalizer 128.
grassbox 54.
grasshopper 56.
grater 103.
greases 203.
green 157.

219

The terms in **bold type** correspond to an illustration; those in CAPITALS indicate a title.

INDEX

green bean 49.
green cabbage 53.
green peas 52.
green pepper 49.
greenhouse effect 28.
greenhouse gases 29.
Greenland Sea 18.
grid system 24.
grille 130.
groin 78.
groove 174, 186.
ground moraine 16.
ground transport 202.
grounding terminal 99.
guard rail 106.
guard, left 178.
guard, right 178.
guardhouse 88.
guava 48.
guide roller 129.
gulf 26.
gum 84, 85.
gutter 92.
guy line 190.
GYMNASTICS 188.

H

hair 79, 162.
hair-dryer 122.
hairbrush 122.
HAIRDRESSING 122.
half note 161.
half rest 161.
half, left 175.
half, right 175.
half-slip 116.
halfback, left 171.
halfback, right 171.
hammer 159.
hammer rail 159.
hammer, carpenter's 108.
hammer, claw 108.
HAND 82.
hand 79.
hand blender 105.
hand cultivator 54.
hand fork 54.
hand mixer 105.
hand protection 216.
handbrake 132.
handgrip 135.
handle 54, 95, 101, 108, 109, 110, 111, 122, 123, 129, 162, 168, 174, 181, 186, 192.
handlebars 137.
handsaw 109.
handset 124.
handset cord 124.
hanger loop 117.
hanging glacier 16.
hanging pendant 98.
HARBOR 142.
hard palate 84.
harmonica 158.
harp 167.
hatch 148.
hatchback 133.
hatchet 192.
head 10, 57, 58, 79, 108, 109, 122, 162, 163, 181.
head linesman 171.
head of water 205.
head protection 216.
headband 128, 129, 181, 187.
headboard 95.
header 93.
headlamp 137.
headland 14.
headlight 130, 135, 139, 140.
headlight/turn signal 132.
headphone 129.
headphone jack 129.
headphone plug 129.
headphones 128.
heart 194.
heart 81.
heartwood 40.
heat production 207.
heat selector switch 122.
heat shield 149.
heat transport pump 206.
heater control 132.
heating oil 203.

heavy duty boot 119.
HEAVY MACHINERY 214.
HEAVY VEHICLES 212.
heel 79, 118, 121, 162, 168, 177.
heel piece 186.
heel stop 185.
heel-piece 187.
heelplate 186.
HELICOPTER 145.
helix 83.
helmet 149, 170, 177, 211.
hemispheres 24.
hen 68.
herbivore's jaw 70.
herbivores 29, 33.
hi-hat cymbal 166.
high bar 189.
high beam 133.
high beam indicator light 132.
high-rise apartment 91.
high-speed exit runway 146.
HIGH-SPEED TRAIN 140.
high-tension electricity transmission 205.
highland climates 21.
highland climates 21.
highlighter pen 150.
highway 27.
HIGHWAY CROSSING 140.
highway crossing bell 140.
highway number 27.
hill 17.
hind leg, butterfly 57, 59.
hind limb 60.
hind toe 75.
hind wing 57.
hinge 93, 186.
hinge pin 213.
hip 79.
hip pad 170.
hitting area 168.
hive 59.
hive body 59.
hock 66, 67.
hockey ball 175.
hockey skate 185.
hockey stick 175.
hockey, playing field 175.
hoisting block 214.
hoisting rope 111, 214.
home plate 169.
home-plate umpire 169.
honey cell 59.
HONEYBEE 58.
honeycomb 59.
honeycomb section 59.
hood 113, 130.
hooded sweat shirt 120.
hoof 67.
HOOFS, TYPES 71.
hook 94, 108, 185, 201, 214, 215.
hopper car 138.
horizontal bar 189.
horizontal movement 195.
horizontal pivoting window 94.
horizontal stabilizer 144, 145.
horizontal-axis wind turbine 209.
horn 132, 138.
horns of giraffe 71.
horns of mouflon 71.
horns of rhinoceros 71.
HORNS, MAJOR TYPES 71.
horny beak 64.
HORSE 67.
horse 70.
horse 188.
horseradish 51.
hospital 216.
hot pepper 49.
hot-shoe contact 125.
hotel 91.
HOUSE 92.
house on stilts 86.
house, exterior 92.
HOUSES, TRADITIONAL 86.
housing 99, 110, 129.
HOVERCRAFT 141.
hub 137, 209.
huckleberry 44.
HUMAN ANATOMY 81.
HUMAN BODY 78, 79.
HUMAN DENTURE 85.
humerus 80.
humid - long summer 21.
humid - short summer 21.
humid subtropical 21.
humidity, measure 23.

hummingbird 77.
hunting cap 113.
husk 52.
hut 87.
hydrant 210.
hydrant intake 210.
hydroelectric complex 204.
HYDROELECTRIC ENERGY 204.
hydroelectric power station, cross section 204.
hydrosphere 20.
hygrograph 23.

I

ice 30.
ice cream scoop 103.
ice cube tray 106.
ice dispenser 134.
ICE HOCKEY 176.
ice hockey player 177.
ice hockey, rink 176.
igloo 86.
ignition key 54.
ignition switch 132.
ilium 80.
in-line skate 185.
inbound line 171.
incandescent lamp 99.
incandescent lamp 208.
incisor 70.
incisors 70.
incoming message cassette 124.
index finger 82.
Indian fig 48.
Indian Ocean 19.
indicators 126.
industrial oil 203.
industrial pollution 32, 33.
inert gas 99.
infield 169.
infiltration 30.
inflator 191.
inflator-deflator 191.
inflorescent vegetables 49.
inner bark 40.
inner boot 185.
inner core 12.
inner table 196.
inner tent 190.
inner, left 175.
inner, right 175.
inorganic matter 29.
insectivores 29.
insectivorous bird 74.
INSECTS 56.
inside 101.
inside left 173.
inside linebacker 171.
inside right 173.
instep 118.
instrument panel 132.
instrument panel 132.
instrument shelter 23.
insulation tiles 148.
interchangeable studs 172.
internal boundary 26.
internal frame 193.
international boundary 26.
internode 36.
interrupted projection 25.
intervals 160.
Io 6.
iris 82.
island 26.
isthmus 26.

J

Jack 194.
jacket 113.
jacket 114.
jalousie 94.
jamb 93.
Japanese persimmon 48.
Japanese plum 46.
jaw 109, 110.
jaw, carnivore's 70.
jaw, herbivore's 70.
jaw, rodent's 70.

JAWS, TYPES 70.
jay 77.
jeans 115.
Jerusalem artichoke 51.
jet fuel 203.
jib 214.
jib tie 215.
jib, flying 141.
jigger topgallant staysail 141.
jigger topmast staysail 141.
Joker 194.
journal box 138.
Jupiter 6.

K

kangaroo 73.
keep 88.
kernel 52.
kerosene 203.
kettle 105.
kettledrum 167.
key 159, 165.
key case 123.
key signature, musical notation 161.
keybed 159.
keyboard 154, 159.
keyboard cable 154.
KEYBOARD INSTRUMENTS 159.
King 194, 195.
King's side 195.
kiosk 135.
KITCHEN APPLIANCES 105.
kitchen scale 201.
kitchen timer 198.
KITCHEN UTENSILS 102.
kiwi 48.
knapsack 123.
knee 67, 78.
knee pad 168, 170, 177.
knee sock 187.
knee-high sock 118.
knife 101, 192.
Knight 195.
knitted hat 114.
knives, types 101.
knob 97, 168.
knob handle 110.
knuckle 82.
kohlrabi 51.

L

label 129.
labial palp 57.
lace 168, 185.
ladder 213.
ladder pipe nozzle 211.
ladle 102.
Lady chapel 89.
ladybug 56.
lagoon 14.
lake 9, 17, 26.
lamb 69.
lanceolate 37.
Land camera, Polaroid® 125.
landing light 145.
landing window 145.
lane 182.
lane number 182.
lane rope 182.
lane timekeeper 182.
larch 43.
large blade 192.
large intestine 81.
last quarter 9.
latch 107.
latch bolt 93.
lateral brush 214.
lateral incisor 85.
lateral moraine 17.
latitude 12.
latitude, lines 24.
lava flow 15.
lava layer 15.
lawn rake 55.
lawnmower 54.
lead-in wire 99.
leading edge 144.
leaf 37.
leaf 34, 36.

leaf axil 37.
leaf margins 37.
leaf node 36.
leaf vegetables 53.
leather end 112.
LEATHER GOODS 123.
leather sheath 192.
leaves, compound 36.
leaves, simple 37.
leaves, types 43.
ledger line 160.
leek 50.
left back 173, 175, 179.
left channel 128.
left cornerback 171.
left defense 176.
left defensive end 171.
left defensive tackle 171.
left field 169.
left fielder 169.
left forward 178, 179.
left guard 171, 178.
left half 173, 175.
left halfback 171.
left inner 175.
left safety 171.
left service court 180.
left tackle 171.
left wing 175, 176.
leg 64, 79, 95, 97, 118, 188.
leg-warmer 121.
lemon 47.
lemon squeezer 103.
lentils 52.
leotard 120.
level 108.
leveling-adjustment foot 153.
lever 105, 109.
license plate light 133.
life raft 141.
lifeboat 141, 143.
lift arm 212.
ligature 165.
light 11.
light bulb 208.
LIGHTING 99.
lightning 22.
lightning arrester 204.
lightning rod 93.
LIGHTS 98.
lily 39.
lily of the valley 39.
limb 40.
lime 47.
limousine 133.
line 160.
line judge 171.
line of scrimmage 171.
linear 37.
linebacker, inside 171.
linebacker, middle 171.
linebacker, outside 171.
linen 95.
lines of latitude 24.
lines of longitude 24.
linesman 173, 176, 179, 180.
linesman, head 171.
lining 113, 121.
lion 70, 72.
lip 66, 67.
liquid crystal display 198.
listen button 124.
lithosphere 20.
litchi 48.
little finger hook 164.
liver 81.
livestock car 138.
lizard 65.
loader 212.
loading hopper 215.
loafer 119.
lobate 37.
lobate toe 74.
lobe 74, 83.
lobster 61.
lock 93, 136.
lock 93.
lock ring 153.
locking device 111.
locking pliers 109.
LOCOMOTIVE, DIESEL-ELECTRIC 138.
log cabin 86.
log chute 204.
loin 67, 79.
long-nose pliers 109.
long-range jet 144.

The terms in **bold type** correspond to an illustration; those in CAPITALS indicate a title.

INDEX

longitude 12.
longitude, lines 24.
loop 112.
loophole 88.
loose-leaf paper 151.
loudspeakers 128.
louver-board 89.
louvred window 94.
loveseat 96.
low beam 133.
lower eyelid 60, 66, 82.
lower fore topgallant sail 141.
lower fore topsail 141.
lower lip 84.
lower mantle 12.
lower shell 186.
lubricating oils 203.
lubricating system 139.
luff 184.
lumbar pad 170.
LUNAR ECLIPSE 10.
lunar eclipses, types 10.
lunar features 9.
lung, left 81.
lung, right 81.
lunula 82.
lyre 158.

M

machicolation 88.
machine hall 204.
magma 15.
magma chamber 15.
magnetic compass 193.
magnetic needle 193.
magnifier 192.
magnifying glass 155.
main engines 148.
main landing gear 144.
main mirror 11.
main tube 11.
main vent 15.
mainmast 141.
mainsail 141.
maintenance 134.
maintenance hangar 147.
male cone 43.
mallet 108.
mallet 166.
mallets 166.
mandarin 47.
mandible 57, 58, 62, 80.
mandolin 158.
mane 67.
maneuvering engine 148.
mango 45.
manned maneuvering unit 149.
manual focusing knob 153.
manual release 187.
map projections 25.
maple 41.
maracas 166.
margin 36.
marine 21.
marine diesel 203.
maritime transport 202.
marker 150.
marker light 134.
Mars 6.
mask 168.
mast 140, 145, 184.
mast foot 184.
mast sleeve 184.
masthead 184.
mattress 95, 191.
mattress cover 95.
maxilla 62, 80.
maxillary bone 85.
maxillipeds 61.
maximum thermometer 23.
measure of air pressure 23.
measure of humidity 23.
measure of rainfall 23.
measure of temperature 23.
MEASURE OF WEIGHT 200.
measure of wind direction 23.
measure of wind strength 23.
measuring spoons 102.
measuring tube 23.
meat 33.
meat tray 106.
mechanical pencil 150.
mechanics bay 134.

medial moraine 16.
median strip 90.
Mediterranean Sea 19.
Mediterranean subtropical 21.
melody strings 158.
meltwater 17.
memory cancel 154.
memory recall 154.
men 195, 196.
MEN'S CLOTHING 112.
men's rest room 216.
Mercury 6.
mercury barometer 23.
mercury bulb 199.
meridian band 152.
merlon 88.
mesocarp 44, 45, 46, 47.
metacarpus 80.
metal frame 159.
metals 33.
metatarsus 80.
METEOROLOGICAL MEASURING INSTRUMENTS 23.
metronome 159.
microscope 155.
microwave oven 107.
middle ear 83.
middle leg 57, 58.
middle linebacker 171.
middle panel 93.
middle toe 74.
midfield line 173.
midrange 128.
midrange pickup 163.
midrib 37.
midsole 121.
Mihrab dome 87.
minaret 87.
minimum thermometer 23.
minivan 133.
minute hand 198.
mirror 134, 135, 152, 155.
mist 22.
mitten 118.
mixed forest 20.
mizzenmast 141.
moat 88.
moccasin 119.
mode selectors 129.
moisture in the air 30.
molar 70.
molar, cross section 85.
molars 85.
monkey 72.
MOON 9.
Moon 6, 10.
Moon's orbit 10.
moons 6.
moraine, ground 16.
moraine, lateral 17.
moraine, medial 16.
moraine, terminal 17.
mordent, musical notation 161.
MOSQUE 87.
motor 54, 110.
MOTORCYCLE 135.
MOUNTAIN 17.
mountain bike 137.
mountain range 9, 26.
mountain slope 17.
mountain torrent 17.
mounting foot 125.
mouse 154.
MOUTH 84.
mouth 60, 78.
mouthpiece 124, 164, 165.
mouthpipe 158.
movable jaw 109.
movable maxillary 64.
movements, chess 195.
mud flap 131, 134.
mud hut 86.
mudguard 16.
muffler felt 159.
muffler pedal 159.
mug 100.
multiply key 154.
multipurpose bottle 193.
multipurpose vehicle 133.
mummy 191.
muntin 94.
museum 91.
MUSHROOM 35.
mushroom, structure 35.
music stand 159.
musical accessories 159.

MUSICAL INSTRUMENTS, TRADITIONAL 158.
MUSICAL NOTATION 160.
musical scale 160.
muskmelon 49.
mute 164.
muzzle 66, 67.
mycelium 35.

N

nacelle 209.
nail 108.
nail nick 192.
nape 75, 79.
nasal septum 84.
national park 27.
natural arch 14.
natural, musical notation 161.
nave 89.
navel 78.
navigation light 144.
neck 64, 67, 78, 79, 85, 162, 163, 188.
neck end 112.
nectarine 45.
negative contact 208.
negative pole 205.
Neptune 7.
net 179, 180.
net 178, 179, 180.
net band 180.
net judge 180.
neutral zone 171, 176.
new crescent 9.
new Moon 9.
nictitating membrane 66.
nightingale 77.
nipple 78.
no smoking 216.
North 27.
North America 18.
North Pole 12.
North Sea 19.
North-northeast 27.
North-northwest 27.
Northeast 27.
Northern hemisphere 12, 24.
Northwest 27.
NOSE 84.
nose 67, 78, 145.
nose landing gear 145.
nose leather 66.
nose of the quarter 121.
nose pad 123.
nostril 60, 62, 67, 84.
notch 200.
note symbols, musical notation 161.
notebook 151.
notepad 151.
nozzle 148.
NUCLEAR ENERGY 206.
nuclear power station 206.
nucleus 10.
number key 154.
number of tracks sign 140.
numeric keyboard 201.
nut 109, 162, 163.
nutcracker 102.

O

oak 41.
objective 155.
objective lens 11, 125, 153.
oboe 165.
oboe 167.
observation window 148.
ocean 9, 26, 31.
Oceania 19.
octave 160.
octave mechanism 165.
odometer 132.
offense 171.
office 134.
office building 91, 143.
office tower 90.
officials' bench 176.
offshore prospecting 202.
OIL 202.
oil tanker 203.
oil tanker 143.

oil terminal 143.
oil, diesel 203.
oil, heating 203.
oils, lubricating 203.
okra 49.
old crescent 9.
olive 45.
omnivores 28.
on-deck circle 169.
on-off switch 105, 122.
on/off button 126, 129.
on/off switch 153.
on/off/volume control 129.
one-person tent 190.
one-toe hoof 71.
onion, pickling 50.
onion, yellow 50.
open strings 158.
operating nut 210.
operator's cab 214.
operculum 60.
optical lens 152.
optical stage 152.
orange 47.
orange 157.
orange-red 157.
orange-yellow 157.
orbiculate 37.
orbits of the planets 6.
orchid 38.
ordinary die 194.
ORGAN OF HEARING 83.
ORGAN OF SIGHT 82.
ORGAN OF SMELL 84.
ORGAN OF TASTE 84.
ORGAN OF TOUCH 82.
ornaments, musical notation 161.
ostrich 76.
outer bark 40.
outer core 12.
outer table 196.
outer toe 74.
outgoing announcement cassette 124.
outlet 99.
output jack 163.
outrigger 210, 213, 215.
outside left 173.
outside linebacker 171.
outside mirror 130.
outside right 173.
outsole 121.
outwash plain 17.
ovary 38.
oven 107.
oven control knob 107.
overcoat 114.
overhead projector 152.
ovule 38.
owl 77.
ox 69.
ozone layer 29.

P

Pacific Ocean 18.
packer body 215.
pad 174.
paint roller 111.
paintbrush 157.
PAINTING UPKEEP 111.
pajamas 116.
palm 82, 118, 168.
palm tree 42.
palmar pad 66.
palmate 36.
pan 200.
pane 94.
panel 93.
panpipes 158.
pantograph 140.
pants 112, 116, 120.
pants 168, 170, 177.
papaya 48.
paper clips 150.
paraffins 203.
parallel 24.
parallel bars 189.
parallelepiped 156.
parallelogram 156.
park 90.
parking area 147.
parking lot 91.
parrot 76.
parsnip 51.

partial eclipse 10.
parts 95.
pass 17.
passenger cabin 141, 145.
passenger car 140.
passenger terminal 143, 147.
passenger transfer vehicle 147.
pastern 67.
patch pocket 113.
patella 80.
pause 126.
Pawn 195.
pay phone 124.
peach 45.
peacock 77.
peak 17, 113, 114.
pear 46.
pear-shaped body 158.
pectoral fin 62.
pedal 136, 166.
pedal rod 159.
pedicel 38, 44, 45, 46.
peeler 102.
peg box 162.
pelvic fin 62.
pen, ballpoint 150.
pen, fountain 150.
pen, highlighter 150.
penalty arc 173.
penalty area 173.
penalty area marking 173.
penalty bench 176.
penalty spot 173.
pencil 150.
pencil sharpener 150.
pendulum bar 159.
peninsula 26.
penis 78.
penstock 204.
penumbra shadow 10.
pepper shaker 100.
percent key 154.
perch 75.
perching bird 74.
PERCUSSION INSTRUMENTS 166.
perforation 125.
pericarp 47.
perpetual snows 17.
personal AM-FM cassette player 129.
personal computer 154.
pesticides 32.
petal 38.
petiole 37.
petrochemicals 203.
petroleum trap 202.
phalanges 80.
phases of the Moon 9.
philtrum 84.
Phobos 6.
phosphorescent coating 99.
photoelectric cell 125.
PHOTOGRAPHY 125.
physical map 26.
piano 167.
piccolo 165.
piccolo 167.
pickguard 163.
pickup selector 163.
pickup truck 133.
pickups 163.
pig 69.
piggyback car 139.
pike 63.
pike pole 211.
pillar 89.
pillow 95.
pillow protector 95.
pillowcase 95.
pilot 139, 140.
pin 99.
pin base 99.
pin block 159.
pine needles 43.
pine seeds 43.
pineapple 48.
pinnatifid 36.
pip 44, 46, 47, 194.
pipeline 202.
pistil 38.
pistol grip handle 110.
pit 45.
pitch 174.
pitcher 169.
pitcher's mound 169.
pitcher's plate 169.
pith 40.

221

The terms in **bold type** correspond to an illustration; those in CAPITALS indicate a title.

INDEX

pivot 193.
pivot cab 213.
placing judge 182.
placket 112.
plain 26.
PLANE 144.
plane projection 25.
plane surfaces 156.
planetarium 90.
planets 6.
planets, orbits 6.
PLANT AND SOIL 34.
plant litter 34.
plastron 64.
plate 192.
plateau 17, 26.
platform 182, 201.
platform ladder 111.
play 126.
play button 129.
player's number 170.
player's stick 177.
players' bench 171, 176, 178, 179.
playing area 143.
playing window 129.
pleated skirt 115.
plexus of blood vessels 85.
plexus of nerves 85.
plug 110.
plug, American 99.
plug, European 99.
plum 45.
Pluto 7.
pocket 112, 117.
pocket calculator 154.
pocket camera 125.
point 101, 185, 196, 197.
point of interest 27.
pointer 199, 200, 201.
poisonous 216.
poisonous mushroom 35.
poker die 194.
polar bear 72.
polar climates 21.
polar ice cap 21.
polar tundra 21.
Polaroid® Land camera 125.
pole grip 187.
pole shaft 187.
pole tip 187.
political map 26.
pollen basket 58.
pollen cell 59.
pollution, atmospheric 30.
pollution, food 32.
pollution, industrial 33.
polo neck 187.
polo shirt 117.
polo shirt 181.
pome fruit, section 46.
pome fruits, major types 46.
pomegranate 48.
pommel 188.
pommel horse 188.
poncho 114.
poop 141.
pop-up tent 190.
poplar 41.
poppy 38.
port hand 142.
portable CD AM/FM cassette recorder 129.
portable cellular telephone 124.
portable fire extinguisher 210.
portable life support system 149.
PORTABLE SOUND SYSTEMS 129.
portal 89.
porthole 143.
position light 140, 145.
position marker 162, 163.
positive contact 208.
positive pole 205.
post 179.
posterior rugae 79.
potato 51.
potato masher 102.
power button 127.
power car 140.
power zoom button 127.
powerhouse 204.
prairie 26.
prayer hall 87.
precipitation 30, 31.
premolar 70.
premolars 85.
preset buttons 126, 127.
pressed area 129.

pressure bar 159.
pressure cooker 104.
pressure regulator 104.
primary colors 157.
primary root 34, 36.
prime meridian 24.
printed document 154.
printer 154.
printout 154, 201.
prism 156.
proboscis 57.
procedure checklist 149.
product code 201.
production of electricity by the generator 205.
production of electricity from nuclear energy 207.
production of electricity, steps 205.
production platform 202.
projection device 214.
projection head 152.
projection screen 153.
projector, overhead 152.
proleg 57.
promenade deck 143.
prominence 8.
propellant level gauge 149.
propeller 143.
propeller duct 141.
prospecting 202.
PROTECTION 216.
protection layer 149.
protective cup 170, 177.
protective equipment 170.
protective girdle 177.
protective helmet 135, 137.
protractor 151.
province 26.
pruning shears 54.
pubis 78.
puck 176.
pulley 111.
pulp 47, 85.
pump 119.
pump island 135.
pumpkin 49.
punch hole 112.
pup tent 190.
pupil 66, 82.
purse 123.
push button 105.
push buttons 124.
push-button telephone 124.
pushpins 150.
pyramid 156.

Q

Qibla wall 87.
quarter 121.
quarter note 161.
quarter rest 161.
quarter-deck 143.
quarterback 171.
quay 142.
quayside crane 143.
Queen 194, 195.
queen cell 59.
Queen's side 195.
queen, honey-bee 58.
quince 46.

R

rack 107.
radar 142.
radial passenger loading area 147.
radiation zone 8.
radiator 139.
radiator grille 134.
radiator panel 148.
radicle 34, 36, 40.
radio antenna 142.
radioactive 216.
radish 51.
radius 80.
rail 93, 97, 140.
railroad 90.
railroad station 90.
rain 22.
rain forest, tropical 21.

rain gauge recorder 23.
rain gauge, direct-reading 23.
rainbow 22.
raindrop 22.
rainfall, measure 23.
rainfly 190.
rake 55.
rake comb 122.
rampart 88.
raspberry, section 44.
rattlesnake 65.
reactor 206, 207.
reactor building 206.
reading start 129.
rear apron 112.
rear brake 136.
rear derailleur 136.
rear light 136.
rear lights 133.
rear shock absorber 135.
rearview mirror 132.
receiver 180.
receptacle 38, 44.
record 129.
record 126.
record announcement button 124.
recorder 165.
recorder 182.
recording tape 129.
recording unit 23.
rectangle 156.
rectangular 191.
red 157.
Red 196.
red currant 44.
Red Sea 19.
red wine glass 100.
red- violet 157.
reed 165.
reeds 165.
referee 171, 173, 176, 178, 179.
refinery 203.
refinery products 203.
refining 203.
reflected heat 28.
reflected ultraviolet rays 28.
REFLECTING TELESCOPE 11.
reflecting telescope, cross section 11.
reflector 136.
REFRACTING TELESCOPE 11.
refracting telescope, cross section 11.
REFRIGERATOR 106.
refrigerator 29.
refrigerator car 139.
refrigerator compartment 106.
reheater 206.
release lever 109.
remote control 126.
remote control 153.
remote control sensor 126.
remote control terminal 125.
remote-control arm 149.
repeat mark 160.
REPTILES 64.
reservoir 105, 204.
reset button 198.
respiratory system protection 216.
rest area 27.
rest symbols, musical notation 161.
restaurant 91.
restricted area 178.
restricting circle 178.
retriever 179.
rev(olution) counter 132.
reverse slide change 153.
revolving nosepiece 155.
rewind 126.
rewind button 129.
rhinoceros 73.
rhombus 156.
rhubarb 52.
rib 123, 213.
rib joint pliers 109.
rib pad 170.
ribbed top 118.
ribbing 117.
ribs 80.
ridge 17.
right ascension setting scale 11.
right back 173, 175.
right channel 128.
right cornerback 171.
right defense 176.
right defensive end 171.
right defensive tackle 171.
right field 169.

right fielder 169.
right forward 178, 179.
right guard 171, 178.
right half 173, 175.
right halfback 171.
right inner 175.
right safety 171.
right service court 180.
right tackle 171.
right wing 175, 176.
rim 123, 135, 137, 178.
rind 47.
ring 35, 107, 123, 164, 189, 198, 201.
ring binder 151.
rings 189.
rink 176.
rink corner 176.
ripper 212.
ripper tooth 212.
river 26.
river estuary 14, 26.
road 27.
road map 27.
road number 27.
roasting pans 104.
rock 14.
rocking chair 96.
rodent's jaw 70.
roller cover 111.
roller frame 111.
rolling pin 102.
roof 59, 92, 131.
Rook 195.
room thermostat 199.
rooster 68.
root 50, 85.
root canal 85.
root cap 36.
root hairs 34, 36.
root of nose 84.
root system 36.
root vegetables 51.
root, primary 34, 36.
root, secondary 34, 36.
root-hair zone 40.
rose 38.
rose 162.
rose window 89.
rotation of the turbine 205.
rotor 209.
rotor blade 145.
rotor head 145.
rotor hub 145.
rubber boot 211.
rudder 141, 143, 144, 148.
ruler 151.
ruler 192.
rump 75.
rung 111.
runner 196.
running shoe 121.
runway 146.
runway line 147.

S

sacrum 80.
saddle 136, 188.
safety binding 187.
safety handle 54.
safety pad 188.
safety rail 138.
SAFETY SYMBOLS 216.
safety tether 149.
safety valve 104, 207.
sail 184.
sail 209.
sail cloth 209.
sail, fore royal 141.
sail, lower fore topgallant 141.
sail, upper fore topgallant 141.
sailbar 209.
SAILBOARD 184.
salad bowl 100.
salad dish 100.
salad plate 100.
salad spinner 103.
salamander 60.
salsify 51.
salt marsh 14.
salt shaker 100.
salty taste 84.
sand island 14.

sandbox 139.
sanitation truck 215.
sapwood 40.
sash window 94.
Saturn 7.
saucepan 104, 192.
sauté pan 104.
saxhorn 164.
saxophone 165.
scale 63, 64, 74, 108, 193, 199.
scale leaf 50.
scale, musical 160.
scales, bathroom 201.
scales, electronic 201.
scales, kitchen 201.
scallion 50.
scampi 61.
scapula 80.
scenic route 27.
SCHOOL EQUIPMENT 152, 154.
SCHOOL SUPPLIES 150.
scientific instruments 148.
scissors 192, 193.
sclera 82.
scorer 178, 179.
scraper 111.
screen 126, 204.
screw 108.
screw 162.
screw base 99.
screwdriver 108.
screwdriver 192.
screwdriver, cross-tip 192.
scrimmage 171.
scroll 162.
scrotum 78.
sea 9, 26.
sea horse 62.
sealed cell 59.
SEASONS OF THE YEAR 20.
seat 97.
seat post 136.
SEATS 96.
second base 169.
second baseman 169.
second dorsal fin 63.
second floor 92.
second hand 198.
second molar 85.
second premolar 85.
second space 178.
second valve slide 164.
second violin 167.
second, musical interval 160.
secondary colors 157.
secondary road 27.
secondary root 34, 36.
section of a bulb 50.
seed 34, 44, 45, 46, 47.
seed leaf 36.
seed vegetables 52.
seeds 75.
segment 47.
segment score number 197.
seismic wave 13.
seismographic recording 202.
self-contained breathing apparatus 211.
self-inflating mattress 191.
semi-circle 178.
semi-mummy 191.
semicircular canals 83.
sensor probe 107.
sepal 38, 44.
serac 16.
server 179, 180.
service area 27, 147, 179.
service court, left 180.
service court, right 180.
service judge 180.
service line 180.
service road 146.
service station 134.
set of bells 166.
set square 151.
seventh, musical interval 160.
shade 98.
shadow 198.
shadow, penumbra 10.
shadow, umbra 10.
shady arcades 87.
shaft 177, 181, 197.
shallot 50.
shallow root 40.
sham 95.
shank 108, 123.
shark 63.

222

The terms in **bold type** correspond to an illustration; those in CAPITALS indicate a title.

sharp, musical notation 161.
sheath 192.
sheath 37, 66, 67.
sheep 69.
sheet 141.
sheet, fitted 95.
sheet, flat 95.
shelf 106.
shell 64.
shell 75.
shield 65.
shin guard 168, 172.
shin pad 177.
shirt 112.
shirttail 112.
shock wave 202.
shoelace 121.
SHOES 119.
shoot 36, 40.
shooting adjustment keys 127.
shorts 115.
shorts 172.
shortstop 169.
shoulder 66, 67, 78, 181.
shoulder blade 79.
shoulder pad 170, 177.
shoulder strap 116, 123, 193.
shovel 55.
shovel 186.
shrimp 61.
shroud 141.
shutter 94.
shutter release button 125.
shuttle 148.
side 141.
side chair 97.
side chapel 89.
side compression strap 193.
side footboard 139.
side light 133.
side molding 131.
side plate 100.
side rail 111.
side vent 15.
side wall 182.
sideline 171, 175, 178, 179.
sight 193.
sighting line 193.
sighting mirror 193.
signal background plate 140.
signal lamp 107.
silk 52.
silos 142.
SILVERWARE 101.
simple eye 57, 58.
simple leaves 37.
single lens reflex (slr) camera 125.
single reed 165.
singles pole 180.
singles sideline 180.
sink-hole 13.
siphon 13.
sistrum 166.
sixteenth note 161.
sixteenth rest 161.
sixth, musical interval 160.
sixty-fourth note 161.
sixty-fourth rest 161.
skate 177.
skate guard 185.
SKATING 185.
skeg 184.
SKELETON 80.
ski 186.
ski boot 186.
ski boot 186.
ski glove 186.
ski goggles 186.
ski hat 186, 187.
ski pants 115.
ski pole 186, 187.
ski stop 186, 187.
ski suit 186, 187.
skid 145.
SKIING 186.
skin 44, 45, 46, 60.
skirt 114, 181.
skull 78, 80.
skylight 92.
skyscraper 91.
sleeping bags 191.
sleeping cab 134.
SLEEPING EQUIPMENT 191.
sleeve 113, 117.
sleigh bells 166.
slide 153.
slide mount 153.

slide projector 153.
slide tray 153.
slide-select bar 153.
sliding door 93.
sliding folding door 92.
sliding folding window 94.
sliding weight 159, 200.
sliding window 94.
slingback 119.
slip joint 109.
slip joint pliers 109.
slipover 117.
slot 105.
slow-motion 126.
small blade 192.
small intestine 81.
snap fastener 113, 118.
snare drum 166, 167.
snout 60.
snow 30.
snowblower 214.
SOCCER 172.
soccer ball 172.
soccer player 172.
soccer shoe 172.
soccer, playing field 173.
sock 118.
sock 170, 181.
sofa 96.
soft palate 84.
soft pedal 159.
soft-drink dispenser 134.
SOIL PROFILE 34.
solar cell 208.
solar cell 154.
SOLAR ECLIPSE 10.
solar eclipses, types 10.
SOLAR ENERGY 208.
solar energy 28.
solar panel 208.
solar radiation 208.
solar shield 149.
SOLAR SYSTEM 6.
sole 118, 185.
solid body 163.
solid rocket booster 148.
solids 156.
sound hole 162.
sound reproducing system,
 components 128.
soundboard 158, 159, 162.
soup bowl 100.
soup spoon 101.
soup tureen 100.
sour taste 84.
sources of gases 29.
sources of pollution 30.
South 27.
South America 18.
South Pole 12.
South-southeast 27.
South-southwest 27.
Southeast 27.
Southern hemisphere 12, 24.
Southwest 27.
sow 69.
soybeans 52.
space 160.
SPACE SHUTTLE 148.
space shuttle at takeoff 148.
space shuttle in orbit 148.
spacelab 148.
SPACESUIT 149.
spade 55, 194.
spaghetti tongs 103.
spanker 141.
spatula 102.
speaker 128, 129.
speaker cover 128.
speed control 54, 105.
speed selector switch 122.
speed skate 185.
speedometer 132.
spent fuel discharge bay 206.
spent fuel storage bay 206.
sphere 156.
SPIDER 56.
spider 56.
spiked shoe 168.
spillway 97.
spillway gate 204.
spinach 53.
spindle 129.
spiny lobster 61.
spiral 129.
spiral bound notebook 151.
spiral-in groove 129.

spire 89.
spit 14.
spleen 81.
splint 193.
split end 171.
spoiler 144.
spoke 137.
spoon 101.
spoons, types 101.
spores 35.
sports car 133.
SPORTSWEAR 120.
spotlight 210.
spreader 123.
spring 20, 109, 188.
spring balance 201.
spring equinox 20.
springboard 188.
sprinklers 207.
spur 17.
square 156.
square 90.
square movement 195.
square root key 154.
stabilizer fin 143.
stack 14.
stacking chairs 96.
stadium 91.
staff 160.
stage 155.
stage clip 155.
stake 190.
stalactite 13.
stalagmite 13.
stalk 44, 45, 46.
stalk vegetables 52.
stamen 38.
stanchion 185.
stand 98, 135, 166.
staple remover 150.
stapler 150.
staples 150.
star diagonal 11.
starboard hand 142.
start button 198.
start wall 182.
starter 54, 182.
starting bar (backstroke) 182.
starting block 182.
starting block 182.
state 26.
station wagon 133.
staysail, jigger topgallant 141.
staysail, jigger topmast 141.
steak knife 101.
steam generator 206.
steam pressure drives turbine 207.
steel bar 189.
steelyard 200.
steering wheel 132.
stem 35, 36, 137, 141, 199.
stem bulb 142.
step 134.
stepladder 111.
steppe 21.
stereo control 129.
STEREO SYSTEM 128.
sterile dressing 193.
stern 143, 184.
sternum 80.
stick 162.
stick eraser 150.
sticks 166.
stigma 38.
stile 93, 97.
stimulator tip 122.
stinger 59.
stipule 37.
stirrup sock 168.
stitching 118, 121.
stock 209.
stock pot 104.
stockade 88.
stocking 118.
stocking cap 113.
STOCKINGS 118.
stomach 81.
stone 45.
stone fruit, section 45.
stone fruits, major types 45.
stool 96.
stop 66, 126.
stop at intersection 216.
stop button 198.
stopwatch 198.
storage compartment 134, 153, 210.
storage door 106.

storage tanks 203.
stork 76.
stormy sky 22.
stove oil 203.
straight skirt 115.
straight wing 144.
strainer 103.
strainer 190.
strait 26.
strap 168.
strap loop 193.
strap system 163.
stratosphere 28.
strawberry, section 44.
street 90.
street lamp 91.
street sweeper 214.
striking circle 175.
string 162.
STRINGED INSTRUMENTS 162.
strings 159, 181.
stroke judge 182.
strokes, types 183.
structure of a flower 38.
STRUCTURE OF A PLANT 36.
STRUCTURE OF THE BIOSPHERE 20.
STRUCTURE OF THE EARTH 12.
strut 209.
stud 121.
studs 174.
stump 40.
stump 174.
style 38.
subarctic climates 21.
subarctic climates 21.
sublimation 30.
submarine pipeline 202.
subsoil 34.
subterranean stream 13.
subtract from memory 154.
subtract key 154.
subtropical climates 21.
sugar bowl 100.
suit 114.
summer 20.
summer solstice 20.
summer squash 49.
summit 17.
SUN 8.
Sun 6, 10, 28.
sun visor 132.
Sun's surface 8.
Sun, structure 8.
sundeck 142.
sundial 198.
sunlight 28.
sunroof 131.
sunspot 8.
super 59.
supply of water 205.
support 11, 23, 97.
surface insulation 149.
surface prospecting 202.
surface runoff 30, 32.
suspender clip 112.
suspenders 112.
suspension spring 138.
swallow 76.
swallow hole 13.
SWEATERS 117.
sweatpants 120.
sweatshirt 120.
swede 51.
sweet corn 52.
sweet peas 52.
sweet pepper 49.
sweet potato 51.
sweet taste 84.
swept-back wing 144.
swimmerets 61.
SWIMMING 182.
swimming pool 143, 182.
swimming trunks 121.
swimming, competitive course 182.
swimsuit 120.
Swiss army knife 192.
Swiss chard 52.
switch 99.
switch 110.
switch lock 110.
swordfish 62.
SYMBOLS, COMMON 216.
SYMBOLS, SAFETY 216.
SYMPHONY ORCHESTRA 167.

T

T-tail unit 145.
tab 123.
TABLE 97.
table 97.
table lamp 98.
tack 184.
tadpole 60.
tag 121.
tail 61.
tail 65, 66, 67, 75, 144, 186.
tail assembly 144.
tail boom 145.
tail comb 122.
tail light 133.
tail shapes, types 145.
tail skid 145.
tail-out groove 129.
taillight 135.
tailpiece 162.
tailrace 204.
take-up reel 129.
talon 74.
tambourine 166.
tank car 139, 203.
tank top 112, 120.
tank trailer 202.
tape 108, 179.
tape dispenser 151.
tape guide 129.
tape lock 108.
tape measure 108.
tapered wing 144.
taproot 40.
tarsus 80.
taste sensations 84.
team shirt 168, 170, 172.
teapot 100.
teaspoon 101.
technical identification band 129.
technical terms 44, 45, 46, 47.
telecommunication antenna 142.
telephone 216.
telephone answering machine 124.
telephone index 124.
telephone set 124.
telephone, cordless 124.
telephone, portable cellular 124.
TELESCOPE, REFLECTING 11.
TELESCOPE, REFRACTING 11.
telescopic boom 210, 215.
telescopic corridor 147.
telescopic front fork 135.
telescopic umbrella 123.
TELEVISION 126.
television set 126.
temperate climates 21.
temperature control 105.
temperature gauge 132.
temperature set point knob 199.
TEMPERATURE, MEASURE 199.
temperature, measure 23.
temple 78, 123.
tempo scale 159.
tendon guard 185.
TENNIS 180.
tennis ball 181.
tennis player 181.
tennis racket 181.
tennis shoe 119.
tennis shoe 181.
tennis, court 180.
tenor drum 166.
TENTS 190.
tents, major types 190.
tepee 86.
terminal box 208.
terminal bud 34, 36.
terminal moraine 17.
tertiary colors 157.
test tube 155.
thermometer 199.
thermometer, clinical 199.
thermostat control 106.
thigh 66, 67, 79.
thigh pad 170.
thigh-boot 119.
third base 169.
third baseman 169.
third valve slide 164.
third, musical interval 160.
thirty-second note 161.
thirty-second rest 161.

223

The terms in **bold type** correspond to an illustration; those in CAPITALS indicate a title.

INDEX

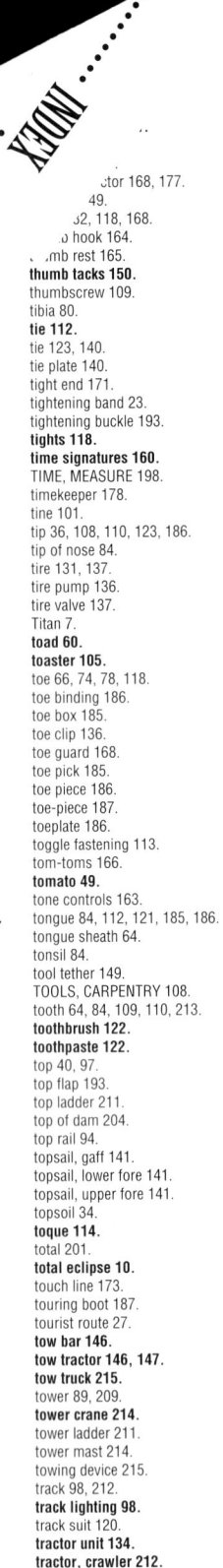

...tor 168, 177.
...49.
...2, 118, 168.
...o hook 164.
...mb rest 165.
thumb tacks 150.
thumbscrew 109.
tibia 80.
tie 112.
tie 123, 140.
tie plate 140.
tight end 171.
tightening band 23.
tightening buckle 193.
tights 118.
time signatures 160.
TIME, MEASURE 198.
timekeeper 178.
tine 101.
tip 36, 108, 110, 123, 186.
tip of nose 84.
tire 131, 137.
tire pump 136.
tire valve 137.
Titan 7.
toad 60.
toaster 105.
toe 66, 74, 78, 118.
toe binding 186.
toe box 185.
toe clip 136.
toe guard 168.
toe pick 185.
toe piece 186.
toe-piece 187.
toeplate 186.
toggle fastening 113.
tom-toms 166.
tomato 49.
tone controls 163.
tongue 84, 112, 121, 185, 186.
tongue sheath 64.
tonsil 84.
tool tether 149.
TOOLS, CARPENTRY 108.
tooth 64, 84, 109, 110, 213.
toothbrush 122.
toothpaste 122.
top 40, 97.
top flap 193.
top ladder 211.
top of dam 204.
top rail 94.
topsail, gaff 141.
topsail, lower fore 141.
topsail, upper fore 141.
topsoil 34.
toque 114.
total 201.
total eclipse 10.
touch line 173.
touring boot 187.
tourist route 27.
tow bar 146.
tow tractor 146, 147.
tow truck 215.
tower 89, 209.
tower crane 214.
tower ladder 211.
tower mast 214.
towing device 215.
track 98, 212.
track lighting 98.
track suit 120.
tractor unit 134.
tractor, crawler 212.
TRADITIONAL MUSICAL
   INSTRUMENTS 158.
traffic island 90.
trailing edge 144.
trailing edge flap 144.
trampoline 188.
transept 89.
transept spire 89.
transfer of heat to water 207.
transformation of mechanical work into
   electricity 205.
transformer 98, 204, 206.

transit shed 143.
transmission of the rotative movement
   to the rotor 205.
transmission to consumers 205.
transparency 153.
transpiration 31.
trapezoid 156.
trapped heat 29.
traveling crane 204.
tray 111.
treble bridge 159.
treble keyboard 158.
treble pickup 163.
treble register 158.
treble tone control 163.
TREE 40.
tree frog 60.
tree, structure 40.
trees, examples 41.
triangle 156, 166.
triangle 167.
triangular body 158.
trifoliolate 36.
trigger switch 110.
trill, musical notation 161.
trip odometer 132.
triple ring 197.
triple tail unit 145.
tripod 11.
tripod accessories shelf 11.
tripod stand 166.
Triton 7.
trolley 214.
trolley pulley 214.
trombone 164.
trombone 167.
tropic of Cancer 12, 24.
tropic of Capricorn 12, 24.
tropical climates 21.
tropical forest 20.
TROPICAL FRUITS 48.
tropical fruits, major types 48.
tropical rain forest 21.
tropical savanna 21.
troposphere 28.
trout 62.
trowel 54.
truck 138, 185.
truck crane 215.
truck frame 138.
TRUCKING 134.
trumpet 164.
trumpet 167.
trunk 40, 79, 131.
trunk, cross section 40.
tuba 164.
tuba 167.
tuber vegetables 51.
tubular bells 167.
tulip 38.
tumbler 100.
tuna 62.
tundra 20.
tuner 128.
tuner 129.
tungsten-halogen lamp 99.
tuning control 129.
tuning controls 126.
tuning fork 159.
tuning peg 162, 163.
tuning pin 159.
tuning slide 164.
turbine 206.
turbine building 206.
turbine shaft turns generator 207.
turbined water draining 205.
turbojet engine 144.
turkey 68.
turn signal 133, 135.
turn signal indicator 132.
turn, musical notation 161.
turning judge 182.
turning wall 182, 183.
turnip 51.
turntable 128.
turntable 213.
turntable mounting 210.
turret 88.
turtle 64.
turtleneck 117.
tusks of elephant 71.
tusks of walrus 71.
tusks of wart hog 71.
TUSKS, MAJOR TYPES 71.
TV mode 126.
TV on/off button 126.

TV/video button 126.
tweeter 128.
tweezers 193.
twig 36, 40.
twist drill 110.
two-door sedan 133.
two-person tent 190.
two-toed hoof 71.
two-two time 160.
tympanum 89.

U

ulna 80.
umbra shadow 10.
UMBRELLA 123.
umbrella pine 43.
umbrella, telescopic 123.
umpire 171, 174, 179, 180, 182.
under tail covert 75.
underground flow 31, 32.
underground stem 50.
undershirt 112.
undershirt 168.
unison, musical interval 160.
unit price 201.
universal step 146.
uphaul 184.
upper eyelid 60, 66, 82.
upper fore topgallant sail 141.
upper fore topsail 141.
upper lip 84.
upper mantle 12.
upper shell 185, 186.
upper strap 186.
upper tail covert 75.
upright 189.
upright piano 159.
upright pipe 210.
Uranus 7.
usual terms 44, 45, 46, 47.
UTENSILS, KITCHEN 102.
uvula 84.

V

V-neck 117.
V-neck cardigan 117.
valley 17.
valve 164.
valve casing 164.
vamp 121.
vanity mirror 132.
variable geometry wing 144.
vaulting horse 188.
VCR controls 126.
VCR mode 126.
VCR on/off button 126.
vegetable steamer 104.
VEGETABLES 49, 50, 52.
vegetables 33.
vein 37.
vein, femoral 81.
vein, subclavian 81.
venom canal 64.
venom gland 64.
venom-conducting tube 64.
venomous snake's head 64.
venous blood 81.
vent, main 15.
vent, side 15.
ventilating fan 139.
Venus 6.
vernal equinox 20.
vernier scale 200.
vertebral column 80.
vertical movement 195.
vertical pivoting window 94.
vertical side band 179.
vertical-axis wind turbine 209.
vibrato arm 163.
VIDEO 127.
video camera 127.
VIDEO ENTERTAINMENT SYSTEM 197.
video monitor 154.
videocassette recorder 127.
videotape operation controls 127.
viewfinder adjustment keys 127.
vine leaf 53.
viola 162.

viola 167.
violet 38.
violet 157.
violet-blue 157.
violin 162.
violin family 162.
visor 135, 140, 187.
visual display 197.
volcanic bomb 15.
VOLCANO 15.
volcano 28.
VOLLEYBALL 179.
volleyball 179.
volleyball, court 179.
voltage decrease 205.
voltage increase 205, 207.
volume control 124, 126, 129, 163.
volva 35.
vulva 78.

W

wading bird 74.
wagon tent 190.
waist 79, 162.
waist belt 193.
waistband 112, 113.
walking leg 57.
Walkman® 129.
wall 9, 47.
wall fixture 98.
wall tent 190.
wallet 123.
wallet 154.
waning gibbous Moon 9.
warming plate 105.
warning device 211.
warning light 140.
warning lights 132.
warning track 169.
washer nozzle 130.
watch, digital 198.
water bottle 136.
water bottle clip 136.
water cools the used steam 207.
water cycle 30.
water intake 204.
water is pumped back into the steam
   generator 207.
water key 164.
water pitcher 100.
water supply point 210.
water table 13.
water tank 139.
water turns into steam 207.
water under pressure 205.
watercolors 157.
watercress 53.
waterfall 17.
watering can 54.
watering tube 214.
watermelon 52.
wax crayons 157.
waxing gibbous Moon 9.
WEATHER 22.
weather radar 145.
web 60, 74, 168.
webbed foot 60.
webbed toe 74.
weeping willow 42.
weight 200, 201.
WEIGHT, MEASURE 200.
West 27.
West-northwest 27.
West-southwest 27.
Western hemisphere 24.
Western meridian 24.
whale 72.
wheel 185.
wheel chock 146.
wheel cover 131.
wheel tractor 212.
wheelbarrow 55.
wheelchair access 216.
whisk 102.
whiskers 66.
White 195, 196.
white cabbage 53.
white of eye 82.
white square 195.
white wine glass 100.
whole note 161.
whole rest 161.

wicket 174.
wicket-keeper 174.
wigwam 86.
WILD ANIMALS 72.
willow 174.
winch 215.
winch controls 215.
wind deflector 134.
wind direction, measure 23.
WIND ENERGY 209.
WIND INSTRUMENTS 164.
wind strength, measure 23.
wind vane 23.
windbag 158.
windbreaker 113, 120.
windmill 209.
WINDOW 94.
window 107, 131, 145, 184.
windows, types 94.
windshaft 209.
windshield 130, 135.
windshield wiper 130.
wing 75, 144, 148.
wing shapes, types 144.
wing slat 144.
wing vein 57.
wing, left 175, 176.
wing, right 175, 176.
winglet 144.
winter 20.
winter solstice 20.
wiper switch 132.
wire brush 166.
wisdom tooth 85.
wishbone boom 184.
withers 66, 67.
wok 104.
WOMEN'S CLOTHING 114, 116.
women's rest room 216.
woodwind family 165.
woofer 128.
worker, honey-bee 58.
worm 214.
wrist 66, 79, 82.
wrist strap 186, 187.
wristband 170, 181.

X

xylophone 166.
xylophone 167.

Y

yard line 171.
yellow 157.
yellow onion 50.
yellow-green 157.
yolk 75.
yurt 87.

Z

zebra 73.
zest 47.
zipper 190.
zither 158.
zoom lens 127.
zucchini 49.

The terms in **bold type** correspond to an illustration; those in CAPITALS indicate a title.